CISTERCIAN STUDIES SERIES: NUMBER ONE HUNDRED FORTY-ONE

Studiosorum Speculum
Studies in Honor of Louis J. Lekai, O.Cist.

Louis J. Lekai, O. Cist.
(Photo by Raff Frano)

CISTERCIAN STUDIES SERIES: NUMBER ONE HUNDRED FORTY-ONE

Studiosorum Speculum
Studies in Honor of Louis J. Lekai, O.Cist.

Edited by
Francis R. Swietek
and
John R. Sommerfeldt

Cistercian Publications
Kalamazoo, Michigan 1993

© Copyright, Cistercian Publications Inc., 1993

The work of Cistercian Publications is made possible in part by support from Western Michigan University to The Institute of Cistercian Studies

Available from
Cistercian Publications (Distribution)
Saint Joseph's Abbey
Spencer, MA 01562

TABLE OF CONTENTS

Foreword 7

List of Plates 11

The Economic Practices of Cistercian Women's
Communities: A Preliminary Look 15
    Constance H. Berman

Twelfth-Century Burgundy: The Great Unknown? 33
    Constance B. Bouchard

Monastic Profession According to Aelred
of Rievaulx 53
    Elizabeth Connor, OCSO

Making Virtues of Vexing Habits 75
    E. Rozanne Elder

American Catholic Historiography Comes of Age 95
    †John Tracy Ellis

An Unknown Illuminated Page from the Statutes
of the Order of Saint Michel in the Ambrosiana
Library in Milan.................................. 113
    Astrik L. Gabriel

The Wharton-Carroll Controversy and the Promise
of American Catholic Life 135
    Thomas W. Jodziewicz

Triumphs of Ecclesiastical Politics in the 1231
Decretum of Andrew II of Hungary 155
    Zoltan J. Kosztolnyik

Martin Luther and Monasticism 173
    Bede K. Lackner, O. Cist.

Conversion to the Monastic Life in the Twelfth
Century: Who, Why, and How? 201
    Jean Leclercq

Recent Scholarship Concerning Cistercian Windows .. 233
    Meredith Parsons Lillich

History: The Bearer of Culture 263
    John Lukacs

The Cistercian Nunnery of Swine Priory: Its Church
and Choir Stalls 275
    John A. Nichols

Father Louis' First Book: *The Spirit of Simplicity* 305
    M. Basil Pennington, OCSO

Cistercians and Bethlehem: A Historical View 321
    Thomas Renna

The Papacy and the Reform of the Cistercian Order
in the Late Middle Ages............................ 337
    Bernhard Schimmelpfennig

Bernard of Clairvaux's Abbot: Both Daniel
and Noah... 355
    John R. Sommerfeldt

A Savigniac Forgery Recovered: Lucius II's Bull
Habitantes in domo of December 5, 1144 363
    Francis R. Swietek and Terrence M. Deneen

Toward a New Provisional Edition of the Statutes
of the Cistercian General Chapter, c. 1119–1189 389
    Chrysogonus Waddell, OCSO

Curriculum vitae of Louis J. Lekai................... 421

Bibliography of Published Works by Louis J. Lekai ... 423

FOREWORD

THE COLLEAGUES AND FRIENDS of Louis J. Lekai, O. Cist., offer this volume of studies to him on the occasion of his seventy-fifth birthday. Those of us who have been privileged to know and work with Father Louis are pleased to have this opportunity to express both our professional esteem and our personal affection for him.

Louis J. Lekai was born in Budapest, Hungary, on February 4, 1916. After completing his secondary education at the cistercian gymnasium of Budapest, he entered the cistercian order in 1934, and over the next seven years completed his philosophical and theological studies in its theological institute at Zirc and Budapest. He also undertook graduate work at the Peter Pazmany University in Budapest, where he was awarded a secondary certificate in history and geography in 1941 and the Ph.D. *summa cum laude* in history and philosophy in the following year.

Father Louis taught in the cistercian gymnasium in Eger from 1942 to 1947. He also served as Lecturer in History at the Eger School of Law in 1943–1944, and was a chaplain in the hungarian armed forces in 1944–1945. He departed Hungary for the United States in October

1947, one of several members of his community appointed to establish a daughter-house in the New World. He and his confrères first settled at the monastery in Spring Bank, Wisconsin. From 1952 to 1956 he was Assistant Professor of History at Canisius College in Buffalo, during which time he became a U.S. citizen. He was instrumental in the establishment, in 1955, of a new cistercian monastery in the diocese of Dallas, which in 1963 would be raised to abbatial status; and in 1956 he was among the founding faculty of the University of Dallas. He served as Associate Professor of History until 1958, when he was named Professor of History, a position which he held until his retirement in 1982. Thousands of alumni fondly recall his teaching, which is said to have combined rigor and good humor in nearly equal measure, and his colleagues in all disciplines cherish memories of his distinguished institutional service and his unfailing wit, charm, and grace.

During his tenure at the University of Dallas, Father Louis also served as prior in the Abbey of Our Lady of Dallas (1967–1975), was a member of a dozen professional organizations, and received research grants from the American Philosophical Association. Over the course of more than a quarter century he also assembled a body of scholarly work remarkable for its breadth, its precision, and its insight. His superb books and articles won him international recognition as the premier historian of the cistercian order, and many of us not only learned from his publications but came to depend on him for advice, which he gave with great generosity and warm friendship. His researches remain one of the fundamental bases for scholarship on the history of the order.

We have chosen to title this collection after a phrase from William of Malmesbury's *De gestis regum Anglorum* 4.337. In a digression on the origins of the cistercian order, William concluded by noting that *sunt hodie monachi Cistellenses omnium monachorum exercitium, studiosorum speculum, desidiosorum oestrum.* The twofold meaning of *studiosorum speculum,* implying both religious zeal and intellectual erudition, seems especially appropriate in reference to Father Louis, a monk of deep piety who is also a scholar of exceptional accomplishment. Moreover, the fact that the phrase derives from the work of the most critically astute and exacting historian of the twelfth century, the era of the medieval renaissance, makes it particularly applicable to a group of essays honoring the man who, in the present century's revival of cistercian studies, is recognized as a special master of the historical art.

The University of Dallas   F.R.S.
                                                      J.R.S.

LIST OF PLATES

Frontispiece   Louis J. Lekai, O. Cist. (Photo: Raff Frano)
Gabriel I.   Milan, Biblioteca Ambrosiana, F. 277 Inferior, no. 59. Louis XI, king of France (1461–1483), represented presiding over a reunion of the Knights of the Order of Saint Michael.
Gabriel II.   Paris, Bibliothèque nationale MS français 5109, fol. A verso. An illuminated page from the *Register* of the criminal process against Charles III, duc de Bourbon (1490–1527).
Gabriel III.   Paris, Bibliothèque nationale MS français 14361, fol. 7 verso. A session of the Order of Saint Michael presided over by the king of France, shown in an illuminated page of the Statute Book of the Order (this copy belonged to the so-called 'official series').
Gabriel IV.   Paris, Bibliothèque nationale MS français 19815, fol. 11 recto. One of

	the sixteenth-century copies of the 'official series'.
Gabriel V.	Paris, Bibliothèque nationale MS français 19816, fol. 9 recto. Another copy of the 'official series' of the Statute Books of the Order of Saint Michael; the king is represented crowned.
Gabriel VI.	London, British Museum MS Harley 4485, fol. 9 recto. Chapter-meeting scene of the Order of Saint Michael; the king is represented crowned.
Gabriel VII.	Paris, Bibliothèque nationale MS français 25190, fol. 1 recto. Henry II, king of France (1547–1559), presiding over the chapter-meeting of the Order of Saint Michael; the chancellor of the order is depicted seated at his desk.
Lillich I.	Fontenay, 1139–1147. Interior view to the east. (photo: J. Feuillie, CNMHS/SPADEM/ARS, New York, 1990)
Lillich II.	Santes Creus, east wall of north transept, bay T N II. (photo: Roland Sanfaçon)
Lillich III.	Santes Creus, west wall of north transept, bay T N V. (photo: Roland Sanfaçon)
Lillich IV.	Sens Cathedral, upper bay of the north tower of the façade. (photo: Françoise Gatouillat)
Lillich V.	Noirlac, fragment now in private collection. (photo: Musées de la ville de Bourges)
Lillich VI.	Maubuisson, excavated fragments. (photo: courtesy of Catherine Brisac)
Lillich VII.	San Pietro, Spoleto, façade. The 'cosmic paradise', combining

List of Plates

	geometric motifs and vegetal ornament. (photo: Patrik Reuterswärd)
Lillich VIII.	La Bénissons-Dieu, north nave. (photo: Meredith Lillich)
Lillich IX.	Knotenkreuz. Romanesque crucifix found in Bergen, Norway. Drawing by P. Blix (after Clasen).
Lillich X.	Mosaic pavement, House of the Phoenix, Antioch. The three knots at the right are inserted into the border where it forms the threshold at the entrance. (photo: Department of Art and Archeology, Princeton University)
Nichols I.	Aerial photograph reproduced by permission of Cambridge University: Department of Aerial Photography, FU 47.
Nichols II.	Diagram of Swine Priory, drawn by John A. Nichols based on physical descriptions of the nunnery in the fifteenth and sixteenth centuries and contemporary remains.
Nichols III.	External view of Swine parish church showing the east end. This and all other photographs, unless otherwise noted, are the author's own.
Nichols IV.	Interior photo of Swine Church.
Nichols V.	East Perpendicular window over the altar.
Nichols VI.	Poulson, *History*, 2:49.
Nichols VII.	Robert and Constance Hilton memorial.
Nichols VIII.	Poulson, *History*, 1:489.
Nichols IX.	Detail of Robert and Joan Hilton memorial.
Nichols X.	Detail of linenfold wooden panel.
Nichols XI.	Misericord of prioress and monkeys.
Nichols XII.	Misericord of mitre-hatted elf.

Nichols XIII.   Misericord of a foliated man.
Nichols XIV.   Misericord of a young woman.
Nichols XV.   Misericord of bearded man with pointed hat.
Nichols XVI.   Misericord of bearded man.
Nichols XVII.   Misericord of man exposing himself.
Nichols XVIII.   Misericord of a beastly face.
Swietek-Deneen I.   Paris, Bibliothèque nationale MS nouv. acq. lat. 2652, fol. 61r.
Swietek-Deneen II.   Paris, Bibliothèque nationale MS nouv. acq. lat. 2652, fol. 61v.

THE ECONOMIC PRACTICES OF CISTERCIAN WOMEN'S COMMUNITIES: A PRELIMINARY LOOK

Constance H. Berman
The University of Iowa

THE QUESTION WHETHER WOMEN were part of the cistercian order in the twelfth and thirteenth centuries is no longer debated as it was as recently as fifteen years ago.[1] Increasingly historians of the Cistercians are accepting such evidences of diversity as the inclusion of women in the order as an index of the early order's strength, rather than seeing divergence from stated 'ideals' as either abberations or the beginnings of decline. For most recent historians of the order, the order's local administrative evidence—its charters rather than its *Statuta*—are the basis for a total rewriting of the early history of the Cistercians. Having affirmed the charter evidence and questioned the evidence of the *Statuta* on other aspects of the order's early history, such historians find little reason to deny the charter evidence for individual communities of women who not only considered themselves Cistercians, but were called Cistercians by contemporary authorities such as the pope.[2]

The twelfth- and thirteenth-century cistercian economy, at least as developed by the order's houses of men, was something new. Indeed, certain aspects of cistercian grange agriculture have been considered among the most important innovations of the early order; they explain its rapid expansion and its wealth. Cistercian houses for men were economically successful because their organization of rural production improved both net and gross yields. For an individual house of men in the order, its ascetic life-style and its reinvestment of savings in land, along with the institution of compact granges, the use of *conversi* as laborers, the practice of transhumant pastoralism, the sale and transport of produce under advantageous conditions in and to nearby towns, and the order's exemption from tithes, all added up to increased profits. These were then available to reinvest in more land and more granges.[3]

Were cistercian women as successful in amassing property and instituting the profitable new cistercian organization of resources? Studies of cistercian economic practice have almost invariably excluded women's communities, although there has been a tendency to see the economies of cistercian women's communities as generally poorer and less-well managed than those of comparable men's houses.[4] If cistercian women did not become as rich, what kept them from sharing the advantages of the order's houses for men? Were there differences in women's religious lives, such as stricter enclosure and the resulting dependence on outsiders, which made establishing a profitable economy more difficult? Differences in early endowment or economic practice could also have had considerable repercussions for later economic viability and consequently may explain the economic problems of female communities in the later Middle Ages. No one has asked whether, within the cistercian order as a whole, communities of women had sufficient endowment or could have managed their properties in ways identical to communities of men.

A close consideration shows that cistercian women's communities were not identical in all respects to those of men. From all accounts we must assume that cistercian women were more strictly enclosed than cistercian men, and that such enclosure had increasingly negative effects on women's abilities to manage their own affairs.[5] Women's monastic communities were in some senses always 'double' communities, always dependent on men as priests and as administrators in a way that men's houses were not dependent on women.[6] While the traditionally 'female' roles within medieval society such as cooking, serving meals, and doing laundry could be taken on by men as acts of penitence, or done by lay-brothers, canon law made it impossible for monastic women to exercise similar 'role-reversal' and take on clerical roles. Moreover, the cloistering of women inevitably hampered their administration of property. We can also suspect that the benefactors of women's communities (most often founded in the thirteenth century) were not as generous as had been the twelfth-century patrons of men's houses.[7]

Just how gender specific were the endowment and administration of property within the cistercian order? How did women's communities differ in their economic organization from those of the order's men? Although there are many aspects of the lives of these women which are lost to historians, there is sufficient surviving economic evidence of the type frequently used in studies of men's houses— the charters of real estate transactions, of donations at the entrance of a daughter or niece, of conveyance of tithes by laymen to support the nuns, and of confirmation of privileges by bishops and popes—to allow us to reconstruct the economic lives of cistercian women.[8] What is provided here is a preliminary assessment, not only in that it draws on well-established general characterizations of the men's houses of the order (although characterizations based on actual practice rather than ideals) and compares those practices to the little which is known thus far about the economic practice of cistercian houses for women, but also in that a comparison is made between cistercian women's abbeys and men's abbeys in two completely different geographical areas.[9] Such a preliminary assessment only underlines the necessity for regional studies in which parallel female and male communities are compared, such as that which I have begun for the ecclesiastical province of Sens.[10]

General characterizations of the cistercian monastery begin with its site in a deserted place, *in locus horroris et vastae solitudinae,* the narrow and inaccessible valley to which the monks (and nuns) retreated from the world and built a new economic world with their hands. It was Bernard of Clairvaux, much more than the original founders at Cîteaux, who elaborated the image of the monastic site in a narrow, isolated valley—an image derived from the writings of the Desert Fathers. As Auberger has shown, the narrow, isolated valley was typical of the sites chosen by Bernard himself,[11] but such small, isolated valleys continued to be the preferred cistercian sites for both men's and women's houses. This is not surprising, since in such valleys were streams sufficiently swift to flow cleansingly through the monastic compound and to run an abbey's mills, but not so large as to cause conflict from other mill-owners or to be close to river traffic which might disturb an abbey's seclusion.[12]

Almost all cistercian monastic complexes had one or more water-mills, but, despite the contentions of historians such as Gimpel, such water-mills were certainly not introduced by the order. Mills had existed considerably earlier, although twelfth-century Cistercians acquired, built, and repaired many throughout Europe.[13] Georges Duby contends that at la Ferté it was revenues from milling which provided a means of subsistence in the earliest years for that daughter-house of Cîteaux, and that milling there may have provided the cash for later expansion.[14] Students of the Cistercians have often considered mills to be one of the many manorial revenues from which the order was attempting to escape, and Bernard certainly characterized mills as places frequented by women.[15] Such water-mills, however, were important to the functioning of the cistercian economy for men's and women's abbeys alike; they ground flour, fulled cloth, crushed bark for tanning, ran the bellows for forges, and could even be used to cut wood and stone. As a result, the relative isolation of cistercian monasteries may not always have been particularly quiet, for water-mills are noisy! Women's communities, like men's, had income and revenues from mills, but there was a subtle difference. Women's houses more often received rents or annuities derived from the profits of mills owned by others.[16] Obviously, such money or flour rents were easily managed, but they were assets only when rents were actually paid. If a mill burned and was not replaced by the owners, as in the case of one owing rents to the cistercian women's house of Lieu-lez-Romorantin, the nuns might have to settle for a fraction of the value of their earlier rent.[17] In contrast, cistercian men actually owned mills, had an incentive to keep them in repair, might seek reparations for damage, and so on.[18] This is perhaps the most striking example of the disastrous consequences to women's communities of donors giving them rents rather than land.

Another 'notorious' manorial revenue in the eyes of cistercian scholars was the ownership of churches and tithes. Despite *Statutes* such as those dated 1134, claiming that the order did not live from the revenues of churches and altars, both cistercian women and cistercian men seem to have profited from gregorian demands that the laity return tithes to the church.[19] For men's houses of the order, the acquisition of churches and tithes was closely tied to the acquisition of land for granges. To some extent this was also the case for women's houses, since lists of churches and tithes acquired often coincide with the parishes where lands were acquired.[20] Repurchase of such tithes was the means by which cistercian men could exercise the exemption from tithes on their own agricultural production. For women's communities of the thirteenth century, however, such tithe exemption was not available, and thus the acquisition of tithes by women's communities was not a means by which to effectively exempt their own cultivation.[21] Moreover, in addition to tithes associated with their granges, there were widespread conveyances of tithes to cistercian nuns in locations where the nuns had not as yet acquired lands.

A good example from the 1210s and 1220s are the tithes given to the women's abbey of Voisins at the instigation of the founder of that house, Manasses II, bishop of Orléans, who appears to have seen such tithes as an especially appropriate source of income for women's houses.[22] Thus, while both men and women of the order had tithes, there were considerable differences in the purposes for which they were acquired.

Although most cistercian houses for both men and women appear to have maintained their ideal of isolation insofar as almost all avoided becoming pilgrimage sites, such abbeys did have considerable ties to the growing cities of their times. The success of cistercian abbeys for men can be attributed, in part, to their almost invariable ties to the urban markets near which they were sited. Ties to these centers included privileges such as exemptions from taxes and tolls on the transport and sale of goods therein, as well as urban properties or rents, and, for the men's communities, urban hospices which provided places for abbots, monks, and *conversi* to stay when contracting business in towns like Toulouse, Montpellier, Nîmes, or Paris. According to the foundation document for the hospice in Nîmes, such houses were to be fully furnished for all the needs of such travelers, with a hospice-keeper who was to greet members of the order 'with a smile', to house their beasts, to provide them a hot meal in a well-furnished refectory, and a dormitory with beds, sheets, pillows, coverlets, and a dormitory light.[23] The cistercian men of Grandselve owned vineyards and gardens in the city of Toulouse which were used as endowment for its hospice there, a hospice which later became a cistercian college.[24] Although I have no evidence of such hospices for nuns, the abbeys of women in the order, like those for the men, certainly did have urban properties: gardens, houses or urban *mansi*, and workshops; all must have produced cash when leased out to tenants. Moreover, some women's houses were sited in the immediate vicinity of trade centers—a fact which has probably made cistercian historians more reluctant to admit that these communities of women were cistercian.[25] The most notable of these abbeys near urban centers was the cistercian women's abbey of Saint–Antoine-des-Champs just outside the gates of Paris. The urban properties belonging to the nuns of Saint–Antoine-des-Champs were extensive, and those properties within the city of Paris must be considered the major source of that community's later financial security.[26] In addition to outright ownership of urban properties, Cistercians of both genders, but particularly women, also acquired rents or annuities on urban properties which they themselves did not own—that is, annual income from the revenues of such urban rights as the hearth tax, mills, market taxes, or tolls at gates.[27] Such rights and properties in cities belie the anti-urban stance of the early order's propaganda. This is also true of cistercian production for urban markets.[28]

The order's production for urban markets is best seen in the most rural of cistercian activities, the order's pastoralism—its sheep-herding, horse-breeding, raising of cows and pigs. It was probably in animal husbandry that both men and women in the cistercian order participated most completely in the economic expansion of the twelfth and thirteenth centuries. In the expanding economy of that period, demand for animal products was much more elastic than was that for cereal; this favored animal producers.[29] For the 'poor' cistercian abbeys of the twelfth century which had received grants of pasture rights from their benefactors, pastoralism was a sure way to wealth; such men's houses gained considerable cash thereby to reinvest in land. The practice of pastoralism *per se* presented none of the sex-specific labor problems otherwise apparent for women's communities, and some women's houses clearly included a strong element of pastoralism in their economies.[30] In such stock-raising there were no practical limitations on the participation of women's abbeys, because both men and women's houses probably hired outside specialists to tend their flocks and herds. However, if the practice of animal husbandry were theoretically as possible for women's communities as it was for men's, it is not clear that donors of pasture rights were as generous in their gifts to women's communities. Once again the difference between the twelfth century and the thirteenth may have been critical, since, in the twelfth century, pasture rights were frequently still under-exploited by both lay and religious groups; that was not the case in the thirteenth, when the value of pasture-rights was well recognized. Moreover, in comparison to men's, women's communities seem to have been more dependent on pastoralism for their subsistence needs and less able than the monks to reinvest the profits of their animal husbandry.

Despite their preoccupation with siting abbeys in relatively isolated places, however, major clearance and reclamation for the creation of new areas of cereal cultivation should not be inferred either from the order's acquisition of woodland pasture rights or from the isolated aspect of their abbey sites. With only a handful of exceptions, I have found no evidence of clearance activities by cistercian men in southern France; indeed, those men may have actively avoided the work of clearance.[31] In contrast, for northern France, houses of cistercian women founded near Chartres in the early thirteenth century seem to have received more uncleared land than did any of the men's houses I have studied.[32] It seems possible that women's abbeys, because they were more desperate for land, had less money to buy land than men and, because they had maintained tenant-families as cultivators, could direct clearance activities which men in the order had neither the inclination nor the labor force to undertake. Indeed, it may well be that in the thirteenth century, when women's houses were founded, they were able to create sites and granges only by clearance. This was not necessarily beneficial. If women did end up directing more clearance efforts, they also received a larger proportion of the last lands to be brought under cultivation, and those were invariably the poorest!

The question of clearance and reclamation, however, must be rigorously separated from that of new lands. As I have shown elsewhere, the isolated valleys which cistercian monks and nuns preferred as sites were often the *assarts, artigues, finages,* or *vagues* already made by the order's predecessors. This was as true for the nuns of Rifreddo in the italian Piedmont as for the monks of Berdoues or Franquevaux in southern France, or for the monks of Pontigny or the nuns of Voisins or Lieu-lez-Romorantin in the north.[33] The best explanation that I have found for the tendency of the order to acquire new lands comes from the region north of Toulouse. There, the monks of Grandselve purchased contiguous strips of formerly marsh-land along the Garonne which had only recently been brought under cultivation.[34] Although probably more fertile than surrounding land at higher elevations, such fields were also subject to periodic flooding. The risk of flood made such lands a poor risk for small-owners, and peasants soon sold those fields. The purchasers were frequently cistercian monks, for only a large religious corporation such as a cistercian abbey could absorb the risk of flood years, and only rich cistercian monks could afford to build dikes and levees to protect those fields. Whether nuns had sufficient cash to make such improvements is less clear.

Whatever the sources of the land acquired, land acquisition by Cistercians, both men and women, resulted in granges. It was the grange, on which *conversi* labored and on which tithe-exempt direct cultivation was instituted, which most characterizes the contrast between the traditional benedictine monastic economy and the economic practices of the new twelfth-century orders.[35] My work on cistercian houses for men has shown that cistercian granges were created by the careful repurchase and reorganization of land which had had a long history of settlement and cultivation. The records for the men's houses show how the consolidation of land rights was accomplished by the gradual repurchase of all existing rights and claims from all earlier claimants to contiguous land. Such compacting of land for a single grange might extend over several parishes. For the men's houses we are talking about hundreds of transactions, sometimes for a single grange. This aggressive acquisition required careful record-keeping, infinite patience and persistence, and considerable cash, and it coincided with recruitment of *conversi* as laborers.[36] Profits from such new granges, with their more efficient use of land and lowered dependency costs, fueled a cycle of land acquisition for men's houses which often lasted over a century.

Initial gifts of land to men and women's houses were similar, but not identical. The thirteenth-century donors to abbeys of women gave those women much less land than the men's houses had received in the twelfth century. Although this needs more study, it appears that, with the exception of those for the actual abbey site, gifts to women's communities were much more frequently of rents and annuities on property, rather than of actual land. Women's communities must, consequently, have had less of an initial base of land from which to build their granges. Moreover, women's communities probably entered the land market with much smaller amounts of cash and did not carry on purchases or keep records of their acquisitions with the same intensity which men's houses did.[37] Stricter enclosure meant that nuns and abbesses were less apt than abbots and monks to leave the cloister to seek the essential gift from a widow on her deathbed or to otherwise solicit gifts and sales of property. It may be too that to many potential donors the nuns could give less in religious services for the dead than could be provided by monks who were also often priests. Women's houses consequently had both much smaller granges and fewer *conversi* to work those granges.

Although smaller granges and fewer *conversi* were in themselves problems, it is with regard to grange usage that the economic practices of cistercian women's houses probably varied most disastrously from an economic standpoint from those of the order's men. Unfortunately, although we know a considerable amount about the actual administration of grange property by the order's men's houses, relatively little has been written about that by its women.[38] Preliminary conclusions from my own study of documents from the diocese of Sens suggest that, although cistercian women had granges, there was relatively little direct cultivation.[39] Women's communities had fewer *conversi*, and numerous lands remained under the cultivation of dependent tenants. Indeed, the documents reveal almost none of the depopulation which characterized the expansion of the men's houses of the order in the twelfth century. Pastoralism appears to have been practiced on a smaller scale by women's abbeys, and their agriculture saw little improvement in yields from increased animals per acre. Moreover, because women's houses were founded after 1215, they did not benefit from the cistercian tithe exemption on direct cultivation which had been so critical to the expansion of the order's communities of men. Finally, if there were less cash for women's communities to purchase land, there must also have been less cash available for any kinds of improvement in agricultural technique, such as introducing more iron tools and heavier plows. Thus, although there are documents suggesting that more pioneering activities were undertaken under the direction of women's communities than of men's, this is not an index of economic health. The lands brought under cultivation in such ways did not constitute an array of granges similar to those amassed by men's communities. Moreover, since such reclamation was done in the late thirteenth century, when there was pressure on the margins of settlement, the lands acquired must have been among the least desirable and most quickly declining in yields. So even such heroic measures did not substantially improve the economic conditions of most women's abbeys.

Despite all these differences from the traditional cistercian economic model for men's houses, cistercian women's communities practiced an administration of endowment which was different from that of the older benedictine economies. The endowment which cistercian nuns received was not so much whole villages as land on the margins and in the interstices of existing villages—types of land often much more in adherence to the order's propaganda than what its men's communities had accumulated in the twelfth century. Cistercian women, even when they received similar endowment, did not have the tithe exemption on their own cultivation, did not have the masses of *conversi* that twelfth-century men's houses had had, and probably could not introduce the substantial numbers of new animals which cistercian men of the twelfth century had. In comparison to either earlier Benedictines or to the men of their own order, cistercian women usually got a smaller number of gifts and had a much greater diversity of rights to rents and annuities—the last considerably less inflation-proof than land. Such dependence on rents and other fixed income made cistercian women more vulnerable to the economic crises of the fourteenth century.

In conclusion, although there were disabilities, such as enclosure, which acted to the detriment of women as managers of their own property, the primary problem for cistercian women's communities of the thirteenth century was insufficient endowment in land. The failure of certain cistercian women's communities in the later Middle Ages was not the result of female ineptitude, but because the job of constructing a viable endowment was so much more difficult in the thirteenth century than it had been in the twelfth, and because the supporters of women's communities (perhaps out of necessity) gave them less land and frequently chose to give them rents and annuities instead. Women could be strong managers, witness Saint-Antoine-des-Champs where the control of substantial real estate in and near Paris was sufficient to keep those cistercian nuns in a position of lordship right up to the French Revolution.[40] For many other communities, however, insufficient property endowment and insufficient funds to add to those properties by purchase made it difficult to survive even the slightest economic downturn. For a number of communities of cistercian women, the economic challenges of the early and middle fourteenth century were fatal; the nuns were suppressed and their holdings turned over to communities of men.[41]

NOTES

An earlier version of this paper was presented with the title, 'Abbeys and Priories of Cistercian Women and the Forces Which Shaped Their Economic Lives', at the Cistercian Studies Conference, Kalamazoo, Michigan, May 1987. I wish to thank Professor Jo Ann McNamara, my co-presenter on that panel, for her suggestions.

[1] On the debate on women within the cistercian order, see Constance H. Berman, 'Men's Houses, Women's Houses: The Relationship between the Sexes in Twelfth-Century Monasticism', in Andrew MacLeish (ed.), *The Medieval Monastery* (St Cloud, Minnesota: North Star Press, 1988) pp. 43–52, especially the first notes.

[2] Jean-Baptiste Auberger, *L'Unamimité cistercienne primitive: Mythe ou réalité?* (Achel: Administration de Cîteaux, Commentarii Cisterciensis; Editions Sine Parvulos VBVB, 1986), addresses the question of the unanimity of practice and even of ideals among early leaders of the order. Auberger's study also demonstrates that such early statutes as are often held up as the order's ideal (in particular those traditionally dated to 1134) contain inconsistencies; they must be considered an amalgam of earlier and later decisions none of which can be precisely dated without external evidence. Although he does not directly address the question of women within the order, it becomes more difficult to deny the early presence of women if one accepts his contention that the founders at Cîteaux, and those who followed them and founded Clairvaux, were far from unanimous in their view of the monastic life or their ideal of reform. In general, historians of the women within the religious orders have increasingly pointed to the abundance of local charter material and papal confirmations of foundations of women's communities as evidence of female participation. In refusing to continue the debate about why women are so infrequently mentioned in the early survivals of General Chapter's *Statuta*, or to be excessively concerned about the precise legal status of women within the order, feminist historians explicitly reject the premise that women are only present in history when they are explicitly mentioned or permitted by patriarchal institutions.

[3] See Richard Roehl, 'Plan and Reality in a Medieval Monastic Economy: The Cistercians', *Studies in Medieval and Renaissance History* 9 (1972) 83–113; and, more recently, Constance H. Berman, *Medieval Agriculture, the Southern-French Countryside, and the Early Cistercians: A Study of Forty-three Monasteries*, Transactions of the American Philosophical Society 76, 5 (Philadelphia, Pennsylvania: American Philosophical Society, 1986).

[4] This is true even of my own work. To have added women's communities to my study *Medieval Agriculture* would have considerably weakened my argument that men's houses of the order rarely conducted their economic affairs according to the generally-presented model. In addition, records for women's communities in southern France are limited, and many of them are not yet catalogued or available in the archives.

On southern french cistercian women, see Marti Aurell i Cardona, 'Les Cisterciennes et leurs protecteurs en Provence rhodanienne', in *Les Cisterciens de Languedoc* (XIIIe-XIVe s.); *Cahiers de Fanjeaux* 21 (1986) 235–67; Marthe Moreau, *L'Age d'or des religieuses: Monastères féminins du Languedoc méditerranéen au Moyen Age* (Montpellier: Les Presses du Languedoc, 1988); and Giselle Bourgeois, 'Les granges et l'économie de l'abbaye de Nonenque au Moyen Age', *Cîteaux* 24 (1973) 139–60. The exceptional study is that by Catherine E. Boyd, *A Cistercian Nunnery in Medieval Italy: The Story of Rifreddo in Saluzzo, 1220–1300* (Cambridge, Massachusetts: Harvard University Press, 1943), in which she asks whether cistercian nuns had 'benedictine' or 'cistercian' economic organization and concludes that their administration was mixed, as discussed below.

[5] On enclosure, see Jane Tibbetts Schulenburg, 'Strict Active Enclosure and its Effects on the Female Monastic Experience (500–1100)', in John A. Nichols and Lillian Thomas Shank (edd.), *Medieval Religious Women*, 1, *Distant Echoes*, CS 71 (Kalamazoo, Michigan: Cistercian Publications, 1984) pp. 51–86; on male administrators for women's communities, see Coburn Graves, 'Stixwould in the Market Place', *Distant Echoes*, pp. 213–35, esp. pp. 215–16.

[6] This point is made especially well by Paulette L'Hermite Leclercq, *Le Monachisme féminin dans la société de son temps: Le monastère de La Celle (XIe-début du XVIe siècle* (Paris: Cujas, 1989), where she says, on page 10: 'Les religieuses ne peuvent jamais se soustraire à la présence masculine. C'est elle qui assure leur direction spirituelle, et la distribution des sacrements, beaucoup plus importances que l'assistance matérielle. La cohabitation est forcément permanente, forcément et irrémédiablement hiérarchisée; la répartition des fonctions place les hommes du côté du spirituel auquel les femmes n'accèdent pas.'

[7] A recurring difficulty in any such comparative study of cistercian men's and women's communities (including my forthcoming one on Sens) is the time lag between foundations; most of those for women's communities occurred almost a century later than the vast majority of men's foundations. See Constance H. Berman, 'Fashions in Monastic Patronage: The Popularity of Supporting Cistercian Abbeys for Women in Thirteenth-Century Northern France', *Proceedings of the Annual Meeting of the Western Society for French History* 17 (1990) 36–45.

[8] Such documents form the basis for a number of studies of communities of men, including Berman, *Medieval Agriculture*. I would like to thank Professor Bernard Barbiche of the Ecole des Chartes for bringing to my attention the extensive collections of papal bulls in the Archives Nationales in Paris for certain cistercian women's communities, including l'Abbaye-aux-Bois, or Franche Abbaye, which is being studied by Brigitte Pipon.

⁹ Details on men's houses come from Berman, *Medieval Agriculture*; and Berman, 'Les cisterciens et le tournait économique du XIIe siècle', *'Bernard de Clairvaux (1089–1153): histoire, mentalités, spiritualité'*, (Paris, 1992) 155–177. On women's communities, in addition to studies cited in earlier notes, see Berman, 'Examples from the Region of Chartres: Economic Activities of Medieval Cistercian Houses for Women', and 'The Urban/Rural World of Cistercian Women', both forthcoming, and 'Women as Donors and Patrons to Southern-French Monasteries in the Twelfth and Thirteenth Centuries', in Constance H. Berman *et al.* (edd.), *The Worlds of Medieval Women: Creativity, Influence, Imagination* (Morgantown, West Virginia, 1985) pp. 53–68. Comparisons to northern England draw on as yet unpublished work undertaken as a researcher in 1985–1986 for the 'Women's Religious Communities, and Lives', NEH-funded project, directed by Professor Suzanne Wemple and Dr. Mary M. McLaughlin.

¹⁰ This larger study, funded by grants from the National Endowment for the Humanities, the National Gallery of Art, the American Historical Association, and the University of Iowa, will be published as *Sisters in Wealth and in Poverty: Endowment and Administration of Cistercian Houses for Women in the Ecclesiastical Province of Sens: 1190–1350* (expected completion date 1996); its terms are outlined in Berman, 'Fashions'.

¹¹ Auberger, pp. 135–65.

¹² Jean Gimpel, *The Medieval Machine: The Industrial Revolution of the Middle Ages* (New York: Penguin, 1976) pp. 3–6.

¹³ In southern France, cistercian houses for men owned considerably more mills than granges—to such an extent that one must conclude that mills were often used as sources of revenue rather than simply for internal needs. See Berman, *Medieval Agriculture*, pp. 87–91.

¹⁴ *Recueil des pancartes de l'abbaye de la Ferté-sur-Grosne: 1113–1178*, ed. Georges Duby (Gap, 1952) pp. 18–19; and Georges Duby, *Saint Bernard: L'Art Cistercien* (Paris: Arts et Métiers graphiques, 1976) p. 106.

¹⁵ A response to Gimpel's assessment of Bernard and mills is that of Jean Leclercq in *Women and Saint Bernard of Clairvaux*, trans. Marie-Bernard Saïd, CS 104 (Kalamazoo, Michigan: Cistercian Publications, 1989) pp. 126–28.

¹⁶ *Cartulaire de l'abbaye de Notre-Dame-de-l'Eau*, ed. Charles Métais, no. 25 (1236) is the conveyance of rights over mills; no. 29 (1241) rents on mills; and no. 35 (1247) a sixth of a mill; *Abbaye royale de Notre-Dame-des-Clairets: Histoire et cartulaire: 1202–1790*, ed. Vicomte de Souancé (Nogent-le-Rotrou, 1894) no. 42 (1236) rents owed on mills, and no. 55 (1267) rents on mills.

¹⁷ Heirs of founders, for instance, reduced the amounts from fulling

mills at Chartres owed to the nuns of Notre-Dame-de-l'Eau-les-Chartres; *Cartulaire de l'Eau* no. 87 (1279).

[18] Contracts concerning mills constructed by men's abbeys sometimes specifically considered how to share revenues or assess damages in case of floods or insufficient water. See *Cartulaire de l'abbaye de Gimont*, ed. Clergeac (Paris: Champion, 1905) no. V–69 (1163); Paris, Bibliothèque Nationale, Collection Doat, vol. 91, no. 7 (1170); and Toulouse, Archives départementales de l'Haute-Garonne, 2 H Calers, no. 11 (1169).

[19] Constance H. Berman, 'Cistercian Development and the Order's Acquisition of Churches and Tithes in Southern France', *Revue bénédictine* 91 (1981) 193–203.

[20] Boyd, p. 45, suggests that some tithes were on manors which the nuns also owned.

[21] By the time that most women's houses were founded, this was a moot point, since the tithe exemption granted by Innocent II to the entire order in 1132 had been all but rescinded—being limited to *noval* lands, gardens, and animal-husbandry—by the Fourth Lateran Council. See Giles Constable, *Monastic Tithes from Their Origins to the Twelfth Century* (Cambridge: Cambridge University Press, 1964) p. 306.

[22] For example, see *Cartulaire de Notre-Dame-de-Voisins*, ed. J. Doinel (Orléans, 1887) no. 23 (1220), which implies the preaching of gregorian notions about lay ownership of tithes. Of the thirty-one conveyances of tithes to the nuns of this abbey, sixteen or seventeen of the gifts came to them during the reign of Manasses.

[23] For a transcription of this very interesting chirograph, see Constance H. Berman, 'Monastic Hospices in Southern France: The Cistercian Urban Presence', forthcoming.

[24] Toulouse, Archives départementales de l'Haute-Garonne, 7E, Collège de Saint-Bernard, *passim*. Published studies of this college include Louis J. Lekai, 'Le Collège de Saint Bernard au moyen âge: 1280–1533', *Annales du Midi* 85 (1973) 251–60.

[25] A point discussed in Berman, 'Urban/Rural'.

[26] For Saint–Antoine-des-Champs's urban rents, for instance, see Paris, Archives Nationales, LL1595 'Cartulaire de Saint-Antoine'.

[27] *Cartulaire de l'Eau* no. 24 (1235), a rent on the tolls of Chartres; no. 50 (1256), and no. 80 (1272), rents to be paid out of general revenues; *Cartulaire de l'abbaye royale du Lieu-Notre-Dame-lèz-Romorantin*, ed. Ernest Prat (Romorantin, 1892) no. 1 (1247), rents to be paid by the *praepositus* of Chartres; and no. 2 (1249), rents on tolls.

[28] As discussed in Berman, *Medieval Agriculture*, pp. 123–25.

[29] Berman, *Medieval Agriculture*, pp. 96–97.

[30] On delivery of wool by english cistercian nuns, for example, see Graves, pp. 227–28.

[31] The isolated aspect of many abbey sites was created by the gradual depopulation of the area immediately surrounding them. Moreover,

the major part of the patrimony used for cereal cultivation was not usually at the abbey site itself, but at granges often located in the most productive cereal lands of the vicinity. Avoidance of clearance is the implication of certain documents concerning the site change to Villelongue by Cistercians of that abbey. See Paris, Bibliothèque Nationale, Collection Doat, vol. 70, esp. nos. 2–7 (all dated 1149); and Constance H. Berman, 'Origins and Foundation Dates for the Filiation of Morimond in Southern France: Gimont, Villelongue, Berdoues, l'Escaledieu, and Bonnefont', Cîteaux 41 (1990) 256–278.

[32] *Cartulaire de Lieu-lez-Romorantin* no. 1 (1247) and no. 24 (1232) are both conveyances of uncleared lands to the nuns of that abbey.

[33] Boyd, pp. 61–67, implies the acquisition of recently-cleared lands in her discussion of 'noval tithes'. Berdoues' acquisition of recently cleared lands is particularly apparent in its acquisition of the hermitage of Artigues. See *Cartulaire de l'abbaye de Berdoues*, esp. nos. 173 (1152) and 266 (1155), as discussed in Berman, *Medieval Agriculture*, pp. 29–30, and in Berman, 'Origins and Foundation Dates'. On Franquevaux, see Berman, *Medieval Agriculture*, pp. 24–25; on Nîmes: Archives départementales de Gard, Franquevaux H 40 ff. For Pontigny, see *Le Premier Cartulaire de l'abbaye cistercienne de Pontigny (XIIe-XIIIe siècles)*, ed. Martine Garrigues (Paris: Bibliothèque Nationale, 1981) no. 370 (1264) (for instance, land adjoining an assart); *Cartulaire de Voisins* no. 146 (1248) is land called 'Assartz'; *Cartulaire de Lieu-lez-Romorantin* no. 242 (1234).

[34] Paris B.N. Latin MS 11011 'Cartulaire de Grandselve', especially the first few pages, as discussed in Berman, *Medieval Agriculture*, pp. 27–28.

[35] Boyd, p. 26 ff., uses the characterizations of benedictine and cistercian economic systems in the italian Piedmont as presented by Francesco Gosso, *La vità economica delle abbazie peimontesi (sec. x-xiv)*, Analecta Gregoriana 22 (Rome, 1940).

[36] *Conversi* recruitment was linked to acquisition of lands on which those peasants had previously been cultivators. The crisis of *conversi* recruitment therefore tended to coincide with the end of expansion; see Berman, *Medieval Agriculture*, pp. 54–57.

[37] Boyd, pp. 147–48, shows that the consolidation efforts of the nuns of Rifreddo were limited, with long periods between purchases.

[38] Boyd, pp. 148–62, characterized the economic practice of the nuns of Rifreddo as partaking of both the benedictine and cistercian types of economies—having both kinds of granges. She can reconstruct to some extent the area of demesne under direct cultivation as opposed to that of the abbey's three manors with tenants, but she can say nothing about the value of tithes. Graves, pp. 228–29, suggests that the successful administration of a large variety of assets contributed to the abbey's modest success, but gives little information on actual land use. Bourgeois, pp. 139–60, shows how the nuns of Nonenque created

a strong group of pastoral granges at the outset, but were forced out of most pasture areas by Templars and Hospitallers. Marthe Moureau, p. 127 ff., describes cistercian women, like the other nuns in her study, owning a diverse group of revenues, lands, mills, tithes, and other properties, but finds nothing about actual administration.

[39] See Berman, 'Urban/Rural', and 'Chartres'.

[40] On Saint Antoine under the ancien régime, see Paris, Archives nationales, no. S*4384, and Depôt des Plans, N4 Seine 2 Atlas de St. Antoine, and the recent exhibition catalogue, *Du faubourg Saint-Antoine au bois de Vincennes: Promenade historique dans le 12e arrondissement: Exposition organisée par le Musée Carnavalet et la délégation à l'action artistique de la ville de Paris: Mairie annexe du 12e arrondissement 26 janvier–20 février, 19 mars-20 avril 1983, and Musée Carnavelet 26 avril-5 juin 1983* (Paris: Les Musées de la ville de Paris, 1983) pp. 24–27.

[41] See, for example, William C. Jordan, 'The Cistercian Nunnery of La-Cour-Notre-Dame-de-Michéry: A Community That Failed', *Revue bénédictine* 95 (1985) 311–20, which describes an abbey north of Sens, and Berman, 'Patronage, Wealth, and The Building of Monastic Churches for Women. The Cistercian Women at La Cour-Notre-Dame-de-Michéry Revisited,' forthcoming.

TWELFTH-CENTURY BURGUNDY: THE GREAT UNKNOWN?

Constance B. Bouchard
University of Akron

A T THE MEDIEVAL CONGRESS at Kalamazoo in 1988, I told an eminent french historian of monasticism that I was working on the Cistercians of twelfth-century Burgundy. 'Why do you want to do that?' he asked. 'Everything about them is already known.'

Although he put it more bluntly than most, his attitude is extremely common. After all, was not Burgundy the heartland of the cistercian order? Have not generations of scholars devoted themselves to the thought and activities of Bernard of Clairvaux? Is not the paradigm of a poor and idealistic order having to accept 'reality' by the middle of the twelfth century well established?

But in fact, as those scholars working on twelfth-century Cistercians *outside* of Burgundy have begun to suspect, the first century of cistercian history in the duchy is remarkably under-studied. I am continuing to work on twelfth-century Burgundy, in spite of such occasional discouragement, and I have recently completed a statistical study of the monks' economic activities. I have found that many aspects of the Cistercians' early history have either never been addressed at all by scholars or else seem to contradict what has long been assumed.

The rather surprising reason for this is that much of the primary evidence has received scant attention. Two-thirds of the monks' charters have never been edited—and even those that have been printed have not previously been examined systematically. While Bernard of Clairvaux's letters, sermons, and treatises are readily available both in excellent modern editions and, in many cases, in translation, and his ideas and spirituality have been widely discussed, there is still no modern scholarly biography of Bernard. While the early cistercian texts, such as the *Carta caritatis*, and the order's legislative pronouncements in their Chapters General have long been available, many of these texts are now being redated and reexamined on the assumption that the form in which we have them is not their original form.[1] It is therefore very difficult for those working on the Cistercians of other areas of Europe, or even the burgundian Cistercians of the thirteenth and later centuries, to compare the developments they find with the 'paradigm' of twelfth-century Burgundy, because such a paradigm is based on a very slim evidentiary base. In many ways, the history of the cistercian order in Burgundy in its first century of existence is 'the great unknown'.

The principal difficulty in 'knowing' twelfth-century Burgundy is the inaccessibility of the sources.[2] The monks of most houses left a large number of original charters, and in many cases a twelfth- or thirteenth-century cartulary. Yet only *one* of the burgundian houses has had all its charters from one of these early cartularies systematically edited.[3] For the nineteen other cistercian houses in the duchy of Burgundy (defined here as contained in the medieval dioceses of Autun, Auxerre, Chalon, and Langres), either there has been no systematic attempt to publish the documents or else that effort so far has stopped two decades or more short of the end of the twelfth century. The rapid increase in the issuance of charters in the later twelfth century means that there are usually at least as many charters for any given house from the final generation of the century as for the rest of the century combined.[4]

Although Cîteaux and three of her 'first four daughters' have been, not surprisingly, the best served by modern editors,[5] Morimond, the last of these daughters, has had no scholarly editions of any of its documents, and the only thorough study of its history is a century and a half old and was written as part of an attempt to recreate french society in a utopian mold.[6] (It was suggested to me at Kalamazoo that, if I insisted on doing burgundian Cistercians, I should concentrate on Morimond.)

But what of the other fifteen cistercian houses in Burgundy? Many of these houses, too, produced a large number of documents. After Clairvaux and La Ferté, the two burgundian houses with the greatest number of surviving documents (both published and unpublished), the next three houses, in terms of existing charters, are Auberive, Fontenay, and Theuley, houses much less well-known today but whose extensive archives attest to their importance in the twelfth century.

A trip (or, actually, trips) to the burgundian archives is therefore necessary, but even french historians may not always be aware of the diverse places in which cistercian documents are to be found. When one thinks of Burgundy, one thinks of the Archives départmentales de la Côte-d'Or in Dijon, but burgundian cistercian documents are also found in the departmental archives of Allier, Aube, Haute-Marne, Haute-Saône, Jura, Nièvre, Saône-et-Loire, and Yonne, as well as in the Bibliothèque nationale in Paris.

I have discovered that the most rewarding archives for studying the Cistercians are two where historians of the twelfth century rarely venture, the archives of Haute-Marne in Chaumont and of Haute-Saône in Vesoul. Other than their convenient locations on the Paris-Basel train line, neither Chaumont nor Vesoul might appear to have much to lure either the scholar or the tourist. Neither has three-star or even two-star sights in the Michelin green guide, and neither is considered a gastronomic capital. There is no printed inventory for the Haute-Marne of series H, the archival series in which most medieval monastic documents are found, and the printed inventory of series H at the archives of the Haute-Saône lists only a handful of documents from one burgundian monastery, that of Theuley.

But in the archives of the Haute-Marne in Chaumont, neatly inventoried on typewritten sheets, is the biggest single extant collection of materials on the burgundian Cistercians, including documents from Morimond, Auberive, Beaulieu, La Crête, Longué, and Vaux-la-Douce. The archives of the Haute-Saône in Vesoul offer the added and very unusual excitement of a peek at documents essentially unseen by the historian's eye. As well as the documents from Theuley inventoried in the series H, there are a large number of documents from Theuley in the series 25 J. The series J is reserved for family papers, generally those of the last century or two, but 25 J at Vesoul is the Collection Jolibois, which includes a large number of medieval documents from monastic houses, seized after the French Revolution and only given to the archives within the last few years. Inventorying the large Collection Jolibois is only beginning, but, armed with persistence and the Jolibois family's own notes, one can at least make good guesses which boxes are likely to contain cistercian documents. The archives in Vesoul also have a microfilm of Theuley's late twelfth-century cartulary, which had long been thought lost but is actually in a private collection.[7]

But the relative inaccessibility of cistercian burgundian documents is not the only reason the history of the order in its original heartland remains so little known. Even more significant is the tendency by modern scholars to assume that, if they did look at cistercian documents from the order's founding houses, they would simply find a confirmation of the outline of cistercian economic and spiritual history which has long been taken for granted. And yet an examination of the burgundian archives reveals that much that has always been assumed about cistercian economic practice is simply not substantiated by the records.

To begin, it has long been taken for granted that the Cistercians were a wilderness order, receiving and cultivating previously uncultivated land, and that part of the reason for their success was their ability to take advantage of rich, unutilized soils.[8] The retrospective account of the foundation of Cîteaux, describing the monks' establishment in a forest far from human habitation, where there was no sound of voices, only of birds,[9] is assumed to apply to all cistercian houses, and to most or all of the twelfth century. Here the monks' desire to retreat from the centers of civilization is taken to have the unanticipated effect of giving them access to land no one else was using, and thus an economic advantage.

Scholars working on Cistercians in areas other than Burgundy have recently begun challenging the universality of this assumption. Records from southern France, for example, indicate that there the monks primarily acquired fields that had long been under the plow.[10] Because the burgundian situation has been so little studied, however, scholars who have attempted to compare the use by the Cistercians in other regions of long-cultivated land with practices in the burgundian heartland have had to try to find explanations for why monks in Provence or Yorkshire should have followed a practice which they believe the order's original houses spurned.

The answer to the dilemma is that in Burgundy, as elsewhere, the twelfth-century Cistercians did not restrict themselves to previously unworked land. The gifts they received most commonly specified 'both cultivated and uncultivated land'. Although the monks did indeed drain some marshes or swamps and clear some woodland, they also took over a number of long-cultivated fields.

The '1134' legislation which described the sorts of property the monks needed did not describe uncleared wilderness; rather, it specified that they should have 'waters, woods, vineyards, meadows, and fields'. Even Clairvaux's records from the first half of the century indicate a variety in the sorts of land among the gifts the monks received. The lord of Vignory, for example, confirmed to Clairvaux anything the monks might obtain that had been held from him in fief, including partial shares of vineyards.[11] Burgundy had been an economic and political crossroads since before the Romans reached Gaul, and, in the twelfth century, it was much too late for any group of monks to hope to find an extensive wilderness within the duchy.

An examination of the Cistercians' unpublished documents indicates that, from the beginning, cultivated land, described as 'fields and meadows' (*agros et pratas*), made up a substantial proportion of the land given to the monks. Large stretches of land were generally specified as including *both* wooded and cleared land (*tam in nemore quam in plano*).[12] Sometimes the land was described in terms of how many days it took to plow (*jornales* or *carrucas*), which certainly suggests long familiarity with plowing it. The land where the monastery of La Bussière was founded in 1131 had already been held by the black monks of Saint-Vivant of Vergy, scarcely a pioneering group, and was described in the transfer documents as including mills, an adjoining *villa*, and a bridge.[13]

All these signs of previous cultivation of the Cistercians' property in Burgundy, it must be noted, should not be seen as a sign that the monks practiced one thing while preaching another. The retrospective accounts of the original vast solitude at Cîteaux have a highly nostalgic character, which is indeed somewhat ironic considering that the monks who drew them up were not actually at Cîteaux in 1098. But the nostalgia was for a past which, if it had ever existed, was already long gone by the 1120s and 1130s.

A tiny handful of monks might have been able in 1098 to find solitude in a patch of marshy woodlands—which Clairvaux's original site is still today. But by the time the New Monastery had begun to expand and to have daughter houses, it was much too late to try to achieve a solitude greater than that of being located in the countryside rather than in the city, where most of the older burgundian monasteries were located. The wilderness experience and the distancing from human affairs, the monks quickly realized, had to be as much mental or moral as physical. They might look nostalgically back at a 'desert' experience, but in practice the burgundian Cistercians, even in the first half of the twelfth century, realized that if they wanted land they were going to have to acquire previously-cultivated land, and they neither objected to nor attempted to avoid such meadows and fields.

Here a lack of detailed knowledge of the Cistercians' archives has made a number of scholars draw some unwarranted conclusions about cistercian property, but there is nothing in the actual records which could be considered particularly startling. After all, neither the Chapters General nor such spokesmen as Bernard of Clairvaux ever objected in principle to receiving land that had long been under the plow. But the unpublished records of the twelfth-century Cistercians also reveal that the monks, from the time the order first began to expand, received sorts of property to which the order at least intermittently objected.

Perhaps the most noteworthy example is the monks' acceptance of dependent peasants. Such peasants were among the sorts of property listed as 'contrary to monastic purity' in the legislation of the Chapter General usually dated to 1134, and also in the *Exordium parvum* and *Exordium cistercii* of a decade earlier, on which this legislation was based.[14] And yet peasants were among the earliest recorded gifts to the Cistercians. The sons of Viscount Raynald of Beaune gave Cîteaux three serfs around 1110, before the house had formed its first daughters, ten or fifteen years before the *Exordium parvum* and *Exordium cistercii* were written.[15] La Crête and Maizières received gifts of peasants in the 1120s, 1130s, and 1140s.[16] By the 1160s and 1170s, peasants were found in a small but significant proportion of all cistercian acquisitions of property.[17]

To some extent, the Cistercians may have had little choice but to accept peasant tenants, in spite of their legislation. Since so much of the land they received was already under cultivation, it was, naturally, being lived on and worked by someone else's peasant tenants. That land enumerated as consisting of a certain number of *mansi*, as much of the land the monks received was, must have long been divided among a number of peasant families, since that land specifically called wilderness or wasteland (*brolium*) in the donation charters was on the contrary never referred to as consisting of a certain number of *mansi* but rather was described by its borders (for example, rivers or roads). When the monks received land consisting of peasant tenancies, they could either take the peasants with it or put the tenants off the land that they and their families had been working. The monks indeed followed the latter course much of the time, but always with the danger of being accused of being depopulators, of depriving innocent peasants of their means of livelihood, a charge to which they were acutely sensitive. In such circumstances, accepting peasants as gifts should not be seen as a sign of decadence but rather as a practical solution to a troublesome problem.

As the Cistercians' records reveal that they received some sorts of property which scholars have generally assumed they did not, so these records also reveal that, even in the first two generations after Cîteaux's foundation, the monks engaged in a number of types of economic activity which the common paradigm of cistercian development would suggest were foreign to the order. As well as receiving property as free gifts in alms, the Cistercians bought land that they needed, leased other land, and engaged in mortgages and pawnbroking from the time that these sorts of transaction first appeared in Burgundy.

Purchasing land was an excellent way for the monks to regularize and consolidate their property. Their grange system of agriculture required compact, contiguous fields, and, if the knights and petty lords who jointly owned stretches of territory were not all willing to make free gifts in alms, the Cistercians could buy the land they needed from them instead.

The complexity of the landholding in Burgundy, even in the first half of the twelfth century, is seen for example in a large donation of land to Theuley in 1142, in which the monks had to acquire the assent of all the individuals who had held parts of the donated land in fief from the donor. If such assent proved difficult to obtain, it was easiest just to buy the land. When the monks of Cîteaux acquired land for their grange at Orsans from a number of different laymen, around the middle of the twelfth century, they drew up a list of exactly what they had offered each one. One third of the laymen gave their land in alms, for the good of their souls, but in two-thirds of the cases they sold their land, for as little as two *solidi*.[18]

Burgundian monasteries had already begun purchasing property to round out their holdings during the eleventh century.[19] Among the cistercian monasteries, there was a surge in the number of recorded purchases of property after about 1130, interestingly at precisely the same time that *conversi* became at all common in cistercian records, again suggesting a close tie between the rise of the cistercian grange system and the monks' interest in buying the property they needed. In fact, my own study of the Cistercians' archival records indicates that, although the decade of the 1150s witnessed the most purchases of property, the decade of the 1130s included more than any other decade until the end of the century.[20] Thus buying land was an integral part of the order's early economic expansion and success.

Again, there is nothing in early cistercian legislation or the writings of men like Bernard of Clairvaux to forbid the buying of land, and yet a number of scholars have taken it for granted that such purchases must have been contrary to the order's spirit.[21] In fact, the Chapter General only began to treat the buying of property as dangerous in the 1180s, and then because a number of abbots became worried that some houses were tying up too many of their liquid assets in land or even going into debt due to over-enthusiastic purchases. In 1182, the Chapter General forbade houses that owed more than fifty marks to buy more land or construct any new buildings; that purchases were here equated with building programs indicates that the assembled abbots' chief concern was not buying property *per se* but rather spending money unnecessarily.[22]

The order did, however, legislate against purchases *per se* in 1191, explicitly equating buying property with greed or materialism. The Chapter General justified the radical step of forbidding further purchases by saying the abbots did so '...to temper cupidity in our order and to avoid a constant interest in acquisition.' But this prohibition proved as difficult to enforce as it had been to keep some houses from going into debt in the first place. The following year, 1192, the ordinances of the Chapter General noted that many houses had 'violated' the prohibition on buying property and waived it in cases of 'necessity'.[23] In practice, the ruling was a dead letter, and cistercian purchases of property in Burgundy increased steadily throughout the final two decades of the twelfth century.

The Cistercians, in addition, leased property for the same reason that they purchased property, because the demands of their grange system required them to acquire compact agricultural units, and they could not wait for the lay landowners to give it to them. Indeed, from the monks' point of view, leasing was in many ways more economically advantageous than buying, since it did not require them to make a large one-time payment. Overall, leasing was the second most common sort of transaction recorded in the archives of the burgundian Cistercians, second only to gifts. It may indeed have been even more common than the records indicate, for many gifts to the monks involve granting them the right to keep the land they had been leasing without continuing to pay the rent, a lease otherwise unattested.[24] Leasing land was not forbidden to the monks during the twelfth century.

Yet, as in the case of purchases of property, scholars have often assumed that the appearance of leases in the monks' records should be taken as a sign that they were losing their original principles.[25] An examination of the documents, however, reveals that leasing was a part of cistercian economic practice from early in the twelfth century. The abbey of Mores, a daughter of Clairvaux, when it was founded in 1132 assembled part of its original holdings as gifts, but also a substantial part by leases, both from laymen and from the black monks of the nearby house of Pouthières.[26]

An additional form of economic exchange revealed by the Cistercians' documents, even though it again was a form of exchange modern scholars often assume they avoided, was taking property in pawn. In return for a lump-sum payment, always less than the sale price of a comparable piece of property, a layman would give a piece of land to the monks with the stipulation that he would repay the amount they had advanced him, generally within six years. If he did not, the monks might keep the land.[27] Pawning property was especially common for men leaving on Crusade, who needed money in a hurry but who still hoped to be able to return and redeem their pledge within six years.

The Cistercians' practice of receiving property in pawn is somewhat different from their practice of buying or leasing property because, although there is nothing in early cistercian legislation to forbid any of the three, the monks only began to receive property in pawn with any frequency after the middle of the twelfth century, whereas the other two practices can be found much earlier. It must be pointed out, however, that the increase in cistercian pawnbroking after 1150 cannot by itself be seen as a sign of incipient decadence, because *no* monks in Burgundy, black or white, received very much property in pawn before this time.[28]

Yet there was always something a little difficult morally about pawns, because it was standard for someone to keep the fruits and income (usufruct) of the land held as a pledge, even if that pledge were redeemed. Around 1150, Pope Eugenius III stated that keeping the usufruct in this way was usurious.[29] In 1157, the cistercian Chapter General declared that houses of the order should not 'receive property in pawn anymore', recognizing that the practice had become common among the white monks. In fact, the monks' records reveal a steady stream of pawned property. In 1180, realizing that the practice was continuing, the Chapter General ordered that those abbots who had received property in pawn should return it by the next year.[30] But these repeated prohibitions had little effect, for the amount of property received in pledge increased steadily during the last two decades of the twelfth century. At best, the monks had the man who pawned his property to them specify that he gave the usufruct as a gift for his soul,[31] so that the transaction could not be seen as usurious.

What does this look at the Cistercians' archives mean for the normally accepted paradigm of the twelfth-century history of the order in Burgundy? I would suggest it indicates how little is actually known about the economic activities of the monks there, and how much opportunity remains for productive research on the monks' property and forms of exchange.

It has commonly been taken for granted that, for the first fifty years or so of the order's existence, the monks practiced subsistence agriculture, clearing and draining wasteland and swamps with their own hands or with the assistance of their *conversi*. During this time, according to the standard paradigm, the monks received their land strictly from gifts in alms. Only in the second half of the twelfth century, this paradigm continues, did the monks begin to 'fall away' from their principles; the death of Bernard of Clairvaux in 1153 is often taken as a convenient turning point. Although this view has been somewhat modified in recent years, from the earlier assessment that decadence was setting in during the second half of the twelfth century to the less harsh judgment that 'ideals' were having to give way to 'reality', there has still been the almost universal assumption that both early cistercian principles and early cistercian practice in Burgundy required the monks to live from previously unworked land, which they received only in alms.

The monks' own records tell a very different story. From the early days of the order, the monks received land that had long been cultivated, sometimes complete with peasant tenants. Rather than always waiting to be given this land, the monks bought or leased what they wanted when their secular neighbors were not willing to make a pious gift. Starting in the middle of the twelfth century, when pawning first became common, the Cistercians quickly became the chief burgundian pawnbrokers, advancing money to Crusaders and others who needed ready cash, in return for a piece of pledged property which the monks had an excellent chance of keeping.

The order's own legislation reflects the Cistercians' willingness to take part in the rapidly diversifying economy of the twelfth century. The earliest statements of the chapters general on the sorts of property suitable for Cistercians, while forbidding serfs, explicitly allowed them all sorts of cultivated as well as uncultivated land. Leasing was never forbidden to the monks as an economic tool in the twelfth century, and purchasing property was only forbidden late and ineffectively, and then primarily because the practice was putting some houses dangerously into debt. Although the Chapter General forbade taking property in pawn some fifteen years after the Cistercians first began to do so,[32] the repeated prohibitions of the later twelfth century, with their apparently ineffectual warnings of what would happen if the abbots did not finally start complying, indicate that a practice that had begun in the first half of the twelfth century, when it was not forbidden, had become too thoroughly integrated into many houses' economic programs to be easily abandoned in the later part of the century.

How has this version of cistercian economic activities in Burgundy remained so little known? It is certainly not because the monks themselves tried to conceal it. Their documents spell out in a precise latin vocabulary whether a transaction was a gift, a lease, a pawn, or a sale.[33] There are far too many of the latter types of transaction, clearly identified as such in the pancartes which the monks assembled for the approval and sealing by the cistercian bishops of Langres and Auxerre, for the monks to have been making any sort of attempt to pass them off as gifts.

Part of the reason scholars have not seen the evidence of these sorts of transaction in the burgundian cistercian records is the relative inaccessibility of these records, as noted above, but part is also because scholars have not been looking. The documents for Cîteaux, Clairvaux, and La Ferté, although not yet edited for the entire twelfth century, have been available in print at least in part for thirty or forty years, and there is a good deal of previously-cultivated land, sales, pawns, and leases in these records. Scholars have assumed that because the Cistercians were an austere and holy order, they would not, at least for the first two generations or so, have become involved in anything so sordid as complicated economic exchange, and therefore the indications of this exchange have been overlooked.

But should the discovery that even the early Cistercians received a diverse mix of property, and received it by many other sorts of exchange as well as by gifts in alms, be taken as an indication that the order was *not* holy and austere? Far from it. The early Cistercians defined themselves by the simplicity of their personal lives, their distance from the bustle of the cities, and their manual labor, not by any rejection of previously-cultivated property or of the practices of buying or leasing the land they needed. Modern scholars might treat successful economic management and holiness of life as antitheses, but, to the early Cistercians and to their lay patrons, the two were perfectly compatible.

Additionally, the increasing participation by the Cistercians in these sorts of economic activity in the second half of the twelfth century, when indeed such activities became more common for all orders of burgundian monks, cannot be treated as an indication that the monks had become decadent or had even given up, reluctantly, their ideals. Since these ideals did not consist of a rejection of economic activity, participation in such activity did not by itself mean that the order had left its ideals behind. Throughout the twelfth century, the Cistercians kept their original austerity in food and clothing. Although their increased wealth made them able to build new and often very large churches after the middle of the century, they built them with rigorous simplicity, without either the elaborate carving found on contemporary burgundian romanesque churches or stained glass.[34]

That the Cistercians' contemporaries continued at this time to consider them as holy monks, whose prayers would find the ear of God, is indicated vividly by the continuing volume of outright gifts to the monks. Gifts in alms continued, throughout the twelfth century, to be the single most frequent sort of transaction recorded in the monks' archives. There were far more gifts to the Cistercians in the second half of the twelfth century, especially in the 1180s and 1190s, than there had been in the first half. In spite of attempts by the Chapter General to freeze the size of the order, the number of cistercian houses increased steadily throughout the second half of the century, as laymen invited the monks to settle on their land and as a stream of converts made possible the foundation of new daughter-houses. Even while the laymen of Burgundy treated the Cistercians as a source of cash if they wanted to sell or needed to pawn some land, they also treated them as pious and holy men, whose prayers they wanted when they died.

This is, perhaps, the one test that matters. As I have attempted to indicate, an examination of the relatively understudied records of the twelfth-century Cistercians in Burgundy reveals as common, from the earliest days, many economic activities often considered later departures from the practices of those earliest days. But it is equally clear that the order's contemporaries, and for the most part the monks themselves, found nothing in this, in the context of their own period, to lower their opinion of cistercian sanctity and holiness. The monks can scarcely be faulted for not conforming to a twentieth-century schema in which spirituality and economic concerns are treated as incompatible opposites, since in the twelfth century such a schema did not exist.

NOTES

[1] Jean-Baptiste Auberger, *L'unanimité cistercienne primitive: Mythe ou réalité?* (Achel, 1986).

[2] For the relative inaccessibility of cistercian documents, see also Constance B. Bouchard, 'Cistercian Ideals versus Reality: 1134 Reconsidered', *Cîteaux* 39 (1988) 221; and *Holy Entrepreneurs: Cistercians, Knights, and Economic Exchange in Twelfth-Century Burgundy* (Ithaca, 1991) introduction. The sources for the twelfth-century history of those cistercian houses in the diocese of Langres are surveyed by Bertrand Joly, 'Les chartes de fondation des abbayes cisterciennes au XIIe siècle dans le diocèse de Langres', *Cahiers haut-marnais* 167 (1986) 107–144.

[3] Martine Garrigues (ed.), *Le premier cartulaire de l'abbaye de Pontigny (XIIe-XIIIe siècles)*, Collection de documents inédits sur l'histoire de France 14 (Paris, 1981).

[4] The archivists of the Archives départementales de l'Aube are slowly and carefully working through Clairvaux's twelfth-century documents. Jean Waquet (ed.), *Recueil des chartes de l'abbaye de Clairvaux, XIIe siècle* (Troyes, 1950–1982). So far, two fascicles have appeared, including editions of all documents through 1173, but three-quarters of the twelfth-century charters remain to be done.

[5] See, besides the editions of documents from Clairvaux and Pontigny cited above, J. Marilier (ed.), *Chartes et documents concernant l'abbaye de Cîteaux, 1098–1182* (Rome, 1961); and Georges Duby (ed.), *Recueil des pancartes de l'abbaye de La Ferté-sur-Grosne, 1113–1178* (Paris, 1953).

[6] Louis Dubois, *Histoire de l'abbaye de Morimond* (Paris, 1851).

[7] The microfilm is catalogued as 1 Mi–3 (R1). There is also a smaller Collection Jolibois at Chaumont, catalogued as series 19 J, and some additional cistercian documents there in the Collection Laloy, series F.

[8] For a typical assessment of the Cistercians as a 'frontier' order, see R. W. Southern, *Western Society and the Church in the Middle Ages* (Harmondsworth, England, 1970) pp. 250–65.

[9] *Summa cartae caritatis*, 1, edd. Jean de la Croix Bouton and Jean Baptiste Van Damme, *Les plus anciens textes de Cîteaux*, Commentarii Cistercienses, Studia et documenta 2 (Achel, 1974) p. 111.

[10] Constance Hoffman Berman, *Medieval Agriculture, the Southern French Countryside, and the Early Cistercians: A Study of Forty-three Monasteries*, Transactions of the American Philosophical Society 76/5 (Philadelphia, 1986) pp. 11–14.

[11] Josephus-Maria Canivez (ed.), *Statuta capitulorum generalium ordinis Cisterciensis*, I, Bibliothèque de la Revue d'histoire ecclésiastique 9 (Louvain, 1933) pp. 14–15, no. 9. Waquet (ed.), *Recueil des chartes de Clairvaux*, pp. 35–39, no. 17.

[12] See, for example, Troyes, Archives de l'Aube, 35 H 5, no. 7, a document from Quincy. See also Benoît Chauvin, 'Réalités et évolution

de l'économie cistercienne dans les duché et comté de Bourgogne au moyen âge', in *L'économie cistercienne: Géographie—Mutations du moyen âge aux temps modernes*, Flaran 3 (Auch, 1983) p. 21.

[13] Dijon, Archives de la Côte-d'Or, 12 H 36. *Gallia Christiana*, 4:89, no. 54. See also Auberger, *L'unanimité cistercienne*, p. 101.

[14] Canivez (ed.), *Statuta*, pp. 14–15, no. 9. Bouton and Van Damme, *Les plus anciens textes*, pp. 77–78, 123. For the dating of these passages in the *Exordium parvum* and *Exordium cistercii*, see Auberger, *L'unanimité cistercienne*, pp. 10–11, 35–56.

[15] Marilier (ed.), *Chartes et documents de Cîteaux*, pp. 49–51, 98, nos. 23, 101. These serfs were ones the viscount had reserved to himself when originally giving the monks some land in 1098. Although Marilier dates the gift from the viscount's sons to c. 1140, perhaps believing the monks would not have received such gifts any earlier, a date around 1110 seems much more likely, as the viscount and all three serfs would scarcely have been alive for forty years after his original gift.

[16] Chaumont, Archives de la Haute-Marne, 5 H 7. *Gallia Christiana*, 4:239, no. 22. Paris, Bibliothèque nationale [henceforth BN], MS nouv. acq. fr. 8680, pp. 5–6. Chauvin is mistaken in stating categorically that cistercian houses in Burgundy received no serfs before about 1160 or 1170, the only exception being the above-mentioned gift to Cîteaux; 'Réalités et évolution', p. 37.

[17] For examples for this period from La Ferté, La Bussière, and Theuley, see Mâcon, Archives de Saône-et-Loire, H 25, no. 6; BN, MS nouv. acq. fr. 8664, fol. 56; and Vesoul, Archives de la Haute-Saône, H 409 and 25 J A13.

[18] Archives de la Haute-Saône, 25 J 1. Marilier (ed.), *Chartes et documents de Cîteaux*, pp. 88–89, no. 89.

[19] Barbara H. Rosenwein, *To Be the Neighbor of Saint Peter: The Social Meaning of Cluny's Property, 909–1049* (Ithaca, 1989) pp. 99–100.

[20] Bouchard, *Holy Entrepreneurs*, chapter 1.

[21] For example, Joan Wardrop, in her study of the Cistercians in Yorkshire, asserts that the order 'must have' been opposed to purchases of property from the beginning; Wardrop, *Fountains Abbey and Its Benefactors, 1132–1300*, Cistercian Studies 91 (Kalamazoo, 1987) p. 70.

[22] Canivez (ed.), *Statuta*, pp. 90–91, no. 9.

[23] *Ibid.*, pp. 142, 147, nos. 42, 3.

[24] For examples from La Crête, Reigny, and Fontenay, see Archives de la Haute-Marne, 5 H 8; Auxerre, Archives de l'Yonne, H 1566; and Archives de la Côte-d'Or, 15 H 9, part 1, fol. 100r.

[25] This is the assumption made, for example, by Robert Fossier, 'L'essor économique de Clairvaux', in Commission d'histoire de l'ordre de Cîteaux, *Bernard de Clairvaux* (Paris, 1953) pp. 109–110. Interestingly, as Fossier notes himself, leases appear in Clairvaux's records under

Abbot Bernard; Waquet (ed.), *Recueil des chartes de Clairvaux*, pp. 4, 66–67, 77, nos. 3, 50, 68.

[26] Charles Lalore (ed.), 'Chartes de l'abbaye de Mores', *Mémoires de la Société académique d'agriculture, des sciences, arts et belles-lettres du département de l'Aube* 37 (1873) 45–49, no. 2.

[27] The terms of a pawn are spelled out clearly in an 1194 document from Auberive; Archives de la Haute-Marne, 1 H 104. For this type of transaction, sometimes called a 'mortgage' by modern scholars, see also Patricia A. Lewis, 'Mortgages in the Bordelais and Bazadais', *Viator* 10 (1979) 23–25; Constance Hoffman Berman, 'Land Acquisition and the Use of the Mortgage Contract by the Cistercians of Berdoues', *Speculum* 57 (1982) 250–53; and Constance B. Bouchard, 'Property Transactions and the Twelfth-Century Cistercians', in *Proceedings of the Eleventh Annual Meeting of the Western Society for French History*, ed. John F. Sweets (Lawrence, Kansas, 1984) pp. 3–4.

[28] Constance Brittain Bouchard, *Sword, Miter, and Cloister: Nobility and the Church in Burgundy, 980–1198* (Ithaca, 1987) pp. 222–23.

[29] Eugenius III, *Letter 550*; PL 180:1567.

[30] Canivez (ed.), *Statuta*, pp. 60, 88, nos. 6, 12.

[31] See, for example, Archives de Saône-et-Loire, H 25, no. 22, an 1179 document from La Ferté recording a pawn.

[32] The earliest fully-described cistercian pawn is from Theuley in 1146, but nothing in the charter suggests that the monks thought they were pioneering a new form of exchange. Archives de la Haute-Saône, 25 J 52.

[33] Bouchard, *Holy Entrepreneurs*, chapter 2. An 1157 charter of Quincy referred to a sale both by the verb *vendere* and the noun *emptio*; Archives de la Côte-d'Or, 17 H 620. For examples of the careful use of the term *cens* to designate a lease, see Archives de la Côte-d'Or, 15 H 9, part 2, fols. 9r–10r, nos. 20–21, documents from Fontenay in the 1130s; and Archives de la Haute-Marne, 8 H 40, nos. 5–6, documents from Morimond in the 1170s. An 1189 charter from Beaulieu distinguished clearly between property given in alms and that given in pawn (*vadimonio*); Archives de la Haute-Marne, 2 H 1.

[34] Bouchard, 'Property Transactions', p. 1.

MONASTIC PROFESSION ACCORDING TO AELRED OF RIEVAULX

Elizabeth Connor, ocso
Abbaye Notre-Dame du Bon-Conseil

IN HIS PREFATORY LETTER to the *Mirror of Charity*, Aelred of Rievaulx explains to Saint Bernard, who had asked and even commanded him to write this work, that in composing it he had taken material partly from his own meditations and partly from notes communicated to his friend and prior, Hugh. These various notes he inserted into his text where they seemed to fit in best,[1] so as to make a coherent ensemble.

One of the sections which is clearly an insertion is Chapter 35 of Book 3, which has been called by Dom Wilmart: 'A Short Tractate on the scope and goal of monastic profession.'[2] Though it must be admitted that this treatise interrupts Aelred's line of development in Book 3, its insertion is not haphazard. Aelred himself states, at the beginning of Chapter 35, that it may not seem pertinent to his subject, but that nevertheless, it is advisable to include it. Furthermore it would hardly be likely that Aelred, in his first major spiritual work, would have been careless about the composition of his opus, especially since he knew that his famous Father Immediate would be examining it closely.

Chapter 35 is a refutation of complaints from a 'certain monk' about the cistercian observance, and is completely in line with the basic thrust of the *Mirror*, which is an *apologia* for the cistercian monastic life as a means of progressing towards the fullness of charity. The question it deals with is, in fact, at the very heart of monastic life, and several of the major themes which run like leitmotifs through the *Mirror* are recapitulated, so to speak, in this Chapter 35. So when Aelred says: 'Although it [the treatise on profession] may not seem completely pertinent to our subject...,'[3] he is perhaps simply being subtle.

The treatise, in dialogue form but with Aelred doing most of the talking, has as starting point the following affirmation of the 'certain monk' whom the context permits us to presume was from a monastery following the benedictine *Rule*:

> I do not hesitate to say that the *Rule* of the monastic state, yes, the virtue of the monastic order, indeed, the essential character of monastic profession itself, consists in those practices which make the monk when all others cease to exist, and without which the others, I will not say do not *make* a monk, but do not even give an idea of what a monk is.[4]

This leads Aelred to say:

> I think it is advisable for us who are called monks to take into account and examine more closely the force of our *Rule*. Since many things are said there about both spiritual and physical [practices], let us investigate by careful questioning which of these the force of the rule and the norm of our profession consist of more particularly.[5]

It is a question of the specific nature of the monastic life, a theme which, during the years following the Second Vatican Council, has occupied many monks and nuns. Before trying to discern this specific nature, however, it is useful to situate the monk among Christians in general. And here we can see that the chapters directly preceding 35 are already a sort of digression from the subject Aelred had been developing in Book 3: the way charity should be practiced in diverse relationships and life situations. In chapter 31 he had been stressing moderation in all things, and was obliged to recognize, when it comes to particulars,

> how arduous and difficult it is to deal with this, when there are as many human aptitudes as there are human beings, and it is very rare to find even two at a time for whom all things are equally suited.[6]

As an illustration of this diversity, in Chapters 32–34 Aelred describes three *ordines* or categories of Christian life. He is quite possibly thinking of Saint Augustine, but a more direct relationship to Saint Bernard's *On Precept and Dispensation* is discernible, as will be brought out in the following pages.[7]

THE THREE ORDERS

Tripartite classifications, fictive as they may seem to us today, were common and familiar to people in Aelred's time. In spite of their limitations, they are useful for the conveyance of a message, and in this case the message will be especially for monks. Aelred begins with a very dense description of the three orders:

> Three orders of human life [*ordines humanae conversationis*] come to mind. The first is natural, the second necessary, and the third voluntary. The first is conceded, the second imposed, and the third is offered to humankind. The first depends on enablement, the second on necessity, and the third on will. To the first grace is due, to the second mercy, and to the third glory.[8]

Since the meaning of these lines is not self-evident, each of the three orders requires some commentary.

The natural order

Fashioned in the image of the Trinity, the first human being was able by his memory to hold fast to God without forgetfulness, recognize him by his understanding without error, and embrace him by his love without self-centered desire for anything else. And so he was happy.[9] He enjoyed the peace which comes from well-ordered being. This was his natural state. The natural order is said to be 'conceded', given, granted, because the human person was created to use the works of creation in a well-ordered way. This *bonum naturae* (= grace) enables the person to do this. It is a power. Humankind was created to be like that. Saint Bernard expresses the same view of human nature: it is 'a natural moral gift' which was corrupted by pride. But

> ...the natural goodness lost by pride is recovered by obedience, and they [humans] learn, as far as in them lies, to live peacefully and sociably with all who share their nature, with all men, no longer through fear of discipline but by the impulse of love.[10]

The person in the natural order, therefore, has attained a certain liberty in his relationship with himself, God, and others.

It is now possible to see more clearly what Aelred meant in the opening paragraph: 'The first order is natural...is conceded...depends on enablement...to it, grace is due.' If grace is due, it is because the *bonum naturae*, the gift, *is* grace.

In his descriptions of the natural order, Aelred remains on a purely moral level. A person is in the 'natural' order who, if he has not committed illicit actions, may make use of everything licit and permitted, as long as he does so licitly. By this Aelred means using everything with moderation, at the proper time and in the proper place, and respecting the circumstances in which one acts and the nature of everything that one uses. In the natural order a person may have possessions and marry: he is not bound to special penitential practices. And Aelred quotes Saint Paul: 'To the pure all things are pure' (Titus 1:15), and 'Nothing which is accepted with thanksgiving should be rejected' (1 Timothy 4:3–4).[11]

The necessary order

The second order is the necessary:

> The necessary order means that someone who has committed illicit acts should restrict himself in the use of things licit. In this restriction, two things should be considered: the measure of satisfaction and the need for amendment. The measure of satisfaction, so that the severity of the mortification may be proportionate to the measure of the fault and that, attentive to the voice of the Baptist, 'we may bear fruit befitting repentance' [Matthew 3:8].[12]

Aelred's initial description of this order needs less clarification: this order *is* 'necessary'; it is 'imposed'. It 'depends on necessity', and 'mercy is due to it'. If a person has sinned, permitted his passions to gain the upper hand, and developed bad habits, he must make the necessary moral effort to return to the Father who, in his mercy, inspires him to undertake these efforts and awaits his prodigal son. 'Mercy is due' in this order, not because of any rightful claim on the part of the creature, but because God's mercy wills that everyone should be saved. Aelred comments only briefly on satisfaction and amendment. Rather, to those struggling against bad habits he recommends Cassian's *Instructions for Renunciants*, in which means of combatting each of the principal vices are given.[13]

The voluntary order

The third order is voluntary:

> There is an unforced holocaust,[14] an acceptable offering, a voluntary sacrifice,[15] when someone makes his way with liberty of spirit upward from the things that are conceded or allowed, through

those which are prescribed, to those which are proposed to all who long for the rewards of greater glory.[16]

It is willingly assumed; it is 'voluntary'. It is not imposed but 'offered'. Assuming it 'depends on [our own] will', 'glory' is its due. It is the order of gratuitousness. Aelred quotes the Lord's invitations: 'If you want to be perfect, go, sell what you own, and give the money to the poor, and come, follow me' (Matthew 19:21). 'There are eunuchs who have made themselves so for the sake of the kingdom of heaven. Let anyone who can accept this, accept it' (Matthew 19:12). And he comments:

> Renunciation of the world, a resolution to observe chastity, and profession of a stricter life are therefore reckoned among voluntary sacrifices.[17] ...Be careful not to reckon this perfection of life—which one undertakes not under compulsion but willingly—to be among things necessary and obligatory, but rather among the voluntary. This necessity, which no one has imposed on him against his will, but to which he has spontaneously submitted himself in his desire for perfection, should be called voluntary and not compulsory.[18]

Saint Bernard, in his work *On Precept and Dispensation*, had already made the distinction between the necessary and the voluntary. The *On Precept and Dispensation* and the *Apology* are, interestingly enough, the only works of Bernard which treat specifically and explicitly of the monastic state. When speaking of the obligation of the *Rule* for those who have professed it, Bernard explains:

> As I see it, the *Rule* of Saint Benedict is proposed to all, but imposed on none. It will be of profit to those who reverently receive it and keep it, but no obstacle to those who pass it by. That which depends on the free will of him who undertakes

it rather than on the authority of him who proposes it, I would definitely consider as a free offering and not as a matter of duty.[19]

This is the order, above all others, which brings the person back to God. If it is an unforced holocaust, it is because God first has enabled the soul to offer it. Charity converts souls because it makes them act willingly.[20]

In his development on free will (Book 1, chapters 9–15), Aelred repeatedly cites Saint Paul's words: 'Not I, but the grace of God with me' (1 Corinthians 15:10); 'It is God at work in you, both to will and to work his good pleasure' (Philippians 2:13).[21]

> That I may be willing to do a good work, it is God who causes even my willing. Then arousing the will itself to seek, to ask, to knock, he gives grace upon grace to complete what the good will chooses.[22]
>
> The will of God is itself his love, which is nothing other than his Holy Spirit by whom charity is poured out into our hearts [Romans 5:5]. It is an outpouring of divine charity and a coordination of the human will with, or certainly a subordination of the human will to, the divine will. This happens when the Holy Spirit, who is the will and love of God, and who is God, penetrates and pours himself into the human will. Lifting it up from lower to higher things, he transforms it totally into his own mode and quality, so that, cleaving to the Spirit by the indissoluble glue of unity, it is made one spirit with him. The Apostle clearly intimated this same thing: 'Someone who cleaves to the Lord', he said, 'becomes one spirit with him'.[23]

For Aelred, the will and love are inseparable.[24] This is a dominant theme in the *Mirror*. All love depends on the accord of two wills. Since the will itself is nothing other than love, and since the summit of the Christian life is found in the accomplishment of the twofold commandment of love of God and neighbor, love implies a well-ordered will. The practices of monastic life are the means of establishing this order in the will. The whole treatise on monastic profession ought to be read in the light of what is said on the voluntary order. But the monastic life is arduous, and a Christian can legitimately and authentically seek God in the natural order. Anyone who desires to embrace the voluntary order, therefore, should

> ... first look carefully into the norm of his promise or resolution, that is, into what it consists of and what it demands. Then let him weigh it in the scales of his experience and discern the strength of both the outward and inward person.[25]

Aelred is echoing the Lord's admonition in the Gospel: 'If a man wants to build a tower...' (Luke 14:28).

WHAT MAKES A MONK

Once the fundamental attitude necessary for the monk is clear, Aelred undertakes to demonstrate the essential character of the monastic life in reply to the black monk who had challenged cistercian observance. What specifically does 'make a monk'? What is the object of the profession promises, that is to say, stability, conversion of life, and obedience according to the *Rule* of Saint Benedict? The virtues? Observances? In the ensuing discussion Aelred analyzes these three categories of monastic obligations. In doing so, he leads his listeners through a verbal labyrinth.

The profession promises

The 'certain monk' had begun confidently, affirming that stability, conversion of life, and obedience according to the *Rule* of Saint Benedict constitute what is essential for the monk. He states with generosity:

> I will strive with complete devotion to fulfill my promises and those things which I have vowed—to the extent that the Lord will grant this to me. But as for the other things, I will try to accomplish them, not as part of the body of our *Rule*, but as practices which support and sustain it.[26]

Aelred does not deny that the objects of the profession promises are essential in the monastic state, but he does question the black monk's reasoning: that they are essential because they do not admit of dispensations, whereas the practices do admit of dispensations—for example, monks in delicate health may be permitted to eat meat.

But, contends Aelred, are such permissions really dispensations? Are they not rather provisions built into the *Rule* because of the diverse characters and capabilities of the monks in any given community? He explains: '[Benedict] taught compassion for the aged and children, not as a dispensation but by the authority of the *Rule* [Ch. 37].'[27] Advancing the hour of their meals is not a question of dispensation from the general rule, but precisely a built-in provision for the aged and children. Furthermore, the argument that essential elements do not admit of dispensations does not hold: Benedict himself sent Maur into Gaul, which was obviously a dispensation with respect to stability, because there is nowhere in the *Rule* an explicit mention of monks being permitted to move from one monastery or place to another. In Aelred's own time, monks did in fact transfer quite frequently from one monastery to another.[28]

As a corollary to the discussion on the promises made at monastic profession, Aelred raises another question which lets us glimpse some of the machinations of monks of his time:

> I would still like to know whether he [the black monk] thinks that the monk professes the first two [stability and conversion of life] according to the *Rule* in the same way as he does obedience, or whether these are professed simply

in an indeterminate way. I would not think the question worthy of inquiry at all, had I not come across some monks who claim they have made profession in such a way—that is, that they have promised only obedience according to the *Rule* and the other two not according to the *Rule* but in some indeterminate way. . . .[29] If the first two are promised in an indeterminate way, the *Rule* of Saint Benedict would seem to differ from other rules only as regards the profession of obedience.[30]

On the one hand, it is obvious that obedience according to the *Rule* of Saint Augustine cannot be different from obedience according to the *Rule* of Saint Benedict; it cannot be tardy or tepid, morose or grumbling.[31] On the other hand, canons and clerics who follow the *Rule* of Saint Augustine are obliged to observe a certain modality of stability and conversion of life.[32] Conversion of life is, in fact, an obligation for all Christians, in virtue of the Lord's teaching in the Gospel.[33] Aelred does not pursue this, since it is clear to him that stability and conversion of life must be viewed in the context of the *Rule* of Saint Benedict if a monk is making profession in a monastery of benedictine *Rule*.

Practice of the virtues

The reply to the question whether practice of the virtues constitutes what is specific to the monastic life must necessarily be negative, because all Christians are obliged by the Lord himself to practice the virtues:

> Does not each [Benedict and Augustine] recommend that charity which Christ recommends in the law and the Gospel? We can ask the same thing about the other virtues. . . .[34] Who in his right mind, in exhorting others to virtue, will say that these precepts are his and not rather those of Christ?[35] . . . Obviously, then, whatever they put into their rules about charity, humility, and the

other virtues, they recommend not as their own precepts, but as the Lord's.³⁶

The precepts of the Rule

These are the 'other things' to which the monk objector alluded at the beginning of the discussion, the 'other things' which he would try to accomplish, not as part of the body of the *Rule*, but as practices which support and sustain it.³⁷ Later in the dialogue, when conversion of life is under discussion, after showing that conversion is a common exigency of all monastic rules and of the christian life, Aelred affirms that

> ...for some diversity to be found among the diverse types of conversion of life which are professed according to the diverse rules, there is nothing to which we may have recourse except those traits which constitute the diversity among the diverse rules.³⁸

And these are: '...How to eat, dress, work, read, keep vigil, sing psalms, correct and be corrected, and other things like this, because they are found to be different in the different rules.'³⁹ Elsewhere, other elements are mentioned: '...Manual labor, the quantity of bread and beverage, the number of portions, the way of dressing, the length of vigils, the quality of the bedclothes, the heaviness of silence, the length of reading, the inflection of psalms, the prolonged fasts, the reception of guests, and anything else of this type....'⁴⁰

Although the 'certain monk' mentions the length of reading, *lectio* as such is nowhere to be found among either the essentials or among the observances which admit of dispensations and are therefore not essential. Aelred

> ...wonder[s] why he said nothing about *lectio*, when he talked about the things that he called not the *Rule* itself but support for it. Since *lectio* can be dispensed, it is clear that, according to him, it does not pertain to the body of the *Rule*.⁴¹

The omission of this primordial practice is ironic, to say the least, but it is consistent with the objector's purpose. He is attacking observances which are physically arduous. Since *lectio* is not so, there would be no need to have a dispensation from it.

The Cistercians recognized the importance of both *corporalia* and *spiritualia* because exterior observances go hand in hand with interior progress. In Book 2 of the *Mirror*, particularly, Aelred explains how the practice of *corporalia*, the yoke and burden of the Lord, is made progressively easy and light as charity grows in the soul.[42] In a sermon for the Assumption,[43] Aelred likens the activities of Mary and Martha to the spiritual and corporal observances, showing that both Mary and Martha must live together in the soul. He treats of the same theme in another sermon in which he uses the image of tunics of wool and of linen to represent the 'active life' (*corporalia*) and 'contemplative life' (*spiritualia*) respectively.[44] Both tunics are necessary. Without the woolen tunic, one will grow cold in one's linen tunic; without a linen tunic, one will find the woolen one too rough and abrasive.

The necessity of the two explains and, one might say, justifies the very down to earth conclusion about what is specific in monastic profession according to the different rules. In the very ordinary, often banal, occupations of each day the monk is called upon to live what he has promised at his profession: stability, conversion, obedience according to the *Rule* of Saint Benedict. He is called on to practice fraternal charity, patience, humility, poverty, gentleness, all virtues recommended or commanded in the Gospel. It is thus that this is his way of following Christ. In a well-known phrase, Aelred has expressed this in his *First Sermon for the Feast of Saint Benedict*: 'For in Christ Jesus he [Saint Benedict] has engendered us through the Gospel.'[45]

Basically, then, it is the combination of doctrine and practice, according to one or another monastic legislator, which constitutes the specific nature of a determined way of monastic life, and this in turn leads to the growth of nuances in the spirit of the diverse ways of monastic life. There is interplay between what the monk does and how he does it. There are differences of interpretation and varying accents.

It is thus that Cistercians find today 'in the Rule of Saint Benedict the practical interpretation of the Gospel' for themselves.[46] And it is in this perspective that, in the dialogue between the novice and Aelred, his novice master, in chapter 17 of Book 2 of the *Mirror*, the neophyte's observations can be understood:

> To summarize many things in a few words, I hear nothing about perfection in the precepts of either the Gospel or the Apostles, I find nothing in the writings of the holy Fathers, I understand nothing in the sayings of the ancient monks which is not in harmony with this order and this profession.[47]

What is said here is a reflection of what Benedict recommended in Chapter 73 of the *Rule* to those who are 'hastening on to the perfection of monastic life': 'the teachings of the holy Fathers... the inspired books of the Old and New Testaments... the [books] of the holy catholic Fathers... the *Conferences* of the Fathers, their *Institutes* and their *Lives*... the *Rule* of our holy Father Basil.'[48]

The essential character of the monastic state and profession, therefore, consists of those things which are promised at profession, the virtues and monastic practices. Even so, Aelred does give preference in this treatise to the practices, for he says:

> If anyone does not agree that the *Rule* consists of these [monastic practices] alone, at least let him admit what cannot be denied except by stubborn obstinacy: that our profession and *Rule* consist of both, that is, of virtues and observances, and let him therefore not refuse to admit that we necessarily practice both.[49]

This insistence on the observances would seem to stem from the apologetic character of the treatise. It needs to be seen in the perspective of his monastic doctrine as a whole. Aelred was never a 'letter of the law' monk or abbot, but he did see the need of defending observances when they were being attacked.

Other questions on the Rule

What should be thought of the monk who keeps the precepts of the *Rule* but does not practice monastic virtues?

> If someone is proud, stubborn, impatient, and yet observes all the things [observances] mentioned above, must we say that he keeps the *Rule* of Saint Benedict?[50]

Aelred's reply is perceptive:

> I maintain that if a monk has committed any of these faults against God's law, he will not be guilty of transgressing his profession if he makes amends for them according to the means prescribed by the *Rule*.[51]

Aelred was probably summarizing the thought of Saint Bernard on this point. In *On Precept and Dispensation*, the abbot of Clairvaux states the principle in this way:

> We may divide all regular observances into two categories: precepts and remedies. Precepts set us to fight against sin, whereas remedies restore us to innocence after we have fallen. These two are both integral parts of the regular life, so that if a professed brother accepts the remedy offered by the *Rule* when he has transgressed some regulation, he has not broken his contract, although he has violated a precept. It is only when both the precept and the remedy have been scorned that I would consider the vow to be violated, the undertaking abandoned, or the contract broken. Thus I judge him safe who, although he offended against obedience, has not despised the remedy

of penance. The limits of the *Rule*, however battered, are not broken so long as the discipline of regular penance is accepted.[52]

Benedict was realistic enough to know that no one is perfect, and so the prescriptions for correction and amendment provided by the *Rule* do constitute ways of observing the *Rule* for those who sometimes fall while struggling in the spiritual combat.

The strictness of the *Rule* is seen in the same perspective; Benedict had written:

> We are going to establish a school of the Lord's service, in which we hope to institute nothing harsh, nothing burdensome. If, however, following the dictates of sound reasoning, for the correction of vices and the preservation of charity, something should turn out to be rather strict. . . .[53]

The goal is fullness of charity, and to leave no ambiguity, Aelred adds the following:

> Is it not true in every institution that the institution itself is one thing and the reason for the institution another? Did he [Benedict] not make a very clear distinction between the institution and the reason for the institution? Does he not declare that the reason for his institution is the preservation of charity and the correction of vices?[54]

The institution itself does not suffice. If the *Rule* is for living persons, it must be interpreted and mediated by a living person: the abbot. All the practices of the *Rule* should conspire towards fostering charity.

What about the case where the practice of a certain observance by a monk would not foster but imperil charity? Aelred gives a clear explanation of dispensation:

> If any one of them [the institutions] in a particular circumstance goes against charity, then

necessity obliges the one to whom granting dispensations has been entrusted so to adapt and arrange everything that this charity—the reason for them all—be not forsaken, but that its fruits be sought in all things. But, unless some extreme necessity obliges him to do so, he should not so arrange things that any established practices are omitted, or that the fixed times assigned for certain practices are shifted around. Otherwise, it will be not dispensation, but disintegration. Yet he may modify certain exercises at certain times to the aptitude and mental state of each person.[55]

This passage is perhaps one of the most important in the dialogue, for it shows Aelred's sensitivity to the needs of both the community and the individual monk. If certain practices prescribed by the *Rule* would be omitted entirely, disintegration of community life would inevitably follow. But the structure must be flexible enough to permit each monk, with his own particular character and aptitudes, to live in a way which nourishes charity within him. 'We allege that [dispensations] can reasonably be granted because they arise from the precepts of a man, but not of God. But it is not within the prerogative of any man that he change or diminish any of the divine precepts.'[56] And, putting into practice himself the moderation he encourages his monks to use, he explains:

We must carefully ward against letting a dispensation—a modification or variation—become in any way destruction. Since the reason for the institution itself is the safeguard of charity and the correction of vices, the dispensation will obviously be reasonable if it furthers this purpose. If, on the other hand, vices are fostered by the dispensation more than by the institution, charity is violated. Even if it may do no harm in itself, the dispensation is surely not without danger.[57]

Aelred incessantly returns to the goal of charity which is of first importance in the monk's existence. Not everyone understands charity in the same way, however. During the discussion, other monks have been listening, and when the subject of strictness of the *Rule* came up, as a means of preserving charity, one of these monk listeners could no longer refrain from speaking up: 'Why do you throw the *Rule* up to me? Have charity and do what you will.... If someone has charity, is he not fulfilling the *Rule*?'[58]

The reader might ask if we are in the twelfth century or the 1960s. Aelred points out that there are very many people in all walks of life who possess charity, but who know very well that they are not committed to the monastic life and keeping a rule. As for monks, it is true that someone who practices charity fulfills the *Rule*, '...if, that is, [the objector] understands what he is talking about.'[59]

> If you have charity it is not necessary for you to be forced to fulfill the promises which your lips have uttered [see Psalm 65:13ff.]. If you scorn fulfilling the things you promised by putting your signature to them and calling on God and his saints as your witnesses, you can be very sure you do not have charity.[60]

Things which are said to be especially characteristic of Basil or Augustine or Benedict are not imposed on all Christians by the authority of the Gospel, but are simply proposed to them. To those who profess these rules, however, they are no longer simply proposed, but they are also imposed.[61] Here again, Aelred seems to have been influenced by Bernard. The following passage from *On Precept and Dispensation* bears this out:

> If a man has once made this free-will offering and promised to be faithful to it in the future, he is henceforth obliged to what he was formerly free to refuse. One is no longer free, but obliged to honor one's promise. He is bound to keep the

vows his own lips have pronounced [see Psalm 65:13ff.; Deuteronomy 23:23], and from his own mouth he will be condemned or justified.[62]

The monastic life is the voluntary order in practice. If a person embraces the monastic state and makes profession according to a monastic rule, it is freely that he does so, making a gratuitous gift of his life to God. Once embraced, the *Rule*'s exigencies are the way of his living out this gift and are binding, of course, in the context of a real community under an abbot. As Bernard says: 'Since you make this offering voluntarily to God, you do your will no violence except by that same will.'[63]

This is true charity. Aelred devoted much of the *Mirror of Charity* to demonstrating that, whereas all charity is love, not all love is charity.[64] He who loves in truth is one who fulfills the great commandment of love of God and neighbor and observes in his relationship with God and man the theological and cardinal virtues. Chapters 8–13 of Book 2 are a long development showing that spiritual sweetness is not a criterion for love of God. It is given sometimes to awaken a person to conversion, or, often, to strengthen him in trial either present or to come, and, exceptionally, as a reward for great holiness. But real love is in the will, turning toward God or away. So 'have charity and do what you will' is a valid affirmation, provided 'one understands what one is talking about.'

This short treatise is of perennial value, it would seem. The questions raised by the black monk are just as timely today as they were in the twelfth century. If the vows, the virtues, and the precepts of the *Rule* are all essential in the monastic life, there is something even more essential, the charity or love with which the monk accomplishes these in the school of service of the Lord which is also a school of charity.

NOTES

[1] Aelred's prefatory letter to the *Mirror of Charity* [Spec car], par. 4, 120–27. All references to the *Mirror of Charity* are to the *Corpus Christianorum, Continuatio Mediaevalis I* edition: *Aelredi Rievallensis Opera omnia*, 1, *Opera ascetica*, edd. A. Hoste and C. H. Talbot (Turnholt: Brepols, 1971). There is an English translation by Elizabeth Connor (Kalamazoo: Cistercian Publications, 1990), Cistercian Fathers 17.

[2] André Wilmart, 'Un court traité d'Aelred sur l'étendue et le but de la profession monastique', *Revue d'ascétique et de mystique* 23 (1947) 259–73.

[3] *Spec car* 3.35.82, 1569.

[4] *Spec car* 3.35.82, 1577–81.

[5] *Spec car* 3.35.82, 1570–75.

[6] *Spec car* 3.31.75, 1401–404.

[7] Augustine, *De libero arbitrio*, 3.1; in *Patrologia Latina* [PL] 32:1121–310. Actually, Augustine spoke of only two *ordines*, the natural and the voluntary, and in a quite different context. Aelred adds a third: the 'necessary', reminiscent of Saint Bernard's *De Precepto et Dispensatione* [hereafter Pre]. See *Sancti Bernardi opera*, edd. Jean Leclercq and H. M. Rochais (Rome: Editiones Cistercienses, 8 vols. in 9, 1963) 3:253–94. English translation by Conrad Greenia, ocso in *The Works of Bernard of Clairvaux*, I, *Treatises I*, Cistercian Fathers [CF] 1 (Spencer, Massachusetts: Cistercian Publications, 1970) pp. 103–150.

[8] *Spec car* 3.32.76, 1414–18.

[9] See *Spec car* 1.3.9, 127–29.

[10] *In Cantica Canticorum, sermo 23*, 6. In *The Works of Bernard of Clairvaux*, III, *On the Song of Songs II*, trans. Kilian Walsh; CF 7 (Kalamazoo: Cistercian Publications, 1983) p. 30.

[11] *Spec car* 3.32.76, 1424–25.

[12] *Spec car* 3.33.79, 1483–88.

[13] Books 5–12.

[14] See Aelred's *Sermo de adventu Domini*, in PL 195:216A-B.

[15] See Bernard of Clairvaux, *In festivitate omnium sanctorum, sermo* 1, 8.

[16] *Spec car* 3.34.80, 1523–27. See also Bernard, Pre 1.2 (CF 1:106).

[17] *Spec car* 3.34.80, 1532–34.

[18] *Spec car* 3.34.80, 1537–42.

[19] Bernard, Pre 1.2; CF 1:106.

[20] Bernard, *De diligendo Deo* 12.34. English translation by Robert Walton in *The Works of Bernard of Clairvaux*, V, *Treatises II*, CF 13 (Washington: Consortium Press, 1974) p. 126.

[21] See Bernard, *Sermo super psalmum 'Qui habitat'* 9 [QH], 1. English translation by Marie-Bernard Saïd in *Sermons on Conversion: Lenten*

Sermons on the Psalm 'He Who Dwells', CF 25 (Kalamazoo: Cistercian Publications, 1981) p. 183.

22 *Spec car* 1.11.31, 463–67.
23 *Spec car* 2.18.53, 983–94.
24 *Spec car* 2.18.53.
25 *Spec car* 3.34.81, 1544–46.
26 *Spec car* 3.35.82, 1590–93.
27 *Spec car* 3.35.85, 1609–612.
28 See *Spec car* 3.35.86, 1645–47.
29 *Spec car* 3.35.88, 1669–75.
30 *Spec car* 3.35.88, 1680–82.
31 See *Spec car* 3.35.88, 1683–86.
32 See *Spec car* 3.35.88, 1679–80.
33 See *Spec car* 3.35.92, 1740–42.
34 *Spec car* 3.35.89, 1701–702.
35 *Spec car* 3.35.89, 1703–704.
36 *Spec car* 3.35.90, 1713–16. See Bernard, Pre 1.2 (CF 1:107).
37 *Spec car* 3.35.83, 1591–93.
38 *Spec car* 3.35.92, 1742–45.
39 *Spec car* 3.35.89, 1706–708.
40 *Spec car* 3.35.85, 1621–25.
41 *Spec car* 3.35.85, 1617–20.
42 *Spec car* 2, chapters 2–7 especially, and 1, chapters 29–30.
43 *Sermon for the Assumption*; PL 195:306.
44 *Sermo de beata Maria*; PL 195:360A.
45 *Sermo in natali sancti Benedicti*; PL 195:239A.
46 'Declaration of the General Chapter of 1969 on the Cistercian Life', *Minutes of the Sessions: 61st General Chapter of the Cistercians of the Strict Observance* (Rome, 1969) pp. 275–76.
47 *Spec car* 2.17.43, 821–26.
48 *Rule* of Saint Benedict, 73:2–5. Translation in *RB 1980* (Collegeville, Minnesota: Liturgical Press, 1981) pp. 295–97.
49 *Spec car* 3.35.94, 1774–79.
50 *Spec car* 3.35.92, 1747–50.
51 *Spec car* 3.35.92, 1751–53.
52 Bernard of Clairvaux, Pre 13.33 (CF 1:130–31).
53 *Rule*, Prologue, 46–47.
54 *Spec car* 3.35.94, 1784–89.
55 *Spec car* 3.36.96, 1830–38.
56 *Spec car* 3.35.95, 1808–811.
57 *Spec car* 3.35.95, 1811–18.
58 *Spec car* 3.35.95, 1790–91, 1794. Charles Dumont's note on this passage in CF 17 reads as follows: '*Habe caritatem, et fac quidquid vis* harkens back to Augustine, *Commentary on the First Epistle of Saint John,*

Tract. 7.8 (PL 35: 2033). This phrase is also found in Peter the Venerable's letter to Saint Bernard (*Ep* 28; PL 189:118D–119A, repeated in 156A; Giles Constable, *The Letters of Peter the Venerable*, I [Cambridge, Massachusetts: Harvard, 1967] 98). The text of Augustine, on the contrary (*Ep Ioh* 7.8), is: *Dilige, et quod vis fac*. Aelred's passage may refer, directly or indirectly, to Peter the Venerable rather than to Augustine.'

[59] *Spec car* 3.35.95, 1799.

[60] *Spec car* 3.35.95, 1801–805.

[61] See *Spec car* 3.35.89, 1710–12. See also Bernard, Pre 4.10 (CF 1:112–13): 'Thus runs the formula of profession: I "promise", not the *Rule*, but "obedience according to the *Rule* of Saint Benedict". According to the *Rule*, and therefore not according to the will of the superior. If, once I have made such a profession, my abbot attempts to impose on me something which is not according to the benedictine *Rule*, and which is also not in accord with the rules of Saint Basil, Augustine, or Pachomius, to what obligation, I ask, have I to conform? I can be obliged to perform only that which I have promised.'

[62] Bernard, Pre 1.2 (CF 1:106).

[63] Bernard, QH 9.1 (CF 25:182).

[64] *Spec car* 3.7.20, 368.

MAKING VIRTUES
OF VEXING HABITS

E. Rozanne Elder
Western Michigan University

JEAN LECLERCQ WRITES of William of Saint Thierry, the author of Book One of the *Vita prima Bernardi*: 'He aimed at presenting Bernard less as a well established historical character, situated with exactitude in a given period and place, and less as a model to imitate, than as a mystery to revere and admire, to fathom if we have received the grace to do so.'[1] Of this there can be no doubt.

Elsewhere Leclercq states that 'In the first book of the *Vita prima* of Saint Bernard, it would seem that William presents an image of the abbot of Clairvaux less in conformity with what we otherwise know of Bernard than with his own temperament.'[2] Then, drawing his information almost entirely from the *Vita antiqua*[3] of William— a work written fifty years after his death by someone who almost surely never knew him but relied on hearsay from a community which had known him only as an old man—Leclercq goes on to characterize the temperament that William is alleged to have projected on to Bernard as 'sickly, troubled, doubting',[4] neurotic,[5] '...depressed and introverted...',[6] 'frail in health, physically fragile, perhaps somewhat unstable, always dissatisfied...a high strung person with all that this entails in weakness in character, but also in sensitivity, psychological richness, and interior resources. . . .'[7] At this I am forced to reluctant disagreement with an eminent scholar to whom I, and so many others, owe so very much. I recognize, of course, that Leclercq is an *amicus Bernardi*, while I am an *amica Guillelmi*, and that this may have something to do with our different interpretations. But, until such time as someone undertakes the 'immense project' Leclercq recommends, that of comparing the *Vita prima* to all the other works of all the biographers,[8] I should like to propose an alternative reading of the motives and techniques of the author of Book One, the chief source we have for knowing how his own contemporaries viewed Saint Bernard, and the composition which determined the tone of the entire *Vita prima*.[9]

If we read the *Vita prima* determined not to be distracted by the miasma of holiness which William has cast about his subject, and if we lay aside any prejudice in favor of Saint Bernard—the handsome, aristocratic, keen-witted, eloquent, well-mannered young man who could have succeeded at any career[10]—and put ourselves instead in the place of, say, *amici Abaelardi*, we discover a Bernard who is—among other things—stubborn, anorexic, and improvident; a young man who lacked practical and pastoral skills, suffered mood swings, sulked or was reduced to tears when frustrated; someone whose behavior irritated and embarrassed his own family; and finally someone who belatedly yielded to a very early yearning for public life.

I am not the first person in eight hundred and fifty years to notice these short-comings, nor the first to suggest that Book One of the *Vita prima* allows us to see criticisms that were, in fact, levelled against Bernard during his lifetime.[11] What I wish to examine is William's reasons for allowing us to see the clay feet of the still-living saint, and also his skill in making virtues by distracting our attention from certain vexing habits.[12]

PERSISTENCE

In chronicling Bernard's repeated refusal to accept a bishopric, William makes a very telling and very general assessment of his character: 'He has never been forced to do anything against his will.'[13] And if we read Book One carefully, we will be struck by the frequency with which he uses forms of the word *instantia* in describing Bernard. Geoffrey of Auxerre, in the *Fragmenta* on which William supposedly built his Life,[14] uses the word only once and then it describes not Bernard, but his sister-in-law, Guy's wife.[15] William uses it almost as a leitmotif. In William's version, Bernard's persistence initially manifests unmistakeable virtue: the noble young Bernard persisted in feigning sleep when a shameless hussy in the buff crawled into his bed.[16] It was his persistence, as well as his eloquence and his prayers, that won his unenthusiastic brothers and relatives to monastic life.[17] In this connection Geoffrey of Auxerre spoke, only once, of his importunity.[18] William also has Bernard admit that only the insistent thought of his mother held him to his own resolve to enter Cîteaux.[19] And once he did enter, only raw determination kept him there.[20]

When Bernard and his band of would-be monks moved to Châtillon to test life in community, Bernard widened his field of candidates by preaching persistently to anyone who would listen.[21] Even as he reveals that mothers hid their sons from Bernard,[22] William draws our attention away from any thought of censuring Bernard's stubborness by laying emphasis on God's preordaining grace.[23] Leclercq observes that convincing all these men, not least his senior brother, to abandon lands and privilege to enter Cîteaux 'would be enough to reveal a very strong, even domineering, personality'.[24] Bredero more bluntly refers to Bernard's 'caractère obstiné, opiniâtre'.[25]

Elsewhere in Book One, William's imputation of stubbornness is less demonstrably virtuous. As a novice, Bernard insisted on extraordinary mortifications.[26] What is more, he would not listen to anyone, not to those who loved him or to those to whom he was bound in obedience, when they admonished him to take better care of himself.[27]

WHEN HIS WILL WAS FRUSTRATED
BERNARD WAS REDUCED TO TEARS OR TO SULKS

Thwarted in his attempt to recruit Hugh of Macon/Pontigny for his cistercian adventure,[28] Bernard was quite literally reduced to tears. William draws our attention immediately to the miraculous rainstorm which followed this petulant—now prophetic—outburst, and which gave Bernard the chance to have his way.[29] Stymied in his determination to join his brethren at harvest time, the frail Bernard 'took to prayer with many tears',[30] until—by God's grace—he was allowed to join the others. When William himself, convalescing in the infirmary of Clairvaux, would not submit to Bernard's instructions, Bernard went into what the impartial reader might construe as a sulk, stalking silently off to Compline.[31] The same incident shows yet another of Bernard's less attractive sides. When William's fever shot up in the night over his tift with Bernard—understandable after a battle of wills with a friend he greatly admired and whose guest he was—it was *summo mane* when Bernard answered William's summons, and then he appeared not for conciliation but for capitulation.[32] Similarly, much earlier, when a wounded, imprisoned Gerard had sent to fetch Bernard, he refused to go to the brother who had refused to become a monk. Both times, William calls our attention to Bernard's prophetic powers,[33] and away from his pique.

BERNARD'S MORTIFICATIONS

From his first year in the monastery, or of leaving the novitiate, Bernard suffered from bad digestion[34] and from constipation.[35] Many scholars, including Leclercq and Bredero, have seen William's account of Bernard's extreme mortification as a hagiographical device.[36] Yet, curiously, the mortification William singled out for attention is something Bernard had concentrated on in his *Apologia*: food.[37] And despite his iron-willed resolution to mortify the senses, the appetites, and the entire body, Bernard developed the curious habit of noting down, after every meal, everything he had just eaten and punishing himself for over-indulgence.[38] In one of his own, later, sermons on the Song of Songs, Bernard ridicules the person who denies himself physical treats and then wastes time and energy in daily reviewing his diet's effect on his digestion.[39] Could this be an older and perhaps wiser Bernard subtly apologizing to his monks for having once tested their patience by this very habit?

Bernard was also an insomniac, complaining throughout his life that time spent in sleep was time wasted.[40] Fasting and keeping vigils are ancient and venerable monastic austerities, and William had no difficulty justifying them, either in themselves or on the grounds that admiration for Bernard's austerities won souls to God. Yet even in declaring that only the impious would condemn them, William betrays that Bernard's 'excesses' were something he did not entirely admire or approve.[41] In the *Golden Epistle*, written at much the same time, William recommended fasts, vigils, and other physical disciplines which help spiritual growth only if practised with discretion:

> If, however, through the vice of indiscretion they are practised in such a way that either the spirit grows faint or the body is enfeebled, and so spiritual things are hampered, the man who so behaves cheats his body of the effect of good work, his spirit of its affections, his neighbor of good example, and God of honor. He is guilty of sacrilege and responsible to God for all this damage.[42]

Even in the *Vita prima*, William did not mask his disapproval, but he has Bernard subsequently see the error of his indiscreet zeal:

> Why do we try to make excuses for what he admits?... He is not embarrassed to accuse himself of sacrilege, to this very day, for having withdrawn his body from the service of God and the brethren, for having rendered it weak and virtually useless by indiscreet fervor.[43]

William also notes that Bernard counselled moderation to his monks.[44] And, in fact, Bernard, in later years, indirectly admitted he had overdone things by counselling his monks to discretion lest in mistaken zeal they ruin their health.[45]

Having, however, ruined his own digestion by indiscreet austerities, Bernard developed a habit which not even William could make attractive or holy:

> His digestion was thoroughly ruined, and he frequently vomited undigested food. This soon became quite annoying to the others, especially in choir at the psalmody, but he did not then and there abandon the gatherings of the brethren; instead, having arranged to have a receptacle set in the ground alongside his stall, he managed for some time in this way to deal with the necessities of his affliction.[46]

OTHER VEXING HABITS

When the monks finally persuaded him to spare them this disgusting sight, Bernard absented himself, for the first of many times, from his community, thereafter joining his brothers only for conversation, consolation, or claustral discipline.[47] Before long his absence—under obedience, William assures us—was almost perpetual.[48] To the intense annoyance of his kinsman,[49] and the ambivalent admiration of his biographer,[50] he was becoming a public person. He was, William reveals, succumbing to a temptation that had, in fact, preceded his conversion.

Bernard entered Cîteaux intending 'there to die from the hearts and memory of his fellows'. God, according to William, had other plans.[51] In Chapter 5, however, William reveals that Bernard had been torn between a preaching career and monastic life from the beginning. Bernard had entered Cîteaux partly to escape his greatest temptation, his pride in his lavish physical and intellectual endowments, and his already budding reputation for holiness.[52] This conflict between desire for renown and holy humility had to be explained away, especially in view of Bernard's later activities. Pastoral concern provided the key:

> The overwhelming concern he had for the salvation of many, which is known to have possessed his breast singlemindedly from the first day of his conversion until the present time...has given rise in his inmost heart to a vehement conflict between holy desire and holy humility.[53]

By having turned attention to Bernard's physical austerities and zeal for souls as signs of his saintliness, William dexterously diverts the pious reader from another shortcoming. Bernard had to be excused from manual labor because of ineptitude.[54] William does not so much as imply that it was Bernard's physical frailty that kept him from common work. He found other, more flamboyant, physical activities while his brothers, cousins, and friends—all men from the same social class as himself who seemed not to experience the same inability and ignorance—did the work monks were expected to share at Cîteaux.[55] Eventually, through prayer and determination, he got the hang of it.

Bernard's apparent lack of practical skills created yet another difficulty William thought it necessary to mention. When Stephen Harding sent the founders to Clairvaux under Bernard's leadership, his companions had very little confidence in his leadership abilities—because, William explains, he was youthful, frail, and inexperienced.[56] Again, William slides deftly past the obvious fact that many of the founders, 'mature and strenuous men, in religion as in the world',[57] were, in fact, Bernard's contemporaries in religion and near contemporaries in age.

Bernard's immature lack of common sense persisted, according to William. Not least annoyed by the young abbot's inattention to practical matters were his own family members. When Bernard's brother Gerard complained to him, sharply, William says,[58] that the monastery lacked provisions for the approaching winter and the funds to buy them, Bernard addressed the problem by falling to prayer.[59] When a donor immediately appeared to resolve the crisis, William rebukes poor, practical Gerard for being faintedhearted, and Bernard's trust in God and the power of his prayer glow in contrast.[60] In Geoffrey of Auxerre's version of this episode, Gerard is neither sharp nor particularly worried, and there is no hint that Bernard was inattentive.[61]

Why would William have embellished Geoffrey's simple tale in a way that invited both reverence and criticism, if there had been no truth in it?[62] In his twenty-sixth sermon on the Song of Songs, Bernard leaves us a fairer picture of the long-suffering Gerard, who, he claims, compensated for his own failings of infirmity, faintheartedness, improvidence, and forgetfulness.[63] Bernard recognized what William did not publicly admit, that it was the ministrations of the uneducated Gerard[64] which enabled him 'to attend to the study of spiritual doctrine so freely and so frequently'.[65] 'Whatever progress I have made, whatever good I have done', Bernard attributed to Gerard.[66] If, as Bernard asserts and Geoffrey implies, Gerard had routinely dealt with practical matters within and without the monastery, and had consulted Bernard only when he was absolutely incapable of handling some matter himself,[67] then the dramatic embellishment William provided may conceivably have come from Gerard himself, driven by exigence to an unwonted and exasperated intrusion on Bernard's studious leisure.[68]

INCOMPREHENSIBILITY TO HIS MONKS

William implies that Bernard habitually took this crisis-intervention approach to financial and material concerns when he records that the monks, 'prudent men' that they were, 'took pains not to lay on Bernard's mind the burden of concern for outward affairs', knowing he was caught up in the delights of paradise and 'too tender' for practical matters. They took reponsibility for provisioning the monastery themselves and resorted to him 'only for their inward consciences, the concerns of their souls' and never for practical matters.[69] Unfortunately, the *plus quam humana puritas*[70] Bernard aimed at also made his spiritual counsel 'barely understood'.[71] In chapter talks and homilies, and in hearing confessions of conscience, the new abbot was demanding, unrealistic, zealous, scrupulous, prejudiced against certain temptations he felt should not bother a real monk, and, in short, so harsh and demanding that the monks had no idea what he was talking about.[72] This is the same Bernard who would later define the abbot's chief responsibility as the tender paternal treatment of faint-hearted and discouraged monks.[73] Bewildered and shocked, his own monks, these *viri vere religiosi, et pie prudentes*,[74] because they lived in the presence of the man William, and they, wanted canonized, 'accused rather than excused themselves' for the lack of communication, the misunderstanding between Bernard's light and their darkness.[75] Finally, Bernard terrified incoming novices by telling them to abandon their bodies outside the monastic courts where only spirits tread, until he was persuaded, or persuaded himself, William does not specify, to content himself with exhorting them to leave concupiscence outside.[76] Leclercq suggests that Bernard's original admonition corresponds more to William's anthropology than to Bernard's,[77] but it is certainly not the teaching of the author of the *Golden Epistle*, who advised novices to treat their bodies with the gentle firmness one shows a sick man and never, on pain of sacrilege, to treat it harshly or indiscreetly.[78]

BERNARD SUFFERED MOOD SWINGS

When, eventually, Bernard realized that he was bewildering and intimidating his long-suffering brethren, he went into a spasm of self-reproach:

When they so humbled themselves at his signals of reproach, he began to suspect even his own zeal regarding brethren so humble, so submissive to his spiritual instruction. He began to shift the blame to his own ignorance and to bemoan not being allowed to remain silent when so incapable of speaking. He began to see how his talk had been not so much of things lofty by human standards as of things unworthy of humanity, even injurious to the consciences of his hearers, and how he had been scrupulously demanding in brethren so simple a perfection he did not even find as yet perfected in himself.[79]

'Extremely distraught and contrite', he decided to retreat 'in solitude of heart and the secrecy of silence' to a life uncluttered with human frailties.[80] William presents this dejected withdrawal as a healthy reaction to facile self-confidence growing from self-forgetfulness in a young man,[81] and declared that 'surely' this is a case where 'charity begot confidence, but humility castigated that confidence'.[82]

WHY DID WILLIAM INCLUDE CRITICISM OF BERNARD IN THE *VITA PRIMA*?

Was William in fact letting us see Bernard's real quirks, as Bredero asserts,[83] or was he, as Leclercq claims, projecting his own neurotic personality onto Bernard, who by contrast appears in his own works as 'an energetic man, quite sure of himself—many people would be inclined to say too sure'.[84] If we do not accept Leclercq's projection thesis, we must ask why William called what may seem to be undue attention to his subject's shortcomings. I would argue that the explanation is threefold.

First, William was not blind to Bernard's very human shortcomings. He had experienced Bernard's stubbornness—when the two disagreed over William's convalescent care,[85] when Bernard refused to allow William to enter Clairvaux,[86] and in the Abelard affair. He had seen the physical effects of Bernard's insistent austerities.[87] By the time he wrote, William had known Bernard some quarter century. Surely he had a more realistic view of Bernard's character than did the much younger Geoffrey of Auxerre, who, as a student,[88] had first fallen under the spell of a fifty-year-old international celebrity in 1140, only five years before he wrote his *Fragmenta*.[89] If William ever had cherished an artificial picture of Bernard, he was rudely jolted from this state of mind by Bernard himself. In a letter to the exasperated abbot of Saint Thierry, Bernard had asked:

> Why then are you struggling to apprehend me and complain that you are not able? You would apprehend if you paid attention; and you can still do so, if you are content to take me as I am and not as you hope I am. . . .I am not able to be what you would like me to be. . . .[90]

William could have cherished no illusion that sanctity was synomyous with affability.

Secondly, William admits, in setting forth his purposes and limiting the scope of his task, that he was recording activities and traits of Bernard which were common knowledge. Consequently they could not be swept under an hagiographical carpet.[91] William knew, as Geoffrey also likely knew, that there were many people living then and sure to survive Bernard, who did not regard Bernard as a saint in the making. 'Is the abbot not a man?', demanded one of Abelard's students, resentful of his imperious treatment of the scholar.[92] Colleagues of Gilbert of Poitiers considered Bernard theologically under-schooled;[93] sycophants at the roman curia smarted under his public character assassination.[94] If this were not so, why would William begin Book One by declaring his account above suspicion of falsehood[95] and conclude it by writing:

> . . .Those who one-sidedly hate, or even simply fail to love, the ones who love them, are

> not being unfriendly or inimical; they are being downright wicked and iniquitous. But someone like Bernard, who diligently loves everyone, is never going to have any enemies at all, though there may be occasions for him to suffer gratuitously some enmity springing from someone else's iniquity.[96]

The challenge before him, therefore, was to create a biography which showed Bernard at his best, the embodiment of reform monasticism and a man of singular personal holiness, without in the process passing over certain vexing habits the still-living subject was known to have. William met the challenge in a masterful way, honestly disclosing Bernard's shortcomings but providing a running hagiographical gloss which draws the readers' attention immediately from Bernard's flaws to God's providence. No one is immune from criticism, he wrote about the same time, 'but you will always have those who praise you and those who calumniate you, as did our Lord as well. . . .'[97]

And finally, William wrote in part to defend the cistercian reform which he had encountered so overwhelmingly in the young Bernard.[98] In Leclercq's words, he aimed 'to propose his own program of monastic reform and to hold up Bernard as the ideal image of the abbot and his community at Clairvaux as a model abbey.'[99] Yet a thread of disappointment runs through the second half of Book One. 'That was the golden age of Cîteaux',[100] William wrote of the time when he stayed with Bernard in his hut and visited Clairvaux for the first time, the time when Bernard was learning through illness and misunderstanding to temper zeal with gentleness,[101] the years when Bernard, *communis vitae seu conversationis ferventissimus aemulator*,[102] lived at Clairvaux in community with his monks:

> Such then, back in those days, under Abbot Bernard and under his teachership, was that school of spiritual studies; such too was the fervor for the Rule's discipline, there in that clearest and

dearest of valleys. It was all his doing, his arranging, his building up of God's tabernacle on earth. . . .[103]

Those days were no longer when William wrote the *Vita prima*.[104] Nowadays—between 1145 and 1148[105]—Bernard was a public figure, always on the road in defense of the Church. The community at Clairvaux, though deprived of his presence, was enjoying sufficiency and peace—not the hard toil and poverty of the founders.[106] Clairvaux had grown, and in 1135 the community moved up the valley, and began an ambitious building programme.[107] William presented all this in the *Vita prima* as God's work,[108] foretold to Bernard in a vision.[109] But, in his *Exposition on the Song of Songs*, William lamented that 'In the wilderness [*in heremis*], palaces are being erected.'[110] And in that same year, he went to Signy, newly founded in the Ardennes, and not to Clairvaux.[111]

In the *Vita prima*, William leaves us in no doubt as to what first attracted him to Bernard: he breathed the air of desert monasticism,[112] he spoke of God from experience, something William had not until then known,[113] and he lived in poverty and simplicity.[114] It was the hovel[115] as much as the 'man of God'[116] which had overwhelmed the benedictine visitor in 1119.[117] Throughout Book One of the *Vita prima* William traced Bernard's public career approvingly, and justified his absence from community by the demands of 'charity and obedience',[118] but he saw them both, and the changes that followed on them, as 'this sad necessity'[119] which had compromised forever the primitive claravallian monasticism he had loved.

NOTES

[1] Jean Leclercq, 'Bernard's First Biographer', pp. 1–21 in *A Second Look at Bernard of Clairvaux*, Cistercian Studies 105 (Kalamazoo, Michigan: Cistercian Publications, 1990) p. 21; published originally in French as *Nouveau Visage de Bernard de Clairvaux: Approches psycho-historiques* (Paris: Les éditions du Cerf, 1976) [hereafter cited as Leclercq, 'First Biographer']. See Adriaan Henrik Bredero, *Études sur la 'Vita Prima' de Saint Bernard* (Rome, 1960 = three articles which appeared in *Analecta Sacri Ordinis Cisterciensis* 17 [1961] 3–72, 215–60, and 18 [1962] 3–59) [hereafter Bredero, Études] p. 241.

[2] Jean Leclercq, 'Towards a Spiritual Portrait of William of Saint Thierry' [hereafter Leclercq, 'Portrait'], in *William, Abbot of St Thierry: A Colloquium at the Abbey of St Thierry*, trans. Jerry Carfantan; Cistercian Studies 94 (Kalamazoo, Michigan, [1987]) p. 205.

[3] Edited by Albert Poncelet in 'Vie ancienne de Guillaume de Saint-Thierry', in *Mélanges Godefroid Kurth* (Liège, 1908) 1:85–96, from MS Lat. 11782 of the Bibliothèque Nationale, Paris. An english translation has been published by David N. Bell, 'The Vita Antiqua of William of St Thierry' in *Cistercian Studies* 3 (1976) 246–55.

[4] Leclercq, 'Portrait', p. 205.
[5] Leclercq, 'Portrait', p. 221.
[6] Leclercq, 'Portrait', p. 209.
[7] Leclercq, 'Portrait', pp. 206–207.
[8] Leclercq, 'First Biographer', p. 19.
[9] Bredero, Études, p. 248.
[10] *Vita prima Bernardi* [hereafter VP] 1.3.6; *Patrologia Latina* [hereafter PL] 185:230B.

[11] Bredero, *Études*, pp. 252–53, Bredero, 'The Conflicting Interpretations of the Relevance of Bernard of Clairvaux to the History of his Own Time'. *Cîteaux: Commentarii Cistercienses* 31 (1980) 53–81, and Bredero, 'William of Saint Thierry at the Crossroads of the Monastic Currents of His Time', in *William, Abbot of Saint Thierry*, p. 114: 'William describes Bernard with his real faults; but he also points out the divine grace which sanctified him, and the impossibility of recounting this religious life to those whose lives were not led by the Spirit of God as his life was.' Leclercq himself points out Bernard's less attractive characteristics in *A Second Look/Nouveau Visage*: see especially chapter 5 (Second Look, pp. 87–101).

[12] As Bredero, *Études*, p. 252, calls them, 'certaines attitudes contestables'.

[13] VP 1.14.69; PL 185:265C.

[14] 'Les fragmenta de Vita et Miraculis S. Bernardi par Geoffroy d'Auxerre', ed. Robert Lechat in *Analecta Bollandiana* 80 (1933) 83–122. The text is hereafter cited as Fragmenta.

[15] Fragmenta 8; *Analecta*, p. 93.

16 VP 1.3.7; PL 185:230D.
17 VP 1.3.13; PL 185: 234D–235A. See VP 1.3.10; PL 185:232, for the details of his campaign.
18 Fragmenta 14; *Analecta*, p. 97.
19 VP 1.3.9; PL 185:234D.
20 VP 1.4.22; PL 185:240A. That Bernard had a sickly constitution could hardly be held against him, except, of course, that it was well known that he brought on his own ill health by his excessive austerities. Not entirely so, claimed William: from his entrance Bernard had a weak constitution. His determination simply delayed recognition of his frailty.
21 VP 1.3.13; PL 185:234D.
22 VP 1.3.15; PL 185:235CD.
23 VP 1.3.13; PL 185:234D.
24 Leclercq, 'First Biographer', p. 13.
25 Bredero, *Études*, p. 251.
26 VP 1.4.20; PL 185:238C. Furthermore, he insisted on these extraordinary mortifications until they became second nature. VP 1.4.20; PL 185:238CD.
27 VP 1.8.38; PL 185:249D.
28 By friends of Hugh who worked very hard to keep Bernard away from Hugh.
29 VP 1.3.14; PL 185:235C. See Fragmenta 11; Analecta, pp. 94–95, where Hugh is also 'flens et eiulans'.
30 VP 1.4.24; PL 185:240D.
31 VP 1.12.60; PL 185:259D.
32 VP 1.12.60; PL 185:260A. If Martinus Cawley (see below, n. 103) is right that *summo mane* = 'high morning' = mid morning (*Bernard of Clairvaux: Early Biographies*, 1, *By William of Saint Thierry* [Lafayette, Oregon (1990)] p. 74, note) then Bernard certainly took his time.
33 By having Bernard remark later that he knew all along that the wound would lead Gerard not to death, but to life (eternal). VP 1.3.11; PL 185:233C.
34 VP 1.4.22; PL 185:239D.
35 VP 1.4.22; PL 185:239D.
36 'But as William was always an author and a thinker of some originality, he tried to cover up the fact that he was adopting the conventional (hagiographical) model. Yet, if we compare his work to earlier or contemporary Lives, and even with the other books of this First Life, we can recognize many a traditional theme in what he says about the way Bernard prayed, became absorbed in meditation, refrained from eating and sleeping, or about his brothers' opposition to his healing activities...' Leclercq, 'First Biographer', p. 5.
37 VP 1.4.22; PL 185:239D. See *Apologia ad Guillelmum abbatem* 9.20; Sancti Bernardi opera [hereafter SBOp], edd. Jean Leclercq et al. (Rome, 8 vols. in 9, 1957–1977) 3:97–98.

[38] VP 1.4.22; PL 185:240A.

[39] *Sermo in Cantica canticorum* [hereafter SC] 30.11; SBOp 1:217: 'What does it profit a man to practice temperance from sensual pleasures and then to waste time every day investigating the many and various combinations and dishes. "Beans," he says, "cause wind, cheese lies heavy on the stomach, milk gives me a headache, drinking water is bad for the heart, cabbage brings on depression, onions led to cholic, fish from stagnant or muddy water hardly ever agree with my constitution."'

[40] VP 1.4.21; PL 185:239C. This is confirmed by Bernard, for example in Sermon 2 for the Octave of Epiphany; SBOp 4:324–25. In SC 7.4; SBOp 1:33, he explained that his reason for singling out sleepiness for castigation was the rude inhospitability it offered the angels who attend the Divine Office.

[41] VP 1.8.41; PL 185:251AB: 'Even if his exaggerations of holy fervor are reproved, his holy excess certainly demands respect in devout minds... [for], even if God's servant has gone overboard in exaggeration, the impression he leaves on devout minds is one not of exaggeration but of fervor.' See Bredero, *Études*, p. 251.

[42] *Epistola aurea* [hereafter Ep aur] 1.11.32; PL 184:328C. For an english translation see *The Golden Epistle: A Letter to the Brethren at Mont Dieu*, trans. Theodore Berkeley; The Works of William of St Thierry 4; Cistercian Fathers 12 (Spencer, Massachusetts, 1971).

[43] VP 1.8.41; PL 185:251B.

[44] VP 1.7.38; PL 185:249CD. In VP 1.7.37 (PL 185:248D–249A) William has the monks of Clairvaux delate Bernard to Bishop William of Châlons for giving more attention to their bodies than to their souls.

[45] *De diversis sermo* 40.7; SBOp 6/1:241.

[46] VP 1.8.39; PL 185:250B.

[47] VP 1.8.39; PL 185:250C.

[48] VP 1.8.42; PL 185:251D. See VP 1.8.42; PL 185:251D.

[49] VP 1.9.43; PL 185:252D. See also VP 1.9.43 (PL 185:253C); VP 1.9.43 (PL 185:253D); VP 1.13.64 (PL 185:262B).

[50] See below, note 102.

[51] VP 1.4.19; PL 185:238A.

[52] VP 1.3.8; PL 185:231D: 'His reluctant brothers had concentrated their energies on his love of intellectual pursuits to dissuade him from entering monastic life.' See, also, VP 1.3.8; PL 185:231D.

[53] VP 1.5.26; PL 185:242A.

[54] VP 1.4.24; PL 185:240D–241A.

[55] VP 1.4.23; PL 185:241B.

[56] VP 1.5.25; PL 185:241CD.

[57] VP 1.5.25; PL 185:241D.

[58] VP 1.6.27; PL 185:242C.

[59] VP 1.6.27; PL 185:242C.

60 VP 1.6.27; PL 185:242D.
61 Fragmenta 20; *Analecta*, p. 100.
62 Bredero and Leclercq both mark William's version as 'a long complaint' which camouflages a reproach to Bernard. Bredero sees it as a literary invention to stress Bernard's holiness. Bredero, *Études*, p. 250: 'Guillaume lui, fit de la conversation des deux frères une longue plainte de Gérard, qui cachait aussi un reproche à l'adresse de saint Bernard.' See Leclercq, 'First Biographer', pp. 6–7.
63 SC 26.4; SBOp 1:172.
64 SC 26.7; SBOp 1:175.
65 SC 26.3; SBOp 1:171. See SC 26.6; SBOp 1:174.
66 SC 26.6; SBOp 1:174.
67 SC 26.6; SBOp 1:174.
68 It was, after all, Gerard who fetched the ailing William from Saint Thierry to Clairvaux, and it is not inconceivable that the two men talked about Bernard on the long trip. VP 1.12.59; PL 185:259A.
69 VP 1.6.27; PL 185:242D–243A.
70 VP 1.6.28; PL 185:243C.
71 VP 1.6.28; PL 185:243C.
72 VP 1.6.28; PL 185:243C.
73 *Epistola* [hereafter Ep] 73.2; SBOp 7:180.
74 VP 1.6.29; PL 185:243D.
75 VP 1.6.29; PL 185:243D. The young Bernard's latent contempt for those who did not share his gifts or his convictions may have exacerbated misunderstanding. Being an insomiac himself, he informed monks who snored or slept sloppily that they were carnal or worldly. VP 1.4.21; PL 185:239C. An older, gentler Bernard couched it differently; see above, note 40.
76 VP 1.4.20; PL 185:238C.
77 Leclercq, 'First Biographer', pp. 15–16.
78 Ep aur 1.7.18; PL 184:320BC. See Ep aur 1.11.32; PL 184:328C, cited above, note 42.
79 VP 1.6.28; PL 185:243D–244A.
80 VP 1.6.29; PL 185:244B.
81 VP 1.8.41; PL 185:251B.
82 VP 1.5.26; PL 185:242A.
83 Bredero, *Études*, p. 252: '. . . Il a osé intégrer certaines attitudes contestables de Bernard dans sa sainteté meme. . . .' See Bredero, 'Crossroads', p. 114: 'William describes Bernard with his real faults; but he also points out the divine grace which sanctified him. . . .'
84 Leclercq, 'First Biographer', p. 18.
85 VP 1.12.60; PL 185:259D.
86 Ep 86; SBOp 7:223–24.

87 VP 1.7.33 (PL 185:246C–247B); VP 1.12.57 (PL 185:258AB); VP 1.12.59 (PL 185:259AB).

88 VP *Admonitio*; PL 185:221–22. Anselme Dimier, *Dictionnaire des auteurs cisterciens*, p. 279: '. . . .En 1140. Il fit partie d'une vingtaine de jeunes clercs que le saint emmera avec lui à Clairvaux.'

89 See below, note 104.

90 Ep 85.4; SBOp 7:222.

91 VP 1, Praefatio; PL 185:226C.

92 Berengarius to the bishop of Mende: 'They say that my tongue is a restless evil, and that there is envy in my mind which spews forth a book against the abbot of Clairvaux. For, they say, he is a man of such holiness that, being already near heaven, he has passed beyond men's opinions of him. Those who say this, although they shine bright in the garb of religion, while they want to be doves without a serpent, steep their tongues in mere folly. Is the abbot not a man?' PL 178:1871C.

93 N. M. Häring, 'The Case of Gilbert de la Porrée Bishop of Poitiers (1142–1154)', *Mediaeval Studies* (1944) 3, cites John of Salisbury's *Historia Pontificalis* 12 (ed. R. L. Poole [Oxford, 1927] p. 27), in which Gilbert advised Bernard to 'procure a better education in disciplinis liberalibus and other preliminary requirements' before dabbling in theology.

94 *De consideratione* 4.4.9–11; SBOp 3:455–57.

95 He claims to have drawn his material from those, monks and ecclesiastics alike, who had personally known Bernard. VP 1, *Praefatio*; PL 185:225D–226A.

96 VP 1.14.71; PL 185:266B.

97 Ep aur 1.1.4; PL 184:311A.

98 VP 1.7.34; PL 185:247CD.

99 Leclercq, 'First Biographer', pp. 7–9. This is truer, I think, than Leclercq's observation (in 'First Biographer', p. 6) that William 'aimed at highlighting the part he [Bernard] played in spreading his Order.' He did chronicle Bernard's role, but not enthusiastically. See below.

100 VP 1.7.35; PL 185:247D.

101 William suggests that Bernard never fully adjusted to lesser mortals or his own limitations, although he did modify his early zeal. VP 1.6.30; PL 185:244C. After his confinement in the hut at the crossroad, Bernard seemed to become more tolerant of his monks. Was his illness and obedience to William of Champeaux a turning point? Perhaps William's own influence softened him? 'Eodem tempore et ego Claram-Vallem, ipsumque frequentare coepi. . .'; VP 1.7.33; PL 185:246CD. According to Leclercq: 'William insists a great deal on this slow maturation [under obedience to William of Champeaux], this educational process, which little by little led Bernard to a correct appreciation of man and his attitude to God, and let him discover that all pleasure is not evil. This runs all through the account, and it certainly corresponds to one

of William's intentions. Does it also correspond to something Bernard experienced?' Leclercq, 'First Biographer', pp. 15–16.

Bredero insists that 'William allows no sense of development [évolution] in Bernard, but then what notion did they have in the twelfth century?' Bredero, *Études*, p. 253. Curiously, according to the VP, after Bernard returned from his convalescence, the monks complained that 'their spiritual father' seemed to be catering more to the flesh than to the spirit. Having learned from Bernard to despise the flesh, they could not understand his new moderation. VP 1.7.36–37; PL 185:248CD–249A. And William backed Bernard up by launching into a sermon which pointed out that God's gifts were to be accepted as they were given.

Could this spiritual father be someone other than Bernard, who is elsewhere and exclusively referred to simply as 'the spiritual father' (VP 1.13.64; PL 185:262CD)?

[102] VP 1.4.23; PL 185:240B.

[103] VP 1.8.38; PL 185:249C. For this turn of phrase, as for several others in these citations, I am indebted to the translation of Martinus Cawley, in *Bernard of Clairvaux: Early Biographies, 1, By William of St Thierry*.

[104] VP 1.8.38; PL 185:249C.

[105] Following G. Hüffer, *Der heilige Bernard von Clairvaux*, I, *Vorstudien* (Münster, 1886)—'. . . les Fragmenta Gaufridi, que Hüffer date avec raison de 1145 . . .'—Bredero dates the Fragmenta Gaudfridi William used as his base to the spring of 1145, and therefore Book One of VP to 1145–1148 (*Études*, pp. 11 and 244, n. 3).

[106] VP 1.7.35; PL 185:247D.

[107] Jean-Michel Musso, 'L'abbaye de Clairvaux', *Les monuments historiques* 145 (1986) 14, credits Bernard with undertaking the construction of 'la véritable abbaye (Clairvaux II)' which he calls 'le prototype—le modèle imposé—des grands établissements de l'ordre cistercien', and again, p. 16, writes of the abbey 'telle qu'elle fut conçue par saint Bernard . . .' He does not, however, provide a source for attributing the new grandeur to Bernard himself.

[108] VP 1.13.62; PL 185:261.

[109] VP 1.7.34; PL 185:247C.

[110] William, *Expositio super Cantica canticorum* 156; ed. M.-M. Davy, *Guillaume de Saint-Thierry: Commentaire sur le Cantique des cantiques* (Paris: Vrin, 1958) p. 189. M. Michaela Pfeifer, O. Cist., 'Auf der Suche nach frühen zisterziensischen Noviziatsschriften: Wilhelms von Saint-Thierry Goldener Brief', Licentiate thesis at San Anselmo, Rome, p. 211, argues that the contemporary *Golden Epistle* similarly reveals William's concern at the 'allzu rasch' growth of the cistercian order. I am indebted for this citation to Jean Leclercq.

[111] Although it is widely assumed that William did not enter Clairvaux because Bernard resolutely refused him permission to do so, our only evidence for this is the oblique reference in Bernard's letter advising him to 'stay where you are and try to guide those over whom you govern.' Ep 86.2; SBOp 7:224, dated by Jean-Marie Déchanet to 'before the Apology' (*William of St Thierry: The Man and His Work*, trans. Richard Strachan; Cistercian Studies 10 [Spencer, Massachusetts, 1972] p. 32, n. 83), and by Leclercq to 'die 9 sept. 1123 vel 1124' citing Damien van den Eynde, 'Les prémiers écrits de s. Bernard', in *Recueil des études sur saint Bernard* 3 (Rome, 1969) pp. 343–422. We do not know that Bernard continued to refuse permission, or that William continued to ask it.

[112] VP 1.7.43; PL 185:247CD.
[113] VP 1.12.59; PL 185:259B.
[114] VP 1.7.33; PL 185:246D. See VP 1.7.35, PL 185:247D–248A.
[115] VP 1.7.33; PL 185:246CD.
[116] VP 1.7.34; PL 185:247BC.
[117] VP 1.7.33; PL 185:246C.
[118] VP 1.14.70; PL 185:265C.
[119] VP 1.8.40; PL 185:250C.

AMERICAN CATHOLIC HISTORIOGRAPHY COMES OF AGE

†John Tracy Ellis
The Catholic University of America

F EW TOPICS HAVE MORE CONSISTENTLY engaged the interest and concern of historians than that of historiography. Nor have Clio's clients in recent decades shown any slackening in that regard. Thus from Oscar Handlin's severe scolding entitled 'History: A Discipline in Crisis', in the 1971 summer issue of *The American Scholar*, to the same journal's summer issue of 1989 in which G. W. Bowersock's article, 'Herodotus, Alexander, and Rome',[1] paid tribute to the father of history, the theme has continued to find its expositors, often as the presidential address to groups like the American Historical Association and the Organization of American Historians.[2] If these essays have had any common denominator, it has been their evidence of the constantly changing perspective of historians, the revelation of what may be called historical fashions, that is, the twists and turns, so to speak, of those on the left, such as the Marxists, to the counter moves of their opponents on the right. Between these ideological extremes, the partisans of the 'new history' have vigorously argued their case, only to be sharply criticized by Gertrude Himmelfarb *et al.*[3] Meanwhile, the practitioners of 'history from below' have drawn an increasing number of disciples, and so in all likelihood will the scene continue to change as new ideas arise and find their followers and then, in turn, give way to something different. It may be a manifestation of the oft-quoted remark of John Henry Newman: 'In a higher world it is otherwise, but here below to live is to change, and to be perfect is to have changed often.'[4]

Mutatis mutandis, the same thing can be said of ecclesiastical historians, with the difference that on the whole the latter have been less prone to change than their counterparts in secular history. Yet one can easily detect differences—and improvement—for example, between the methodology of Eusebius of Caesarea (d. c. 339), often called the father of church history, and the heightened dependence on original sources and more careful research and interpretation of Saint Bede (d. 735), who is generally thought of as the father of english history and the first significant author in the evolution of english church history. Should anyone have any doubt about the current concern of historians with historiography, they have only to consult the June 1989 issue of the *American Historical Review*, where eight different authors air their differences about how history should be interpreted and written, not always, I regret to say, to the enlightenment of history's professionals and fans. In fact, the more I have pondered some of those essays, the more have I valued the approach of historians like William H. McNeill, Owen Chadwick, and, in the realm of more strictly religious history, the late David Knowles and Christopher Dawson. In other words, it is the broad perspective employed by these historians that enables the student to achieve what Newman had in mind when he declared:

> ...The study of history is said to enlarge and enlighten the mind, and why? because, as I conceive, it gives it a power of judging of passing events, and of all events, and a conscious superiority over them, which before it did not possess.[5]

The history of any people at any time is conditioned by the circumstances in which they find themselves. Thus the missionary era in what was to become the United States produced no notable narrative histories between the 1540s, when the earliest friars arrived in what came to be called the Southwest, and the birth of the Republic in the 1770s. But during those years there were compiled outstanding original sources such as the *Jesuit Relations* and the numerous letters, diaries, etc. of the franciscan friars and other missionary groups. Nor were the early decades of the organized catholic community after John Carroll's episcopal consecration in 1790 much better in that regard. For example, John Carroll Brent's *Biographical Sketch of the Most Rev. John Carroll* in 1843, Charles I. White's biography of Elizabeth Seton in 1853, and Henry de Courcey's *The Catholic Church in the United States: A Sketch of its Ecclesiastical History* (1856)—to cite only three works from this period—left much to be desired by way of critical use of sources, archival research, and objective evaluation and interpretation. Yet that is not meant to disparage these early efforts, for to do that would be to violate one of history's perennial rules, namely, that human beings and events must be judged by the standards of their own time and not by the standards of a later age.

The first faint suggestion of a professional approach in history among american Catholics came with a relatively untrained layman, John Gilmary Shea (1824–1892). Motivated by a deep love of the Church and her history in this country, Shea published numerous articles and books, edited collections of original documents, and helped to found the United States Catholic Historical Society of New York in 1884, the same year in which the American Historical Association was established. Shea was a tireless researcher who worked against great odds, such as personal poverty, lack of appreciation of his efforts, and uncertain health. In 1888, Shea touched on some of these problems in a letter to John Farley, then secretary of the archbishop of New York, when he said:

> *The Life and Times of Archbishop Carroll* is, as you know, ready; and it has cost me great labor, absorbing all my leisure and impairing my health seriously. It covers an important period, and really the history of the Church during it has not hitherto been known. Not only are errors and misrepresentations corrected, but whole chapters are new contributions.
>
> I have made the volume so large and expensive, that I am in considerable debt; and I see no way out except to have another appeal for patrons of the work.[6]

The Carroll biography to which Shea referred was the first volume of his *magnum opus*, the *History of the Catholic Church in the United States*, the final volume, the fourth, being published in 1892, some months after his death. In all, Shea's titles numbered nearly 250 and established his name as the preeminent historian of american Catholicism, an achievement that won him in 1883 the Laetare Medal of the University of Notre Dame, the first person on whom it was conferred. It was richly deserved, to be sure, as was the posthumous honor bestowed by the American Catholic Historical Association in 1944 in marking their silver jubilee by the institution of the John Gilmary Shea Prize given annually for an outstanding work in church history.

During the quarter century between Shea's death and World War I, a number of studies appeared on the history of dioceses and religious congregations of men and women, for example, histories of the dioceses of Vincennes and Fort Wayne by the german-born Herman J. Alerding (1845–1924), third bishop of Fort Wayne. While these studies were of some use to future historians in the sources they gathered, they were not scientific works in the sense that they were not well organized, nor did they show anything approaching an objective and critical spirit. In a word, they were products of the period when the ghetto mentality still held the catholic community captive, an age when to admit the errors and mistakes of bishops, priests, and religious was thought to lend comfort to the Church's enemies such as the American Protective Association and, later, the Klu Klux Klan.

With the opening, in November 1889, of the Catholic University of America, the status of ecclesiastical sciences in general was improved, but church history did not at first partake in this advance. For altogether good reasons John Gilmary Shea had hoped to be named to the faculty, but clericalism prevailed, and Augustine F. Hewit, CSP, superior of the Paulists, a learned convert but with no qualifications in history, was chosen to lecture in church history. Nor was the second choice, Thomas O'Gorman (1843–1921), a priest of the archdiocese of Saint Paul, much of a gain. That was evident with the publication of his *History of the Roman Catholic Church in the United States*, which was largely a condensation of Shea's work down to 1866 and thereafter a wooden account of little worth, a book that was scarcely a source of pride to Catholics as Volume IX of the interdenominational American Church History series. It was no loss to scholarship when this protegé of Archbishop John Ireland was named bishop of Sioux Falls in 1896. One wonders if O'Gorman was one of those Ireland had in mind a few years before when he counseled John J. Keane, rector of the University: 'You must educate your professors, and then hold on to them—making bishops only of those who are not worth keeping as professors.'[7]

By this time, however, the prospects for church history at the new university had brightened with the appointment in 1888 of Thomas J. Shahan (1857–1932), chancellor of the diocese of Hartford, to undertake graduate studies abroad. He returned in 1891 and began to teach church history until administrative duties absorbed more and more of his time and energy, culminating in 1909 with his appointment as the fourth rector of the institution. Meanwhile Shahan was at pains to see that church history was not abandoned by securing the permission of the archbishop of Philadelphia for one of his promising young men to join the faculty. Peter Guilday (1884–1947) was thus enlisted and took his doctorate at the Catholic University of Louvain. With Guilday's arrival in Washington in 1914, a new and energetic chapter in american catholic history was inaugurated. True, Guilday's training had been in european church history, but Shahan advised him to focus on american catholic history, which he did with courses in the Church of Europe on the side, so to speak.

In his enlightening essay, 'Peter Guilday: The Catholic Intellectual in the Post-Modernist Church', David O'Brien of the College of the Holy Cross has described Guilday as the man who 'provided a living bridge between the drive for scholarship and intelligent leadership in the Church',[8] an appropriate way in which to summarize Guilday's notable contribution. It would not be exaggerating to say that with the thirty-year old priest's advent to Washington a new and promising era opened for american catholic history. If the content of his courses was rather thin, he more than made up for that deficiency in other ways. For example, in April 1915, there appeared the inaugural issue of the *Catholic Historical Review*, a quarterly journal that reached its seventy-fifth volume in January 1989, a scholarly periodical the quality of which has made it a prime exhibit of american catholic history having 'come of age'. Although Thomas Shahan was at first the nominal editor, from the outset it was Guilday who was the principal directing hand behind the enterprise, a post he filled until declining health compelled him to resign the editorship in 1941. I was then named editor and continued to 1963, when the present editor, Robert Trisco, took over, a man whose high standards have guaranteed the *Review*'s fine reputation in scholarly circles.

Although small groups had from time to time founded catholic historical societies, notably in Philadelphia and New York in the 1880s, in spite of their national titles they remained in large measure local enterprises. Their contribution, however, was real in stimulating interest in catholic history in their respective regions and, too, in publishing original sources that might otherwise not have seen the light. There had been no truly national organization among Catholics, and it was that goal that Guilday had in mind in assembling in Cleveland, in December 1919, about fifty professional historians who there founded the American Catholic Historical Association, which has continued uninterruptedly to sponsor the *Catholic Historical Review* and to hold meetings in Christmas week and in the spring in various locations, at which learned papers are read by a wide range of historians. These papers have frequently been published at a later date, and in several cases in the early years they came out in book form, for example, the papers read at the Ann Arbor meeting in December 1925, which appeared as *Church Historians* (New York: P. J. Kenedy & Sons, 1926) with a foreword by Peter Guilday. The Association has for the past seventy years served as a clearing house for catholic historical interests as well as representing the general catholic community in relations with the American Historical Association and its affiliated societies. Its activities have been hampered by the lack of support, a fact clearly evidenced by its 1989 membership of 1,090 out of an estimated catholic population in the United States of over 54,900,000.

Monsignor Guilday not only promoted Clio's cause nationally through the *Review* and the Association but as well through his seminar in which dozens of graduate students were trained who, in turn, carried their training nationwide in seminaries, colleges, and universities. From that seminar there were published thirty-three doctoral dissertations that treated a wide variety of topics on the american catholic past. Meanwhile Guilday steadily pursued his personal research and writing with major biographies of John Carroll, first archbishop of Baltimore, in 1922, and of John England, first bishop of Charleston, in 1927, to mention only two of his works. All in all it was a striking achievement that placed american catholic history on a firm scholarly footing for the first time, a foundation that built on the significant contribution of John Gilmary Shea *et al.* I had good reason to know how much was owed to Shea and Guilday when, in 1941, I was asked to succeed the latter as editor of the *Review*, secretary of the Association, and teacher of american catholic history.

By the 1940s the history of Catholicism in the United States had come to engage the efforts of an increasing number of scholars whose research and publications flourished far beyond the Catholic University of America. A dozen or more names come to mind, but at the risk of omitting women and men of deserved merit I must confine mention to only a few lest this become a mere litany. For example, there was the talented literary convert, Theodore Maynard (1890–1956), who, though not a trained historian, contributed a number of semi-popular biographies of prominent figures such as Orestes Brownson, Simon Bruté, *et al.*, that won a rather wide audience of readers and served to broaden Catholics' knowledge of their religious past. Regional studies were advanced by the archival research that enriched the numerous publications of Carlos E. Castañeda (1896–1958) on Texas and the Southwest, the same being true of Maynard J. Geiger, OFM (1901–1977) for California and Gilbert J. Garraghan, SJ (1871–1942) for the Middle West. True, the principal focus of Geiger and Garraghan was their own religious order, about which they showed a certain bias, something that the layman Castañeda escaped, but these historians were reasonably objective and certainly dedicated to constructing their narratives on original sources. In other words, they were historians and not hagiographers, as had been true of so many who had preceded them.

In any survey of american catholic historiography, special mention must be made of Thomas T. McAvoy, CSC (1903–1969) of the University of Notre Dame. Early in this century, Notre Dame's librarian, James F. Edwards, conceived the idea of a national catholic archive, and in consequence he brought to Notre Dame numerous manuscript sources from the archdioceses of Cincinnati and

New Orleans as well as from other diocesan collections. Having earned his doctorate at Columbia University in 1940, Father McAvoy took over as archivist and professor of american catholic history. Up to his death nearly thirty years later, he made significant additions to Notre Dame's collections with the result that, with the single exception of the archives of the archdiocese of Baltimore, Notre Dame became the most important location of archival sources for the catholic history of this country. Meanwhile McAvoy continued his personal research while serving as chairman of the Department of History and as editor of the *Review of Politics*. His most notable book was *The Great Crisis in American Catholic History, 1895–1900* (Chicago: Henry Regnery Company, 1957), a detailed account of the so-called heresy of Americanism.

Thomas McAvoy's outstanding contribution to Notre Dame's reputation as a center for american catholic historical studies was not allowed to die with his death. One of his prize students, Philip Gleason, has made his own distinguished contribution to that tradition, as have Jay P. Dolan, Director of the Cushwa Center for the Study of American Catholicism, and Marvin R. O'Connell, whose biography of John Ireland, archbishop of Saint Paul, won deservedly high praise in 1988, although the talented author's field is european rather than american history. Those of us in american catholic history would warmly welcome any 'intruder' who would match the skill in research, literary grace, and balanced interpretation of a Marvin O'Connell. In fine, the University of Notre Dame ranks near the top in its fostering of a sophisticated and professional approach in this field, the evidence of which is seen in the stimulation offered by the Cushwa Center's varied programs, the publications of the University's press, and the scholarly productions of its historians, for example, Jay Dolan's *The American Catholic Experience: A History from Colonial Times to the Present* (Garden City: Doubleday & Company, Inc., 1985) and Philip Gleason's *Keeping the Faith: American Catholicism Past and Present* (Notre Dame: University of

Notre Dame Press, 1987), to name only two works of which Thomas McAvoy would have been proud.

The 'coming of age' of this discipline has been due to a number of factors, among which the development of graduate studies among Catholics has played a leading role. The years after World War II were notable in that regard, with Saint Louis University, Fordham, Notre Dame, and other catholic institutions offering more and varied programs. Thus John B. McGloin, sj (1912–1988), of the University of San Francisco, historian of California Catholicism, was trained at Saint Louis, as was Christopher J. Kauffman, author among other works of highly praised histories of the Knights of Columbus and the american Sulpicians. A prime exhibit of the maturing of american catholic history is the six-volume work, *Makers of the American Catholic Community* (New York: Macmillan Publishing Company, 1989) of which the same Christopher Kauffman was the general editor. Others like Thomas McAvoy and his confrère, Thomas E. Blantz, csc, went to secular universities such as Columbia where the latter produced his able monograph on Francis J. Haas (1889–1953) and is now at work on a biography of the important lay scholar, George N. Shuster (1894–1977).

Few have done more to advance the field of american catholic history than Colman J. Barry, osb. From his 1953 doctoral dissertation, *The Catholic Church and German Americans*, he adhered to a high professional standard in a continued series of publications that include a history of his own religious community of Saint John's Abbey, Collegeville, a perennially useful collection of *Readings in Church History* in three volumes, a biography of Aloisius Muench, the first american catholic churchman to serve as an apostolic nuncio, and a history of the Church in the Bahamas, a benedictine mission. Here again I am taking the risk of doing an injustice to some by naming names, for there were, indeed, others besides Barry who made their mark during this period, among whom the name of Annabelle M. Melville stands out. This first woman

President of the American Catholic Historical Association has set a high standard for ecclesiastical biography in her lives of Elizabeth Seton, John Carroll, Jean Cheverus, and Louis William DuBourg.

Were I asked to summarize my concept of ecclesiastical history having 'come of age', I should be inclined to put it this way. First, it must be honest and real with every effort to portray persons and events as they were and as they happened. No historian can achieve that goal with perfection, but one must come as close as one possibly can, and that regardless of the bias and prejudice that inhabits every human being on the score of ethnic heritage, race, religion, and national origin. Pope Leo XIII stated the ideal in his letter on historical studies of August 1883, in which he borrowed Cicero's formula and declared:

> The first law of history is to dread uttering falsehood; the next not to fear stating the truth; lastly, that the historian's writings should be open to no suspicion of partiality or of animosity.[9]

Like all ideals it has seldom been realized in full; in fact, I would be tempted to say that no ideal has been sinned against more frequently with the mistaken notion that the exposure of churchmen's weaknesses and mistakes would harm the Church. I never found the reverse of this attitude better expressed than in a letter of Jean-Baptiste Lacordaire, OP, to l'Abbé Henri Perreyve, professor of church history in the Sorbonne, in which he said:

> Ought history to hide the faults of men and Orders? It was not in this sense that Baronius understood his duty as an historian of the Church. It was not after this fashion that the Saints laid open the scandals of their times. Truth, when discreetly told, is an inestimable boon to mankind, and to suppress it, especially in history, is an act of cowardice unworthy of a Christian. Timidity is the fault of our age, and truth is concealed under

pretense of respect for holy things. God indeed has conferred upon His Church the prerogative of infallibility, but to none of her members has he granted immunity from sin. Peter was a sinner and a renegade, and God has been at pains to have the fact recorded in the Gospels.[10]

In the literature on american Catholicism numerous works could be cited in which the truth was concealed about bishops, priests, and religious, as well as about institutions and movements in the sense Newman had in mind when speaking of faulty church history:

> I mean the endemic fidget which possesses us about giving scandal; facts are omitted in great histories, or glosses are put upon memorable acts, because they are thought not edifying, whereas of all scandals such omissions, such glosses are the greatest.[11]

This major handicap to sound history has in good measure been put behind us. One can find this open and honest approach in outstanding biographies of prelates such as Marvin O'Connell's *John Ireland and the American Catholic Church* (Saint Paul: Minnesota Historical Society Press, 1988) and Thomas J. Shelley's *Paul J. Hallinan, First Archbishop of Atlanta* (Wilmington: Michael Glazier Inc., 1989). It shows up as well in the articles in the *Catholic Historical Review*, and in the more recent periodical, begun in 1980, *U.S. Catholic Historian*, the winter 1987 issue of which was devoted to 'Reflections on Catholic Historiography'.

Another feature of current ecclesiastical history is the emphasis given to research in manuscript sources as they have been found in archives of the Church both here and abroad. James Hennesey, sj, built his important monograph, *The First Council of the Vatican: The American Experience* (New York: Herder and Herder, 1963) on archival sources, and the same author's superior general work, *American Catholics: A History of the Roman Catholic*

Community in the United States (New York: Oxford University Press, 1981), reflects a similar high regard for original sources. The same can be said for the works of Gerald P. Fogarty, SJ, especially *The Vatican and the American Hierarchy from 1870 to 1965* (Stuttgart: Anton Hiersemann, 1982) and *American Catholic Biblical Scholarship: A History from the Early Republic to Vatican II* (San Francisco: Harper & Row, Publishers, 1989).

A further consideration for mature history is the taking cognizance of environmental factors—the avoidance of writing history in a vacuum, which was a fairly common characteristic of the histories of dioceses, religious communities, and movements many years ago. That is no longer true, as the works of Jay Dolan give evidence, as well as the histories of movements like that of lay trusteeism exemplified in Patrick W. Carey's *People, Priests, and Prelates: Ecclesiastical Democracy and the Tensions of Trusteeism* (Notre Dame: University of Notre Dame Press, 1987).

Thus in biographies, in periodicals, in the history of dioceses, religious communities, and catholic movements generally there has been a marked improvement in the last generation or two. This improvement has been so marked, in fact, that John Gilmary Shea would be astonished were he to see both the quality and the quantity of serious writing today on the catholic history of the United States.

The changed mentality that helped to bring about this improved condition in the study of american Catholicism was very well expressed in a letter of H. Stuart Hughes, then a professor at Harvard, to my friend, John Whitney Evans of the College of Saint Scholastica, Duluth. I have quoted it more than once, and I do not hesitate to do so once again. Writing in 1966, Hughes stated:

> Before the war, Catholic graduate students in history at Harvard were few in number, mostly undistinguished, and on the margin of intellectual exchange; the rest of us treated them with politeness, but it would not have occurred to us

> to discuss religious or philosophical matters with them (and perhaps they themselves would have been embarrassed to do so). Today my Catholic graduate students are some of the very best I have, they are right in the center of student life, and they do not hesitate to discuss the most prickly topics frankly and cordially.[12]

It has been from minds such as those described by Stuart Hughes that much writing in catholic history has come during the past quarter century, minds that demonstrated superior professional training, an emancipation from the strictures of the preceding age, and the almost revolutionary change that came about in catholic circles as a sequel to Vatican Council II.

An accompaniment of the post-conciliar years has been a new vocabulary, for example, the expression 'people of God' brought anew into common use. To be sure, there has been little conscious connection between the 'people of God' and the current fashion of 'history from below', yet the one blends well with the other and fosters a mutual understanding that is useful to the believer who finds inspiration and support for his or her belief in history. Long before the 'people of God' and 'history from below' had become popular and meaningful, Gregory Dix described the importance of the masses of humankind in a moving passage:

> To those who know a little of Christian history probably the most moving of all the reflections it brings is not the thought of the great events and the well-remembered saints, but of those innumerable millions of entirely obscure faithful men and women, every one with his or her own individual hopes and fears and joys and sorrows and loves—and sins and temptations and prayers—once every whit as vivid and alive as mine are now. They have left no slightest trace in this world, not even a name, but have

passed to God utterly forgotten by men. Yet each of them once believed and prayed as I believe and pray, and found it hard and grew slack and sinned and repented and fell again. Each of them worshipped at the eucharist, and found their thoughts wandering and tried again, and felt heavy and unresponsive and yet knew—just as really and pathetically as I do—these things.[13]

Throughout this essay I have tried to show how american catholic history has matured and won a respectable place and name in professional circles. I have thought the best way of illustrating that theme was to cite examples of publications of various kinds that exemplify that type of history. If I am convinced that genuine progress has been made in that regard, I am under no illusion concerning the distance we still have to travel to bring about a community of Catholics in this country reasonably well informed about their religious heritage. Here I find the laity much more eager to learn the Church's story in the Republic than is true of the clergy. I sometimes wonder if this well educated laity do not sense the importance of the Church's history as a support for their faith. There is no doubt in my mind of the connection between the two, and I have often stated that, next to the light of the Holy Spirit, I find my knowledge of ecclesiastical history the strongest foundation on which to rest my belief. One of the most distinguished church historians of the English-speaking world saw it likewise, namely, David Knowles (1896-1974). I bring this essay to a close, then, with the learned Benedictine's comment, a view in which I fully share. Dom Knowles maintained:

> Yet while it is true that faith is a gift of God and that the gospel can be preached and heard by little ones and by the unlearned, it is also true that once we begin to consider the part of human endeavour in the matter of understanding and penetrating the truths of faith and the ways of God, a knowledge of history is, after theology

and the study of Scripture, the most valuable of all mental possessions. The background of classical and oriental civilization, the moment of peace in the empire that embraced almost the whole world as it was known to the Mediterranean peoples, the early opposition and the final capitulation of the government of the Empire to Christianity—all this sets the Christian message so clearly forth against the confusion and poverty of human thought and endeavour that the argument from history is one of the strongest arguments of the apologists for the divine origin of the Church. Indeed, a familiarity with the early history of the Church does far more than serve as a setting to the gospel narrative; it gives the Christian of today a new kind of hindsight into the economy of salvation.[14]

Notes

[1] Oscar Handlin, 'History: A Discipline in Crisis', *The American Scholar* 40 (1971) 447–65; G. W. Bowersock, 'Herodotus, Alexander, and Rome', *The American Scholar* 58 (1989) 407–414.

[2] For the American Historical Association, see C. Vann Woodward, 'The Future of the Past', *American Historical Review* 75 (1970) 711–26; Gordon Wright, 'History As a Moral Science', *American Historical Review* 81 (1976) 1–11; Bernard Bailyn, 'The Challenge of Modern Historiography', *American Historical Review* 87 (1982) 1–24.

[3] Gertrude Himmelfarb, *The New History and the Old* (Cambridge: The Belknap Press of Harvard University Press, 1987).

[4] John Henry Newman, *An Essay in the Development of Christian Doctrine* (New York: Doubleday and Company, 1960) p. 63.

[5] John Henry Newman, *The Idea of a University*, ed. Ian T. Ker (Oxford: At the Clarendon Press, 1976) p. 119.

[6] 'John Gilmary Shea Discusses His Problems and Methods in Writing the *History of the Catholic Church in the United States*, March, 1885-September 26, 1890', Shea to Farley, October 18, 1888, in John Tracy Ellis (ed.), *Documents of American Catholic History* (Revised and enlarged edition, Wilmington, Delaware: Michael Glazier, Inc., 1987) 2:427–28.

[7] Ireland to Keane, Rome, April 26, 1892, in Patrick Henry Ahern, *The Catholic University of America, 1887–1896: The Rectorship of John J. Keane* (Washington: The Catholic University of America Press, 1948) p. 50.

[8] David O'Brien, 'Peter Guilday: The Catholic Intellectual in the Post-Modernist Church', in Nelson H. Minnich, Robert B. Eno, ss, and Robert Tisco (edd.), *Studies in Catholic History in Honor of John Tracy Ellis* (Wilmington, Delaware: Michael Glazier, Inc., 1985) p. 261.

[9] *The Tablet* (London), 62 (September 1, 1883) 322.

[10] Lacordaire to Perreyve, April 2, 1855, in Joseph T. Foisset, *Vie du Père Lacordaire* (Paris: Lecoffre fils et Cie, 1870) 2:532.

[11] John Henry Newman, *Historical Sketches* (London: Longmans, Green and Company, 1906) 2:231.

[12] H. Stuart Hughes to John Whitney Evans, Paris, November 4, 1966. I wish to thank Professor Hughes and Father Evans for permission to quote this letter.

[13] Gregory Dix, *The Shape of the Liturgy* (Westminster: Dacre Press, 1945) pp. 744–45.

[14] David Knowles, 'The Need for Catholic Historical Scholarship', *Dublin Review* 232 (1958) 122–23.

AN UNKNOWN ILLUMINATED PAGE FROM THE STATUTES OF THE ORDER OF SAINT MICHAEL IN THE AMBROSIANA LIBRARY IN MILAN

Astrik L. Gabriel
University of Notre Dame

THE AMBROSIANA LIBRARY in Milan has a collection of illuminated manuscript fragments, historiated initials, half and full page illuminations (F. 277 inferior)—mostly cut out of unidentified manuscripts ranging from the thirteenth to the sixteenth centuries.* Among them there is a hitherto unknown single leaf, full page illumination representing Louis XI, king of France (1461–1483), presiding over a meeting of the knights of the Order of Saint Michael, surrounded by fifteen standing knights, eight at his right and seven at his left.[1] The beardless king is seated under a canopy and is vested with a royal blue mantle, decorated with fleur de lis, lined with ermine over a red surcoat showing a grayish robe underneath. He is holding the royal scepter in his right hand and the 'Hand of Justice' in his left (see Plate I).

The fairly large and long nose of the king indicates that the miniaturist intended to depict Louis XI, the founder of the order. However, the form of hats and their clumsy shoes with the large tips worn by the knights reveal that it was painted during the reign of Francis I (1515–1547). The walls are hidden by a blue curtain adorned with fleur de lis. The three knights in the foreground are vested in black, gold, and grayish mantles. Their hats are black, except for three knights, who display red.

All of them, including the king, are wearing the distinctive emblem of the Order of Saint Michael, double golden chains composed of shells. In the middle hangs the figure of the archangel Saint Michael, shown vanquishing the dragon. The entire scene is in a golden architectural frame with two winged putti blowing horns on the tops of the renaissance columns. One putto in the middle of the lower margin is holding a garland fastened to two heads. Six lines are inscribed with bastard script starting with an illuminated initial 'L', the first lines of the Charter of Foundation of the order.[2]

THE FOUNDATION OF THE ORDER

The Order of Saint Michael was established by Louis XI with an ordinance dated August 1, 1469, from Amboise. Two additional ordinances were added and were promulgated on December 22 and 24, 1476, respectively. The number of knights was fixed at thirty-six. It had four officers: chancellor (always an ecclesiastic), treasurer, clerk (*greffier*), and the royal herald of arms (*heraut roi d'arms*). The ordinance identified by name only fifteen knights as 'nos freres et compaignons', headed by the brother of the king, Charles de France, duke of Guyenne, and John II, duke of Bourbon.[3]

The distinctive mark of the order was a golden chain of shells with a figure of Saint Michael victorious over the dragon.[4] The ordinance described the uniform to be worn by the knights during the ceremonies: long white mantle, lined with ermine, trimmed with embroidered shells, crimson chaperon or shoulder ban.

The statutes of the order were to be inscribed in a book illustrated with an 'histoire', an illuminated page representing the founder Louis XI and the original fifteen knights. Two such books were prepared, one for the king and the other for his brother. The king's (own) copy (Paris BN. MS fr. 19819),[5] brilliantly painted in a harmonious composition by Jean Foucquet, conforming to the instructions, depicted Louis XI seated and vested in the uniform of the order with the knights standing around him, all wearing their long white mantles and veloured crimson colored shoulder bands, as specified in the ordinance of 1469, and the golden chain with the figurine of Saint Michael. The four officers standing in the background were represented by Foucquet without golden chains.[6] A much inferior copy of the same scene was made for Charles of France (BN. MS Clairambault No. 1242, p. 1421).[7] The splendid illumination and composition of Foucquet established the model for subsequent but much inferior artists for the decoration of the statute books under such french kings as Charles VIII (1483–1498); Louis XII (1498–1515); Francis I (1515–1547), and Henry II (1547–1559).

However, not all the statute books had the illustrations representing the french monarch presiding over the chapter of the order.[8] The statute book (Vienna, NB 2637) prepared for Louis XII, containing the 1476 ordinance, shows the king pointing to the insignia of the order: large white mantle, veloured crimson shoulder band, and the golden chain with the figurine of Saint Michael.[9]

THE OFFICIAL SERIES OF THE STATUTE BOOKS IN THE TIME OF FRANCIS I

With the reign of Francis I, the splendor of illuminated statute books suffered considerably. This was a period of mass production of the statute books by able practitioners for the members of the order. An 'official series' painted by the same atelier was inaugurated by a copy sent to Henry VIII, king of England. The latter was knighted in the Order of Saint Michael by Francis I and was presented with an illuminated copy which is now in the Museum of Records Office in London. Louis XI is shown seated, holding only a scepter in his left hand and surrounded by the knights. An evidence of a remote iconographical influence of Foucquet's original miniature is a white greyhound painted in the center of the composition.[10]

The illuminations showing the reunion of the knights under the presiding king in the 'official series' seem to be influenced by the artist of an elaborate and pleasing full-page hors-texte miniature (Paris BN. MS fr. 5109, fol. A verso) heading the *Register* of the criminal process of Charles of Bourbon in 1527. The twelve peers of France have the same gestures as the knights of the 'official series' of the statute books. The architectural frame, the stylization of the columns, the winged putti seated on the top, the features of Francis I are painted like those of Louis XI; the shoes, the placement of the windows, reflect the techniques displayed in the 'official series' (see Plate II). The steps of the throne have a shell as a decorative motif exactly like the Ambrosiana minature and a copy in Paris (BN. MS fr. 14361, fol. 7 verso) (see Plate III). On the lower margin of the *Register* the arms of France are surrounded with the double chains of the Order of Saint Michael.[11] The illuminated page of the Ambrosiana is the product of an atelier that executed the 'official series' of the statute books. Relatively speaking, the Ambrosiana illumination is the most elaborate artistic work among the nine known copies.[12]

Besides the Ambrosiana folio (F. 277, no. 59), miniatures showing the chapter meetings of the Order of Saint Michael are painted in:

Paris, BN. MS fr. 14361, folio 7 verso;[13]
                14365, folio 8 recto;[14]
                19815, folio 11 recto;[15] (see Plate IV)
                19816, folio 9 recto;[16] (see Plate V)
                19818, folio 11 recto;[17]
Trivulziana   1394, folio 9 recto;[18]
London, Harley 4485, folio 9 recto;[19] (see Plate VI)
Cheltenham   1323.[20]

I have examined seven copies in original of the 'official series'. I have not seen two manuscripts in original, the Cheltenham 1323 and London, Harley 4485. I have, however, obtained reproductions. The Turin manuscript, Gallicus XXX, was destroyed during a fire in 1905 and apparently belonged to the same 'official series'.[21]

The nine copies of the statutes, or ten if we include the somewhat different composition of the chapter scene as shown in the copy sent to Henry VIII,[22] display the following common features: (1) They depict the king seated holding a scepter and the Hand of Justice. Usually he wears a black flat hat *à la mode* Francis I[23] except in three copies where he is wearing a royal crown. In nine he is not wearing the originally prescribed ceremonial white mantle with crimson shoulder bands but is represented wearing mantles of different colors with double gold chains displayed on his shoulders. The knights are standing before the king, except in Paris BN. fr. 19816, folio 1 recto, where they are shown seated on benches, five at the right side and five at the left of the king. (2) The number of the knights grouped around the king is usually ten, two on either side, standing in the background, and three on either side in front, or twelve,[24] in threes farther back and in threes facing each other or looking at the king. In the miniature executed during the reign of Louis XI the number of knights is eighteen.[25]

The uniqueness of the Ambrosiana illumination consists in the fact that it is the only one in the official series in which the number of knights is fifteen, corresponding to the number of the originally constituted fifteen knights listed by name in the charter of foundation of August 1, 1469.[26] In the composition of the interior of the chapter room, the Ambrosiana miniature is unparalleled in the series because the artist did not paint windows but covered the wall with a blue curtain decorated with fleur de lis. All the other copies depict two or four windows.[27] Under the iconographical influence of the illuminated page of the statute book executed for Louis XII,[28] in the foreground of which a knight is carrying a cane, the 'official series' of the statute books also depicts, though inconsistently, one sometimes two, even three knights displaying a cane or baton.[29] In the Ambrosiana illumination only one knight has a cane. Originally, it was the symbol of the grand master of the order. Later on, to show the importance of the dignitaries of the kingdom of France among the members of the order, the artist depicted knights other than the chancellor carrying canes.

DATE OF THE COMPOSITION OF THE AMBROSIANA MINIATURE

The date of the Ambrosiana illumination, along with the execution of the other manuscripts of the so-called 'official series' discussed above, should be placed in the first half of the reign of Francis I, who ruled from 1515 to 1547. Several reasons support dating the illumination to around 1522–1523: (1) The style of hats and shoes worn by the knights reflects the taste of the period of Francis I. (2) The knights are represented in the statute books painted for Louis XI[30] (also in that of his brother, Charles of France, duke of Guyenne[31] and in the exemplar of Louis XII[32]) as wearing only one row of shells in the shape of a golden chain. Francis I changed it to a double row of chains during the first chapter meeting of the order held after his crowning in September 1516. He called the chapter of the order together for March 3, 1516. The invitation was sent by Francis I to Artus Goufier, seigneur de Boissy, grand master of the order. He prescribed a double row of golden shells attached one above the other with the figurine of Saint Michael in the middle pendant. He did so in memory of Anne de Bretagne (1477–1514) who was the mother of his wife, Claude. The silk knots that held together the original gold cord of Louis XI were replaced by buckles (*fermail*).[33] (3) One of the copies in the 'official series' (BN. MS fr. 14365, folio 8 recto) has an inscription on the upper edge of the fleur de lis curtain: 'François par la grace de Dieu Roy de Fra[nce]'. In the Cheltenham manuscript the drapery is spangled with capital 'F's, the initial of Francis I.[34] (4) Finally, there is archival evidence that some kind of 'industrial production' of the statute books of the Order of Saint Michael was ordered by the royal court. On January 9, 1523, Estienne Coland or Collault, illuminator (*enlumineur*), gave a receipt to Antoine Tavard, 'chevalier Roy d'Armes' of the Order of Saint Michael and 'Valet du Chambre du Roy', for the amount of seventy-two Tours pounds for having made and delivered six books containing the chapters, statutes, and ordinances of the order. The six copies were intended to be bound in velour 'tanné' because Pierre Le Jay, a Paris merchant, sold two 'aulne'[35] of velour (about 2.37 meters) on the same day, January 9, 1523, to the same Antoine Tavart to cover the six books containing the 'Chapitres, Statuts et Ordonnances de l'Ordre du Roy notre Sir'.[36]

Twelve additional statute books must have been ordered, because, on January 22, 1522, the same Antoine Tavart, 'chevalier Roy d'Armes' of the order, acknowledged having received eighty-six 'écus d'or soleil' from Nicolas de Neuville, 'Conseiller du Roy' and 'Secretaire de ses finances', to pay the copyists, illuminators, and binders for twelve books to be written, illuminated on parchment, covered with velour. These books, containing the statutes and ordinances of the Order of Saint Michael, were to be distributed later to the members of the order on the command of the king.[37]

The text copied into these statute books contained not only the original ordinances of Louis XI given on August 1, 1469, at Amboise, consisting of sixty-six articles, but also the additions ordered on December 22 and December 24, 1476, given 'au Plessis du Parc les Tours', augmenting the number of articles to ninety-two. After December 24, 1476, the seat of the order was no longer at Mont-Saint-Michel, but the knights used the Chapel of Saint Michel in the Royal Palace in Paris. The October 14, 1512 copy printed by Guillaume Eustache, 'à l'enseigne des deux sagittaires', already has ninety-eight articles.

The only thing which is not quite clear is how many statute books were requested: twelve or eighteen? The receipt of Estienne Coland, of January 9, 1523, seems to imply that the books had already been made 'pour avoir fait' and delivered 'livré 6 livres'. On the other hand, the January 23,

1523 receipt given by Antoine Tavart speaks of copyists, illuminators, and binders who will write, illuminate, bind, and cover the twelve books 'qui feront 12 livre'. Can we assume that eighteen books were ordered? This is exactly the number of knights visible on the oldest representation of the order painted by Foucquet (BN. MS fr. 19819, folio 1 recto).

There are nine known copies of this 'official series' showing the chapter scene, or ten if we may add the copy executed for Henry VIII. Three further statute books in this group have no significant illustrations,[38] and three others display coat of arms, illuminated initials, and marginal illustrations[39] but not the chapter scene. Therefore, we have fifteen copies accounted for. The Ambrosiana miniature belongs to the 'official series' and must have been produced around 1523.

PROVENANCE OF THE AMBROSIANA ILLUMINATED PAGE

The Ambrosiana F. 277 inferior collection of illuminated folios with historiated initials and full-page miniatures does not betray any signs regarding its provenance. Going through the above listed manuscripts of the statutes of the Order of Saint Michael in the Bibliothèque Nationale, I did not find any mutilated copies. Durrieu, in his description of the illuminated manuscripts of the Thomas Phillipps Collection at Cheltenham in 1889, signaled a manuscript No. 4314 similar to Cheltenham 1323 containing the statutes of the Order of Saint Michael. However, he indicated that the traditional representation of the chapter reunion of the knights was cut out from this manuscript.[40] In all probability we may presume that the illuminated folio of the Ambrosiana F. 277 inferior no. 59 is the miniature that once adorned the Cheltenham MS 4314.[41] It was a long pilgrimage for a folio detached from its mother manuscript. It went from Paris to England and through adventurous paths, finally finding its place and peace in the Ambrosiana Library, Milan.

STATUTE BOOKS OF LATER DATES

As an epilogue let us mention that the order regained its splendor and old reputation during the reign of Henry II (1547–1559), thanks to Cardinal Charles de Lorrain, appointed chancellor of the order by Henry II on May 19, 1547. Henry II, by an order dated June 1548, restored the traditional attire of the order: the white mantle and crimson colored shoulder band. The number of knights at that time was eighteen. The chapter scene under Henry II is shown in a miniature of the statute books executed for Cardinal Charles de Lorrain, chancellor of the order. This copy is in the Bibliothèque Municipale of Saint Germain-en-Laye. The chapter scene shows the king, Henry II, surrounded by his knights. As an innovation in the representation of the chapter scene, we see the chancellor seated at the feet of the king at his desk with the symbols of his office, the seal and a container of wax.[42]

Three more statute books illuminated after Henry II achieved considerable fame. One was supposedly executed for Edward VI (1547–1553), the young king of England, to whom the golden chain was sent in July 1551.[43] Three more manuscripts were illuminated in this series ordered by Henry II, showing the king presiding over the chapter and the chancellor at his desk together with the other officers of the order present (see Plate VII).[44]

The most remarkable example of an illuminated printed copy is the statute book of Martin de Bellay, brother of Jean and Gullaume du Bellay, received as knight of the order in 1555. It shows the reception of a new knight kneeling before the chancellor. The king is seated and surrounded by knights. He is holding the distinctive chain of the order, a single row of golden shells, in his left hand and looks ready to put it on the shoulders of a candidate.[45]

The renaissance of the order during the reign of Henry II did not last for long. The prestige of the order slowly declined. During the reign of Louis XIV and during the eighteenth century, it was still bestowed as a sign of recognition on great artists: painters such as Hyacinth Rigaud, the sculptor Pigall, and the architect Mansard, who became knights of the Order of Saint Michael. The order was suppressed by the French Revolution but was revived during the Restoration. It finally became extinct during the Revolution of 1830.

The illuminated page of the Ambrosiana with its bright and cheerful colors helped the survival of the memory of the order, preparing the transition from the aristocracy of birth to the aristocracy of spirit—from Jean II le Bon, duke of Bourbon (1426–1488) to Jean Baptiste Pigall (1714–1789), the eminent artist. The latter is better known through the strip-tease-infected 'Place Pigalle' in Paris than through his knighthood in the order under the patronage of the first knight, Saint Michael, 'Sainct-Michel archange, premier chevalier, qui pour la querelle de Dieu victorieusement batailla contre le dragon', Saint Michael, archangel, the First Knight, who, for the cause of God, victoriously fought the dragon.**

NOTES

* Research for this study was carried out thanks to a grant given to the University of Notre Dame, Ambrosiana Collection, by the Samuel H. Kress Foundation, and by a travel grant of the University of Notre Dame, the Very Reverend Dr. Edward A. Malloy, CSC, President; Dr. Timothy O'Meara, Provost; and Dr. Roger A. Schmitz, Vice President and Associate Provost.

[1] Milan, Biblioteca Ambrosiana, Sala Rosa, F. 277 inferior no. 59. Single leaf, size 170 x 257 mm., illuminated on recto with text following on verso.

[2] 'Loys par la grace de/ dieu Roy de france scau[oir]/ faisons a tous presens/ et aduenir que pour la/ tresparfaicte et singuliere amo[ur] que/ auons au noble ordre et estat de/.' *Ibid.*, fol. recto.

[3] Le Marquis de Pastoret, *Ordonnances des Rois de France de la Troisième Race, recueillies par ordre chronologique* (Paris: Imprimerie Royale, 1820) 17, 236–55.

[4] '...Ung collier d'or fait à coquilles lassées l'une à l'autre d'un double laz, assises sur chainectes ou mailles d'or, au milieu duquel sur ung roc aura ung image d'or de monsieur [monseigneur] Sainct-Michel, qui reviendra pendant sur la poictrine....' *Ordonnances*, 17, 238, items 3 and 4.

[5] Statute Book of the Order of Saint Michael, illuminated before May 20, 1472, parchment, 29 folios, 205 x 150 mm. (formerly Saint-Germain, Harlay 407): L. Auvray and H. Omont, *Catalogue général des manuscrits français: Ancien Saint-German français, III, Nos. 18677–20064 du Fonds français* (Paris: Ernest Leroux, 1900) p. 411.

[6] Comte Paul Durrieu, 'Les manuscrits des Statuts de l'Ordre de Saint-Michel', *Bulletin de la Société française de reproductions de manuscrits à peintures* [henceforth *SFRMP*] 1 (1911) 17–47. Miniature reproduced on plate 1. Also from the same author: 'Une peinture historique de Jehan Foucquet: Le roi Louis XI tenant un chapitre de l'Ordre de Saint-Michel', *Gazette archéologique: Revue des Musées Nationaux* 14 (1889) 61–80, pl. 14; Camille Couderc, *Album de portraits d'après les collections du Départment des Manuscrits, Bibliothèque Nationale* (Paris, n.d.) p. 39, no. LXXXVIII; reproduced by Pierre Champion, *Louis XI* (Bibliothèque du XVe siècle, no. 34) (Paris, 1927) pl. XIII, between pp. 216 and 217; and by Henry Martin, *Les joyaux de l'enluminure à la Bibliothèque Nationale* (Paris, Bruxelles, 1928) p. 114, fig. CIII.

[7] Reproduced by Durrieu, *SFRMP* 1 (1911) 18, pl. II.

[8] Statute Books produced during the reign of Louis XI (1461–1483) without the chapter scene: Paris, BN. MS français 5745, executed for Jean II le Bon, duke of Bourbon; BN MS fr. 19817 made for Jean de Baudricourt, marechal of France; the MS BN. fr. 14363 was delivered on October 27,

1493, for Charles VIII (1483–1498); under Francis I (1515–1547) MS BN. fr. 14364; Arsenal 5100.

[9] Vienna, Österreichische Nationalbibliothek, MS 2637, XVth cent. end, parchment, 1 plus 58 folios, 228 x 167 mm. Full-page miniature showing the king of France among the knights pointing to the insignia of the Order of Saint Michael on folio 11 verso. Reproduced Durrieu, *SFRMP* 1 (1911) pl. V; also the description in Otto Pächt and Dagmar Thoss, *Französische Schule I*: *Textband*, Österreichische Akademie der Wissenschaften, Phil.-Hist. Klasse., Denkschriften, Band 118 (Vienna, 1974) pp. 92–93 with abundant bibliography, and reproduced by the same in the companion *Tafelband*, Abb. 160. Other illuminations: folio 12 recto (Abb. 161); folio 47 verso (Abb. 162); and 58 recto (Abb. 163). I am very grateful to Dr Eva Irblich at the Österreichische Nationalbibliothek, Manuscript Department, for the much appreciated scholarly cooperation in providing me with new photographs of the illuminated pages of this manuscript.

From the same atelier that produced the Vienna copy MS 2637 made for Louis XII (1498–1515) came another splendidly illuminated statute book, now in the Pierpont Morgan Library, MS no. 20, executed probably even earlier during the reign of Charles VIII (1483–1498) for the duke of Bourbon, likely Jean II le Bon (1420–1488). I described this manuscript and determined its provenance in my study 'A Statute Book of the Order of Saint Michael in the Pierpont Morgan Library, New York City' in *Miscellanea Codicologica F. Masai Dicata*, edd. P. Cockshaw, *et al.* (Ghent, 1979) pp. 481–89 and plates 63, 64, and 65.

[10] Reproduced by Durrieu, *SFRMP* 1 (1911) pl. VI. C. Maxwell Lyte, *Catalogue of Manuscripts and Other Objects in the Museum of the Public Record Office* (London, 1905) p. 28, case F., no. 64, as reported by Durrieu.

[11] 'Registrum processus criminalis ac aliarum expeditionum in suprema parlamenti curia agitatarum contra et adversus Carolum de Borbonio', XVIth cent., parchment, folios 484 plus flyleaf A and folio 228 bis (formerly 9719[3], Colbert 2548). *Catalogue des manuscrits français, Tome quatrième, Ancien fonds nos. 4587–5525* (Paris: Firmin-Didot, 1895) p. 562, col. 2.

[12] Ten if we count the London Museum of Record Office copy among the 'official series' ordered during the reign of Francis I. A copy was destroyed by the 1904 fire in Turin (MS Gallicus no. XXX).

[13] Statute Book of the Order of Saint Michael, XVIth cent. parchment, 36 folios, 250 x 175 mm, bound in blue Morocco leather. H. Omont, *Bibliothèque Nationale: Catalogue général des manuscrits français: Ancien Supplément français, III. Nos. 13091-15369 du Fonds français* (Paris: Ernest Leroux, 1896) p. 182.

[14] Statute Book of the Order of Saint Michael, XVIth cent., parchment, 51 folios, 250 x 165 mm., bound in contemporary parchment. H. Omont, p. 182. Reproduced by Durrieu, *SFRMP* 1 (1911) pl. VII.

An Unknown Illuminated Page 125

¹⁵ Statute Book of the Order of Saint Michael, XVIth cent., parchment, folios 67, 205 x 138 mm. Bound in fawn colored calf leather (formerly Saint-Germain, Gesvres, 129). L. Auvray and H. Omont, *Cat. manuscrits francais III. Nos. 18677–20064*, p. 410 (see Plate IV).

¹⁶ Statute Book of the Order of Saint Michael, XVIth cent. parchment, folios 50, 250 x 180 mm. Red leather binding (formerly Séguier-Coislin, Saint-Germain français 1401). L. Auvray and H. Omont, p. 410 (see Plate V).

¹⁷ Statute Book of the Order of Saint Michael. The miniature is blurred and hardly visible. XVIth cent., parchment, folios 58, 225 x 160 mm. (formerly Séguier-Coislin, Saint-Germain français 1827). On folio 2 verso the coat of arms of Montmorency; L. Auvray and H. Omont, p. 411.

¹⁸ Statute Book of the Order of Saint Michael, beginning XVIth cent., parchment, folios 54, 237 x 172. Giulio Porro, *Trivulziana: Catalogo dei cod. manoscritti* (Torino, 1884) p. 415; *Kunstschätze der Lombardei: 500 vor Christus/1800 nach Christus*, Kunsthaus Zürich, November 1948/März 1949, no. 268; Caterina Santoro, *I codici miniati della Biblioteca Trivulziana* (Milano, 1959) pp. 120–21, no. 124. Chapter scene reproduced Tav. CIV; *I tesori della Trivulziana* (Milano, 1962) p. 16, tav. XLI; *I codici medioevali della Biblioteca Trivulziana* (Milano, 1965) pp. 294–95, no. 437; Giulia Bologna, *Miniature francesi e fiamminghe della Biblioteca Trivulziana* (Milano, 1976 p. 98; chapter scene, folio 9 recto, reproduced on p. 58.

¹⁹ The folio 9 recto, chapter scene is reproduced by Durrieu, *SFRMP* 1 (1911) pl. VIII; see p. 31. I obtained black and white, also colored, reproductions thanks to the British Library, London, England.

²⁰ Described by Paul Durrieu, 'Les manuscrits à peintures de la Bibliothèque de Sir Thomas Phillipp à Cheltenham', *Bibliothèque de l'École des Chartes* 50 (1889) 411. The Statute Book displays the coat of arms of the Du Bellay Family from Anjou.

²¹ Or L. V. 39; *SFRMP* 1 (1911) 31.

²² London, Museum of Records Office. The chapter scene is reproduced by Durrieu, *SFRMP* 1 (1911) pl. VI.

²³ The king of France is shown wearing a crown in the following manuscripts: Trivulziana MS no. 1394, folio 9 recto; London, British Museum, Harley MS no. 4485, folio 9 recto; BN. fr. 19816, folio 9 recto; BN. fr. 19818, folio 11 recto.

²⁴ Ten knights are depicted in the following manuscripts: Trivulziana, MS no. 1394, folio 9 recto; London, British Museum, Harley MS no. 4485, folio 9 recto; Paris, BN. fr. 19815, folio 11 recto; BN. fr. 19816, folio 9 recto; BN. MS fr. 19818, folio 11 recto; Cheltenham, MS no. 1323. Twelve knights are shown in Paris, BN. MS fr. 14361, folio 7 verso; and BN. MS fr. 14365, folio 7 verso.

²⁵ Paris, BN. MS fr. 19819, folio 1 recto; Clairambault, MS no. 1242, p. 1421.

[26] The artist complied with the stipulation of the charter of foundation of August 1, 1469, and depicted the chapter scene with the fifteen knights: '...Au commencement desquels livres sera faicte une histoire de la représentation du souverain et desdicts quinze chevaliers premièrement mis et nommez par nous audict ordre', *Ordonnances*, 17, 243, item 24.

[27] Two windows are depicted in the following copies: Paris, BN. fr. 14361, folio 7 verso; BN. MS fr. 14365, folio 8 recto; BN. MS fr. 19816, folio 9 recto. Four windows are painted in Trivulziana MS no. 1394, folio 9 recto; London, British Museum, Harley MS no. 4485, folio 9 recto; Paris, BN. fr. 19815, folio 11 recto; BN. fr. 19818, folio 11 recto.

[28] Vienna, Österreichische Nationalbibliothek, MS 2637, folio 11 verso; see *SFRMP* 1 (1911) 26 and pl. V.

[29] Only one knight carries a cane while standing at the left side of the king in the following manuscripts: Ambrosiana, F. 277 inferior, no. 59 recto; Paris, BN. fr. 14361, folio 7 verso; BN. fr. 19815, folio 11 recto. Two knights have batons, one standing at the right side and the other at the left of the king: London, British Museum, MS Harley no. 4485, folio 9 verso. Three knights are shown with batons, two at the right side of the king and one at his left: Paris, BN. MS fr. 14365, folio 8 recto. No baton is visible in the chapter scenes of the following statute books: Trivulziana, MS no. 1394, folio 9 recto; Paris, BN. MS fr. 19816, folio 9 recto. In BN. MS fr. 19818, folio 11 recto, it cannot be determined if any knight carries a baton, because the illumination is washed away and remains indistinct.

[30] Paris, BN. MS fr. 19819, folio 1 recto, personal copy of Louis XI, painted by Jean Foucquet. See note 5.

[31] Made for Charles de France, duke of Guyenne, brother of Louis XI. Paris, BN. MS Clairambault, no. 1242, p. 1421. Reproduced by Durrieu, *SFRMP* 1 (1911) pl. II.

[32] Vienna, Österreichische Nationalbibliothek MS No. 2637, folio 11 verso. See note 9.

[33] 'Le Roy François I au 1er chapitre qu'il tint en Septembre 1516 changea les Equillettes et noeuds de soye noire en longs fermaux et Cordelieres d'or en mémoire de St. Francois'; Paris, BN. MS Clairambault, no. 1242, p. 1419.

[34] I have not seen the Cheltenham manuscript. I am referring to Durrieu, *SFRMP* 1 (1911) 31.

[35] One aune was 1,888 meters at Paris.

[36] Paris, BN. MS Clairambault, no. 1242, pp. 1630-31.

[37] '...Pour celle somme estre baillé aux écrivains, Enlumineurs et Relieures qui feront 12 livres en parchemin esquels seront declaréz contenus et écrits les articles statuts et ordonnances audit ordre, lesquels 12 livres qui seront écrits, enluminéz reliéz et couverts de Velour Le Roy notre Sire a ordonné estre bailléz et delivréz à aucuns de Messieurs les chevaliers dudid Ordre....' *Ibid.*, p. 1629.

[38] Statute books with no significant illumination and illustrations: Paris, BN. MS fr. 24013; BN. MS fr. 25188; BN. MS fr. 25189.

[39] Statute books with marginal illustration, displaying either coat of arms or illuminated initials: Paris, BN. MS fr. 14362; BN. MS fr. 14364; BN. MS fr. 19817. No chapter scene was depicted in these manuscripts.

[40] Paul Durrieu, 'Les manuscrits à peintures de la Bibliothèque de Sir Thomas Phillipps à Cheltenham', *Bibliothèque de l'École des Chartes* 50 (1889) 411: under no. LXXXIII: 'mais le feuillet sur lequel était peinte la miniature traditionnelle a été coupé.'

[41] *Catalogus Librorum Manuscriptorum in Bibliotheca D. Thomae Phillipps. Bart. A. D. 1837* (Typis Medio Montanis, 1837) p. 68, under no. 4314: 'Statutes of the Order of St. Michel. Thin fol. V. S. XVI'.

[42] Reproduced by Durrieu, *SFRMP* 1 (1911) pl. XI. See pp. 33–34.

[43] London, Collection of Sir George Holford. Described by Durrieu, *SFRMP* 1 (1911) 38–39, pl. XII.

[44] Statute books written and illuminated during the reign of Henry II (1547–1559) a quasi 'official series': Paris, BN. MS fr. 25190, Chapter scene on folio 1 recto, reproduced by Durrieu, pl. XIII. Copy no. 69 in the 1878 Auction-sale of Firmin Didot is also described by Durrieu, p. 41, together with Sainte-Geneviève MS no. 1688.

[45] Paris, BN. MS Clairambault, no. 1242, p. 1891. See Durrieu, p. 43.

** I should like to express my appreciation to Dr Angelo Paredi, Honorary Director of the Ambrosiana Library at Milan, for his scholarly cooperation and for the kind permission to reproduce the miniature F. 277 inferior, no. 59.

Milan, Biblioteca Ambrosiana, F. 277 Inferior, no. 59. Louis XI, king of France (1461–1483), represented presiding over a reunion of the Knights of the Order of Saint Michael.

Paris, Bibliothèque nationale MS français 5109, fol. A verso. An illuminated page from the *Register* of the criminal process against Charles III, duc de Bourbon (1490–1527).

Paris, Bibliothèque nationale MS français 14361, fol. 7 verso. A session of the Order of Saint Michael presided over by the king of France, shown in an illuminated page of the Statute Book of the Order (this copy belonged to the so-called 'official series').

An Unknown Illuminated Page

Paris, Bibliothèque nationale MS français 19815, fol. 11 recto. One of the sixteenth-century copies of the 'official series' [see note 15].

Paris, Bibliothèque nationale MS français 19816, fol. 9 recto. Another copy of the 'official series' of the Statute Books of the Order of Saint Michael; the king is represented crowned [see note 16].

London, British Museum MS Harley 4485, fol. 9 recto. Chapter-meeting scene of the Order of Saint Michael; the king is represented crowned.

Paris, Bibliothèque nationale MS français 25190, fol. 1 recto. Henry II, king of France (1547–1559), presiding over the chapter-meeting of the Order of Saint Michael; the chancellor of the order is depicted seated at his desk.

THE WHARTON-CARROLL CONTROVERSY AND THE PROMISE OF AMERICAN CATHOLIC LIFE

Thomas W. Jodziewicz
The University of Dallas

As THE AMERICAN REVOLUTION came to an official end with the signing of the Treaty of Paris in the fall of 1783, the prospects for Catholics in the new United States of America seemed far brighter than at any previous moment in the history of England's former colonies in the New World. Religious freedom was to be one of the hallmarks of the new republic, and this liberty was even to be extended to the denomination most resented and feared by the protestant majority during the one and one-half centuries of colonial rule. While few Catholics were ever actually found outside Maryland and Pennsylvania before the Revolution, the english prejudice against Roman Catholicism had been alive and well within the dominant colonial culture. In Maryland, the colony founded in part, ironically, to serve as a haven for Catholics in the early seventeenth century, persecution and political and social disabilities had appeared by mid-century and were flourishing by the 1690s. Laws were enacted against public catholic religious services and missionary activity, catholic education and voting rights were prohibited, and catholic immigration was heavily fined in order to discourage any would-be visitors. These laws were not always enforced, but their existence, and periodic vitality, served to remind Maryland's Catholics that they were welcome in the colony only if they kept their religious views and practices to themselves. To the north, especially in puritan New England, an unexamined, visceral anti-catholic bigotry was part of the very warp and woof of colonial life, a colorful staple in sermons and books, and an ever-present chord to be touched in the face of the french catholic menace that periodically descended upon these colonies from Canada during the four imperial wars between 1689 and 1763.[1] As late as January 10, 1776, Thomas Paine could touch that anti-catholic emotion in his celebrated pamphlet *Common Sense*, sure of its usefulness in his argument for independence and sure of its generally-accepted resonance in colonial american society.[2] At that very moment, however, colonial interest was beginning to turn toward possible french and spanish assistance in the struggle against Britain, an assistance which was eventually, and significantly, forthcoming. But it was not only political necessity but also the logic of republican and revolutionary ideology—Bernard Bailyn's 'contagion of liberty'—which muted religious intolerance and the remaining sectarian disabilities in the american polities, and by the end of the war freedom of religion was an announced public reality in the various states. Disabilities against full catholic participation in politics remained—for example, in New Jersey, Connecticut, Georgia, and North Carolina Catholics could not hold public office—but the closet door had been opened, and prospects did appear to be brightening for Catholics in the United States as the Revolutionary War came to its close.[3]

From the catholic point of view, all of this was exciting and, of course, promising, but other difficulties were also prominent in 1783 and 1784: in short, the Church in America was badly in need not just of legitimacy and toleration but also of organization. Before their suppression as an order in 1773, the Jesuits had been the principal priestly presence in Maryland and Pennsylvania. Nominally under

The Wharton-Carroll Controversy

the authority of the Vicar Apostolic of the London District since 1753, most of these Jesuits had remained in the United States after the order's suppression. But practical and then official independence from Great Britain, and the perceived anti-jesuit posture and policies of the Vatican's Sacred Congregation of the Propaganda, created a context of confusion and outright suspicion of outside authority and governance among the twenty or so rather sensitive ex-Jesuits still living and working in the United States. From Rome's perspective, the american situation was unique:

> For the first time in its long history the Holy See was confronted by the necessity of providing an ecclesiastical rule for a small group of its adherents living in the midst of an overwhelming Protestant population in a country that had adopted a republican form of government and that was located over 3,000 miles away.[4]

Taking the american lead in this urgent matter of the appropriate relationship between american Catholicism and Rome was John Carroll of Maryland.

Part of a prominent Maryland catholic family—his brother Daniel would be one of the framers of the United States Constitution in 1787, his cousin Charles a signer of the Declaration of Independence in 1776—John had left his native country in 1748 at the age of thirteen to pursue his education in european schools.[5] He was a Jesuit and had been ordained in 1771. He had subsequently returned to Maryland in 1774, the year after the order's suppression, to minister to his fellow Maryland Catholics. His abilities and connections had led to his participation in an unsuccessful diplomatic mission to Canada in 1776, along with his cousin Charles, Benjamin Franklin, and Samuel Chase, to seek support for the american cause. By the end of the revolution, John Carroll was recognized as a leader in the american catholic community, and, when Benjamin Franklin was approached in Paris in 1784 by a papal representative and asked for the name of a possible head of the american missions, Franklin had mentioned Carroll. Extremely sensitive to perceived anti-jesuit attitudes at the Vatican as well as acutely aware of traditional anti-catholic feelings in the United States, Carroll reluctantly accepted his subsequent appointment, in the summer of 1784, by the Prefect of the Sacred Congregation of the Propaganda as superior of American Missions.[6] Within five years, and, on the vote of his fellow priests in the United States, Carroll would be confirmed by Pius VI as the first Roman Catholic bishop of the United States.

Carroll's task, first as superior of the American Missions, and then as bishop, and archbishop, of Baltimore, a diocese which included most of the United States east of the Mississippi River under his jurisdiction, was a daunting one. Organization of the american Church and a shortage of priests were among the large number of fundamental difficulties Carroll had to face and deal with before his death in 1815. Complicating his heavy pastoral burden, yet at the same time encouraging him in his efforts, were the peculiar historical circumstances within which he self-consciously worked. Official representative of a Church lately tolerated but long suspect in America as authoritarian, anti-freedom, and anti-individual rights, John Carroll envisioned a particular american Catholic Church. While recognizing the spiritual primacy of Rome, this church would at the same time make its peace with the new republic in which the ideals of religious freedom, separation of church and state, and extended lay participation in church governance were in the process of realization.[7] Over the next thirty years, events would perhaps temper the new superior's hopes and plans for such an american Roman Catholic Church, but, in the summer of 1784, the future seemed rather bright for Carroll and his fellow Catholics.[8] At that very moment, fragile and promising at the same time, a pamphlet originally published in England explaining the apostasy of a former Jesuit was published in Philadelphia. *A Letter to the Roman Catholics of the City of Worcester*, written by Charles Henry Wharton, a distant relative of John Carroll, was a proverbial bombshell.[9] Not only was Wharton's defection to the Anglican Church a concern, but the pamphlet also contained sentiments, in Wharton's explanation of his departure from the Catholic Church, which brought into question the fundamental validity of an authentic catholic presence in the new republic. With little enthusiasm Carroll decided to respond publicly to Wharton's *Letter*.

Given the long duration, if sporadic enforcement, of the persecution of american Catholics, and the relatively brief moment of somewhat grudging toleration, John Carroll's entry into public controversy was a recognized risk. As he admitted to Charles Plowden, the latter's friends who had entertained earlier suspicions about Wharton, who had recently returned to Maryland, had been correct, and Carroll, in his initial hopes regarding his relative, wrong: 'He not only has renounced his Religion, but has published a pamphlet, which, under the colour of apology, is a malignant invective & misrepresentation of our tenets.' Encouraged by his fellow priests, Carroll wrote a reply during the summer of 1784, despite a lack of both time and the necessary resources.[10] Five months later, on February 17, 1784, again writing to Plowden, Carroll expanded on the reasons for his *Address to the Roman Catholics of the United States of America, by a Catholic Clergyman*:

> You have heard of Wharton's proceeding and probably seen his pamphlet. Notwithstanding all advices from you and others, I still hoped, that his conduct in England was owing to great vivacity, and a more liberal view of many things, than some of us educated in Colleges ever dare take. I was loth to attribute it to the motives, which he has since avowed in his publication. I dare say, that you will, on perusing it, find it carries marks of being written long before it was published. The exultation of Protestants, and discouragement of R.C. compelled me to enter

the lists with him. I wrote a hasty answer, amidst continual avocations, & almost without any materials but those, which my memory suggested.[11]

Carroll's effort, in fact, was a double-edged apologetic: he did offer a series of replies to Wharton's assaults on a variety of catholic doctrines and beliefs.[12] But, in addition, the very mode of his reply, a pamphlet put together with an obvious and due respect for reasoned discourse and composed and delivered in a calm, measured, indeed tolerant, tone, indicated of itself the suitability of american Catholics for the new republic and their acquiescence in the founding principle of religious toleration. Speaking for a faith historically viewed in America as antithetical at its very core to freedom and individual rights, Carroll chose to participate in a public debate not only to rally his newly-emancipated fellow Catholics, but to provide direct evidence that Catholics were in fact not dangers to the republic. On the contrary, they were citizens fully capable of subscribing to, and being cultivators of those very values of free inquiry and religious toleration near the very center of the american experiment. Still, to seek to demonstrate the compatibility of Roman Catholicism and the american circumstances of religious liberty, pluralism, and toleration, and the separation of church and state, without succumbing on the other hand to a religious indifferentism was a risky business given the long-standing american hatred of his faith.[13]

In his *Letter to the Roman Catholics of the City of Worcester*, Charles Wharton admitted to much personal suffering and many difficulties in his move away from the Roman Catholic faith.[14] He did want, though, to share his motives for leaving that church. In a rather telling aside, he explained that he did not intend to raise doubts in the minds of those Catholics whose faith was bottomed on 'mature deliberation, and rational enquiry'.[15] As hard experience had lately proven to him, his own Roman Catholic faith had not been so bottomed. Contacts with Protestants, good people whom Rome had nevertheless consigned to eternal damnation and persecution through the teaching that there was no salvation outside the Roman Catholic Church, had raised doubts in his mind.[16] Once this belief had become for him questionable, and in fact no longer supportable, Wharton had been set free from 'the boasted infallibility of a living authority'.[17] Increasingly as this 'dead weight of authority' was removed, charity speedily replaced the roman tendency to persecute the otherwise-minded.[18] Open finally to the full use of his human reason operating on revelation, and his individual conscience, rather than a mere acquiescence to authority, Wharton entered into a full inquiry into religious truth. Addressing himself to Scripture alone, armed only with his reason and his conscience, Wharton had progressed to the point where he could find no valid scriptural basis for such catholic doctrines and beliefs as those concerning transubstantiation, the power to forgive sins or auricular confession, purgatory, and the Church's infallibility.[19] These doctrines, and others, he found to be in direct contradiction to the 'only means' that God had given man for arriving at truth, 'our senses and our understanding', or, more simply, reason applied to Scripture, 'the sole standard' for a Christian's beliefs.[20] Wharton's hope was that his former fellows in the Roman Church might also one day awaken, set aside their prejudices, and 'begin to think for themselves'.[21]

Aside from the immediate personal qualities of Wharton's *Letter*, his work fits quite nicely into the traditional framework of american anti-Catholicism as described by Archbishop Martin John Spalding of Baltimore over two generations later: 1) Catholics were portrayed as 'intolerant and proscriptive' regarding religion; 2) Catholics were deemed to be 'enemies of republican institutions and friends of a foreign despotism' in politics.[22] Wharton's principal charges of anti-intellectual freedom, exclusivity regarding salvation, and infallible authority can be comprehended within this framework with a discernible emphasis on the Church's alleged intolerance and irrationality, realities that resulted in congregations filled with those unable 'to think for themselves'. Poor risks these would be in a republic only as strong and secure as its citizens were thoughtful, independent, and, in short, democratic. Indeed, after a brief moment of toleration of these Catholics in America, approximately until the late 1820s, Wharton's charges would find new life in a revived anti-catholic and anti-foreign bigotry in the 1830s–1850s, again in the 1890s, and yet again in the post-World War I period.[23]

Whatever the difficulties under which he labored during the summer of 1784, Carroll did produce a point-by-point refutation of Wharton's arguments in the course of which it became plain, for example, that the latter's passion had not necessarily translated into a careful or disinterested use of sources.[24] While the details of Carroll's *Address* are significant, the form of the reply, and its very tone—calm, dispassionate, and logical rather than authoritative, strident, and *ad hominem*—were even more significant. As Carroll recognized, religious controversy did not appeal to many: 'Mankind have conceived such a contempt for it, that an author cannot entertain a hope of enjoying those gratifications, which in treating other subjects may support his spirits and enliven his imagination.' But even more to the point of his own situation, Carroll 'could not forget in the beginning, progress, and conclusion of it, that the habits of thinking, the prejudices, perhaps even the passions of many of my readers would be set against all the arguments, I could offer.' Wharton's efforts, though, had wounded Carroll deeply, and it was not merely his personal apostasy: his public paper 'had imputed to us doctrines foreign to our belief, and having a natural tendency to embitter against us the minds of our fellow-citizens.' In truth, 'It did not become the friend of toleration to misinform, and to sow in minds so misinformed the seeds of religious animosity.' Despite his own carefully-composed expressions regarding the ultimate limitations of human reason, Carroll's *Address* was a reasoned and critical response meant to reassure catholic and non-catholic Americans alike that

Catholicism was not an irrational exercise of naked authority over blinded and cowering adherents hardly fitted for life in a new republic 'so blessed with civil and religious liberty'. Carroll was about a vindication of catholic beliefs, then, but he was also providing evidence, and offering himself as evidence, that american Catholics were good and useful neighbors in the new republic, a country where religious harmony was developing, a happy circumstance

> which if we have the wisdom and temper to preserve, America may come to exhibit a proof to the world, that general and equal toleration, by giving a free circulation to fair argument, is the most effectual method to bring all denominations of christians to an unity of faith.[25]

Significantly, John Carroll's defense of american catholic civil credentials placed him firmly within what one recent author has described as the english catholic Enlightenment. Consciously seeking to distance themselves from the counter-reformation Church's antipathies towards religious pluralism, secularization, and the empirical method, certain english catholic thinkers in the late eighteenth and early nineteenth centuries sought to re-connect reason and faith in the context of the new intellectual age, the Enlightenment. The efforts of such as John Lingard, Joseph Berington, Charles Butler, John Kirk, and John Fletcher were directed toward a synthesis of Roman Catholic faith and Enlightenment thought, premised on a lockean anthropology of pre-existing rights and contract theory, regarding church-state relations, theology, ecclesiology, history, and religious practice. In short, these individuals accepted, by means of a critical and scientific methodology, political secularization or separation of church and state, religious liberty or toleration, and a contractual theory of civil as well as, to some extent, ecclesiastical government. John Carroll not only accepted these european ideas, but he found himself in a position, and a place, to put them into practice.[26] In the pluralistic United States, Catholics influenced by these ideas were called on to steer an ecumenical course between religious or doctrinal indifferentism and the equally dreaded shoals of 'ecclesiological exclusivism'. But, to say the very least, Wharton's *Letter* once again called into question the validity, and the viability, of any catholic participation in this important american venture.[27]

Carroll's treatment of reason in his *Address* is essential to his response to Wharton, for, without a demonstrable commitment to rational inquiry, Catholics would indeed appear to be dangers within a republic open to individual rights and dependent upon the free exercise of and respect for man's intellectual and spiritual liberties. Carroll assured his fellow Catholics that the Church enjoined its members, both priests and laity, to examine the grounds of their religion to the best of their abilities and to arrive at a 'reasonable' obedience. Quoting from 1 Peter 3:15, Carroll asked how otherwise could any Catholic 'give an answer to every man, that asketh you a reason of that hope that is in you?'[28] Indeed, the duties of the clergy to inform and to instruct were clear in the matter, and 'if we have been deficient in the discharge of either,... if we have flattered your passions, or withheld knowledge from your minds, we have certainly deviated from the obligations of our state, and the positive injunctions of our church.' Any claims that the Catholic Church sought 'to keep her votaries in ignorance' were 'groundless'.[29] Wharton himself was well aware of the fact that his charge that Catholics could not read protestant works was false, Carroll continued, since they had both been exposed to these sources in their jesuit seminary days.[30] Surely protestant and catholic churches did seek to protect their unlearned and uninformed 'by a jealous zeal... from the artificial colourings of real or supposed error', but this was only natural and hardly prejudicial to the principles of 'free inquiry' and 'rational investigation' which Carroll and Wharton had both experienced.[31]

As for Wharton's portrayal of the supposed catholic belief that there was no salvation outside that church as both an effective stop to open inquiry (since there was no truth to be pursued outside the Church) and an occasion for an alleged persecution of those outside the fold (a deserved suffering), Carroll presented a distinction between being in the actual communion of the Church and being a member of the Catholic Church. The latter he described as 'all those, who with a sincere heart seek true religion, and are in an unfeigned disposition to embrace the truth, whenever they find it.'[32] Citing such authorities as the Council of Trent, Saint Thomas Aquinas, Saint Augustine, Francisco de Suarez, as well as contemporary european theologians, protestant and catholic, Carroll explained the catholic position regarding such as the possible salvation of unbaptized infidels, the true nature of heresy as a disorder of an obstinate and perverse will and not merely an error of one's judgment, and the importance of the conscience of the individual.[33] As he suggested, the issue, in a pluralistic society, was an important one, and he wanted to be sure 'to free you [his fellow american Catholics] from the imputation of uncharitableness in restraining salvation to those of your own communion.'[34] And as to the charge of a consequent persecution of those allegedly damned folk outside the Church, Carroll himself could see no ready connection between the two ideas, but he was willing to admit 'that protestants and catholics equally deviate from the spirit of their religion, when fanaticism and fiery zeal would usurp that controul over men's minds, to which conviction and fair argument have an exclusive right.'[35]

In turn, Carroll dismissed the position, advanced by Wharton, that Catholics could not engage in a candid inquiry regarding religion because they did not begin their investigation with the essential 'indifference to the truth or falsity of a tenet', as an illogical position. That only a supposed perfect neutrality or even an attitude of disbelief was requisite to such inquiries was an error and indeed even ridiculous. And the authority to whom Carroll appealed for support in this matter was an eighteenth-century protestant author, John Leland, a tactic Carroll employed several times in his paper: 'It is sufficient [Leland wrote] to a candid examination, that a man apply himself to it [a rational investigation] with a mind open to conviction, and a disposition to embrace truth, on which side soever it shall appear, and to receive the evidence that shall arise in the course of the trial.'[36] Yet there was another side to the circumstance of reason—'this excellent gift of our provident and bountiful Creator'—and Carroll was not about to pretend otherwise so as to create the false image of a religion of which the competent, and complete, arbiter was reason. Wondering how Wharton, using reason alone, could convince for example a Deist, who rejected the infallibility of Scripture, of the truth of such mysteries as the Incarnation or the Trinity, Carroll's reply was an admission of reason's limitations. Rather than Wharton's contention that 'the most rational religion must always be the best', Carroll countered with examples of the great difficulties which followed from 'extending the exercise of reason to matters beyond its competency'. While a Catholic could, and should, honor and develop God's 'excellent gift' of reason, then, he must also understand the ultimate necessity for faith.[37]

Regarding Wharton's denial of the Church's infallibility, and hence his construction of an apparently open field for personally judging the truth of various catholic doctrines, Carroll argued that Christ had established a church and endowed it with an authority which necessarily, of its very nature, must be free of error regarding the faith. To say otherwise, contended Carroll, was to admit that Christ had not provided well for his followers, and to deny the efficacy of the Holy Spirit or Comforter sent to abide with his Church forever (John 14:16–17). Fully aware of human fallibilities, including those of a recent pope who had participated in the horrid suppression of the jesuit order, Carroll positioned infallibility 'in the body of bishops united and agreeing with their head, the bishop of Rome.'[38] The exercise of this authority was not only historical—practiced and public—but could be traced through apostolic succession to the very group of men to whom Christ had given the initial responsibility and power to teach and to baptize all nations, a peculiar prerogative of Roman Catholicism.[39] And all of this was opposite to any notion of private judgment and the obvious and consequent disarray and confusion possible in 'a country blessed like this with unlimited toleration... giving equal countenance to the professors and teachers of every denomination of christians.'[40] Realizing the fundamental significance of the locus of religious authority as well as the sensitivity of his non-catholic readers and neighbors regarding this matter, not only for religious but political reasons, John Carroll offered much more discussion of this issue than the preceding barebones description. Consciously, and usually limiting himself to the defensive, to a specific response or series of related responses to Wharton's specific charges and arguments rather than a full-fledged and broad-gauged theological offensive, Carroll nonetheless devoted a bit over a third of his *Address* to the question of the spiritual authority of the Church.[41] While he therefore did not here touch precisely on the concerns about a Catholic's ultimate political loyalties—an issue not raised by Wharton—his own current suspicions regarding Rome's pretensions to the exercise of any non-spiritual authority can be logically inferred from his text.[42]

As for catholic doctrines such as transubstantiation, purgatory, and auricular confession, Carroll argued that once the question of an infallible church authority was decided, such matters were by the very nature of the means of their delivery by this authority to be deemed authoritative; yet he would respond to Wharton's particular arguments.[43] This he proceeded to accomplish through use of a variety of resources and methods: history; the Church Fathers; textual analysis, including fuller and more accurate and critical presentation of texts cited by Wharton; and accurate presentations of exactly what the Church taught about these articles of faith.⁴⁴ As already noticed, Carroll was quite aware that his presentation would not be convincing to all: '... The habits of thinking, the prejudices, perhaps even the passions of many of my readers would be set against all the arguments I could offer; and that [moreover] the weaknesses, the errors, the absurdities of the writer would be imputed to the errors and absurdity of his religion.' Driving his effort, then, was no intention to draw attention and acclaim to himself. Nor was it, alone, an effort to vindicate his fellow Catholics and to reassure them in their faith. In the end, Carroll's *Address* was an effort to assert the legitimacy of a benign and civic-minded catholic presence in a new republic 'so blessed with civil and religious liberty'. This liberty and religious toleration, important as they were, however, were not ends in themselves. Rather, and this would seem in fact to be Carroll's principal point in the entire Wharton matter, this context of freedom would be 'the most effectual method to bring all denominations of Christians to an unity of faith.'⁴⁵

In the following year, Wharton published in Philadelphia *A Reply to an Address to the Roman Catholics of the United States of America*, but Carroll had 'no inclination to enter the lists again' as it appeared his *Address* had served to confirm his fellow Catholics in their faith. To continue the debate, he feared, would revive 'a spirit of controversy' which might 'add fuel to some sparks of religious animosity, which are visible at present amongst us'.⁴⁶ The Wharton-Carroll exchange was not to be the future archbishop's only foray into public debate, but it was not only the first and most lengthy of his apologetical efforts but also the most significant for several reasons.⁴⁷ In his *Address*, John Carroll took on himself the task of replying to an attack on specific catholic doctrines and the validity of the Church's teaching authority. The historical setting, a new nation dedicated to liberty, and currently working out the structures for religious freedom and toleration, was full of promise and opportunity for the previously persecuted catholic minority. To become involved in religious controversy was to run a decided risk of reawakening ancient, but well-worn, prejudices. Carroll took that risk because truth mattered in two ways. If american Catholics were to become full partners in the republican experiment, their beliefs needed to be seen for what they truly were, not the caricatures offered by Wharton. Not many others would become convinced in this instance of the truth of Catholicism, despite Carroll's best efforts, and he recognized that circumstance. His appearance in print, however, also signalled in itself the readiness of american Catholics to participate openly and wholeheartedly, and equally, in the affairs of the new nation. At ease himself with religious liberty and intellectual freedom, and with the separation of church and state, John Carroll intended his *Address*, in some of its specifics and in the overall effect of its presentation, to demonstrate the truth that there was no necessary contradiction between american and catholic. Reality was often beset by tensions, and tensions, creative at times, would develop historically between the two realities. But in John Carroll's vision of 1784, what America and Catholic stood for at their authentic best was not antithetical, but rather complementary, each to the other, and graced with hope and promise. It is yet a challenging vision.

NOTES

[1] Regarding early american anti-Catholicism, see Sr Mary Augustina Ray, *American Opinion of Roman Catholicism in the Eighteenth Century* (New York, 1936); John Tracy Ellis, *Catholics in Colonial America* (Baltimore, 1965); Thomas More Brown, 'The Image of the Beast: Anti-Papal Rhetoric in Colonial America', in Richard O. Curry and Thomas M. Brown (edd.), *Conspiracy: The Fear of Subversion in American History* (New York, 1972) pp. 1–20; Stephen J. Vicchio, 'The Origins and Development of Anti-Catholicism in America', in Stephen J. Vicchio and Sr Virginia Geiger (edd.), *Perspectives on the American Catholic Church, 1789–1989* (Westminster, Maryland, 1989) pp. 85–103.

[2] In his demythologizing of the institution of monarchy, Paine provided a readily-available and guilty association:

> That the Almighty hath here [1 Samuel] entered his protest against monarchical government is true, or the scripture is false. And a man hath good reason to believe that there is as much of kingcraft, as priest-craft in withholding the scripture from the public in Popish countries. For monarchy in every instance is the Popery of government.

Thomas Paine, *Common Sense*, ed. Isaac Kramnick (New York, 1986) p. 76.

[3] Bernard Bailyn, *The Ideological Origins of the American Revolution* (Cambridge, Massachusetts, 1967) chap. 6. See also, Thomas O'Brien Hanley, *The American Revolution and Religion: Maryland, 1770–1800* (Washington, D.C., 1971). In the first federal census (1790), Catholics numbered approximately 35,000 in a total population just under four million.

[4] Ellis, *Catholics in Colonial America*, p. 423. A vicar apostolic was a papal delegate or representative in a diocese which did not enjoy the benefit of the usual, established ecclesiastical hierarchy; the Sacred Congregation of the Propaganda directed the Church's missionary activities.

[5] Biographies include Peter Guilday, *The Life and Times of John Carroll: Archbishop of Baltimore (1735–1815)* (New York, 1922); and Annabelle M. Melville, *John Carroll of Baltimore: Founder of the American Catholic Hierarchy* (New York, 1955). See also Melville, 'John Carroll of Baltimore: A Bicentennial Retrospect', *The Catholic Historical Review* 76 (1990) 1–17.

[6] In a celebrated instance, in a letter (April 10, 1784) to a frequent correspondent, the English ex-Jesuit Charles Plowden, Carroll let loose his pent-up emotions, both as an ex-Jesuit and as an American, regarding roman authority:

> But this you may be assured of; that no authority derived from the Propagda will ever be admitted here; that the

Catholick Clergy & Laity here know that the only connexion they ought to have with Rome is to acknowledge the pope as the Spirl [Spiritual] head of the Church; that no Congregations existing in his states shall be allowed to exercise any share of his Spirl authority here; that no Bishop Vicar Apostolical shall be admitted; and if we are to have a Bishop, he shall not be *in partibus* but an ordinary national Bishop, in whose appointment Rome shall have no share.

Thomas O'Brien Hanley (ed.), *The John Carroll Papers* (Notre Dame, Indiana, 3 vols., 1976) 1:146. See also Carroll to Ferdinand Farmer [December 1784]; *Carroll Papers*, 1:155–58. [7] See two articles by James Hennesey: 'An Eighteenth Century Bishop: John Carroll of Baltimore', *Archivum Historicae Pontificae* 16 (1978) 171–204; 'The Vision of John Carroll', *Thought* 54 (1979) 322–33.

[8] For a rather pointed discussion of this particular moment in american catholic history, see Jay P. Dolan, *The American Catholic Experience: A History from Colonial Times to the Present* (Garden City, New York, 1985) chap. 4.

[9] Carroll and Wharton were first cousins once removed: Thomas W. Spalding, 'John Carroll: Corrigenda and Addenda', *The Catholic Historical Review* 71 (1985) 513–14.

[10] Carroll to Plowden, September 18, 1784; *Carroll Papers*, 1:150. See also Carroll to Plowden, September 26, 1783; and Carroll to Plowden, April 10, 1784; *Carroll Papers*, 1:77, 146–47. The controversy, and its european phase, can be followed in Guilday, *Life and Times*, pp. 116–33; and Melville, *John Carroll*, pp. 89–94.

[11] *Carroll Papers*, 1:167–68.

[12] While Carroll was aware of the dangers of public religious controversy (see below), he did not counsel nor did he practice religious indifferentism, or a rounding of doctrinal edges, in order to promote some sort of lowest common denominator Christianity. He promoted charitable dealings with non-catholic Christians, but he was ever aware that truth must not be surrendered in the name of a mere good fellowship. See his 'Sermon on Occasion of Possessing His Pro-Cathedral' (1790); *Carroll Papers*, 1:476–78. The historical tendencies in american Christianity toward a sort of religious homogenization, based in part on a doctrinal indifferentism, are discussed in Daniel J. Boorstin, *The Genius of American Politics* (Chicago, 1953) chap. 5. Boorstin acknowledged the lesser assimilation and hence lesser americanization of both Catholicism and orthodox Judaism in the early 1950s, a circumstance perhaps more problematic today. On the other hand, there is a viewpoint that this lesser americanization is a boon to a revitalized american enterprise: see Richard John Neuhaus, *The Catholic Moment: The Paradox of the Church in the Postmodern World* (New York, 1987).

[13] For stimulating discussions of Carroll's, and american Catholicism's ecumenical tendencies during this period of the early Republic, see Joseph P. Chinnici, 'American Catholics and Religious Pluralism, 1775–1820', *Journal of Ecumenical Studies* 16 (1979) 727–46; and Joseph Agonito, 'Ecumenical Stirrings: Catholic-Protestant Relations During the Episcopacy of John Carroll', *Church History* 45 (1976) 358–73. Ironically, the basic issue of separation of church and state in the United States was not apparently settled until the dis-establishment of New England's Congregational churches in the first part of the nineteenth century.

[14] Charles Henry Wharton, *A Letter to the Roman Catholics of the City of Worcester, from the Late Chaplain of That Society* (Philadelphia, 1784) pp. 6–7.

[15] Wharton, *Letter*, p. 5.

[16] Wharton, *Letter*, pp. 9–11.

[17] Wharton, *Letter*, p. 12.

[18] Wharton, *Letter*, p. 13.

[19] Wharton, *Letter*, p. 23.

[20] Wharton, *Letter*, pp. 23, 27.

[21] Wharton, *Letter*, p. 37. He did suggest though, that something good was happening in the catholic community:

> From my own observation I am happy to assure them, that the Roman church in this, as well as in many other particulars is daily undergoing a silent reformation. The dark monsters of persecution and bigotry are retreating gradually before the light of genuine religion and philosophy.

Wharton, *Letter*, p. 12.

[22] Robert Gorman, *Catholic Apologetical Literature in the United States (1784–1858)* (Washington, D.C., 1939) pp. 1–2. Gorman suggests as a third reason for american anti-Catholicism the belief that these Catholics harmed material prosperity due to the group's cultivation of ignorance, superstition, and immorality.

[23] See Vicchio and Geiger (edd.), *Perspectives*, pp. 85–103; Ray Allen Billington, *The Protestant Crusade: 1800–1860* (New York, 1938); Donald Kinzer, *An Episode in Anti-Catholicism: The American Protective Association* (Seattle, 1964). According to John Tracy Ellis, Arthur M. Schlesinger, Sr., once told him: "'I regard the prejudice against your Church as the deepest bias in the history of the American people.'" Ellis, *American Catholicism* (2nd ed., Chicago, 1969) p. 151.

[24] For examples, see *Carroll Papers*, 1:112, 113, 116–19, 120–27, 128, 130–31, 133–34.

[25] *Carroll Papers*, 1:139–40.

[26] See Joseph P. Chinnici, *The English Catholic Enlightenment: John Lingard and the Cisalpine Movement, 1780–1850* (Shepherdstown, West

Virginia, 1980); and Margaret Mary Reher, *Catholic Intellectual Life in America: A Historical Study of Persons and Movements* (New York, 1989) chap. 1.

[27] According to Joseph P. Chinnici:

> Within the context of the eighteenth century, the Enlightenment challenged Catholics to both a project of intelligibility—an attempt to make Catholic belief and practice understandable to the Age of Reaso—and a socio-political anthropology, a redefinition of the structures of church and state in terms of the new view of the person.

Chinnici, 'American Catholics', p. 729. Chinnici argues that this early american catholic effort to participate in the american project, derailed after 1830 by increased catholic immigration and renewed anti-catholic bigotry, has been revived by developments emanating from Vatican II. Among these are the work of John Courtney Murray, sj, on the Declaration of Religious Freedom; Chinnici, pp. 745–46.

[28] *Carroll Papers*, 1:84.

[29] *Carroll Papers*, 1:83.

[30] *Carroll Papers*, 1:86.

[31] *Carroll Papers*, 1:85–86.

[32] *Carroll Papers*, 1:87. Chinnici suggests that Carroll's position, which distinguished between toleration and religious indifferentism, was heavily dependent on Saints Augustine and Robert Bellarmine and was in line with the thinking of other enlightened Catholics, such as Joseph Berington and Arthur O'Leary. A stricter definition of church, and the reality of *extra ecclesiam nulla est salus*, was advanced by such as John Gother, Stephen Badin, and Richard Challoner; 'American Catholics', pp. 739–44.

[33] *Carroll Papers*, 1:89–91.

[34] *Carroll Papers*, 1:89.

[35] *Carroll Papers*, 1:92.

[36] *Carroll Papers*, 1:84–85.

[37] *Carroll Papers*, 1:94–95. In addition, Carroll noted that 'The vainest therefore of all controversies, and the most ineffectual for the discovery of truth, is, to dispute on the metaphysical nature of the doctrines of Christianity.' *Carroll Papers*, 1:93.

[38] *Carroll Papers*, 1:105–106. This quotation is used to suggest the apparent difficulty John Carroll would have had with the pronouncement of papal infallibility at the future Vatican Council I (1869–1870). Two points need to be made: 1) Carroll admitted that some already believed in papal infallibility, 'but with this opinion faith has no concern, every one being at liberty to adopt or reject it, as the reasons for or against may affect him' (*Carroll Papers*, 1:105–106); 2) Carroll noted in

his *Address* that doctrine develops over time, and sometimes only when some traditional or implicit truth needs to be defended from heretics (*Carroll Papers*, 1:107–108, 120, 125, 138). Carroll also noted the obvious historical concurrence of human peccability and infallibility in faith (*Carroll Papers*, 1:99–100).

[39] *Carroll Papers*, 1:115–16.

[40] *Carroll Papers*, 1:114.

[41] *Carroll Papers*, 1:95–116. And, as elsewhere, Carroll suggested other authors who pursued the particular issue with far more completeness (*Carroll Papers*, 1:95).

[42] See above for Carroll's ideas regarding the american Catholic Church.

[43] *Carroll Papers*, 1:115–16.

[44] *Carroll Papers*, 1:116–34. In a telling (and timeless?) aside, Carroll noted: 'Our faith is formed on the public doctrine of the church, and not on the opinions of private theologians.' *Carroll Papers*, 1:133.

[45] *Carroll Papers*, 1:140.

[46] *Carroll Papers*, 1:191. In this letter to Charles Plowden (June 29, 1785), Carroll expressed some disappointment with Wharton's *Reply* and the author's continued scholarly shortcomings:

> ... Like his letter, [it] is written with spirit and elegance, and interspersed with many sentimental passages. He has boldly denied facts, which I did not expect, that any one now a days would have the effrontery to dispute: he has explained away his misquotations: he has vindicated particular passages in his letter by keeping his own words out of sight. ...

See also Carroll to Joseph Berington, September 29, 1786; *Carroll Papers*, 1:217–18. Interestingly, Wharton's quite laudatory entry in the *Dictionary of American Biography*, by Harris Elwood Starr, refers to the *Reply* as 'a vigorous and well-documented pamphlet'. Dumas Malone *et al.* (edd.) (New York, 10 vols., with supplements, 1964-) 10:26–27. See Guilday, *Life and Times*, p. 127; and Melville, *John Carroll*, pp. 93–94.

[47] For the other instances, see Guilday, *Life and Times*, pp. 112–15; Melville, *John Carroll*, pp. 84–89; *Carroll Papers*, 1:259–61; 365–69.

TRIUMPHS OF ECCLESIASTICAL POLITICS IN THE 1231 *DECRETUM* OF ANDREW II OF HUNGARY

Zoltan J. Kosztolnyik
Texas A&M University

Archiepiscopus Strigoniensis praemissa legitima admonitione nos vinculo excommunicationis, et eos innodandi habeat potestatem.
The 1231 *Decretum* of Andrew II

AT THE END OF 1218, Andrew II of Hungary (1205–1235) returned home from his crusade to the Holy Land.[1] The crusade—if it can really be called a crusade; one could rather speak of an excursion, of an irresponsible and unplanned military expedition[2]—ended abruptly, in total failure.[3] Because he wished to excuse himself before the papal curia, Andrew sent two churchmen to Rome: the archpriest Benedict from Győr, and Stephen, the archdeacon from Féhérvar, to inform the Holy See that it was on account of an outbreak of domestic disorders and bloody uprisings that he had to conclude his mission without accomplishing his goal.[4] Social upheavals continued to spread in the country, however; it was fearful to observe the numbness of the population at a time when the monarch continued to donate goods from the crown domain—goods he could not retrieve without breaching his oath of office.[5]

Following an appeal from Archbishop John of Esztergom, Pope Honorius III declared void any royal oath related to donations the king had recently made;[6] Rome placed the realm under its protection against exploitations by ismaealite merchants, who were favored by the royal court.[7] It was the exchange of letters with, and the dispatch of ambassadors to the curia that may have led to drafting of resolutions known as the 1222 *Decretum*, known as the (hungarian) Golden Bull, at the annual law day held on August 20, 1222.[8] Therefore, the bull, this Decree of 1222, long regarded as the first document of constitutional life in Hungary, developed from the turbulent political and social upheaval of Andrew II's reign.[9]

The embezzlement of crown lands had undermined royal authority; the king's reeves, nominally royal appointees, now inherited their offices; many of the new landholders had gained control over local government. Inheritance of offices of authority by royal reeves and donations made from the crown domain had weakened the political-social status of the king's (lesser) service nobility, the *servientes regis*. The new territorial potentates began to enact laws in their respective regions—at no little expense to the public good, or, at least, to the prestige of the monarch.[10] The king, who had lost his domain, had to seek new sources of revenue by farming out—to outsiders, that is, to foreigners—the collection of the *regale*, salt tax, and toll (the thirtieth of the value of the merchandise concerned)—thereby making unbearable the lives of the poorer segments of society.[11]

The 1222 Decree called for attending to the grievances of the lay element of the population: the service (lesser) nobility and all free men;[12] it defined the rights and privileges of the lesser nobles and of all free men and women and made binding decisions to improve conditions in the realm.[13] Andrew II had dealt with ecclesiastical complaints in an earlier document, in which he determined the privileges the Church held in courts of law and in matters of taxation; simultaneously, he had forbade servants to enter ranks of the clergy, and had asserted that a cleric must not, out of sheer greed, preoccupy himself with business unworthy of his vocation.[14]

The individuals who had drafted the 1222 Decree found historic precedents for determining the concept and the meaning of freedom for the king's service nobles in the tradition that surrounded the legislation and memory of the first Hungarian king, St Stephen I (d. 1038),[15] even though Stephen's *leges* provided little foundation for this, saving only his decrees dealing with family inheritance.[16] Contrary to the by then established hungarian custom,[17] Andrew II issued the decree, as if symbolically, on his own authority, without mentioning the council and the assembly; *nos igitur...concedimus tam eis, quam aliis hominibus regni nostri libertatem a sancto rege concessam*.[18] The monarch asserted his and his nobles' rights against those of the high nobility,[19] thereby hoping to end disorder in the realm and bring freedom to every inhabitant.[20]

Interestingly, the resistance clause of the Decree that forced the king to keep his promises[21] was not of hungarian origin,[22] nor did it display any resemblance with the conclusion of the english Magna Carta.[23] The right of resistance was customary in Aragon.[24] Constance, the queen of Emery I (1196–1204), the elder brother and predecessor of Andrew II, was the daughter of Alfonso II of Aragon.[25] Because of this, close relations existed between the two royal courts at the time.[26]

None of the seven copies of the Decree (one directly addressed to the papal curia[27]) have come down to posterity —not even in the papal archives[28]—and the sole existing copy of the text is a 1318 transcript preserved in the archiepiscopal archives in Esztergom.[29] One may draw the conclusion that, even though the monarch had issued the Decree, the Golden Bull of 1222—the date certainly proven from the letter, dated December 15, 1222[30]—it was not, must not have been, his serious intention to observe and keep the written promises he had made.[31]

The Decree did not restore peace or inner tranquility in the country. It did not bring to a halt the continued alienation of crown lands and landed goods, though it did limit the abuses connected with it; nor did it open up new resources of revenue for the king.[32] As evidenced by the note Andrew II sent to the curia shortly after the promulgation of the Decree, its execution became impossible because the majority of the country's nobility refused to obey him, as they regarded his son Béla, the heir to the throne and junior king, as the legitimate ruler.[33]

Pope Honorius III answered the royal complaint in a writ addressed to the members of the hungarian hierarchy instructing them to excommunicate anyone who dared to revolt or otherwise commit treason against the anointed monarch.[34] Another letter of complaint went to the Holy See: during the annual law day held and presided over by the king (or, by his palatine)[35] the people there assembled had made demands the king found unwise to fulfill. The populace wanted him to dismiss all of the hated noble officials from their posts, confiscate all of the nobles' properties and landholdings, and evenly distribute them among the populace. Their attitude forced the monarch to take a public stand: he must either give in to their demands and deny justice its course, thereby undermining his own authority, or, ignoring the protest, expose himself and his supporters to the wrath of the populace.[36]

In the already cited letter, the curia gave prompt reply by instructing the bishop of Eger and two cistercian abbots of the realm[37] to make their position public before the multitude gathered together on the annual law day: the demands on the ruler were to be declared improper. They were to tell the multitude that law and justice demanded that nothing be done against the persons and goods of the nobles.[38]

Similar difficulties arose with the marriage problems of Béla the junior king (the later Béla IV, 1235–1270). During the return journey from the Holy Land, Andrew II had arranged the engagement of Maria, daughter of Theodore Lascaris, emperor of Nicea, to his son and heir, Béla, and had taken and educated her at his court.[39] The couple were married, but King Andrew soon realized that his realm would benefit more from a different marriage alliance. Therefore, Béla unexpectedly announced to the curia that, on coming of age, he had decided not to marry his fiancée—more properly, to live with his wife—and requested that the pope dispense him from the marital engagement his father had made earlier.[40]

The pontiff commissioned three hungarian noblemen to conduct an inquiry into the case.[41] The result of the investigation was that the terms of Béla's request did not correspond to reality. On reaching legal age, Béla and Maria had lived together peacefully as husband and wife for two years, when, 'on suggestions received from some evil people,' Béla dismissed his wife.[42] Rome now ordered Béla to take her back,[43] and Béla complied with the papal demand.[44] By obeying the pope Béla angered his father; Béla was forced to flee to Austria in the fall of 1223.[45]

The Holy See intervened at this point; the pope asked the king to seek reconciliation with his son and treat him with the respect due to the heir of the throne by letting him participate in governmental decisions.[46] The king was also to treat fairly Béla's adherents who had faithfully followed him out of the country.[47] The pontiff also wrote letters to the bohemian king[48] and the austrian duke,[49] and sent instructions to the hungarian hierarchy requesting their support for ending enmities between the royal father and his princely son.[50] Indeed, shortly hereafter Andrew II made peace with his son.[51]

At this time Andrew II also had an unfriendly encounter with the Teutonic Knights. In 1211, the knights had been settled with his permission in the Barca region with the intent that they defend southeastern Transylvania and the realm from the Cumans.[52] The Knights had undoubtedly fulfilled their obligations; furthermore, they had populated the area with foreign settlers and raised it to a high level of material civilization and socio-spiritual culture. And yet, the Knights had asked Rome for privileges additional to those they had already held from the hungarian court in their region. They had requested, for instance, that the curia exempt them[53] and their region from the spiritual jurisdiction of the archbishop of Esztergom, thereby placing them directly under the supervision of the Holy See.⁵⁴ In 1224, the Knights had requested anew that the curia acquire and hold in possession their Barca land;⁵⁵ in return, they would recognize and accept the direct supremacy of the Holy See. In acknowledgment thereof, they would pay one gold mark to the pope and one to the cardinals in Rome. In offering an explanation for their request, they had emphasized that settlers would be more willing to settle and remain in a territory that enjoyed direct supervision of, in fact, ownership by the Roman See.⁵⁶

Interestingly, Andrew II at first supported the Knights' request. The royal court found nothing in the nature of the request sent to Rome that disturbed the territorial and political interests of the crown. Consequently, on April 30, 1224, the papal curia officially took charge of the Barca land held by the Knights, and accepted their offer of two gold marks per annum to the pontiff and the cardinals.⁵⁷ Merely for the sake of legal formality, the curia reminded Andrew II that he had to hand over the Barca land *ad precum tuarum instantiam, ad preces tuas*. Thus, the monarch, who had previously raised no voice in protest, could not now argue that the Knights were actually questioning the rights of the crown by placing the region under the protective ownership of the Holy See.⁵⁸

The Knights cancelled all of their obligations to the crown and, by military force, expanded the frontiers of the Barca land. Against this the king took countermeasures. In early 1225, he led an armed expedition to the southeastern corner of Transylvania, besieged and occupied a fort, and caused serious damage to the Knights, whom he had now ordered to leave the area immediately.⁵⁹

The Knights in turn wrote Rome that the curia could not allow them to abandon their territory without the permission of the pope and of the grand master of the order. Their petition was answered by Rome in a letter sent to the hungarian court to the effect that the king should display good will toward the Knights, pay them indemnity for damages caused them, and officially re-settle them on Barca land.⁶⁰ The Holy See further authorized three cistercian abbots to visit the area and determine on the spot the borders of the region that belonged to the Knights.⁶¹ The pope sent Count Christopher Urach, bishop of Portuenso, as delegate to the court of Andrew II, to warn the king that the pope could not abandon the Knights—regardless of how deeply he appreciated the dignity of the monarch's position. In matters that pertain to God, no earthly monarch may receive special treatment from the curia: *non debemus tamen deferre homini contra Deum.*⁶²

Under the impact of the sternly worded letter from Rome, Andrew II expressed willingness to re-settle the Knights in his territory, on the condition that they return the disputed areas: lands adjacent to the Barca land they had occupied by force.⁶³ The king dispatched envoys to Rome to discuss the issues involving the Knights; the Knights refused, however, to comply with the royal demand, and King Andrew, in a rather abrupt manner and without awaiting further communication from Rome, permanently expelled them from his country.⁶⁴ Andrew II did not alter his decision even when the curia, urged by the master of the Knights in the Barca land (who had hurriedly visited Rome), encouraged him to seek reconciliation with the Knights.⁶⁵

In the relations between Church and the hungarian court, the occupancy of the archiepiscopal see of Esztergom now caused a swirl of diplomatic dust. In the archiepiscopal election of 1225, the cathedral chaper at Esztergom split into two parties; one nominated the bishop of Csanád, the other the bishop of Nyitra. Pope Honorius III refused to confirm either candidate but allowed the chapter of canons to hold a second election.⁶⁶ The results remained the same, and, obeying a papal summons, the canons of the chapter dispatched two of their members to the papal curia. Listening to their report, the pontiff, on his own, named Robert, bishop of Veszprém, as archbishop of Esztergom.⁶⁷ Archbishop Robert took possession of his see without undue delay.⁶⁸

The new archbishop now requested Rome that he be permitted to carry out missionary work among the cuman population in Moldavia—a mission that had been requested by the cuman nobles of that region. Archbishop Robert asked that he be given the rank and privileges of a papal delegate for the area and, at the same time, be dispensed from his crusading vow.[69] He fulfilled a fruitful mission among the Cumans,[70] and, as legate, ordained Theodore, a dominican, as bishop for the converted Cumans.[71]

At the same time Archbishop Ugrin of Kalocsa also achieved success with his missionary endeavor among the 'heretics' in Bosnia; with the approval of the curia, he established for them a bishopric at Szerem.[72] The archbishop held high ambitions: he hoped that through the new bishop he would be able to place the greek orthodox faithful in the region under his metropolitan jurisdiction. Rome reacted cautiously: if the Greek Orthodox already had a bishop who was willing to submit to Rome, his ecclesiastical authority was to remain intact.[73] Rome decided to investigate and sent Aegidius, a papal chaplain, as legate to Hungary.[74] Aegidius sojourned in the realm from 1228 to 1231, and gained respect from the hungarian clergy.[75] The legate frequently took care of legal business among the bishops, cathedral chapters, and monastic communities.[76] He could not influence the monarch however.[77] It may have been due to this lack of direct understanding between the king and the papal envoy that the curia received negative reports from Aegidius, in about 1230, about the rather difficult and confusing conditions, especially for clergymen, in Hungary. This may also explain why the curia requested a report on conditions prevalent in the country from the archbishop of Esztergom.[78]

The situation in Hungary was, undoubtedly, serious: religious faith had been lost among the faithful; freedom had been trodden under foot by government officials; royal authority had disappeared. Jews and Moslems, who blindly trusted royal protection, had oppressed the christian population, married Christians, kept christian slaves. The Muslims had, in fact, enticed Christians to convert to Islam. The court had made the clergy pay taxes and appear before royal courts in any legal matter. The Church had lost property and income. In response, the curia gave the archbishop severe instructions: establish a firm stand toward the non-christian elements who had abused their free status in society.[79] One may argue that it was on the grounds of this papal directive that the revised version of the 1222 Decree had to be promulgated in 1231;[80] this guaranteed security for churchmen and members of the lay estates and authorized the archbishop of Esztergom to excommunicate the king were he to breach the law of the land.[81]

The Decree of 1231 provides evidence of the growing prestige of churchmen in the country; on the annual law day (August 20), the bishops, too, were now expected to appear, next to the king or his palatine, and listen to the grievances of the population.[82] The bishops now controlled governmental functions, supervised courts of law, and kept the palatine under observation.[83] The 1231 Decree left out the articles of the Decree of 1222 that did not correspond to the needs of the clergy or imposed hardships on them.[84] In the concluding paragraph of the Decree of 1222, it was the palatine who had been entrusted with carrying out its provisions; that was why he had, supposedly, kept a copy of it, so that neither he nor the monarch, nor even the nobles, could dare to dissent from its articles.[85] But, in 1231, it was the archbishop of Esztergom who was authorized to place the king or his son(s) under sentence of excommunication, were he, or they, to break the law, and this under the assumption that a public outcry would improve royal behavior.[86]

The security clause proved to be ineffective. The archbishop of Esztergom wished to spare the monarch, his person and office, from embarrassment; he excommunicated the royal advisors instead and placed the country under an interdict.[87] However, it is evident from a letter, dated February 25, 1231, that the king did not mend his ways; in fact, Andrew II raised a protest in Rome because of the scandals that had involved him.[88] Dénes [=Dionysius] the Palatine (whom the archbishop of Esztergom had earlier excommunicated because he had confiscated church property and supported non-Christians at the expense of native Christians),[89] Rembald, grand master of the Templars in Hungary,[90] and Simon (a newcomer from Aragon and now) reeve of Győr,[91] were members of the royal delegation sent to Rome, taking the king's letter with them.[92] The delegation assured the curia of the king's unending devotion to the Church, in whose service the king had fought wars in distant countries, but complained that the king's services remained unappreciated by the Holy See.[93]

The writ, a classic example of diplomatic double talk, was successful: on July 22, 1231, the curia ordered the archbishop of Esztergom to undertake no further action against the king until the arrival of a new papal delegate.[94] In a letter dated a month later, the Roman See assured King Andrew that no one could excommunicate him without previous papal authorization.[95]

The new papal delegate, Jacob Pecora of Picenze, a Cistercian and cardinal of Palestrina, was a well educated man; he had pursued his studies at Paris and had served as papal emissary to Emperor Frederick II.[96] In the fall of 1232, the cardinal summoned a gathering of hungarian bishops at Buda.[97] There, he and the bishops transcribed the papal letter of March 31, 1231,[98] and the resolutions of the law day of the same year, together with the writ of excommunication of the king's advisors by Archbishop Robert of Esztergom. They forwarded the collected material to Rome.[99] The cardinal must have wished to make it easier for Archbishop Robert to justify his behavior and actions toward the king before the Roman See.[100]

The delegate's activities turned out positively, as far as the king was concerned. After some lengthy discussions—

carried out through emissaries; the king avoided personal contact with the cardinal—Andrew II acknowledged the justification of ecclesiastical demands from the country's hierarchy, and signed the Treaty of Bereg (a hamlet located in the woody northeastern part of the realm) in the fall of 1233.[101] In signing the treaty, the monarch attempted to rectify the written promises he had made, though did not fulfill, in the Decree of 1231. On the personal request of the delegate, the monarch also took a second oath that he would punish heresy and conversions to the jewish faith and islamic religion, and tolerate no disobedience toward the Holy See.[102]

NOTES

[1] The compiler of the *Chronicon pictum*, c. 175, creates the impression that the monarch, having earlier received a papal invitation, 'quod mandatum acceperat dum esset adhuc dux', only 'visited' the Holy Land: 'Terram Sacram visitavit ad mandatum papae.' See E. Szentpétery (ed.), *Scriptores rerum Hungaricarum* (Budapest, 2 vols., 1937–1938) [cited hereafter as SSH] 1:465, 10–14. H. Roscher, *Papst Innocenz III und die Kreuzzüge* (Göttingen, 1969) p. 140ff., deals with the background in depth; Albericus Trium Fontium, *Chronicon*, in G. H. Pertz (ed.), *Monumenta Germaniae historica, Scriptores* (Hannover, 30 vols., 1826 etc.) [cited hereafter as MGH SS] 23:905, 8–14; 905, 42–47, hinted at the westerners' lack of interest in joining ranks with the Hungarians. Compare with the writ of Innocent III, dated December 14, 1215, in A. Potthast (ed.), *Regesta pontificum Romanorum* (Berlin, 2 vols., 1875) [cited hereafter as Potthast] n. 5009. Dandalo's *Chronicon Venetum*, 10.4.29, speaks of Andrew II as a crusader, 'cruce designatus', who went to Tripoli; Dandalo expresses himself with diplomatic caution; see L. A. Muratori (ed.), *Scriptores rerum Italicarum* (Milan, 1728) 12:339. On the other hand, Thomas of Spaleto, *Historia Salonitarum*, c. 26, mentions cooperation between the king and the Germans; MGH SS 29:577. See also R. Röhricht, *Studien zur Geschichte des fünften Kreuzzüges* (Innsbruck, 1891) p. 24ff., for an outline of coordinated activities between the king and the duke of Austria; T. C. VanCleve, 'The Fifth Crusade', in R. E. Wolff and H. W. Hazard (edd.), *The Later Crusades, 1189-1311*, vol. 2 of K. S. Setton (ed.), *A History of the Crusades* (Philadelphia, 4 vols., 1955 etc.) p. 337ff. Andrew spent three months in the Holy Land. See SSH 1:466, 1; and Petrus Ransanus, *Epithoma rerum Hungararum*, ed. P. Kulcsár (Budapest, 1977) pp. xvi and 1215. The *Chronicon pictum*, MS fol. 62'b, in a 'P' initial, depicts Andrew II as a crusader; see D. Dercsényi, *Chronicon pictum: Képes Krónika* (Budapest, 2 vols., 1963) vol. 1 (facsimile). After several delays, Innocent III did set 1217 as the year for this crusade; see his writ of February 3, 1213, in J.-P. Migne (ed.), *Patrologiae cursus completus, series latina* (Paris, 221 vols., 1844–1855) [cited hereafter as PL] 216:757ac; Potthast, n. 4669. H. E. Mayer, *Geschichte der Kreuzzüge* (3rd ed., Stuttgart, 1973) p. 195, mentions only briefly the 'crusade' of Andrew II.

[2] See *L'Estoire d'Eracles empereur*, in *Recueil des historiens des croisades* (Paris, 16 vols., 1841–1906), *Historiens occidentaux* (Paris, 5 vols., 1894–1895) [cited hereafter as RHC Occ] 2:321ff., esp. p. 323f.; R. Röhricht, 'Die Kreuzzugsbewegung in Jahre 1217', *Forschungen zur deutschen Geschichte* 16 (1876) 139ff.; Oliver Scholasticus, *Historia Damiatina*, ed. H. Hoogeweg in *Die Schriften des Kölner Domscholasters, späteren Bischofs von Paderborn und Kardinal-Bischofs von S. Sabina Oliverus*, vol. 222 of the *Bibliothek des litterarischen Vereins in Stuttgart* (Tübingen, 1894) [cited hereafter as

Oliver, *Damiatina*] p. 162f.; W. Wattenbach, *Deutschlands Geschichtsquellen im Mittelalter* (6th ed., Berlin, 2 vols., 1893–1894) 2:446, n. 2.

³ On this 'lack of success', see Oliver, *Damiatina*, p. 168; Eracles, RHC Occ, 2:325; James de Vitry, *Epistolae, III, 1216–1221,* ed. R. Röhricht in *Zeitschrift für Kirchengeschichte* 15 (1894–1895) 568f. W. Junkmann, 'Mag. Oliverius und der Kreuzzug von Damietta', *Katholische Zeitschrift* 1 (1851) 99ff., 205ff. See, further, I. de Thurocz, *Chronica Hungarorum*, edd. E. Galántai and J. Kristó (Budapest, 1985) p. 136f.; c. 100. Thomas of Spaleto spoke of poisoning; MGH SS 29:578f.; S. Katona, *Historia critica regum Hungariae stirpis Arpadianae* (Pest-Buda, 7 vols., 1779–1782) 5:287f.; further, J. P. Donovan, *Pelagius and the Fifth Crusade* (Philadelphia, 1950) p. 29ff.

⁴ See A. Theiner (ed.), *Vetera monumenta historica Hungariam sacram illustrantia* (Rome, 2 vols., 1859–1860) [cited hereafter as Theiner] n. 32; E. Szentpétery (ed.), *Regesta regum stirpis Arpadianae critico-diplomatica* (Budapest, 2 vols., 1923–1961) [cited hereafter as RA] n. 355, and the response of Pope Honorius III on March 5, 1219; Potthast, n. 6001; Theiner, n. 33; Katona 5:319.

⁵ As, for example, RA, nn. 357, 358; See G. Fejér (ed.), *Codex diplomaticus Hungariae ecclesiasticus ac civilis* (Buda, 44 vols., 1829–1842) [cited hereafter as CD] 3/1:285; and G. Wenczel (ed.), *Arpádkori új okmánytár* [New Document Collection of the Arpadian Age] (Pest, 12 vols., 1860–1874) [cited hereafter as AUO] 7:157.

⁶ Most probably, reference is made to this in CD 3/1:194; compare with papal writs addressed to Béla, junior king, and the archbishop of Kalocsa in Potthast, nn. 7443 and 7444; Theiner, nn. 126 and 127, or CD 3/2:47 and 68; Katona 5:469.

⁷ On this, two papal letters, Potthast, nn. 6639 and 6640; Theiner, nn. 58 and 59, and CD 3/1:312 and 313.

⁸ RA, n. 379; text in S. L. Endlicher (ed.), *Rerum Hungaricarum monumenta Arpadiana* (Sankt Gallen, 2 vols., 1849; one vol. repr. Leipzig, 1931) [cited hereafter as RHM] 2:412ff.; H. Marczali (ed.), *Enchiridion fontium historiae Hungarorum* (Budapest, 1901) 134aff.; K. Csiky *et al.* (edd.), *Corpus Iuris Hungarici: Magyar Törvénytár* (Budapest, 10 vols., 1896 etc.) 1:130ff.; G. Érszegi, 'Az Aranybulla [Golden Bull]', *Fejér megyei történeti évkönyv* [History Yearbook of County Fejér] 6 (1972) 5ff., esp. 14f.; W. Näf, 'Herrschaftsverträge des Spätmittelalters', *Quellen zur neueren Geschichte* (Bern, 1951) p. 7ff.

⁹ I. G. Bolla, 'Az Aranybulla-kori társadalmi mozgalmak a Váradi Regestrum megvilágitásában [Early Thirteenth-century Social Movements in Hungary in the Light of the Record in the Várad Register]', *Acta Universitatis Scientiarum Budapestiensis*, sectio historica 1 (1959) 84ff. For the text of the 'Várad Register', see RHM 2:640ff.

[10] See AOU 6:399ff., esp. p. 400. For Andrew II thanking Archbishop John of Esztergom for his steadfast loyalty, see RA, n. 350; CD 3/1:257.

[11] B. Hóman-Gy. Szekfü, *Magyar történet* [Hungarian History] (6th ed., Budapest, 5 vols., 1939) 1:490f.; Gy. Székely, *Magyarország története: elözmények s magyar történet 1242-ig* [History of Hungary: Prehistory and Hungarian History Until 1242] (Budapest, 1984) p. 1322ff.; Gy. Kristó, *Az aranybullák évszázada* [A Century of Golden Bulls] (Budapest, 1981) *passim*; Gy. Györffy, 'Ungarn von 895 bis 1400', *Europäische Wirtschafts- und Sozialgeschichte im Mittelaler*, vol. 2 of H. Kellenbenz (ed.), *Handbuch der europäischen Wirtschafts- und Sozialgeschichte* (Stuttgart, 1980) p. 625ff.

[12] Andrew II attempted to improve their public and social status; see the 1222 Decree, aa. 4, 10, 19; RHM 2:413, 414, 415; Marczali, *Enchiridion*, p. 134aff.; Gy. Györffy, *Wirtschaft und Gesellschaft der Ungarn um die Jahrtausendwende* (Vienna-Graz, 1983) p. 102ff.

[13] 'Concedimus tam eis, quam aliis hominibus regni nostri libertatem a sancto rege concessam.' RHM 2:413; Marczali, *Enchiridion*, p. 134a.

[14] RA, n. 378; RHM 2:417ff; Theiner, n. 190; CD 3/1:379ff.

[15] '... Libertas tam nobilium regni nostri, quam etiam aliorum, instituta a sancto rege Stephano.' RHM 2:412; Marczali, *Enchiridion*, p. 134a.

[16] See a. 4; Marczali, *Enchiridion*, p. 136a; RHM 2:413. Compare with Stephen's Laws, 2:2; RHM 2:321; Marczali, *Enchiridion*, p. 77f. On the 'filial quarter', see A. Murarik, *Az ösiség alapintézményének eredete* [Origins of 'Aviticitas'] (Budapest, 1938) p. 163ff. This was deduced from the Roman *lex falcidia*; see F. Eckhart, 'Vita a leánynegyedröl' [Debate on the 'Filial Quarter'], *Századok* 66 (1932) 408ff.; J. Holub, 'La "quarta puellaris" dans ancien droit hongrois', in *Studi in memoria di Aldo Albertoni* (Padua, 1935) 3:275ff. Their arguments were based on Emperor Justinian's *Institutiones* 3.1.16; see P. Krueger et al. (edd.), *Corpus Iuris Civilis* (Berlin, 3 vols., 1895–1899) vol. 3.

[17] As, for example, Stephen's Laws, aa. 1:15, 31, 34; 2:14 (note 'secundum nostri senatus decretum'). See RHM 2:315ff., and Marczali, *Enchiridion*, p. 72ff. It is known that Béla I did summon a public assembly in 1060; *Chronicon pictum*, c. 94; SSH 1:359, 20–22. Another example: 'placuit regi et omnium concilio' in Coloman the Learned's *Decretum*, a. 1; RHM 2:361; Z. J. Kosztolnyik, *From Coloman the Learned to Béla III (1095–1196): Hungarian Domestic Policy and Its Impact Upon Foreign Affairs* (New York, 1987) p. 237f.

[18] RHM 2:412; Marczali, *Enchiridion*, p. 134a. It further says that those of foreign birth may not obtain high public dignity in the realm 'sine consilio regni'. See a. 11; Marczali, *Enchiridion*, p. 138a; RHM 2:414.

[19] 'Nos igitur eorum petitioni in omnibus satisfacere cupientes, ut

tenemur...'; 'Et...hec nostra tam concessio, quam ordinatio sit...in perpetuum valitura'; *loc. cit.*, preface and a. 31.

[20] When, on August 20, he personally takes part in the law day; there, '...Et omnes servientes, qui voluerint, libere illuc conveniant'; *loc. cit.*, a. 1.

[21] '...Tam episcopi, quam alii iobagiones ac nobiles regni, universes et singuli, presentes et futuri,...statuimus, quod...'; a. 31, *loc. cit.* A. Timon, *Ungarische Verfassungs- und Rechtsgeschichte* (2nd ed., ed. F. Schiller; Berlin, 1904) p. 124f.

[22] Thus, the king complained to Rome, some nobles dared disobey him. This is evident from a papal reply; see Potthast, n. 6870; Theiner, n. 70.

[23] For the text, see W. Stubbs (ed.), *Select Charters of English Constitutional History* (8th ed., Oxford, 1895) p. 296ff. See also B. Lyon, *A Constitutional and Legal History of Medieval England* (New York, London, 1960) p. 310ff.; C. R. Cheney, *Innocent III and England*, vol. 9 of *Päpste und Papsttum* (Stuttgart, 1976) pp. 303ff. and 375ff.

[24] 'Rex eris, si recte facis, et si non facis, non eris.' See V. Balaguer, *Instituciones y reyes de Aragon* (Biblioteca Museo-Balaguer, 1896) p. 48; Timon, p. 124f.; R. B. Merriman, 'The Cortes of the Spanish Kingdoms', *American Historical Review* 16 (1911) 485ff. In Aragon, the idea of resistance remained unknown until 1287; see F. Kern, *Gottesgnadentum und Widerstandsrecht im frühen Mittelalter* (rev. ed. by R. Buckner; Munich, Cologne, 1954) p. 210, n. 452; H. Mitteis, *Der Staat des hohen Mittelalters* (8th ed., Weimar, 1968) p. 417.

[25] The wife of Emery was the daughter of Alfonso II, and a sister of Peter II. See H. Svrita (J. Zurita), *Indices rerum ab Aragoniae regibus gestarum ab initiis regni ad annum MCDX* (Caesaraugustae, 1578) 1:84. On the death of her husband, Queen Constance married Emperor Frederick II; she died in 1222 (*ibid.*, p. 103).

[26] Reeve Simon of Györ was born in Aragon. See RA, n. 393; CD 3/1:393; RA, n. 443; CD 3/2:140.

[27] See a. 31, in Marczali, *Enchiridion*, p. 143a; RHM 2:416f. One of the recipients, Pontius de Cruce, was grand master of the Templars in the realm and had accompanied the king on the crusade (RA, n. 143). The Hospitallers (of St. John) were established in the realm during the reign of Géza II; see D. Fuxhoffer and M. Czinár, *Monasteriologiae regni Hungariae* (Pest, 2 vols., 1858), II, 134ff. A member of the order, Julius Guncel(lus) 'de gener Kán', regularly witnessed the writs issued by Béla the junior king (RA, nn. 567, 570, 572, 574, etc.) and became archbishop of Spoleto in about 1220; MGH SS, 29:579, 33–37, and 580, 7–8.

[28] V. Fraknói, *Magyarország és a Szentszék* [Hungary and the Holy See] (Budapest, 3 vols., 1901–1903) 1:341.

[29] RA, n. 379. For the text of the 1351 *Decretum*, see Csiky, *Corpus*

Iuris 1:166ff.; Marczali, *Enchiridion*, p. 216ff. F. Döry (ed.), *Decreta regni Hungariae* (Budapest, 1976) p. 124ff., provides a better reading of it, esp. of a. IX. See further, F. Somogyi and F. L. Somogyi, 'The Constitutional Guarantee of 1351: The Decree of Louis the Great', in B. S. Vardy (ed.), *Louis the Great, King of Hungary and Poland* (New York, 1986) p. 429ff.

[30] The date is certainly proven from the letter of Pope Honorius III dated December 15, 1222. Potthast, n. 6900; CD 3/1:390f.; Theiner, n. 73; Székely, *Magyar történet*, p. 1330f.

[31] For example, despite the provisions of the 1222 Decree (a. 24), jewish officials had remained at their posts; CD 3/2:48. As early as 1221, Rome had warned the hungarian court about the preeminence of foreigners in Hungary and had encouraged the court to further the emancipation of slaves. Potthast, nn. 6939–40; Theiner, nn. 58–59.

[32] CD 3/1:407ff.; Hóman-Szekfü 1:497f.

[33] As is evident from the papal writ dated July 4, 1222; Potthast, n. 6870.

[34] *Ibid.*; CD 3/1:388f.; Theiner, n. 70.

[35] The 1222 Decree, a. 1, *loc. cit.*

[36] As is revealed in the papal writ cited in note 30 above.

[37] See L. J. Lekai, *The White Monks* (Okauchee, Wisc., 1953) p. 38; Lekai, 'Zirc 800 éve [The Abbey of Zirc 800 Years Old]', in D. Farkasfalvy (ed.), *Ciszteri lelkiség: Zirc alapításának 800 évfordulóján* [Cistercian Spirit: On the 800th anniversary of the Foundation of the Abbey of Zirc] (Eisenstadt, 1982) p. 7ff.; M. Heimbucher, *Die Orden und Kongregationen der katholischen Kirche* (3rd ed., Paderborn, 2 vols., 1933) 1:687ff.

[38] Theiner, n. 73; Székely, p. 1330f.; K. Pennington, *Pope and Bishops: The Papal Monarchy in the Twelfth and Thirteenth Centuries* (Philadelphia, 1984) p. 13ff.

[39] Theiner, n. 32.; MGH SS 29:579, 4–5; 23:911, 37–40.

[40] Theiner, n. 33; Potthast, n. 6001.

[41] Potthast, n. 6845; CD 3/1:384; Theiner, n. 67.

[42] '...Malivolis suggestionibus perversorum'; Theiner, n. 85.

[43] Theiner, n. 93; Potthast, n. 7174.

[44] Potthast, n. 7152; CD 7/5:234.

[45] Potthast, n. 7177; Theiner, n. 94.

[46] Potthast, n. 7189; Theiner, n. 97; CD 3/1:433.

[47] Potthast, n. 7190; Theiner, n. 98; CD 3/1:436. The loyal supporters of Béla must cause no further misunderstanding; Potthast, n. 7191; Theiner, n. 99; CD 3/1:437.

[48] Potthast, n. 7179.

[49] Potthast, n. 7177; Theiner, n. 94; and Potthast, n. 7193; CD 3/1:438.

[50] See the papal writ addressed to Robert of Veszprém; Potthast, n. 7175; CD 3/1:432. Also to Ugrin of Kalocsa; Potthast, n. 7176; CD 3/1:433. To the bishop of Vác, Potthast, n. 7178; Theiner, n. 95.

[51] Potthast, n. 7189; Theiner, n. 97; CD 3/1:435.

52 RA, n. 261. Redrafted at the papal curia, April 26, 1231; Potthast, n. 8728; Theiner, n. 169. The 1211 charter; RA n. 124; CD 3/1:106ff.; see further, CD 3/1:379ff.; F. Zimmermann and C. Werner, *Urkundenbuch zur Geschichte der Deutschen in Siebenbürgen* (Hermannstadt, 1892) 1:11ff. and 17f.

53 See Potthast, n. 6918; CD 3/1:405; and Potthast, n. 7115. Theiner, n. 87: 'nullum praeter Romanum pontificem habent episcopum.'

54 Potthast, n. 7116; Theiner, n. 88.

55 Potthast, n. 7229; Theiner, n. 108.

56 This petition was acknowledged by a papal bull; Potthast, n. 7232; CD 3/1:459f.: '... praelati Hungariae, ut ordinem Hosp. S. Mariae Teutonicorum exceptum et incolas in terra Burce nullo modo molestent.'

57 Potthast, n. 7231; Theiner, n. 106.

58 Potthast, n. 7431; Theiner, n. 124.

59 Potthast, n. 7427; Theiner, n. 122.

60 Potthast, n. 7494; Theiner, n. 135.

61 Potthast, n. 7428; Theiner, n. 125.

62 Potthast, n. 7432; Theiner, n. 123; CD 3/2:43f.

63 As may be concluded from a papal writ; Potthast, n. 7494; Theiner, n. 128; CD 3/2:53f.

64 This is recorded in the papal letter, of October 27, 1225, mentioned above; CD 3/2:58f.; Theiner, n. 135. The tone of the letter is not too friendly.

65 Potthast, n. 7531; Theiner, n. 136; CD 3/2:74ff. Later, Pope Gregory IX, in Potthast, n. 8991; Theiner, n. 183.

66 As of March 17, 1225; in Potthast, n. 7382; Theiner, n. 116. Katona, *Historia critica* 5:481.

67 Potthast, n. 7646; Theiner, n. 140; CD 3/2:27f. Also, a letter of March 13, 1226, in Potthast, n. 7545; Theiner, n. 139.

68 Potthast, n. 7547; Theiner, n. 141. The pontiff died on March 18, 1226 (Potthast 1:677) and was succeeded by Hugo Anagni: Gregory IX.

69 He obtained it, witness the papal writ dated July 31, 1227, in Potthast, n. 7984; Theiner, n. 154; CD 3/2:109ff.; Katona, *Historia critica* 5:109f.

70 Potthast, nn. 8153 and 8154; Theiner, nn. 156 and 157.

71 Potthast, n. 8155; CD 3/2:154ff.

72 Potthast, n. 8318; CD 3/2:155f.; Theiner, n. 158.

73 At a later date, March 20, 1232: '... miramur non modicum'; in Potthast, n. 8899; Theiner, n. 178; CD 3/2:244.

74 Potthast, n. 8348; CD 3/2:157f.

75 Katona, *Historia critica* 5:544f.

76 As, for example, the papal letter of May 15, 1230, in Potthast, n. 8554; Theiner, n. 164.

77 As of August 15, 1230; Potthast 1:725. Also, Potthast, n. 8430; Theiner, n. 160; CD 3/2:165f.

[78] Potthast, n. 8671; CD 3/2:241ff.; Theiner, n. 168.
[79] Potthast, n. 8668; Theiner, n. 165; further, Potthast, n. 8670; Theiner, n. 166.
[80] RA, n. 479; RHM 2:428ff.; Marczali, *Enchiridion*, p. 134bff.; Theiner 1:105ff., esp. p. 109f. (n. 187); Hóman-Szekfü 1:507f.; Katona, *Historia critica* 5:628ff.
[81] Marczali, *Enchiridion*, p. 142b; RHM 2:432.
[82] *Ibid.*, art. 2.
[83] *Ibid.*, aa. 3, 17, and 8—in that order.
[84] Decree of 1222, a. 21, *loc. cit.*
[85] 'Septimum apud palatinum, . . . quod ipsam scripturam pre oculis semper habens, nec ipse deviet in aliquo in predictis, nec regem, nel nobiles, seu alios consenciat deviare . . .'; Decree of 1222, a. 31, *loc. cit.* Compare with the Decree of 1231, a. 3; Marczali, *Enchiridion*, p. 135b.
[86] ' . . . Premissa legitima admonitione nos vinculo excommunicationis et nos innodandi habeat potestatem'; Decree of 1231, conclusion. See Marczali, *Enchirdion*, p. 142b; RHM 2:432. To be put into effect; see Theiner 1:107ff. (n. 187); compare to Potthast, n. 8668; Theiner, n. 165.
[87] On this, see the papal writ of February 28, 1231, in Potthast, n. 8670; Theiner, n. 166.
[88] RA, n. 485; CD 3/2:299ff.; Theiner, n. 180; Katona, *Historia critica* 5:641f.
[89] See RA, n. 439; AOU 6:440ff.
[90] In 1222, the grand master may have been Pontius de Cruce, who had accompanied Andrew II on his crusade. RA, n. 353; Theiner, n. 143. Rembald (RA, n. 485) had previously visited Rome; Potthast, n. 7431; Theiner, n. 124.
[91] RA, nn. 393 and 443; CD 3/2:397 and 140, respectively.
[92] See above, note 88.
[93] ' . . . Cum tam ego, quam regni mei incolae ab uberibus mellificiis sanctae matris ecclesiae tamquam filii degeneres excludamur'; Theiner, n. 180.
[94] Potthast, n. 8975; Theiner, n. 181.
[95] As of August 22, 1232; in Potthast, n. 8991; Theiner, n. 183.
[96] Potthast, n. 8993 (and compare to n. 8023); Theiner, nn. 185 and 186, respectively.
[97] See Fraknói 1:53f.
[98] Potthast, n. 8671; Theiner, n. 168; CD 3/2:303f.
[99] Potthast, n. 9273; Theiner, n. 196; CD 3/2:371.
[100] Potthast, n. 9274; Theiner, n. 197; CD 3/2:372.
[101] RA, n. 599; CD 3/2:316ff.; Theiner, n. 208.
[102] RA, n. 604; Theiner, n. 209. Compare with Potthast, n. 9272, and Theiner, n. 195; Katona, *Historia critica* 5:708.

MARTIN LUTHER AND MONASTICISM

Bede K. Lackner, O. Cist.
University of Texas at Arlington

HISTORIANS TODAY TEND to agree that Martin Luther was a religious and oratorical genius and an expert on the human heart. Unfortunately, less clarity prevails among them about other aspects of the great reformer's life and work. Thus, with regard to monasticism, it should at last be realized that Luther was not a monk in the strict sense of the word but, rather, a religious, a member of the Augustinian Hermits whom Pope Pius V would attach to the mendicant orders in 1567. The monastic vows of stability, conversion of morals, and obedience became in the non-monastic religious orders—among them the mendicant orders—the vows of poverty, chastity, and obedience, vows which Luther professed as a young adult but subsequently combatted as a reformer. Thus, when Luther assailed monastic vows, he actually meant religious vows. And when he talked about monasticism, he did not differentiate between early monasticism, which was not clericalized, and medieval monasticism which, after the eleventh century, ordained its monks to the priesthood and reinforced traditional monastic chastity with priestly celibacy, from which church law allowed no exception or dispensation. This means that Luther argued not so much against the monk, but against the monk-priest, and, when he reasoned against perpetual vows—above all, the vow of celibacy—given his time-bound knowledge of monastic history, he was simply unmindful of how the medieval clericalization of the monastic order had decisively changed the nature of the monastic commitment to celibacy.

These preliminaries are necessary for a proper understanding of this paper. Its thesis may be summarized as follows: the reformer is generally portrayed as a mortal enemy of monasticism. Indeed, Luther said and did many things on individual occasions which may, or could, be used in support of such a characterization. Yet, as will be pointed out in some detail, Luther's actions and utterances on the subject of monasticism are, on balance, much more positive and nuanced. To put it briefly: as all the experts agree, the reformer was greatly affected by monasticism. This can be deduced, above all, from his spirituality and from the exclusively biblical orientation of his prayer life. Because of this, he admired the monastic heroes and saints and clearly admitted their accomplishments. Moreover, he himself wished to be a good monk. He fought against abuses and obstacles and, in a way, 'lost' his monastic vocation precisely because he wished to uphold the monastic ideal against increasingly overwhelming odds. His criticism of abuses was quite often inspired by a hidden or misguided love and a desire to offer help. One could even say that the reformer remained a 'monk' all his life. No one sees Luther as a mere layman or family man; he was more than that. There is in him the undeniable additional element of a total (monastic?) surrender to God and a total devotion to the cause of God. In many ways Luther remained, throughout his life, a product of the monastery who, even after the break, was quite willing to preserve the genuine good found in christian monasticism.

In attempting to understand Luther, one must also consider whether Luther's statements—for instance, on monasticism, women, marriage, the peasants, the Turks, or the Jews—should be taken in their specific context as inspired perhaps by emotions of the moment or, rather, in their totality. In addition, one should avoid vernacular translations—including english ones—which abound in inaccuracies.[1] Instead, one should consult and refer to the authentic text of the Weimar Edition (Weimar Ausgabe: WA). A new english translation of Luther's treatise on monasticism is, therefore, indispensable if one is to do justice to its famous author in that language.

Martin Luther began to think seriously about monasticism at least by the year 1505. After completing his basic studies at the University of Erfurt as a *magister artium*, he enrolled, heeding his father's wish, in the faculty of law. He ended his legal studies a few weeks later when, in a storm near Stottersheim, fearful for his life and salvation, he made the vow 'Help me, Saint Anne, I shall become a monk' and entered, in haste, the convent of the Augustinian Hermits on 17 July 1505. Although Luther took his vow under great stress, he felt bound by it, in spite of his father's opposition and the remonstrances of his friends. Luther's attitude seems understandable only if we assume that he had previously, and, possibly, for a long time, considered the option of becoming a religious. How could he have made a sudden vow of this nature and have kept it if he had never thought about this possibility before? It is, therefore, quite likely that, prior to his sudden decision, Luther had weighed the idea that his salvation might be more secure in a monastery than as a layman in the world. Moreover, in the summer of 1505, Martin was almost twenty-two years old, mature enough to have an idea about his vocation without needing his father's permission to enter the religious life. As Martin described his father's opposition many years later, Hans Luther was 'fearful about my weakness because I was then...just entering my twenty-second year—that is, to use Saint Augustine's words—still "clothed in hot youth." '[2]

The Erfurt convent, which had some seventy members, belonged to the strict (that is, reformed) observance of the Augustinian Hermits. It was not wealthy. It was one of the more than thirty monasteries of the Saxon Congregation governed, since 1504, by a new constitution which sought to strengthen the members' commitment to the *vita communis*, the ideal of Saint Augustine.[3] Luther was a postulant for about two months and then began the year-long trial period or novitiate, as prescribed by the augustinian *Rule* and canon law. His novice master was, as Luther recalled in 1532, 'a truly outstanding man and, under his damned cowl, a true Christian.'[4] After this year of probation and formation, during which one could leave freely, Luther pronounced his religious vows in 1506, vows which were, at that time, final and permanent. He promised to live 'without personal possessions', 'in chastity' and 'obedience' according to the *Rule* of Saint Augustine 'until death'.[5] Hence, when Luther wrote to his father in 1521, 'it is almost sixteen years since I became a monk, taking the vows against your will and without your knowledge',[6] he could not possibly have meant it literally, for more than a full year had elapsed between his entrance and the subsequent profession of his vows.

The novice thoroughly familiarized himself with the *Rule* of Saint Augustine which prescribed the *vita communis*, the 'common life', the imitation of the life of the early christian community in Jerusalem as described by the *Acts of the Apostles*. The *Rule* also called for unanimity, communal ownership, prayer, fasting, good discipline, obedience, and the duty to fight the vice of pride. During the early years of his religious life Luther cherished the monastic vows and upheld the augustinian ideal of community life.[7] He vigorously defended the augustinian *Rule* against the humanist Jakob Wimpfeling who questioned Augustine's authorship: 'Why are you fighting, old man and miserable worm? Why do you correct the Church of God? Why do you propose such utterly impure lies?'[8] Moreover, Martin was an exemplary religious who took his duties and obligations quite seriously. As he remembered later in life: 'It is true, I was a fervent religious and strictly kept the rules of my order.' 'I wanted to be a holy and fervent monk and prepared myself with great piety for Mass and prayer.' 'I have diligently read all of the pope's books.'⁹

Accordingly, Luther was most generous in his praises of the religious life. In 1507, the year of his ordination to the priesthood, he characterized it as 'a beautifully reposeful and divine life.' In 1515, he added: 'I believe that, in two hundred years, it has never been better to become a religious than just now.'¹⁰ The suggestion that Luther was ill-humored, a troublemaker, or a reluctant practitioner of religious obedience is, therefore, nothing but a legend. As Josef Lortz, a prominent modern catholic historian, has concluded, Luther's religious life was 'correct' until 1517.¹¹ Even Heinrich Denifle, the acerbic dominican critic of the reformer, has had to admit: 'Indeed, in all his religious life Luther never spoke a syllable against true monasticism.'¹²

There were reasons for this. For one, the community's rule prescribed a regular study of the Scripture. Thus, unlike the practice in many other monasteries, the Bible was not kept from the young religious. As Luther himself reminisced, in the monastery 'the monks gave him a Bible bound in red leather. He made himself so familiar with it that he knew what was in every passage and when some passage was mentioned, he knew at once where it was to be found.'¹³ On another occasion he added: 'After I entered the monastery, I began to read the Bible and to reread it over and again.'¹⁴ Accordingly, he concluded: 'If boasting would amount to anything, I could boast as well. For I have spent days and nights in this study, and I must remain a student of this subject. I resume it every single day.'¹⁵ In time he acquired a prodigious knowledge of the Bible and was able to quote long passages from memory without any difficulty. But more important than this 'formal' control was his *personal* rapport with the Bible. He came to call it his 'bride', and so cherished this intimacy that the Bible quickly took a hold on his whole being.¹⁶

But this was not his only monastic legacy. In his religious community Luther grew as a man of prayer. He ascribed to prayer an importance which cannot be overstated.

This explains why, throughout his life, he remained within the great prayer tradition of monasticism. This also explains why, even after the break, Luther continued to be the familiar 'Pater Martin Luther'. He continued to recommend what had been obvious to him from the recitation of the monastic prayer hours: 'It is good to let prayer be the first thing in the morning and the last thing at night.' In his inimitable way, he called for a prayer that was truly genuine: 'If the snout blabbers but the heart is not there, the glory of God will be violated.' In addition, he stressed the importance of meditation, the material of which was to be drawn from the Ten Commandments, the Psalms, the Lord's Prayer, and the words of Scripture. This meditation was to proceed through four states: (1) a consideration of the doctrine or teaching of the passage at hand; (2) thanksgiving and gratitude elicited by this reflection; (3) an examination of one's own life coupled with a petition for forgiveness because, as he insisted: 'He who does not confess [his sins] is not a Christian'; and (4) the opening of the heart in order to make a petition or request.[17] Luther used and molded the material of his meditation into a 'little crown'—an expression which could easily remind some readers of the prayer beads of the Rosary. Of course, the central point in Luther's spiritual life was the First Commandment, which proclaims the sublime majesty of God—a God of anger, but also of love, as shown by Jesus on the cross—hence Luther's lifelong struggle for the glory of God which, not many years later, would be echoed by his great counterpart, Ignatius of Loyola, who also issued the call: *Omnia ad majorem Dei gloriam*.[18]

Luther's superiors judged Martin to be a reliable and talented member of the congregation and sent him, therefore, to study at the university. In time, the friar obtained the doctorate and became a professor.[19] In his early lectures (on the *Psalms*, *Romans*, and *Galatians*), and even between 1517 and 1519, Luther held on to traditional monastic views, which Bernhard Lohse has characterized as 'Festhalten am monastischen Ideal'. Luther retained, for instance, the traditional distinction between commandments and precepts as well as the differentiation between monks and laymen; he also believed in the possibility of spiritual advancement, in the special worth of the monastic state and the vows of chastity and obedience, and in the importance of free works, without which, according to tradition, no person can be saved.[20]

Moreover, Luther fought for his monastic convictions by speaking out against all kinds of abuses prevalent in contemporary religious houses. At first he tended to criticize individuals or certain types of monks. Among the latter he singled out the so-called *observantes*, the modern-day followers of the Pharisees, who relied excessively on a meticulous observance of the rules and on external religious discipline. He warned them against the danger of self-assertion and of not noticing that, beneath the cloak of humility, pride in its many forms may actually be hiding. The proud believe that they fulfill the law out of their own righteousness and, therefore, do not admit sin. They seek Christ in a carnal way, not to be saved by him, but to convince themselves that they are already saved. He also condemned the egotism of those monks who joined God for the sake of gaining secular honors, or to acquire spiritual advantages in the life to come. Besides, he reproached those monks, who, seeking 'perfection', fled the company of the poor, as the worst of all monks. For in their selfish love, they gave up true love and, pursuing individual salvation, remained unconcerned about the salvation of others; thus, they violated the *lex Christi*, the law of Christ, namely, the love of neighbor. For true love binds the Christian to his neighbor so that, in the question of salvation, there is no room whatsoever for any autonomous Christianity. Finally, he strongly denounced externalism in prayer.[21]

After 1517, Luther's criticism became more general. He censured a long list of vices: the lukewarm performance of the prayer hours, monastic greed, the seeking of temporal rewards from God, quarrels about observances, reliance on personal works, practicing vices under the cloak of piety, gluttony, the failure to proclaim the word of God, and the multiplication of godless vows to attain security and thus be freed from the need of relying on God alone.[22] By 1520, he came to the conclusion, expressed in his *Address to the Christian Nobility*, that there were too many monasteries which simply drained Germany of talent and revenue. According to Luther, the best thing would be to have no monasteries at all.[23]

But Friar Martin was also critical of himself. Already in the fall of 1516, he wrote: 'I ought to have two secretaries, for I hardly do anything all day long but write letters. For that reason I do not know if I am not always repeating the same thing. I am preacher at the monastery and table reader. Every day I am asked to preach in the parish church. I supervise the studies of the students; I am vicar of the district, and that means eleven times prior. I am in charge of the fish pond at Leitzkau; I represent the people of Herzberg at the court of Torgau; I lecture on Paul and I am assembling [material for] a commentary on the Psalter.... Seldom does full time remain for my reciting of the [prayer] hours and for celebrating Mass.'[24] In 1519, he told Johann von Staupitz, his religious superior: 'I am a man exposed to and enveloped by society, gluttony, carnal excitement, negligence, and other bothers, beside those which weigh upon me on account of my office.'[25] In the following year he complained: 'I know that I do not practice what I teach.'[26] And, in 1521, he openly confessed: 'Poor man that I am, I grow cold in spirit. I... am lazy in prayer. Let us watch and pray.'[27] Later in his life, he summed up his experiences: 'When I was a monk I was overworked.'[28]

In addition to being overburdened, Luther was also weakened by his asceticism and immoderate self-chastisements: 'I have martyred myself and tortured myself to pieces; I did not eat, I wore no [warm] clothing and I froze.'[29] Hence, he concluded: 'If I had continued much longer I would have tortured myself to death with vigils, prayer, reading, and other work.'[30] He asked himself in

1539: 'Why did I burden my body with fasts, vigils and the cold? Because I strove to be certain by such works of attaining the forgiveness of my sins.'[31]

Luther was, clearly, an exemplary religious who took his duties and responsibilities very seriously. But, as time went on, he became increasingly aware of his own insufficiency and, in corresponding measure, of the overwhelming greatness of God. This awareness, foreshadowed already in his description of the utter confusion he felt during his first Mass, gradually paralyzed him. Almost thirty years later he explained his experiences: 'Even though I lived irreproachably as a monk, I felt myself to be a sinner before God, and my conscience greatly troubled me. I could not believe that he was placated by my satisfaction. I did not love—indeed I hated—*that* God who punished sinners.'[32] Even confession did not ease his troubled conscience: 'I used to be contrite, to confess and sedulously perform my allotted penance. And yet my conscience could never give me certainty; I always doubted and said: "You did not do that correctly. You were not contrite enough. You left that out of your confession." The more I tried to remedy an uncertain, weak, and afflicted conscience with the traditions of men, the more I found myself each day uncertain, weak, and troubled.'[33] He revealed with an amazing frankness: 'When I was a monk, I immediately believed that it was all over with my salvation every time I experienced the concupiscence of the flesh, that is to say, an evil movement against one of the brethren, of envy, or anger, or hatred, or of jealousy, and so forth. I tried various remedies. I went to confession every day, but that did not help me at all. For this concupiscence of the flesh was always returning so that I could never find peace, but was everlastingly tormented with the thought, "You have committed such and such a sin; you are still a prey to jealousy, to impatience and the rest. It did you no good to receive holy orders, and your good works are simply useless."'[34] He was convinced that 'we are unable to pray [properly] and will not be heard unless we are wholly pure and without sins, like the saints in heaven.'[35] Looking back on these trials, he wrote in 1534: 'I have been a monk for fifteen years. Yet I derived no consolation from my baptism but always thought: "When will you become pious and do enough that you will find a merciful God?"'[36]

These experiences coincided with a gradual change in Luther's theology, especially after his 'Tower Experience', and his new understanding of the Church and religious life. (The latter topic has been extensively treated by Bernhard Lohse, in his *Mönchtum und Reformation*.) Actually, from the very beginning of his religious life, Luther had an independent view of ascetical practices. He had his doubts about late medieval teachings on humility. Nor did he greatly stress, as had been customary, that the monastic vows were another baptism that wiped away sins. He did not use the then traditional terminology about the human body and the state of marriage. And, while he talked about progress and spiritual growth, he clearly disliked excessive demands made in the name of obedience.[37]

The same thing could be observed in his lectures. Already in his first *Lectures on the Psalms*, Luther did not characterize the monastic life as a special imitation of Christ, the apostles, and the Jerusalem community. The implication was, since the New Testament is binding on all Christians, there is little justification for the monastic virtues as distinct from the demands of the Gospel, or for the belief that the monastic life as such was more meritorious than the life of a layperson. He also called for a new understanding of the relationship between baptism and the monastic vows. In the *Lectures on Romans*, Luther again stressed the oneness of the christian life and rejected every attempt to set up a more perfect way in the following of God's will. Man only has the choice of listening to God or refusing to listen, to turn disobedient.[38]

In these lectures Luther also developed a clearer understanding of concupiscence, which caused him to abhor the idea of spiritual progress. Moreover, he began to stress the idea of christian freedom, a gift of divine grace. In the

Lectures on Galatians Luther proclaimed that perfection and holiness are not merely the business of monks, for there are saints also in the world. This means that a person's status in life made no difference in this regard. He saw in the idea of spiritual growth not so much a belonging to a state of perfection as, rather, an effort to strive toward perfection.[39] And while he still believed that without works—prayer, fasting, vigils, good acts—no one would be saved, he explained that no one will be justified on the basis of his works but, rather, on the basis of an 'inner justification' which will grow in the measure in which external justification decreases. Hence, there is no difference between the rich and the poor, or between one monastic order or another. Estate, rank, and order do not produce faith. Differentiations—for instance, the distinction between layman and monk—are actually obstacles to a truly christian life. Luther also pointed out that there is already an essential link between the monastic vows and baptism, so that these vows could not claim to be a second baptism.[40] Then, in 1518, Luther developed a new understanding of church law. To him the 'spiritual Church' was ruled by divine law, while the 'general Church' was a society governed by human law. The laws of the Roman Church are therefore, human laws, and its vows—for instance, the vow of celibacy—are mere human promises. Since the vow of celibacy has no scriptural basis, it is not a divine law.[41] In 1519, Luther made a comparison between marriage and the monastic vocation. The latter is, obviously, a life of greater suffering, even though it has its advantages: 'For, a religious state, if it stands right, shall be of sufferings and torment, that he [the monk] may have more exercise of his baptism than in the married state, and that, by such torment, he may accustom himself to receive death joyously, and thus soon attain the end of his baptism.'[42] In 1520, in the *Address to the Christian Nobility*, Luther again stressed that the monastic vows had not been instituted by Christ but were human inventions which transformed man's free service into a permanent bondage. He urged that no more monastic vows be taken or at least that no one should enter a monastery before the age of thirty. And he expressed the hope that no more monasteries would be established. But, since there were still too many of them, he suggested that they be combined by uniting, for instance, ten convents into one house, though the very best remedy would be to have no monasteries at all.[43] Finally, he concluded, in his pamphlet *On the Babylonian Captivity of the Church*, that the monastic vows were contrary to the freedom which has been given to the Christian in baptism.[44]

These were clearly new teachings. Seeking to pinpoint the turning point, Sarenac has proposed that Luther gave up the traditional monastic ideal already in his *Lectures on Romans* (1515–1516), in which he spoke about a monasticism that resembled its medieval counterpart only in name.[45] However, at that time Luther did not call for a reformed monasticism, but merely proposed different motives for which the monastic state should be embraced. Years later, in 1519, Luther still accepted the orders and monasteries that were then in existence and did not talk about a new type of monasticism. Even in March 1520, he still held that the monastic vows were more binding than church law. And in his *Address to the Christian Nobility* he allowed the monasteries to serve as schools, as he thought things had been in the early Church. All this shows that Luther did not reject monasticism or the monastic vows in the period between 1520 and the spring of 1521. But he proposed new ideas: the linkage of the monastic vows to baptism and the claim that canon law was of human, not divine, origin, which soon caused Luther to take more fateful steps.[46]

Matters progressed rapidly during Luther's stay at the Wartburg. The turbulences at Wittenberg, the revolutionary theses of Karlstadt about priestly and monastic celibacy, statements made by Melanchthon on the monastic life, the wholesale marriage of priests and monks, and the question of celibacy in the case of priests and religious who opted to remain in the religious life, caused Luther to take up the question of monastic vows once again, in a more systematic fashion, and to draft, in September 1521, his *Themata de votis*, presenting two series of theses on the monastic vows for public scrutiny.

In the *Themata* Luther argued that, since man is justified by faith, vows made for the purpose of obtaining salvation are blasphemous sins against the faith. Vows enchain man's conscience. And, as experience shows, hardly anyone has made his vows with the right intention. Hence they should be given up, and monks should 'fall away' from their vows for the sake of their salvation. For the prerequisites of a vow are faith and freedom. This evangelical freedom is a divine gift which is given to man in baptism. It retains a life-long validity and may not be restricted by any attachment to a certain type of work, place, thing, or person. From this it follows that vows must not be observed as binding obligations but as free undertakings. This freedom remains before God, whether one has taken monastic vows or not. In fact, God does not recognize a vow that is opposed to the freedom of the Gospel, a freedom man cannot give up even if he wishes to do so. Luther additionally stressed that the monastic vows are not real vows, because already in baptism man has vowed to cultivate a spirit of poverty and obedience; hence there is no difference between a monk and a layman. And, if poverty and obedience are not justifiable as perpetual vows, neither can chastity be made into such a vow. Thus the *Themata* deprived the monastic state of everything that would raise it above the layman's vocation or make it a state of higher perfection. It simply became one vocation (*Beruf*) a person could choose.[47] But, even in that case, the vows must be free, whether they are observed temporarily or in perpetuity. For they remain within the context of the faith and christian freedom.[48]

Already before the publication of the *Themata*, on 6 August 1521, Luther wrote to Spalatin: 'Good Lord! Will our people at Wittenberg give wives even to monks? They will not push a wife on me!'[49] But the exodus continued, and, in November, thirteen religious left the community of Wittenberg in what Luther called a 'tumultuous exodus'.[50] Moreover, Luther experienced difficulties of his own at this particular period of time, for he told Melanchthon, on 3 August 1521: 'You should know how greatly I am tormented.'[51] Somewhat later he confided to Johannes Lang: 'Physically I am healthy and well cared for, but I am also thoroughly buffeted by sins and temptations.'[52]

All these experiences caused Luther to finalize his views about the monastic life. Accordingly, he wrote to Nicholas Gerbel, on 1 November 1521: 'Philip and I have a powerful conspiracy concerning the vows of monks and priests; they have to be abolished and made void.... For nothing sounds worse to my ears than the words "nun", "monk", and "priest."'[53] On 11 November, he advised his friend Georg Spalatin: 'I have decided to attack monastic vows and to free the young people from that hell of celibacy.... I am writing partly because of my own temptations and partly because I am indignant.'[54] Luther completed his definitive statement on the subject, *De votis monasticis judicium*[55] in November 1521. He did not intend it to be a controversial writing but simply wished to help monks and nuns, those who had left their convents and those who were on the point of doing so, to develop clarity of conscience. Luther viewed it as a major work and claimed: 'The pamphlet is in my opinion the most solid of all that I have written and, if I may boast, even invincible.'[56] In its five parts Luther argued that the monastic vows are contrary to Scripture, the faith, evangelical freedom, the commandments, and human reason (*ratio*).

In the first section he proposed that monastic vows are dangerous, 'because they are without the authority and example of Scripture.' But, where God's commission is absent, no vow or rule may be set up by man. And, since the will of God, found in Scriptures, is the same for everyone, its injunctions may not be divided into counsels for monks and precepts for all others. Nor may the christian life called for by the Gospel be divided into a perfect state for monks and an imperfect state for the christian people. For whatever the Gospel enjoins is binding on everyone. Besides, there is no justification in Scripture for singling out poverty, chastity, and obedience as 'evangelical counsels', and the Church has no authority to change the Gospel, which is common to all. Thus, what the monk professes in his vows is actually demanded of every Christian, and the latter must rely not on externals but on Scripture.[57]

In the second instance, Luther contended that the monastic vows are contrary to the faith. They are not an expression, or outgrowth, of the faith which trusts in God's mercy, seeks justification from Christ alone, and fulfills the baptismal commitments free of human encumbrances. For they are man-made and, relying on 'law' and 'work', deny Christ. They do not forgive sin. They do not provide personal growth or growth in the faith. To bring the faith to fruition is part of everyone's baptismal responsibilities and not an obligation taken on by man-made monastic vows.[58]

Thirdly, Luther claimed that the monastic vows are irreconcilable with the liberty given by the Gospel to every Christian. This liberty is a baptismal gift and entails both internal freedom—freedom of conscience—and freedom from works, and may not be given up or be made into a vow. And since God did not prescribe any vows, only free vows are acceptable to him, that is, vows which are not made necessary for justification and salvation. Vows must be free and may, therefore, be given up. Thus celibacy may not be made into a permanent vow, but all should instead uphold their common 'virginity of the faith'. Because perpetual vows are against the basic freedom of a Christian, Luther proposed this solution: 'Go ahead and take whatever vows you wish to take, as long as you do no injury to the mandate of liberty.'[59]

Luther's fourth argument was that perpetual vows are contrary to the commandments of God. They are, above all, against the First Commandment, which demands fullness of faith and leaves no room for any particular sanctity to be procured through individual works. Moreover, vows also violate the commandment of loving one's neighbor—one's parents and fellow men—for, through the vow of obedience, they restrict the monk to the love of his religious superior and confreres. They prevent him from keeping the divine commandment to love all men. Thus, the love of God and love of neighbor, called for by baptism, become impossible to attain.[60]

In the last place, Luther set out to prove that the monastic vows are challenged even by human reason. For, by standard practice, impossible vows are routinely dispensed, and religious superiors grant numerous exemptions in individual cases. However, no dispensation is ever given from the vow of celibacy, even if it should become an unbearable burden. But, if dispensations are legitimately granted in certain cases, they must be given in all cases, since Scripture knows nothing about perpetual vows. Thus, to divide the vows into absolute vows and non-essential vows is a human invention. Reason suggests, therefore, that 'all vows are temporary and changeable'.[61]

In *De votis monasticis* Luther considered the raison d'être of monasticism and used, for the first time, an argument based on human reason (*ratio*). His conclusion was that a vow remains binding only in the sense of the jewish Law—which had been abrogated by Christ. Thus, the decisive point in the whole treatise was the argument of evangelical freedom which, he insisted, 'is of divine right'.[62] Accordingly, any vow made against this freedom is null and void; hence it is wrong to say that the religious life is necessary to obtain salvation. A true monk is, thus, the Christian who lives simultaneously both under the vows and free of them. This means monastic vows should be made with the proviso that there remains the freedom to leave the monastery if this should be warranted. As examples Luther gave: 'I vow to thee obedience, chastity, and poverty, together with the whole *Rule* of Saint Augustine until death. I do it of my own free will, which means that I would be free to change my mind if it seemed good.'[63] Or: 'I take the vow of chastity for as long as it is possible to keep it; if, however, I am unable to keep it, then let me be permitted to marry.'[64] Whereas previously Luther had opposed the idea that a monk might give up a vow—for instance, the vow of chastity—in case he was unable to fulfill it, explaining that a complete fulfillment of the commandments was simply impossible, he now proclaimed that the option of marriage makes the fulfillment of the commandment of chastity possible. He explained it thus: 'But if I am able to observe the commandments of God but not the vows, then the vow must recede so that the commandments may remain and vow and commandment not be transgressed in license.'[65]

With all these assertions, and especially with his emphasis on christian freedom, Luther called for reforms which undermined monasticism. He allowed the possibility of making vows but denied that they had any permanent binding force. This clearly destroyed the very foundations of traditional monasticism.[66]

Given the widespread concubinage that had discredited both celibacy and the religious state throughout sixteenth-century Europe, the preceding arguments proved quite attractive to many of Luther's contemporaries. But the reformer felt uncomfortable at the sight of so many religious leaving their monasteries who, no doubt, made use of his newly proclaimed principle of christian liberty: 'I see that many of our monks are rushing out [of the monastery] for the same reason for which they had entered, namely for the sake of the stomach and the comfort of the body. Through them Satan seeks to raise a big stench against the good odor of our words.'[67] However Luther himself wished to remain in the cloister. As he told Wenzeslaus Link on 18 December 1521: 'I shall of course remain in this state, unless this world of ours becomes a different one.'[68] Still, in 1522, the augustinian chapter gave its members the freedom to leave the order and regulated the lives of those who wished to remain by assigning to them the task to teach the Scripture or else pursue manual labor to provide for the livelihood of the teaching brethren.[69]

After publishing *De votis monasticis*, Luther did not again discuss monasticism in any great detail. He remained somewhat ambivalent on the subject. He argued in this famous treatise: 'I wish that all monasteries were uprooted, extinguished, and abolished, as indeed they ought to be.'[70] In 1523, he similarly proclaimed: 'All monasteries ought to be completely annihilated or abandoned.'[71] In the same year, he helped nine cistercian nuns escape their convent at Nimbschen in Saxony, as he explained in a letter to Leonhard Koppe, a citizen of Torgau.[72] In 1525, he married one of these nuns, Katharina von Bora, thus making a complete break with his former way of life.[73] Five years later, he expressed satisfaction that 'Since I attacked the monastic life... the monks have become fewer.'[74] In 1531, he rejoiced that he was no longer a prisoner of his monastic past and that he had changed so much that whenever he saw a monk with his bodily eyes he thought he was beholding a monster.[75] Finally, in 1540, he boasted that the papists would not get any monk from the great number of students 'here in Wittenberg'.[76]

Yet, in spite of such strong words, Luther was not entirely negative toward monasticism. He revered, for instance, the heroes of the monastic past and often extolled Bernard of Clairvaux: 'I regard Saint Bernard as the most pious of all monks and prefer him to all the others.' The abbot of Clairvaux '... was a man so pious, holy, and chaste that I think he deserves to be put ahead of all other monks.' Luther believed that Bernard is saved because he was a true monk who placed his trust in Christ and, in spite of his monastic vows, lived in christian freedom.[77] Even in *De votis monasticis* he allowed: 'If there were such Bernards in monasteries, they could be tolerated because they would, on their part, observe the serious injunctions of Paul.'[78] To Albrecht, the margrave of Brandenburg, he wrote in December 1523: 'If monastic orders declared their laws and regulations to be a matter of choice and did not require the... congregations to fulfill them as something necessary and useful for salvation or life, then they ought to be tolerated.'[79] And, in 1530, he told the clergy of Augsburg: 'I have not put the monks down by an uprising, but by my doctrine.'[80] Four years later he confessed: 'I have truly neither wished nor done evil to the papists, but I only sought to point them to Christ the truth.'[81] In like manner he explained in 1535: 'In truth, we persecute no one; we oppress or kill no human being.'[82] In 1538, he spoke in support of the nuns of Herford, whom he described as 'very pious maidens who had always lived in unity from the labors of their hands.' He argued: 'One should allow such nuns to stay at their pleasure, like the rural monasteries which princes founded for noble persons. . . . I should especially like to see the rural monasteries and those that have been endowed to stay, to take care of noble persons and poor ministers. Nor have I proposed anything else from the beginning.'[83] Incidents like these have caused Nicolaus Heutger, a modern lutheran scholar, to conclude: 'The Reformer [was] basically conservative. In a number of utterances, including *De votis monasticis*, he would give the monasteries a chance to continue, although with a different prefix, for instance, by assigning to them educational tasks.'[84]

Luther's views, as ultimately formulated in *De votis monasticis*, have been analyzed by Scheel, Sarenac, Lohse, Denifle, Grisar, Esnault, and Kurten (that is, by both Protestants and Catholics) from a theological point of view.[85] Other commentators have endeavored to reduce Luther's position to one root. Thus, according to Carl Volz, Luther's '. . . primary concern was the irreconcilability of monasticism with the doctrine of grace.'[86] In Heutger's view, the reformer '. . . called for a witness of the faith not in the exceptional situation of the monastery, but in the very center of daily life: in the family and in the performance of one's personal vocation.'[87] And Volz adds: 'It was axiomatic with Luther that all Christians, including monks, are equal in the sight of God.'[88]

Attempts like these are incomplete because they fail to take into account the totality of Luther's experiences.

They also leave the basic question—the individual's role in salvation—unresolved. For, while there is but one Mediator in the New Testament, the question remains: do humans, must humans, in some way participate in their own salvation? Can man and woman make some contribution to the glory which the Savior of humankind renders to the almighty Father? Is there some room for human decisions that would enable individuals to determine how they can best answer what God wants from them in the fulfillment of the First Commandment? Finally, is it legitimate to make a distinction between those requirements of the Gospel, which everyone must fulfill, and those demands which men and women may seek to fulfill as nearly as possible, by doing all that is in their power and then hope that God will complete what these human efforts are not able to achieve?[89] But these questions must be decided by theologians, not historians, although the verdict of the theologians will clearly affect the work of the historians.

In the meantime, the conclusion is already at hand for the historian: Luther was quite serious about his religious life and the vows he had pronounced in 1506. But, in time, he took his own sinfulness and the sad situation of the Church and of the monastic order so seriously that he was thrown into a crisis of conscience, which gradually drove him to new theological insights and revolutionary measures.[90] Unlike Erasmus, Thomas More, or Caritas Pirckheimer—who were, undoubtedly, as mindful of the then prevalent abuses—Luther came to the conclusion that only a separation, a radical reform, could remedy the situation.

But Luther also realized and implied repeatedly that monasticism would continue in the Church of Rome. The astonishing thing is that some monastic elements—for instance, monastic prayers, customs, community exercises, marian devotions, and celibacy—survived, during the sixteenth and seventeenth centuries, even in Lutheranism.[91] In our own day monasticism flourishes in the Greek Orthodox Church, the Church of England, *and* in Lutheranism—with its *Diakonissen* and the *Darmstadter Marienschwestern* devoted to a life of charity and reparation.[92] It also flourishes, as the example of Taizé shows, even in modern Calvinism.

Too often Luther and his impact are judged on the basis of whether he is viewed as a saint or as a heretic. Actually, as Reinhold Schneider has observed: 'We will probably never be able to say about Luther what ought to be said.' Yet, notwithstanding his personal weaknesses—his excessive polemicism, his intolerance, and his occasionally vulgar vocabulary—Luther remains to us a man filled with a supreme enthusiasm for God. He was aglow with an all-consuming fire: the fire of being moved by God. He was a listener, a translator, and an interpreter of the Word. He was a man of prayer, a man with a singing heart. He was a preacher and a catechete. He was, in a word, an impressive witness of his living God.[93] And, all things considered, Luther had no other ambition than to belong exclusively to God. But could not and should this not be said of every monk?[94]

NOTES

[1] In the translations, words are sometimes mistranslated, the monastic vocabulary is at times disregarded, critical expressions are explained away, adjectives become superlatives, and meanings are stretched to present the reformer as a superhuman being. But these attempts are clearly injurious to both Luther and the truth.

For the critical edition, see *D. Martin Luthers Werke: Kritische Gesamtausgabe* (Weimar: Böhlau, 58 vols., 1883–1948; hereafter cited WA). The three parallel series of this *Weimarer Gesamtausgabe* include the *Tischreden*, or Table Talk (Weimar, 6 vols., 1912ff.; hereafter cited WA, Tr); the *Briefwechsel*, or Letters (Weimar, 6 vols., 1930ff.; hereafter cited WA, Br); and the *Deutsche Bibel*, German Bible, 12 vols. For the 'American Edition' (hereafter AE), edited by Helmut T. Lehmann, see *Luther's Works* (Philadelphia: Fortress Press, 55 vols., 1955ff.). This edition includes the *Letters* (1963ff.) and *Table Talk* (1967).

[2] WA 8:573; AE 48:331. In his *Table Talk* Luther proposed another possible motive: 'My parents kept me under very strict discipline, even to the point of making me timid. For the sake of a mere nut my mother beat me until the blood flowed. By such discipline they finally forced me into the monastery.' WA, Tr 3:410, n. 3556A; AE 54:235. Luther described his father's opposition in a letter to Melanchthon, dated 9 September 1521: 'I remember when I made my vow, my earthly father was terribly angry.' WA, Br 2:385; AE 48:301. See also WA, Tr 1:295, n. 623 (AE 54:109) and WA, Tr 3:410f. (AE 54:234). But, following his own counsel, Luther told his father: 'I was so certain of the justice of my cause that I heard you only as a man and strongly defied you [*fortiter contempsi*].' WA 8:574; AE 48:332. Eventually his father was reconciled (WA, Br 2:384; AE 48:301) and 'bowed to the will of God'. *Letter to Hans Luther*, 21 November 1521; WA 8:575; AE 48:332. In his student days Luther had an accident that was somewhat similar to the trauma of 1505; he referred to it in WA, Tr 1:46.

[3] Josef Lortz, *Die Reformation in Deutschland* (Freiburg i. Br.: Herder, 1948) 1:157f. See also *Lexikon für Theologie und Kirche* (Freiburg i. Br.: Herder, 1957) 1:1086f.

[4] Heinrich Denifle, *Luther and Lutherdom: From Original Sources*, trans. Raymond Volz (Somerset, Ohio: Torch Press, 1971) p. 423.

[5] The full text of Luther's vow was: 'I, Brother Martin, make my profession and vow obedience to almighty God and the blessed Mary, ever virgin, and to you, brother Winand, prior to this monastery, [acting] in the name and on behalf of the Prior General of the Order of the Brother Hermits of the holy Bishop Augustine and his lawful successors, to live without [personal] possessions and in chastity, according to the rule of the same blessed Augustine, until death.' WA 8:564. See also

Lortz, *Die Reformation* 1:158f., which gives the german text and Prior Winand's reply.

⁶ WA 8:573; AE 48:331.

⁷ 'At first I devoured, not merely read Augustine.' WA, Tr 1:140, n. 347; AE 54:49. On Luther's religious life, see Bernhard Lohse, *Mönchtum und Reformation*: *Luthers Auseinandersetzung mit dem Mönchsideal des Mittelalters* (Göttingen: Vandenhoeck & Ruprecht, 1963) p. 214f; and Lortz, *Die Reformation* 1:160. In 1507 Luther was ordained to the priesthood and celebrated his first mass. WA, Br 1:10f.; AE 48:3f. See also WA, Tr 2:133, n. 1558; AE 54:156.

⁸ WA 9:12. See also Lohse, p. 214, n. 2.

⁹ WA 38:143. In WA 20:672, Luther revealed: 'I myself was a monk without any complaint.' For similar references, see WA 22:305f.; WA 37:611; WA 40:2; and WA, Tr 1:220, n. 495, and Tr 1:240, n. 595.

¹⁰ Denifle, p. 427, n. 1437 (and, 3, n. 15); WA 3:275.

¹¹ Lortz, *Die Reformation* 1:159.

¹² Denifle, p. 43.

¹³ About his early study of the Bible, Luther recalled in 1531: 'At that time no other study pleased me so much as sacred literature. With great loathing I read physics.' WA, Tr 1:44, n. 116; AE 54:13f.

¹⁴ WA, Tr 3:598, n. 3767.

¹⁵ WA 29:583. In 1532 he revealed: 'For some years now, I have read through the Bible twice every year.' WA, Tr 2:245.

¹⁶ 'The Epistle to the Galatians is my dear epistle. I have put my confidence in it. It is my Katy von Bora.' WA, Tr 1:69, n. 146; AE 54:20.

¹⁷ See, above all, Luther's admirable treatise *Eine einfältige Weise zu beten für einen guten Freund* (1535). It is addressed to 'Peter Balbierer', his barber Peter Beskendorf. WA 38:358–75. For other references on prayer, see WA 58 (index):121–24. In 1530, Luther wrote to some pastors in the city of Lübeck: 'Among the most important things you must constantly impress on yourselves as well as on the people, however, are the prayers and litanies [of the saints], both private and public: for purity and fruitfulness of the Word, for common peace, [good] government, and for all the other matters [about which] you can read in the litany.' WA, Br 5:220f.; AE 49:263. Luther's 'rosary' is reproduced in Vergilius Ferm, *Pictorial History of Protestantism* (New York: Philosophical Society, 1957) p. 23. See also Johannes Merz, 'Martin Luther: Seine Frömmigkeit und Spiritualität: Als Angebot an den heutigen Menschen,' a paper read during the Luther memorial in Würzburg, Germany, on 24 June 1983; and Denifle, p. 107.

¹⁸ Merz, above, n. 17.

¹⁹ Lortz, *Die Reformation* 1:159. Luther invited his confrères to the graduation ceremony (18–19 October 1512): 'I beg you to honor me with your presence, if it can be done with any ease, and to partake in this my

solemn "parade"—I am honest —for the sake of decorum and the honor of our Order, and especially of our district.' WA, Br 1:18; AE 48:6f.

[20] Lohse, pp. 228ff., 311ff., and 325ff.

[21] Lohse, pp. 220ff., 267ff., 294ff., 315ff. According to Denifle, 'Luther depicted the monks as gourmands, guzzlers, rakes, libertines, and idlers'; p. 341. A comprehensive list of contemporary monastic abuses is found in Lortz, *Die Reformation* 1:87, 89, and 92. See also Josef Lortz and Erwin Iserloh, *Kleine Reformationsgeschichte* (Freiburg i. Br.: Herder, 1969) p. 59.

[22] Lohse, pp. 315, 316, 337–41; Lortz-Iserloh, p. 279.

[23] WA 6:416. See also Martin Luther, 'Address to the Christian Nobility', in *Three Treatises from the American Edition of Luther's Works* (Philadelphia: Fortress Press, 1970) p. 60f.; Lohse, p. 349; and Lohse, 'Luthers Kritik am Mönchtum', *Evangelische Theologie* 20 (1960) 413ff.

[24] WA, Br 1:72; AE 48:27f. Denifle, p. 35.

[25] WA, Br 1:344f.; AE 48:110. WA, Br 2:397; AE 48:319. See also Denifle, p. 108 (with documentation).

[26] Quoted by Denifle, p. 109, n. 219.

[27] WA, Br 2:388; AE 48:307. WA Tr 1:220, n. 495; AE 54:85. See also Denifle, pp. 111–13. Luther also sustained violent attacks from the devil: 'I have many evil and astute demons with me; they "amuse" me, as one says, but in a disturbing way.' *Letter to Spalatin*, 1 November 1521; WA, Br 2:399; AE 48:323f. To Gerbel he wrote on the same day: 'Believe me, in this leisurely solitude I am exposed to a thousand devils. . . . Often I fall, but the right hand of the Most High raises me again.' WA, Br 2:397; AE 48:319. And, already in April 1521, he complained about other plights: 'I am sitting here [at the Wartburg] all day, idle and drunk.' WA, Br 2:337. This the AE renders as 'I am sitting here all day, drunk with leisure.' AE 48:225.

[28] Denifle, p. 389.

[29] WA 37:611.

[30] WA 38:143.

[31] Denifle, p. 387.

[32] WA 8:574, and WA 22:305f. Ian D. Siggins, *Luther* (New York: Barnes and Noble, 1972) p. 77. Erwin Iserloh, *Luther und die Reformation* (Aschaffenburg: Pattloch, 1974).

[33] WA 40:2.

[34] Philip Hughes, *A Popular History of the Reformation* (Garden City, New York: Doubleday, 1959) p. 95; John Dillenberger, *Martin Luther: Selections From His Works* (Garden City, New York: Doubleday, 1961) pp. 11, 148. In 1533, Luther recalled: 'I often made confessions to Staupitz. . . about really serious sins. He said: "I don't understand you." This was real consolation! Afterward, when I went to another confessor, I had the same experience. In short, no confessor wanted

to have anything to do with me. Then I thought, "Nobody has this temptation except you", and I became as dead as a corpse.' WA, Tr 1:240, n. 518; AE 54:94.

[35] WA 22:305ff.

[36] WA 37:11. See also WA 1, 558, where Luther reveals: 'I know of a man who had suffered [the pains of eternal torments] in the shortest possible time, so great and infernal that "no tongue nor pen can show."'

[37] Lohse, pp. 219, 225; Denifle, p. 39.

[38] Lohse, pp. 277, 300f.

[39] Lohse, p. 277.

[40] Lohse, pp. 313, 339.

[41] Lohse, p. 342f.

[42] See WA 2:736: 'He who binds himself to the married state walks in the cares and sufferings of that state, wherein he has burdened his nature, that it may be habituated to love and sufferance, avoid sin, and prepare so much for death, which he might not so well be able to do out of that state. But he who seeks greater suffering and wishes shortly by much exercise to prepare himself for death, and desires soon to attain the works of his baptism, let him bind himself to chastity or to a religious order. For a religious state, if it stands right, shall be of suffering and torment, that he may have more exercise of his baptism than in the married state and that, by such torments, he may soon accustom himself to receive death joyously, and thus [soon] attain the end of his baptism.'

[43] WA 6:416f., 438f., 468. Martin Luther, *Three Treatises*, pp. 38, 61f., 110. See also Lortz, *Die Reformation* 1:158; and Lohse, p. 349f.

[44] 'It is impossible to say how much that most widespread delusion of vows detracts from baptism and obscures the knowledge of Christian liberty. . . . Vows should either be abolished by a general edict, especially those taken for life, and all men recalled to the vows of baptism, or else everyone should be diligently warned not to take a vow rashly' (*Three Treatises*, p. 198). For 'It is certain that none of them [saintly monks] was saved through his vows and his religious life; they were saved through faith alone by which all men are saved' (*Three Treatises*, p. 201). See also WA 6:538f.; Lohse, pp. 350, 353f.; 361; and Vilmos Vajta, *Luther und Melanchthon: Referate des Zweiten Internationalen Lutherforschungskongresses Münster, 8–13. August 1960* (Münster, 1961).

[45] V. Sarenac, *Luthers Kritik an den Mönchsgelübden bis zum Ablass-Streit* (Diss. theo., Jena, 1940) p. 60.

[46] Lohse, pp. 310, 343, 344, 347, 349, 378; Vajta, pp. 129–32.

[47] Lohse, p. 378; Vajta, p. 132.

[48] WA 8:323ff. For a brief outline of the *Themata de votis*, see Lohse, pp. 357–62. About the thesis Luther wrote to Nikolaus von Amsberg on 9 September 1521: 'I am enclosing theses on the vows. Although there is nothing new among them for which you people may be looking, still

they will be new and shocking to [our] enemies if they are published. . . . Here I have used material which is reliable and sufficient to assure consciences and liberate them from their vows.' WA, Br 2:390; AE 48:310f.

[49] 'At mihi non obtrudent uxorem!' WA, Br 2:377; AE 48:290. See also WA, Br 2:413; AE 48:356.

[50] Kurt Aland, *Die Reformatoren* (Gütersloh: Gerd Mohn, 1980) p. 31.

[51] 'Vides, quantis urgear aestibus' ('You see, then, with what great passions I am afflicted'). WA, Br 2:375. This is translated by AE 48:287: 'You see what great unrest disturbs me!' See also WA, Br 2:403 (AE 48:328) and Hartmann Grisar, *Martin Luther: His Life and Works*, ed. Frank J. Eble (Westminster, Maryland: The Newman Press, 1961) p. 201.

[52] WA, Br 2:413; AE 48:357. According to Erik H. Erikson, Luther developed '. . . a demonological preoccupation with the lower parts of his body.' *Young Man Luther: A Study In Psychoanalysis and History* (New York: W. W. Norton, 1962) p. 232. This and similar characterizations are clearly unsound and far-fetched.

[53] WA, Br 2:396f.; AE 48:321f.

[54] WA, Br 2:403; AE 48:328. See also WA 8:564. Luther told Spalatin on 22 November 1521: 'It is certain that the monastic vows must be condemned now, if only for this one reason: the Word of God is not treated in the monasteries.' WA, Br 2:405; AE 48:337f. Further references are found in WA, Br 2:403; AE 48:328.

[55] *De votis monasticis judicium*; WA 8:573–669; AE 44:243–400.

[56] *Libellus omnium quos scripsi etiam me teste munitissimus, et quod ausim gloriari, invictus*; WA 8:569. See also WA 8:565.

[57] WA 8:578–91; AE 44:251–72. Lohse, pp. 364–66.

[58] WA 8:591–604; AE 44:373–95. Lohse, p. 366.

[59] WA 8:604–617; AE 44:295–316. Lohse, pp. 366–68.

[60] WA 8:617–29; AE 44:317–36. Lohse, p. 368.

[61] WA 8:629–66; AE 44:336–96. Lohse, p. 368f.

[62] WA 8:613.

[63] WA 8:614; AE 44:311. See also WA 8:605; Lohse, p. 369; Lortz-Iserloh, p. 58.

[64] WA 8:633; AE 44:341.

[65] WA 8:632; AE 44:349. Lortz-Iserloh, p. 58.

[66] Lortz-Iserloh, 58; Lohse, pp. 369, 377.

[67] WA, Br 2:488. Luther told Lang on 18 December 1521: 'I do not approve of that tumultuous exodus.' WA, Br 2:413; AE 48:356. See also Lortz-Iserloh, p. 58.

[68] WA, Br 2:415; AE 48:359.

[69] Beresford J. Kidd, *Documents Illustrative of the Continental Reformation* (Oxford: Clarendon Press, 1963) p. 99f.; Aland, p. 31.

[70] WA 8:624; AE 44:327. Denifle, p. 379.

[71] WA 8:679.

⁷² Wa, Br 3:898; WA 15:86ff. See also Denifle, pp. 121–27 ('The Duping of the Nuns'), and Grisar, p. 233ff.

⁷³ WA, Br 3:540; AE 49:115. Luther informed Johann Briessmann, a fellow reformer, about his marriage: 'I have now testified to the Gospel not only by word but also by deed: I have married a nun to spite the triumphant enemies who yell "Hurrah, hurrah!" [I have done this] so that it does not seem that I am yielding.' WA, Br 3:556; AE 49:123. To Nikolaus von Amberg he listed further reasons: (1) 'to silence evil mouths'; (2) 'to obey my father's wish'; (3) 'to confirm what I have taught'; and, (4) to accept the will of God ('God has willed and brought about this step. For I feel neither passionate love nor burning for my spouse, but I cherish her'). WA, Br 3:541; AE 49:117. He invited Staupitz to the wedding banquet. WA, Br 3:540; AE 49:115f. About his wife Luther commented in 1531: 'I have often observed that other women have more shortcomings than my Katy.' These shortcomings '...are outweighed by many great virtues.' WA, Tr 1:17, n. 49; AE 54:8. See also Grisar-Elbe, pp. 173–89. According to Nikolaus Heutger, we thus find 'a Cistercian lady [nun] in the first Protestant rectory.' 'Zisterzienserkloster in der Zeit der Reformation', in *Die Zisterzienser: Ordensleben zwischen Ideal und Wirklichkeit* (Bonn: Rheinland Verlag, 1980) p. 276. In 1532, Luther reminisced: 'God knows, I never thought of going so far as I did. I intended only to attack indulgences. If anybody had said to me when I was at the Diet of Worms, "In a few years you'll have a wife and your household", I wouldn't have believed it.' WA, Tr 2:165, n. 1654; AE 54:160.

⁷⁴ Denifle, p. 381.

⁷⁵ Lortz 1:417.

⁷⁶ WA, Tr 4:263, n. 4368; AE 54:335. Denifle, p. 332.

⁷⁷ WA 54:85; WA 39 (II):168. See also Carl Volz, 'Martin Luther's Attitude Toward Bernard of Clairvaux', in *Studies in Medieval Cistercian History*, Cistercian Studies 13 (Spencer, Massachusetts: Cistercian Publications, 1971) pp. 186, 198f.

⁷⁸ WA 8:622; AE 54:325.

⁷⁹ WA, Br 3:218; AE 49:65.

⁸⁰ Denifle, p. 381.

⁸¹ Denifle, p. 380.

⁸² Denifle, p. 380.

⁸³ WA, Tr 4:89, n. 4031; AE 54:312.

⁸⁴ Heutger, p. 255.

⁸⁵ For the references, see Lohse, pp. 206, n. 24, 356, 361, and 363. See also Grisar-Eble, p. 202, n. 21.

⁸⁶ Volz, p. 196. Additionally, François Vandenbroucke has singled out the importance of a faith that is worthy of Christ: 'Luther will have reason to cry out for an authentic faith, resting on pure motives,

something more worthy of Christ, to replace those superstitious means of arriving at salvation.' See *Why Monks?*, Cistercian Studies 17 (Washington, D.C.: Consortium Press, 1972) p. 15.

[87] Heutger, p. 255.

[88] Volz, p. 197.

[89] See Klaus Wittstadt, 'Martin Luther—frommer Mönch und Reformator'; Herbert Immenkotter, 'Bange Frage nach einem gnädigen Gott'; Hans-Bernhard Meyer, 'Nicht Gebote, sondern Weisungen'; Walter Brandmüller, 'War Glaubenspaltung die einzige Möglichkeit?', in *Sonntagsblatt* (Würzburg: Summer, 1983). Further, see Iserloh, p. 50f.

[90] Norbert Summer, 'Zorn aus Gottes Liebe', *Fels* 14 (1983) 148.

[91] Heutger, p. 256ff.

[92] Today, there is also a lutheran monastery in the state of Michigan.

[93] WA, Tr 1:146, n. 352; WA, Tr 2:11, n. 1258; WA, Br 5:639. See also Paul-Werner Scheele, 'Wir dürfen Luther Bruder nennen.' Address at Nuremberg on 24 June 1983, reported in *Sonntagsblatt* (Würzburg: Summer, 1983).

[94] Even today, christian monasticism could greatly benefit from Luther's struggles and insights. For instance, it should apply wise principles of selection in the admission of its candidates and place the monastic vows within the individual's baptismal commitments. The monastic life must simply be a practical implementation of the Gospel, a living commentary on the Bible. Monastic prayer must come from the heart and be nurtured by Scripture. Externalism, legalism, and all forms of superstition should be forever banished. 'Evangelical freedom' deserves to be cherished, because a monk has not only obligations and duties but, also, very real rights and, as a child of God, always retains his human dignity. Moreover, it would be beneficial to update the still unresolved question of authority and obedience and stress the primacy of the Gospel over man-made laws. Monastic 'specialization' should never be seen as a barrier to a broader apostolate. Finally, monasticism should be able to prove that a life of celibacy, as a gift of God, is truly 'evangelical', if it is sustained, as it always needs to be, by divine grace.

The list, which could be multiplied, clearly summarizes Luther's contribution and challenge: Luther taught and provoked monasticism to justify its existence, its actions, and its values on the basis of Christ and the Gospel.

CONVERSION TO THE MONASTIC LIFE IN THE TWELFTH CENTURY: WHO, WHY, AND HOW?

Jean Leclercq
Abbaye Saint Maurice, Clervaux

P ASSED IN ALL WALKS of life in medieval society, including urban society, to life in the country. An example is offered by those men and women who during the twelfth century, a period in which cities were expanding, entered monasteries. This raises the problem as to what this 'conversion', to use the word found in the *Rule* of Saint Benedict, really meant. After having edited and studied various texts on the subject, the time has now come to survey the varieties of this religious phenomenon, to discern the factor unifying them all, and to situate them in relation to the spirituality of one of the greatest of monastic centuries.

Two considerations stand out as one approaches this research. First, the problem raised here is very complex. The twelfth century cannot be understood apart from those which went before, in particular the eleventh. The facts of conversion are many and varied, and they differ somewhat from one another geographically, and, even within a same country, from one generation to another. It is not easy, consequently, to draw up a typology. Then too, we must not forget that the spiritual life is that of men and women who share in the culture of a given society with its social, economic, and political structures. Any order which we might attempt to introduce into all these facts is necessarily artificial. But the sources we have do suggest some sort of order. Before considering the reasons motivating all these men and women who came to the monastic life, we must ask 'Who were they?' Before 'why?' and 'how?', we must ask 'who?' We cannot, of course, draw up a complete 'Who's Who' on the subject, but we can distinguish several categories of people.

We know that the numbers of such people were legion. However, for the tens of thousands of cases that existed, we have only a few hundred documents.[1] Some concern well-specified personal conversions; others have a programmatic and general value. Each document should be examined in keeping with the literary genre which it reflects. Several partial syntheses still remain to be done before it will be possible to go about an exhaustive study of the subject. Here I shall suggest something more akin to a research programme and give a summary of the results already obtained.

WHO?

Who were these men and women entering monastic life in the twelfth century?

1. On this subject the first question to be asked for this period—as for the middle ages in general, and probably for every age—concerns the social stratum to which they belonged. It seems that many, perhaps even the majority, belonged to the aristocracy, of which there were many degrees. Once monasticism had been organized in the West, the temptation crept in very soon to give preferential privilege to noblemen, to the detriment of those who did not belong to nobility or who came from a servile condition. Legislators and reformers did their best to set up equality between all, and this is to be noticed particularly in the *Rule* of Saint Benedict.[2] However, social pressures were such that, throughout the middle ages, and even later,

certain monasteries were reserved for the members of aristocratic families, and these people were given preference in all monasteries, especially when it was a question of the abbacy. And it even came about that this fact was justified in theory.[3] In the later periods of the middle ages, this 'custom' was considered by some as a 'privilege' according dispensation from an essential prescription found in the *Rule* of Saint Benedict, whereas in reality it was a form of corruption.[4]

In dealing with the twelfth century, we must at once make a distinction between the old monasteries and those belonging to the new orders which came into existence at that time. The former belonged to traditional monasticism and made up what the papal chancellery, from the thirteenth century onward, called the 'Order of Saint Benedict'. In recent times they have been called 'Benedictines', but when this word was coined, in the seventeenth century, it applied to all those monks and nuns—Cistercians and others—who lived under the *Rule* of Saint Benedict. Since this modern name is convenient, it will be used here. But at the beginning of the twelfth century other orders were founded—the Cistercians, the Carthusians, the Grandmontains and others—and they made up a new type of monasticism, often considered by the traditional monks as being innovative. The members of this 'new' monasticism generally wore a habit of natural-colored, undyed wool; they were first called grey monks, then white monks, whereas the monks belonging to the old order were called black monks.

In the eleventh century, the reform of many monasteries was possible only through the help of noble families, and it was often they who instigated the reform. This meant that the majority of recruits came from these families, even though other people were not excluded. In many cases, groups of people, sometimes composed of several dozens from a same family, were 'converted' in this way to the monastic life. The motivation of such conversions was the desire to reform a monastery, and, often enough, economic disadvantage played a part too. At least one of the aims of reform and foundations in that period was to bring together all these 'converts' coming from various social ranks and 'even to do away with the differences between the free and the non-free'.[5]

This state of affairs continued in the twelfth century, and it was scarcely changed in the new orders. Among the Cistercians, the *Life* of Amadeus of Hauterive, who died towards the year 1150, is throughout one long illustration of this fact.[6] Among all these converts of unequal social rank and different culture, a distinction was made between the 'monks' properly speaking and the others diversely named *fratres exteriores, fratres barbati, donati,* and especially *conversi*. In the twelfth century, this distinction and the name *conversi* became an institution among the Cistercians, the Carthusians, and others. The conversion of bourgeois and villains is attested, especially from the end of the twelfth century.[7] It is known that educated clerics became lay-brothers, but this was prohibited by a cistercian General Chapter in 1215.[8] Among all these new-comers to monastic life there were bachelors, widowers, and married men who, by common consent, had separated from their wives. Among the nuns there were virgins, widows, and married women separated from their husbands with consent. In the west of France at least twenty per cent of the nuns were widows, and at the cluniac Abbey of Marcigny, they made up fifty per cent of the community.[9] The cultural level of these men and women varied greatly. Educated clerics became monks, and Clairvaux even recruited two architects.[10]

2. A second question enlightening us as to 'who' entered the monasteries at this period concerns the *age* of the recruits to monastic life. The first distinction to be made is that between adults and children. The latter were boys and girls who, often at a very early age—from five onward—were 'offered' to the monastery by their parents. For this reason they were called 'oblates'. Sometimes even before the child was born, its fate was decided, especially if it were not wanted. This was also a way of getting rid of

surplus girls. It even happened that, as soon as a woman was noticed to be with child, it was declared that 'If it is a girl, she shall be a nun.' But economic reasons or problems concerning succession of inheritance also led many families to act in this way after the birth of a child, boy or girl, especially if it happened to be ugly or deformed, or if for one reason or another it had no chance of getting on the marriage market. It seems that the greater number of members of benedictine communities were former oblates. This is a practice which went on until at least the seventeenth century.[11] There is nothing which permits us to say that, on the whole, the results were not good. A witness for the twelfth century is the historian Orderic Vitalis. In 1141, recalling memories of his youth, the days when, almost sixty years earlier, he was ten years old, he wrote:

> And so, O God of glory, who ordered Abraham to leave his country, his father's house and kindred, you inspired my father Odeler to give me up and surrender me wholly to you. Weeping, he gave a weeping child to Rainald the monk, and sent me into exile for your love—nor ever after saw me. A small boy did not presume to contradict his father, but I obeyed him in all things, since he promised me that I should possess paradise with the innocent.[12]

Such a moving witness as this gives us grounds for reacting against the idea sometimes put forward that there was no affection between children and parents.[13] Furthermore, an expert on matters concerning the anglo-norman world, Christopher Brooke, after having quoted this text, adds: 'Orderic's life as a monk was happy, like Eleanor of Castile's as a queen and a wife.'[14] In such cases there was no personal 'conversion' at the beginning, but the whole pedagogy of the *Rule* of Saint Benedict and the entire claustral observance tended to bring about this spiritual experience in a continuous, lifelong process. It was quite normal, then, that conversion should occur at one or other moment in life. Sometimes adult conversions have been called 'late vocations', whereas, in fact, the oblates had 'delayed vocations'.

At the beginning of the twelfth century, Cistercians, Carthusians, and most of the new orders, and later on certain older monasteries, accepted oblates only in exceptional cases, for example, the child of an adult entering the monastery.[15] (From the middle of the twelfth century, there were certain infringements of this rule.) The earliest age for entry, first fixed at fifteen, was raised to twenty.[16] Many of the *iuvenes* were young nobles who had found no other occupation than fighting in one form or another—wars or tourneys—and had found no opportunity to marry. But their age and civil status permitted a process of personal conversion before entering the monastery. Obviously, their psychology was very different from that of monks who had lived in the monastery from early childhood.[17]

In all orders applications for entry came from adults of a more advanced age. This was called *moniage* in the romance tongue, and it was sometimes the case for trouvères and troubadours.[18]

Lastly, we must mention the many laymen who asked to receive the monastic habit when they thought that they were approaching death. They were the aged or the incurably sick. And even in such cases, the fact of living apart from their wives in their last days required great detachment. Among other examples we can quote the moving scene between Ansoul of Maule and his wife, who made no secret of the hardness of separation.[19] Such *moniages* could also be the case for knights at the height of their strength but mortally wounded in war or during a tourney.[20] And it was even sometimes necessary to hasten their monastic clothing in a race against death.[21] Whatever their age, all these men had one thing in common: the desire to die in the habit, as monks. It was as though they took out an insurance policy for eternal life and took this way of getting into heaven by an emergency entrance. This was called a clothing or a profession *ad succurrendum*.[22]

3. Having considered the social condition and the age of the 'converts', we may also ask whether this fact of conversion was any different for those men and women who entered monastic orders and those who entered canonical orders, the Premonstratensians and other orders of regular canons,[23] or the communities of women religious which were more or less attached or affiliated to them. Whatever the more or less clear distinctions which the theorists of these orders put forward at that time and which historians have since presented, conversion was very much the same in both instances. The aims of monastic and canonical institutions were in part different, but entering into any one of them always supposed the same break with secular life—either clerical or lay—and led to the beginning of a 'claustral' existence, even though some members of canonical orders lived outside the monasteries themselves, like the cistercian laybrothers who lived in the granges. Thus we find texts where the words 'monk' and 'canon' are interchangeable.[24] There were adults, too, who converted to the eremetical life, living either alone, independently, or in some group of hermits already formed.

WHY?

1. *Documentation*. Why did all these people convert to the monastic life? There must have been reasons specific to each person and each category. But were there also some reasons common to all, or at least to many? How can we know? It is on this aspect of the problem of conversion that we are the most abundantly informed by explicit, numerous, and varied texts, each one of which must be used with the precautions called for by its literary genre: treatises, stories, poems, sermons, biblical commentaries, biographies, and especially letters. We may not suspect as a foregone conclusion that authors of all these were lacking in sincerity. One must read and re-read these texts one by one in the frame of mind which they suppose in the men

and women for whom they were written, that is to say without any systematic skepticism.

Among the letters, there is one special category which calls for special attention: I have suggested calling them 'vocation letters'. In a former study, written sometime back, I established the list of those which had already been published at that time.[25] Other letters have been published since. Some are still waiting to be published, such as those transmitted by several benedictine manuscripts of the twelfth century and which, though they have not yet appeared in print, we may examine here.[26] All these documents are letters in which a monk exhorts one or more persons living the secular life to come and join the cloister. Some of these letters originate in benedictine circles: for example, Elmer of Canterbury writes along these lines to a monk, but also to his own sister. However, most vocation letters come from cistercian circles, especially Clairvaux. Saint Bernard has left us several. Nicholas of Clairvaux, who was his secretary for some years, composed a series of such letters; they are much less personal, less beautiful, less convinced, and less convincing than those of his master. An anonymous novice of Clairvaux wrote a short but charming one. Other vocation letters came from the Carthusians. Letters encouraging perseverance may also be put into this category; they are written to monks who are already converted but hesitate to remain in their state of life.

Were all these texts simply recruitment propaganda? There is no doubt that Saint Bernard did all he could to draw men to Clairvaux.[27] And even after his death several men who had in one way or another benefited by his influence came to 'die at Clairvaux', as an expression which became proverbial put it.[28] Saint Bernard is supposed to have worked a miracle by blessing beer which he offered to a group of young knights who, out of curiosity—more exactly, moved by the desire to see him—had made a detour to Clairvaux between two tourneys. Shortly after they had left, beer and blessing having had their effect, they came back to the monastery for good. This same marvelous fact was soon told about the abbey of Orval, daughter house of Clairvaux, and still today renowned for its beer.[29] We may wonder, then, whether propaganda for the cistercian life did not inspire some of the vocation letters. A certain number became part of a collection of model letters, for example in a formulary of Pontigny. We may also wonder whether others were not stylistic compositions or 'homework' given to novices or pupils: 'Write a letter to a friend inviting him to come to the monastic life.' Were they all addressed to real people or were they intended for imaginary and anonymous readers? One of the reasons why this literature is interesting is that it raises problems which are perhaps unsolvable. But at least we can be sure of the context, and it is that we must now examine together with the context in which other documents were written.

They all contain a real doctrine. To attempt to summarize this would necessarily lead to a dry and cold account which would require illustrations from dense, sometimes tender, often poetic texts. They must be set in the order suggested by the very nature of them; we must start with the motivations most frequently mentioned, then consider the other motivations in descending order of importance.

2. *Doctrine*. At the origin of all these different motivations is something very aptly expressed by the word 'vocation'. 'Conversion' is a result of a 'call' to change; it is a putting into practice of what the Gospel and all spiritual tradition have called *metanoia*, a word inadequately rendered by the Latin *paenitentia* by which it is generally translated. To convert oneself is not only to change one's life-style but also to reverse one's scale of values. It means judging by other norms than those dictated by nature. This radical change is the fruit of a gift coming from the Father of lights, from Christ, and from the Holy Spirit. Such a gift is expressed by the verb *vocare*, to call. It is the 'grace of Christ' or 'divine grace' which *calls*. This verb is sometimes repeated several times in a few lines and contrasted with anything which attempts to make a person *revocare*—

refuse or retard—the answer to be given. A vocation is an 'inspiration from God', a 'spiritual inspiration': the Spirit is there with his invisible light, the voice of Christ speaks to the conscience, and the conscience must be in a disposition of docility to answer, sufficiently liberated to adhere to this free service of God. A human intermediary—the friend who sends the letter—can exhort, invite, urge, entreat, stimulate this encounter between the divine Caller and the called, but he cannot himself call, nor in any way force or constrain. Saint Bernard describes such an intermediary as a servant, a 'minister'; as a formula of feudal law put it, he can give 'help and counsel', but that is all.

The call to conversion is personal and comes from Christ. Love and desire for God, sometimes explicitly mentioned, are always personalized, referred to Christ, to the 'Good Jesus', to his cross. It is he who is to be preferred before all others, even parents. 'I am the Way, the Truth, and the Life', he said. These words, quoted on the first page of Saint Bernard's first treatise, *On the Steps of Humility*, are directly applicable here. One must unite oneself to his passion and his cross to take part in the glory of his resurrection. Christ is the model and the efficacious principle of all those virtues to be put into practice by the 'convert'. It is the humility of Christ which enables one to renounce the pride of the world; his poverty strengthens one to resist the attraction of riches and their lure. According to a traditional formula, the 'convert' is to 'follow naked the naked Christ'[30] and be attracted, drawn to him, as he himself says in the Gospel of John. As Jesus said when on earth, he again says: 'Come'. And his invitation is obeyed. The entire mystery of redemption is shown to be realized in the vocation.[31] It is one of the means of interiorizing all objective and universal realities of the christian life and of making them one's own. 'The love of Christ is at stake', writes Saint Bernard; 'The sweetness of Christ will be there.' And he goes on to give a very tender mother image of God—as did other spiritual writers: 'Suck not so much the wounds of Christ, but rather his bosom; he will be for you a mother, and you will be for him a son.'[32]

Any other reasons invoked in justifying the call to monastic life are secondary; the important thing is desire for personal union with the Lord. Before mentioning these other reasons, we must point out their major source, namely Holy Scripture, the same source from which came all that we have already described. Occasionally reference is made to what Saint Jerome wrote in some of his letters about the monk's vocation.[33] We find more frequent mention of the psychological and religious analysis of a vocation given by Saint Benedict in the Prologue of his *Rule*: the monastic vocation is a call to 'seek God', 'to combat under Christ the King.' All these ideas are biblical in inspiration. We find textual borrowings from Scripture, for many of these vocation letters are simply a tapestry of biblical quotations and reminiscences. We find one at practically every line in Matthew of Rievaulx and others like him. The Gospel verses most frequently used are those which mention a call to leave everything in order to follow Jesus. Saint Paul too is much quoted. Then, after the texts, there are the biblical models: everyone who, in the Old Testament, is related to have come back to God is held up as an example. In the New Testament, the Prodigal Son is mentioned with particular frequency: he had wandered away into the 'region of dissemblance', but through self-knowledge—knowledge of his wretchedness and his own capacity for conversion—he came back to his father. Gilbert of Hoyland, commentator on the *Song of Songs*, applies these texts and images to the monastic vocation. Admittedly such a process is artificial, but in a cultural milieu entirely fashioned by the Bible, it was quite natural for authors to use its language.

The call from God to imitate Christ is the basic motivation. There are other reasons and, through the workings of grace, they fit harmoniously into the human psychology of the 'convert'. A vocation is thought to be a result of an awakening to the fact that we are all sinners or a consequence of the desire to expiate personal sin. The fear of death and judgement, the possibility of damnation and the hope of heaven, are all so many motivations for a return to God. The love of the heavenly homeland, of eternal life, of the true Jerusalem—that which is above; desire for happiness, desire to share in divine bliss—first in this life then in the life to come, all these thoughts move a man to conversion. The contrast is noted between the cares of this life and the inner peace possessed by those men and women who live in the cloister, the contrast too between the punishment which has befallen those who rejected the call of God and the reward assured to others. To draw someone to the monastic life, the writer of a vocation letter describes the unutterable joys tasted in the cloister, especially union with God in prayer. One of the letters of Guigues the Carthusian is simply one long hymn to joy. But to attain such joy it is sometimes necessary to show a courage similar to that of the martyrs.

In these letters we find praise of the virtues practiced in the order to which the addressee is being invited: contemplation, by which one imitates Mary sitting at the feet of the Lord and listening to his word; brotherly love, the joys of the common life—though this is considered with realism: the community is made up of humans, not angels. The value of a vocation for the body of the faithful is not forgotten; by the example given in renouncing the world, especially if he is young and rich, a person becomes 'the fragrant perfume of Christ', as Saint Bernard says, following Saint Paul. The prayer of intercession raised to heaven by the monk is profitable to all; this corporate aspect of a vocation is sometimes developed at length.

We may wonder whether the theme of 'contempt of the world' is frequent in such letters? This may not be supposed *a priori*. In one instance where such suppositions have been made, the texts quoted make no mention of such contempt.[34] One does indeed find this theme, but it is neither dominant nor obsessive, and it is never considered as being sufficient in itself. But probably the true notion of the *contemptus mundi*, at least in twelfth-century monasticism, covers all aspects, negative and positive, of a very complex attitude leading a person to leave the secular way of life and to adopt that of the cloister. 'Certainly, it is not evil to despise gold; philosophers of this world have done so. But to renounce oneself to follow the Crucified One, that indeed is great. . . . The Lord is my heritage, and therefore [that is, in comparison with the Lord] the world has become for me worthless.'[35] Each of these words, borrowed from the Bible, is full of vigor. 'More than contempt, they suggest an idea of "separation", of "distance", necessary for the realization of the monastic vocation.' But above all they are indicative of an absolute preference for God.[36]

Another consideration is often joined to all these doctrinal ones, and it is indeed very lovely even though it is more of the psychological order: friendship. A friend invites a friend to come and share his life. He writes of the joy there would be for both to go on living together, doing the same things for God. Since they have been inseparable in the world, why not continue to be so in the cloister? 'Had I become archbishop of Reims, you would already have joined me. Hasten now to your friend, the novice of Clairvaux, and what you would have done for the world, do it now for God.'[37] Lastly—but it is an exception—Nicolas of Clairvaux paints, for potential candidates for the monastic life, a glowing picture of the attractions of life at Clairvaux, the pleasant site, the quality of the community: 'Many of the men here are powerful, noble, cultivated, delicate. There is even one of the king's brothers.' Saint Bernard does not appeal to any such motivations.

Profane literature is a source of information which must not be neglected, though we must use it with prudence.[38] Several of these texts date from later than the twelfth century, but they witness to conceptions and practices of an earlier tradition. They convey to us ideas which were prevalent in lay and even worldly circles. As might be expected in romances, one of the reasons for conversion is disappointment in love, sorrow caused by the death of a wife or a mistress, or, for a woman, the death of the knight to whom she was married or who was her lover. Some are said to have entered the monastery to escape a forced or unattractive marriage. Others because they are unable to assume the duties incumbent on a knight; his companions say: 'Let's put him in the monastery; there he will be fed without having to beg.' 'There too he will be able to pray for the sins of us all.' He will have an easy life, enjoy the pleasures of the cloister. The poor and the peasants are said to find something to eat in the cloister and are thus freed from the worry of finding food and clothing. Possibly this reason did have some part to play occasionally, as in the case of the laybrother mentioned by Humbert of Romans; at his clothing, the abbot put the ritual question: 'What do you ask?' And he is said to have answered: 'White bread—and often.'[39]

However, even in this courtly literature, a man becomes a monk for religious reasons: 'For God', it is written several times; to save one's soul, to get to heaven, to hasten to God, to make one's soul sober and chaste. The idea of expiation for past sins is frequent. Vocation continues to be considered as a gift from God, and one answers to the call in all liberty, 'if God gives the grace and the will.' One of the conditions required is sometimes mentioned: to be able to sing and to read—in Latin, of course. As a proof of having good health, the candidate is sometimes asked to come to the monastery on foot or on horseback.[40]

Thus, one sees, there is a long list of motivations given to justify entering a cloister of monks, canons, or nuns. And on the whole there is agreement between these different reasons stated in literary witnesses which, however, vary greatly from one another.

HOW?

Now, how did all this theory of monastic conversion work, if one may put it that way? How did it fit into a praxis? Two fields must be considered: psychology and social data, especially economics. Concerning psychology, the texts reveal two things: first, they show that to answer a monastic call was not considered all that easy, and, secondly, they give us a glimpse of the way in which this inner struggle was settled.

1. The first thing one notices in the texts is that the divine call meets with various *obstacles*. That stemming from fleshly desires is mentioned but not over-stressed. It is taken for granted that the power of being able to love according to the flesh, or the 'habit of sin', is felt but controlled. The attraction of 'temporal glory' is at least as strong, especially for those whose social status opens the prospect of a good secular or ecclesiastical career. In some families, a relative—a prelate, an archdeacon, a cantor, or some other cathedral dignitary—fosters ambitions of this sort. Having completed one's studies assures a fine future from a human point of view; as such studies are considered dangerous—dangerous too because they fill the mind with 'arguments and sophisms' which are foreign to that simplicity of heart so necessary for a life of prayer. The present possession of worldly goods, the attraction of all the wealth which could be amassed in the future are also reasons one may hesitate to reply to the divine call. Lastly, the desire to remain free from the constraint of observances is an occasion for singing the praises of that true liberty which consists in serving God with joy and love. All these objections are passed in review and refuted. They seem to have been frequent.

Other objections occur less frequently in the texts. The first is the 'severity of the order', the difficulty of the observance. But it seems too that the courage which accompanies the grace of a vocation gives the necessary strength to face up to this hardship. Another objection, minor but not unfounded, is the bad example of those who leave the monastic life, especially when, once they have returned to the world, they prosper. The answer to this objection is that it is better to consider the more numerous examples of perseverance. Sometimes an argument brought forward is an objection about celibacy dating from the most ancient times: what would happen if everyone became a monk? And, in particular, who would then carry out pastoral duties? Lastly, there is one other stumbling block: the fact that abbots, starting with Saint Bernard, are so frequently absent from their monasteries. Does this not lead one to think that these abbots feel more useful outside than at home?

Such objections raised against the monastic vocation come generally from the family or other outside circles. Consequently, it is they who must be dealt with to answer the call, and a break must be made with these milieux. Quite often we find stress laid on the fact of having to give up affection for parents or children. The very mention of this supposes that this affection really existed. And it is confirmed in the case of oblates. We read that a father hesitated to let his son leave and tried to dissuade him. Other parents feared that their child would later come to regret his decision and leave the monastery. Stephen of Paris, in his *Commentary on the Rule*, commenting on the passage in which Saint Benedict says that the *petitio* should be wrapped with the child's hand in the altar cloth, remarks that it is the mother who takes the first place in this rite because 'The son is loved by the mother more tenderly; it is all the more necessary, then, that the mother's consent to the oblation be more marked.'[41] For adults, it is noted more than once that an obstacle is 'adulation from relatives'; they put up opposition out of affection. And the monk must bear with their estrangement if he is to follow his vocation. Odo of Ourscamp congratulates his sister because her son—his own nephew—has become a monk.[42] Such indications, though they may sometimes be brief and made in passing, are always meaningful and prove that ties of affection existed for youngsters as well as between parents and their grown children. Not everything can be put down to mere chilly juridical relations.

2. Can we now get an idea of what was, so to speak, the *psychological mechanism* of conversion, faced with the many reasons which were put forward either for or against it? We

can do no more than describe briefly this process. Normally it was not easy and required courage. Furthermore, it was a slow process. Elmer of Canterbury, for example, has left us a kind of psychological analysis of what went on.[43] Others have described the phases of this inner drama in terms which help us reconstruct the journey from the fear of judgement to the meeting with the kindly Judge, to joy and the repose of union with God and contemplation.[44]

Considering the texts as a whole, we notice a series of stages in the process of conversion. Not every person, monk or nun, necessarily went through each one in the order which we shall give. Or, at least, not everyone was aware of the stage he or she was going through. But, in those who were conscious of what was happening, we notice a logical and chronological sequence. The call from God gives rise to the intention, the purpose—the *propositum*—to answer it. It is talked over with another person who is, in this sense, a friend. With the friend's help and in his or her presence the 'convert' commits himself by a promise—*promissio, sponsio, votum*—which is something like a temporary vow. There is never an over-hasty decision. Sufficient time is given for reflection, and sometimes there is a certain amount of hesitation. It is at this stage that obstacles and objections crop up. The confidant helps to overcome them. The alternatives—to answer or to refuse this call—having been weighed, a lucid choice is made, and this leads to a free decision. Such a process is merely the practice of an anthropological theory set out by Saint Bernard and other writers in their doctrinal writings. It is a matter in particular of restoring the image of God which, though it cannot be effaced, is disfigured. In this way a 'new creature' comes into being, to use Saint Paul's words, and the soul enters into the intimacy of the Lord Jesus, and 'savors his sweetness'.

To the obstacles coming from within are added those from without, the obstacles rooted in the institution itself, if we are to judge by a text which is a norm in such matters and sums up well all that has just been said. We find this text at the beginning of the *Rule of the Master* which inspired Saint Benedict when he wrote his own *Rule*. It was made into a treatise called *On the Novices Who Convert in Their Heart*, and it is in this form that it is found in, for example, two benedictine manuscripts from the region of Florence in the twelfth century.[45] According to the title and in keeping with the text of the two ancient rules mentioned, this exhortation is made to novices who have already entered the monastery. But it also shows us the trials which they suffered before entering and those that beset them once they entered.

The newcomer is not to be given easy entrance. The text copied in the twelfth century adds more obstacles to those already mentioned by Saint Benedict when he spoke of the way to deal with the would-be postulant. Everything must be done to discourage him, and he must be warned of all that will be asked of him by his conversion. The difficulty is very aptly situated, not on the level of the austerity of life, but on the level of essentials: the mortification of self-will in all its natural spontaneity in order that it be submitted to the will of the abbot. This requires obedience, patience—in the strongest sense of this word—and thus a sort of martyrdom. As an incentive to accept this, many biblical quotations are brought forward to encourage the candidate. These quotations speak of the love of God and the hope of a future reward. In keeping with the *Rule*, which must be read to the candidate, there will be a lifelong separation from parents, and he will suffer many temptations which he must overcome. Toward the end of the text it is again said that the novice must not be given the habit too soon, before he has been warned of all that is in store for him; easy vocations are to be sifted out.

Was this principle often observed, we may ask. In the *Life of Amadeus of Hautecombe* it is narrated at length how he and his sixteen companions were received by the abbot 'with a face which put on an air of severity.'[46] He talked to them along the lines of all that we have just described and in words that were anything but encouraging. After another conversation, during which the abbot again talked of austerity, he left them to think things over. Amadeus rallied the flagging spirits of his companions. The next day when the abbot came back, they repeated their request to enter and were admitted. All this was entirely in keeping with the provisions made by ancient rules and tradition. The programmes they laid out remained in all their vigor, at least in the cases considered exemplary. Before this, the programme had become a hagiographical theme, and for it to be able to become one, monks had to take pains to copy it, keep it, and read it in public or in private. There, as in every other document concerning the vocation, gospel themes are abundant. They are valid, originally, for every christian vocation, but were applied by a long tradition to monastic conversion. To these gospel themes are added those handed down by ancient monastic rules. We may wonder whether all this is not just literature and not fact. And, after all, why not literature *and* fact? The document we are considering here is only one of many which give us a glimpse of the way people thought about that so very complex phenomenon mentioned in the title: conversion. This is not just a change from one exterior way of living to another, but a deep down returning of the heart to God.

After the problem of conversion proper, there is the question of formation: once one has become a monk or nun, once he or she has entered the monastery, the convert must still learn the job, so to speak. He or she must become a monk in every fiber of his or her being and not just because he or she wears the habit. This formation is a lifetime's work, going far beyond the novitiate. Moreover, conversion itself is never completed, but it is especially during the first years that one learns the theory of what it means to live according to the vocation one has received. That too is part of the 'how' of conversion. It concerns a vast field with its own spiritual, juridical, and psychological aspects. To move from an existence led according to profane standards to a life based on a new scale of values, religious values, supposes a kind of destructuring, an unmaking of a person in order to rebuild, restructure, remake that 'new creature' of which Saint Bernard and many others speak. This process has already been considered in other studies dealing either with the period of initiation or the important role played by the community itself in formation under the guidance of counsellors.[47] Teaching must be backed up with living example.

The doctrinal and psychological aspects recalled so far are all present in the texts we have at our disposal. Should we now suspect that there are other motives, other problems left unsaid in these documents and which belong to the realm of the subconscious, things that do not come to the surface because they are repressed and are therefore all the more important because they are more profound and, precisely, unexpressed? Could it be that the conversion of so many thousands of men and women is simply an outcome of repression? Would the key to everything—including, and especially, the mystery of prayer and union with God—be a desire for political power or the need to give outlet and balance violent aggressitivity? Some sophisticated conjectures have from time to time been put forward along these lines, and they have been transformed into certitudes. It is for historiography, on condition of its remaining scientific, to verify to what extent such conjectures have an objective foundation.

3. *The donation.* It now remains for us to consider one of the most delicate questions connected with conversion: that of the donation which accompanied the entry of a person into the monastery. Fortunately this has recently been the object of an extremely well-informed, well-researched, careful, and intelligent study carried out by Joseph H. Lynch.[48]

More than once in profane poetry, we find donations mentioned in terms of 'hogsheads of wheat', or presents consisting of objects in gold, arms, in ready money.[49] In the spiritual writings used here, such references are very rare. In a letter exhorting total detachment from the world, Elmer of Canterbury writes to a friend that the way to this detachment is to give away all his earthly goods in 'large alms'. But he does not say that they must be given to a monastery.[50] Toward the end of the twelfth century, Stephen of Paris, commenting on the *Rule* of Saint Benedict for the monks of Monte Cassino, says to a father or a mother who is too poor to make a donation: 'You suffer in not being able to make a donation with your child. You would do so, for the soul of your son and your own soul, if you had any earthly possessions. But you have nothing to offer as a little gift [*munusculum*] with your son. God does not feed on earthly goods; he has no need of temporal food and drink. What he wants and desires is your own self. So, with your child, offer the affection of a sincere, humble, devout heart so that this affection may become something real. Affection changes, indeed, when holy works follow holy desires.'[51] To make a donation with the oblation of a child is, then, still considered as being normal and honorable, an occasion for joy in privation which needs some consolation. A little earlier, in a passage quoted above, Stephen speaks tenderly of the gentle affection of a mother for her son. This is clear evidence. But there is something exceptional about it. According to the greater number of spiritual texts dealing with entry into monastic life, it seems that either the donation did not exist, or else it was not worth mentioning, as though it were of little or no importance.

However, we do have the dossier assembled by Joseph Lynch. In about 125 charters taken from forty-two cartularies, and in many other historical sources, he has noticed, for the twelfth century, some two hundred or so mentions of donations accompanying entry into the monastic life of child oblates or adults. In these texts, 'The religious element was generally present.'[52] From 1120 onward the custom of making a donation began to be criticized; it was pointed out that it could foster cupidity in the monks who received the would-be novice and pride in the convert who made the gift or was the occasion for it. But it is not so much the practice itself which was condemned as the abuses to which it led. Soon canonists took over the matter and made it the subject of a disputed question; the gift was considered a form of simony and condemned as such. In 1163, for the first time, a council held at Tours prohibited the practice. Then Pope Alexander III repeated the prohibition, while decretal masters strove to justify it with all their might. Thus, throughout the twelfth century, though the donation was an accepted practice, it was also subject of debate among the learned. It was ignored or, at least, not mentioned by spiritual masters; neither Saint Bernard nor others give any hint of its existence.

This leads us inevitably to ask how the silence of spiritual writers can be reconciled with the facts found in other sources of information. Were all the discussions on this matter simply school questions raised by canonists? Surely not. But were the abuses denounced as general as the polemists would lead us to think? There is scarcely any proportion between the tens of thousands of entries into the monastic life, on the one hand, and, on the other, the few hundred charters noting the donations, a few dozen mentions in the glosses made by canonists—which have never been edited, and were probably very little known in their own times—or in the better known *summae* which were later published. It is true that the texts of spiritual writers are scarcely more numerous than this sort of document. But several of them—the letters of Saint Anselm, Saint Bernard and others—were more widely diffused. And what of the entries into monastic life which are not mentioned in the charters? Were the donations too insignificant to be noted in writing? Or perhaps they gave no cause for controversy. In any case, in monastic doctrine, a donation is never mentioned either as a motive for a vocation or as giving special rights to the new monk and his family. Perhaps, when making the recommendation to combat the obstacle created by wealth, writers were aiming at the detachment necessarily implied by the making of a donation. Was the problem raised by the canonists really 'lived' by monks and nuns, abbots and abbesses as a whole? Did it really give rise to spiritual crises? So far, all that we have in answer to these quite different questions is a series of conjectures. What went on in the depths of hearts is a secret known only to each individual conscience and to God.

CONCLUSION: THE RESULTS

By way of conclusion are we now in a position to judge the results of the very complex process called conversion? Though we have texts penned by spiritual writers who teach what should be—or ought to be—a real conversion, the converts themselves are silent on the way things really happened. We have scarcely any information other than that dealing with exceptional cases—examples of holiness or of failure; they tell us little about the every day facts, the common lot.

Certainly there were some conversions which, if we may say so, were a 'success', and some were a 'failure'. Dissatisfaction among monks and nuns is seen mainly in three groups. The first is the most frequent and is found among those who ask to transfer from one order to another.[53] It seems that nearly all known cases concern monks, not nuns. During the twelfth century a juridical procedure for dealing with such cases was installed little by little, and it even became precise and complex. But these legal formalities have only second place: the first place is given to spiritual problems about which we have a certain amount of information. In all these cases, the choice is not between leaving the regular life or staying in it, but of persevering in another observance, normally a stricter one, *arctior*. This then is rather a confirmation of vocation than a failure.

A second category of dissatisfied monks and nuns were composed of those who ran away for a longer or shorter period; they were called fugitives. Both monks and nuns absconded in this way, but there were more cases among the monks.[54] It seems that such cases were not rare, though it is impossible to have any idea of the number or even the proportion of fugitives in comparison with those who stayed. They nearly always came back. They gave rise to a great deal of literature: letters calling them back to the monastery or asking abbots to welcome them kindly—three or even more times; lamentations in form of prayer over their leaving; treatises and rituals of reconciliation.[55] Saint Anselm, for example, has left seven letters about monks—who sometimes left as a group—a nun, a princess, and perhaps even an abbot. Saint Bernard often preached indulgence towards all these people; the greatest minds were also those who had the most compassion.

A touching example is that of a regular canon, an adult who behaved 'like a child'—that is, like a son—and left to spend a few days with his mother. It is rare that we find hints that the fugitive ran off with some of the monastery's goods. Toward the end of the twelfth century, a monk contested the validity of the oblation his parents had made of him.[56] With former oblates and converted adults, the fact of absconding—like *transitus*—is sometimes presented as being a temptation to be overcome. Peter the Venerable thus describes the case of a monk who was homesick for his country; this case has recently been the object of some interesting remarks.[57] In one of his letters, Alan of Tewkesbury (d. 1202) advises an abbot to avoid anything in his way of governing that might cause his monks to wish to leave.[58]

Finally, a third group of monks who left were the apostates; they were those who left and did not come back. There do not seem to have been many such cases, probably in part because it must have been difficult to get back into secular life after having been in the religious state. However, some of the monks—and even the nuns—who left got married. Even in those days, the bishop of their diocese was asked to show kindly understanding toward them.[59]

Were all those who stayed happy? In men's communities some discontent manifests itself when lay-brothers rebelled. But what they contested was not the monastic life itself but certain observances, in particular the status—both material and juridical—of those who were not monks juridically.[60] There are very few texts in which we read of monks complaining of their lot. Among the women, the *Chanson of the Nonne* describes a little nun, shut up in the cloister against her will, lamenting over her unhappy state and sometimes calling with all her strength for a friend to come and deliver her. On this type of text 'we have examples from the twelfth century onward.'[61] Such cases are mentioned more frequently in romances than anywhere else. This was a literary theme which tempted more than one talented writer. One such poem, charming in its way, more amusing than moving, might well have been composed, in Latin, by a humorous cleric gifted in satire.[62]

May we presume that the majority of monks and nuns were happy in their vocation? Two facts are certain: especially among women, we notice that some of those who 'converted' to the monastic life preferred it to the servitude and violence which they might have met in marriage, especially when this marriage was more or less forced on them. Furthermore, and especially for the lay-brothers and for the nuns, the activities occasioned by the administration of conventual affairs was a promotion giving opportunity for responsibilities in practical or administrative business which the majority would never have had in secular life. They were always obliged to renounce attachment to such affairs.[63] However, this was a favorable opportunity, surely, to practice that the Gospel says: 'Seek first the Kingdom of God, and all the rest will be given to you over and above.'

Whatever may be the actual truth about these countless personal mysteries which, in the end, elude the historian, he or she is obliged to acknowledge that a whole doctrine of vocation—elaborated in view of an ideal, but even so proposed very realistically—is to be found inserted in a context of cultural and institutional data and that this more or less successful solution came down across the centuries.

NOTES

¹ A certain number of these texts are dispersed in the volumes of *Analecta monastica* I-VII, which appeared in the collection *Studia Anselmiana* between 1948 and 1965. These volumes will be designated here by the abbreviation *Anal*. Others are to be found under the title *Textes sur la vocation et la formation des moines au moyen âge*, in *Corona gratiarum: Miscellanea patristica, liturgica et historica Eligio Dekkers O.S.B. XII Lustra complenti oblata* (Bruges, La Haye, 1975) 2:168–94 (designated here as *Corona*). In this and the following notes, titles not preceded by the name of an author are those of publications in which I have dealt at greater length with subjects which can be only briefly mentioned here. The references given to particular texts will be done as examples of many others.

² Texts and facts are quoted under the title 'The Problem of Social Class and Christology in St Benedict', *Word and Spirit: A Monastic Review* 2 (1980) 33–51.

³ 'Nobiltà' in *Dizionario degli Istituti di Perfezione* [hereafter designated DIP], edd. G. Pellicia and G. Rocca (Rome, 1983) 6:311–17.

⁴ Texts in Laetitia Boehm, 'Papst Benedikt XII (1334–1342) als Förderer der Ordensstudien: Restaurator—Reformator—oder Deformator regularen Lebensformen', in *Secundum Regulam Vivere: Festschrift P. Norbert Baekmund, O.Praem*, ed. Gert Melville (Windberg, 1978) p. 306.

⁵ Such is the conclusion reached in the study by Joachim Wollasch, 'Parenté noble et monachisme réformateur: Observations sur les "conversions" à la vie monastique aux XIe et XIIe siècles', *Revue historique* 284 (1980) 3–24.

⁶ Ed. M.-Anselme Dimier, *Vita venerabilis Amedaei Altae Ripae*, in *Studia monastica* 5 (1963) 265–304.

⁷ Texts in Paul Scheuten, *Das Mönchtum in der altfranzösichen Profandichtung (12.–14. Janrhundert)* (Münster in Westf., 1919) pp. 24–25: Mönchberuf, Eintritt.

⁸ M.-J. Canivez (ed.), *Statuta Capitulorum Generalium Ordinis Cisterciensis* (Louvain, 1933) 1:448, 82.

⁹ G. A. Loud, 'Nunneries, Nobles and Women in the Norman Principality of Capua', *Annali Canossiani* 1 (1981) 52.

¹⁰ Robert Fossier, 'L'essor économique de Clairvaux', in *Bernard de Clairvaux* (Paris, 1953) p. 101.

¹¹ Catherine Rosenbaum-Dondaine, 'La réforme bénédictine en Franche-Comté au XVIIe siècle: Son idéal', *Revue de la Bibliothèque nationale* 2 (1982) 20–26.

¹² Quoted in the translation given by Christopher N. L. Brooke, *Marriage in Christian History: An Inaugural Lecture* (Cambridge, 1968) p. 26.

[13] Henri Platelle, 'L'enfant et la vie familiale au moyen âge', *Mélanges de science religieuse* 39 (1982) 67–85.

[14] Brooke, p. 26.

[15] An example is quoted in Ferruccio Gastaldelli, *Richerche su Goffredo di Auxerre: Il compendio anomino del Super Apocalypsim* (Rome, 1970) p. 10.

[16] Joseph H. Lynch, 'Cistercians and Underage Novices', *Cîteaux* 24 (1973) 283–97.

[17] *Monks and Love in Twelfth Century France* (Oxford, 1979) pp. 8–26.

[18] 'Monks and Hermits in Medieval Love Stories', *Journal of Medieval History* 18 (1992) 341–356.

[19] Text quoted and commented on in *Monks on Marriage: A Twelfth Century View* (New York, 1982) pp. 19–20.

[20] Texts in Joseph H. Lynch, *Simoniacal Entry into Religious Life from 1000 to 1260: A Social, Economic and Legal Study* (Columbus, 1978) pp. 53–54.

[21] Lynch, *Simonical Entry*, p. 29.

[22] 'La vêture ad sucurrendum d'après le moine Raoul', *Anal* 3 (1955) 158–68, with bibliography.

[23] Gert Melville, 'Zur Abgrenzung zwischen Vita canonica und Vita monastica: Das Überstrittsproblem in kanonistischen Behandlung von Gratian bis Hostiensis', in *Secundum Regulam vivere*, pp. 205–243. Stefan Weinfürter, '"Vita canonica" und Eschatologie: Eine neue Quelle zur Selbstverständnis der Reformkanoniker des 12. Jahrhundert aus dem Salzburger Reformkreis', in *Secundum Regulam vivere*, pp. 155–56, 164.

[24] For example, in a manuscript of the cistercian abbey of Vauclair of the twelfth-thirteenth century, Laon 71, in the text of chap. VII of the *Rule* of Saint Benedict, the word *monachus* is replaced by *canonicus*. A treatise for novices attributed to Hugh of Saint-Victor was used and interpolated by Gerard Itier, prior of Grandmont, as has been pointed out by Pierre Riché, 'Sources pédagogiques et traités d'éducation', in *Les entrées dans la vie: XIIe congrès de la société des historiens médiévistes de l'Enseignement supérieur public* (Nancy, 1961) p. 22. Later, in his constitution *Ad decorem* on the studies of regular canons, Benedict XII took up again the text of his constitutions addressed to monks, in writing *canonicus* instead of *monacus*, *praelatus* instead of *antistes*; Boehm, 'Benedikt XII', p. 287.

[25] 'Lettres de vocation à la vie monastique, VI', *Anal* 3 (1955) 169–97. 'L'authenticité de l'épitre 462 de S. Bernard ad noviter conversos', in *Sapientiae procerum amore: Mélanges Médiévistes offerts à Dom Jean-Pierre Müller O.S.B...*, ed. Theodor Wolfram Köhler (*Studia Anselmiana* 63 [1974]) pp. 81–96.

[26] These letters are conserved in several twelfth-century manuscripts. They will be quoted here according to that of Saint-Omer, 8.

[27] M. Anselme Dimier, 'S. Bernard et le recrutement de Clairvaux',

Revue Mabillon 42 (1952), 17–30, 56–78; *S. Bernard pêcheur de Dieu* (Paris, 1953).

[28] M.-A. Dimier, 'Mourir à Clairvaux', *Collectanea Ordinis Cisterciensium Reformatorum* 17 (1955) 272–85.

[29] 'Spiritualité et culture à Orval au siècle de S. Bernard d'après les manuscrits', in *Aureavallis* (Orval, 1975) p. 76.

[30] Giles Constable, '"Nudus nudum Christum sequi" and Parallel Formulas in the Twelfth Century: A Supplementary Dossier', in *Continuity and Discontinuity in Church History: Essays Presented to George Hurston Williams* (Leiden, 1970) pp. 83–91.

[31] Un chartreux, *Lettres des premiers chartreux*, II; Coll. Sources chrétiennes, 274 (Paris, 1980) pp. 127–37.

[32] Bernard, *Epistola* 322.1; *S. Bernardi opera* (Rome, 1977) 8:257. Other witnesses to the same sense are found in Carolyn Walker Bynum, *Jesus as Mother: Studies in the Spirituality of the High Middle Ages* (Berkeley: University of California, 1982).

[33] 'S. Jérome docteur de l'ascèse, d'après un centon monastique', *Revue d'ascetique et de mystique* [*Mélanges Marcel Villers*] 25 (1949) 140–45.

[34] Michel Rouche, 'Saint Anthelme et la spiritualité érémitique de l'action', *Le Bugey* (1979) 325–31.

[35] MS Saint-Omer, 8, fol. 210v–211v.

[36] Un chartreux, *Lettres des premiers chartreux* 2:35.

[37] 'Lettres de vocation', p. 173.

[38] Scheuten, pp. 33–34.

[39] 'Comment vivaient les frères convers', *Analecta Cisterciensia* 21 (1965) 239.

[40] Lynch, *Simoniacal Entry*, p. 54.

[41] *Corona*, p. 174.

[42] *Anal* 3 (1955) 152–53.

[43] *Anal* 2 (1953) 106.

[44] *Anal* 3 (1953) 184–86.

[45] Ed. Gregorio Penco, 'Un nuovo manoscritto italiano della Regula Magistri', *Benedictina* 18 (1971) 227–33.

[46] M.-A. Dimier, *Vita V. Amedaei*, pp. 281–83.

[47] 'Formazione', DIP 4:131–36. 'Noviziato', DIP 6:442–48. 'Spiritual Guidance and Counselling According to St Bernard', in *Abba: Guides to Wholeness and Holiness, East and West*, ed. John R. Sommerfeldt (Kalamazoo, 1982) pp. 64–87.

[48] Lynch, *Simonical Entry*.

[49] Scheuten, p. 33.

[50] *Anal* 2 (1953) 100.

[51] *Corona*, p. 174.

[52] Lynch, *Simonical Entry*, p. 50.

[53] M.-A. Dimier, 'S. Bernard et le droit en matière de "transitus"',

Revue Mabillon 43 (1953) 48–82. Recent bibliography in G. Malville, 'Zur Abgrenzung....'

[54] Under the title 'Pour l'histoire de l'encyclique de S. Bernard sur la croisade,' *Etudes de civilisation médiévale, IXe-XIIe siècle* [*Mélanges E.-R. Labande*] (1974) 489–90, I have published, after the MS Copenhagen Gb. Kgl. 1571, 4°, a letter of Sydo, provost of the regular canons of Neumünster from 1176 to 1201, about a nun.

[55] 'Documents sur les fugitifs', *Anal* 7 (1965) 87–145.

[56] *Anal* 7 (1965) 120–21.

[57] Denise Bouthillier and Jean-Pierre Torrell, 'De la légende à l'histoire: Le traitement du "miraculum" chez Pierre le Vénérable et chez son biographe Raoul de Sully', *Cahiers de civilisation médiévale* 25 (1982) 89–91.

[58] *Anal* 7 (1965) 119.

[59] This is the case in the document quoted in note 54.

[60] 'Comment vivaient les frères convers', quoted in note 39.

[61] Pierre Bec, *La Lyrique française au moyen âge (XIIe-XIIIe siècles)* (Paris, 1977) 1:74–75. The rareness of these texts seems to be confirmed by the fact that there is no mention of them in either the songs edited and commented on, or in the bibliography found in *Vox Feminae: Studies in Medieval Women's Song*, ed. John F. Plummer (Kalamazoo, 1981).

[62] This text, conserved in a single manuscript, which is of the twelfth century, has been edited by Peter Dronke, *Medieval Latin and the Rise of European Lyric* (Oxford, 1968) pp. 357–58.

[63] 'Medieval Feminine Monasticism: Realities versus Romanticism', in *Benedictus: Studies in Honor of St Benedict* (Kalamazoo, 1981) pp. 63–70. Especially in G. Andenna, 'Il monachesimo Cluniacense femminile nella "Provincia Lombardia"', in *Cluny in Lombardia: Atti del Convegno di Pontida, 22–25 aprile 1977* (Cesena, 1979) pp. 331–80.

APPENDIX

A recent publication has drawn attention to texts in which a certain category of adult conversions to monastic life, certain *moniages*, are criticized and often caricatured, namely the conversion of knights.[1] In this literature, which is of the epic genre, knights are reproached with changing 'orders', passing from the order of knights to the monastic order and thus choosing an easy life, whereas it would have been much more courageous to stay on and fight in the knightly order.[2] Thus, while a writer like Saint Bernard did his best to sublimate knightly aggressiveness by transposing it to the ascetic level, an attempt is made to drag these 'ridiculous *moniages*' down to natural violence. But this did not prevent many men from entering the cloister. We may wonder, then, whether this propaganda was really efficacious. Such anti-monastic satire reveals, if nothing more, that conversion was not self-evident to all; in some it met with strong opposition.

It is very difficult to verify to what extent there was really much opposition to the *moniage* of knights. It would seem that such resistance was rather a facile exploitation of an already ancient literary theme, for we find it already in the monastic comedy of the ninth century with the poem *Waltharius*.[3] Whatever the truth of that, neither Bernard nor any other spiritual writer on conversion protested against or refuted such opposition. The interest shown by certain historians today might lead one to think that such literature was very widespread. However, for each century and in each language there are very few texts attested to by the manuscripts—which are themselves not very numerous. Were these texts read? Did many people know about them? There is nothing to show this. But at least we know the intentions of the authors of such literature. What were they? Rather than to discourage knights from becoming monks, their aim was to criticize monasticism, not so much in itself—they even esteemed it—but rather the way it was lived. They denounced real or imagined abuses that they might be reformed. Furthermore, satire of cenobitic monasticism often led to praise of the eremitic life, and this too was more or less real or idealized. In this way these *moniages* were *hermitages*, if one may so name conversion to a hermit life.

Many of the details given by these writers about hermits agree with those revealed by courtly literature.[4] Satire about church people has always been part of christian folklore. It is even a sign of the healthiness of faith in free societies in which fundamental religious convictions are neither suspected nor attacked. To the extent that the eremitic life, generally lived in common by small groups, is an authentic form of monasticism, and the complement of the cenobitic life, any praise would surely have had the effect of drawing some knights away from the world into a hermitage. This does not seem to have been frequent.

NOTES TO THE APPENDIX

[1] *Les chansons de gestes du cycle de Guillaume d'Orange*, III, *Les Moniages: Hommage à Jean Frappier*, edd. Ph. Menard et J.-Ch. Payen (Paris, 1983).

[2] This motivation appears already in a few poems mentioned in note 38.

[3] In *Les chansons de gestes...*, there are indications of the evolution of the literary genre, the chronology of successive redactions of the 'cycle', the manuscript tradition of certain witnesses. For example, for the *Moniages Guillaume I* and *II*, which are of the twelfth century, we know only of two incomplete manuscripts for the first, and seven—of which only two give the complete text—for the second; Jean Frappier, *Le Moniage Guillaume*, pp. 19–20.

[4] 'Monks and Hermits in Medieval Love Stories,' (above, n. 18).

RECENT SCHOLARSHIP CONCERNING CISTERCIAN WINDOWS

Meredith Parsons Lillich
Syracuse University

A DECADE HAS PASSED since the publication of Zakin's fundamental study, *French Cistercian Grisaille Glass*, a pivotal work in scholarly interpretation of cistercian fenestration.[1] Rejecting the arguments that colorless glass was simply more economical,[2] and that unfigured windows were just reductions or puritanical simplifications of contemporary gothic taste, Zakin sought in the writings of Saint Bernard for references of significance for cistercian fenestration: light, whiteness, symbolism of the number three (the Trinity) and the circle (the Godhead), references to flowers and the lily, and to divine measure and order.

The present discussion seeks to survey recent scholarly work related to cistercian windows and to assess our current understanding of their importance and meaning—or lack thereof. Where has recent scholarship led us?

WINDOW OPENINGS

The preference is obvious in early cistercian buildings for round oculi, and for triplet window arrangements of various kinds (Zakin, pp. 149–52): two lancets and an oculus, three equal lancets below an oculus, two matching lancets grouped with a third of different size, and so on. Certainly the Cistercians held no monopoly in the medieval world on such standard forms and patterns, but clearly they found them meaningful. Even late *rayonnant* windows in cistercian churches and cloisters often take the form of oculi topping lancets in threes or multiples of three.[3]

But Fontenay, second daughter of Clairvaux, has other very prominent patterns of fenestration as well. In the west façade, the three lancets are supported by a group of four, possibly suggesting Bernard's four ways in which God can be comprehended: length, breadth, height, and depth.[4] The view toward the altar of Fontenay (see Plate I) is dominated by five equal lancets for which an even more expicit explanation is to be found in Bernard's *Parable 6*:

> These five themes on which we reflect in contemplation are viewed through five windows. A window is a space in a wall. If the wall is unbroken, there is no window. If there is only a space without a wall there is no window. A wall which contains a space is called a window.
>
> Christ's humanity was like a wall which yet allowed his divinity to shine forth within that humanity. Therefore, Christ is a window. Indeed five windows may be pondered in him: his incarnation, his way of live, his teaching, his resurrection and his ascension. It is through these five realities that the things spoken of regarding contemplation are seen.[5]

The unadorned interior of the church of Fontenay is so completely dominated by its patterns of window openings that their usefulness in contemplation seems impossible to question. And Fontenay (1130–1147) was built within Bernard's lifetime and possibly under the saint's supervision.[6]

VITREA ALBAE FIANT

While quoting Bernard in explanation of Fontenay is clearly defensible, the search for bernardine texts to illuminate a symbolic basis for cistercian grisailles—none surviving before c. 1160–1170—was criticized in 1986 by the young english scholars Christopher Norton and David Park:

> ...In the absence of explicit statements by the Cistercians themselves as to how they understood the architectural forms and decorative details, considerable care is required not to read too much into their writings.... Until we know, for instance, whether the interlace and foliate motifs characteristic of later twelfth-century glass and tiles are a new development of that period or a continuation of earlier forms, it would be dangerous to adduce texts of St Bernard as evidence for their interpretation.[7]

The student of medieval aesthetics knows all too well that such ultra-conservative insistence on explicit historical documentation is bound to lead us nowhere. Medieval men had no aesthetic language per se, and the field of medieval aesthetics, like medieval philosophy, is inextricably bound to coeval theological thought. Norton and Park also betray a total lack of sympathy with the spiritual values of contemplation. Is it possible, or useful, to assess the environment of a cistercian church without trying to understand the goals and quality of monastic contemplation? It is reassuring to read, in another study in the volume edited by Norton and Park, the words of C. H. Talbot recognizing that the Cistercians '...attempted to spiritualize art, to divest it of its purely sensuous appeal and, in so doing, make it worthy of the Divine Being for whose service it had been created.'[8]

The earliest cistercian statute requiring that 'Windows are to be made white, and without crosses and pictures', formerly believed to date 1134, is now assigned to the Chapters General of 1149–1150, just before Bernard's death. Conrad Rudolph has cogently argued for such a date, further refining the dating of c. 1145–1151 adopted by Christopher Holdsworth.[9]

Thus it is a matter of the greatest importance that Richard Marks, also in the Norton and Parks volume, has published 'the earliest firm evidence of Cistercian espousal of white glass' from the cartulary of Rievaulx and dated between 1139 and 1143.[10] The incident relates to a proposed takeover by the Cistercians of an augustinian priory. The departing Augustinians were to be allowed to take not only their liturgical objects but also 'fenestras vitreas coloratas... pro quibus illis albas faciemus.' Thus documentation exists of the cistercian preference for white glass well within Bernard's lifetime and in a milieu—Rievaulx—closely associated with him. While the earliest surviving cistercian grisailles of c. 1160–1170 follow Bernard's death in 1153, the statute before his death and particularly Marks' important discovery in the Rievaulx cartulary put the matter on solid ground. We may, after all, refer to cistercian white glass as bernardine.

WHITE OR COLORLESS?

Conrad Rudolph, however, in his discussion of the statute referred to above, argues that 'Color symbolism does not seem to have played any active role in the choice of *vitrea albae*.'[11] Certainly such symbolism is not mentioned in the spare legislative Latin of the statutes. But Bernard's potent symbolic usage of *alba* and *candidus* has suggested otherwise (Zakin, pp. 153–52). Louis Lekai has pointed out that 'Saint Bernard's attitude toward monastic art proved to be decisive over Cistercian artistic endeavors.'[12] In attempting to define that attitude—in other words, Bernard's aesthetics—Emero Stiegman has concluded that the saint's central aesthetic principle was 'an uncompromising spiritual authenticity', or, put another way, the central drive for and pursuit of self-knowledge which marks monastic contemplation. To begin to know one's self is to begin to approach God. The opposite of self-knowledge (*notitia sui*) is *curiositas*, a distraction toward lesser goals.[13] One must ask, then, are Bernard's windows white—or are they colorless? Stiegman has concluded in another study that, in Bernard's view of the inner world—which carries one simply to the presence or absence of God—color is irrelevant, a distraction which suggests only gradations of reality. The sheer presence or absence of light, the contrast between natural sunlight and darkness, is the best image of the spiritual life.[14]

Though light imagery is basic to all religious belief, and was particularly so in the twelfth century, brightness is its distinguishing quality in cistercian literature. Examples of Bernard's light imagery were discussed by Zakin (pp. 144–49), and were further collected and analyzed in 1982 by Melczer and Soldwedel.[15] They emphasize that Bernard's common imagery is of a divine light which is not painful and dazzling but '...that man, in the higher stages of monastic contemplation, is indeed able to bear.' And, while Bernard's light imagery may have been influenced by Augustine, the two saints differed on the subject of color, a positive element to Augustine, to Bernard a distraction. Thus we are on firm ground in attributing the cistercian preference for colorless glass to Bernard, and in recognizing it as more than a puritanical economy or a functional reduction of the physical environment.

'IMPOSSIBLE D'ETRE PAUVRE AVEC PLUS DE NOBLESSE'

Mâle's oft-quoted words describe the famous early cistercian grisailles executed in blankglazing, that is, with patterns formed without painting, by leads alone. Clearly, blankglazing provides more 'brightness', since nothing is added to the glass surface to impede the passage of light. Zakin studied the blankglazing of Obazine, La Bénissons-Dieu, Pontigny, Bonlieu, Noirlac, and Beaulieu, and noted a tantalizing 1517 description of Clairvaux: '...et sont les verrières de voir blanc seullement.'[16] In Germany she listed blankglazing from Eberbach, Haina, Marienstatt, and Namedy. The earliest of these survivors are now dated c. 1160–1170 and the latest around 1250.[17]

A recent and important addition to this list is the extensive ensemble of blankglazed windows in Santes Creus (see Plates II-III), recently being studied by Joan Vila-Grau for a forthcoming volume of the Corpus Vitrearum for Catalonia.[18] Though consecrated in 1211, the church of Santes Creus was not fully in use until 1225, and presents an impressive ensemble of blankglazing at a fairly late date and in a part of Europe 'not previously heard from'.

Because relatively few grisailles of any kind, cistercian or not, have survived from before the second quarter of the thirteenth century, it has remained an open question whether the Cistercians invented blankglazing or simply adopted and refined a standard—perhaps even secular—type of window filler. Zakin's viewpoint (pp. 177-78, 183-96) was that the sophisticated cistercian use of blankglazing influenced non-cistercian monuments as early as the late twelfth century, particularly in Burgundy and Champagne, close to the cistercian heartland. In 1983, Naomi Kline's dissertation adopted and refined Zakin's position, proposing that the four blankglazed designs among the numerous grisailles of the benedictine abbey of Orbais in Champagne were derived from Pontigny.[19]

In 1985, Françoise Gatouillat, profiting from the work of the census of burgundian stained glass (published in 1986), reviewed the question of blankglazing in non-cistercian milieux in Burgundy. Among the examples known from nineteenth-century publication, but no longer extant, are the parish church of Migennes, the collegiate churches of Montréal and of Saint-Martin de Chablis, and the Hôtel-Dieu of Sens.[20] These losses have been offset, however, by two recent and important discoveries of blankglazing made during the work of the census.

Cistercian-type blankglazing, identical in pattern to the two designs recorded from the Hôtel-Dieu of Sens (Zakin, plates 182-83), survives in the small church of Cudot (Yonne). Founded c. 1170 by the archbishop of Sens and sited adjoining the cell of the female mystic Saint Alpais (d. 1211), Cudot enjoyed donations and attentions from several french queens. A second discovery of cistercian-type blankglazing, even employing one of the same designs, is in an upper tower window of the façade of Sens cathedral, constructed after a fire of 1184 (see Plate IV). The existence in Burgundy of so many non-cistercian examples of blankglazing reactivates the old question of whether the Cistercians influenced others or simply adopted a local method of window glazing. We shall return to this question.

Blankglazing fell from favor in France by the mid-thirteenth century, a rare exception being the blankglazed grisailles of Beauvais cathedral, in hemicycle band windows that Michael Cothren has dated c. 1268–1272.[21] While acknowledging their cistercian antecedents, he suggests that blankglazing was used for its increased legibility in windows so distant from the observer's eye.

In the Rhineland, a simplified form of non-cistercian blankglazing in a zigzag, interlace pattern—known in french as *à bâtons rompus*—continued in popularity. Colored glass usually forms the background of the interlace pattern, and colored figures are occasionally set directly into the interlace. To Zakin's example at Coisdorf (Zakin, pp. 192–93, plates 190–91) can be added such blankglazing from the Ritterstiftkirche in Wimpfen im Tal, c. 1270–1280 (now in the Hessisches Landesmuseum in Darmstadt), several churches in Alsace dated to the last quarter of the thirteenth century, and the cistercian abbey of Altenberg at the beginning of the fourteenth century.[22] By the time this rhenish type of blankglazing had reached Lorraine, in the fourteenth-century glazing of the transepts and nave of Toul cathedral (published in 1985 by Michel Hérold),[23] no direct cistercian heritage is likely.

But to return to the famous early cistercian blankglazed patterns. Is there another way to approach the problem of what, if anything, the Cistercians indeed invented? The non-cistercian blankglazing mentioned in the paragraphs above is, almost without exception, some kind of geometric interlace. While the question will never be solved, it does seem reasonable to accept that the Cistercians adopted this type of blankglazed pattern from general glazing practice, just as they made early and extensive use of (but did not 'invent') the pointed barrel-vault of burgundian romanesque architecture. *Why* they adopted—and developed with such great sophistication—geometric interlace blankglazing is another question, to which we shall return at the end of this paper. It is of greater significance at this point to stress that cistercian blankglazing, unlike other kinds,[24] is not limited to geometric interlace but also includes a distinctive group incorporating obvious vegetal or floral motifs.

FLOWER OF THE FIELD AND LILY OF THE VALLEY

Among the texts collected by Zakin in reference to stylized floral imagery in cistercian grisailles (Zakin, pp. 154–61) is Bernard's commentary on the *Song of Songs* 2.1:

> Truth however is a beautiful lily, remarkable in its brightness... and its brightness is of eternal light, its splendor and form is the essence of God.[25]

Many beautiful blankglazed patterns of stylized flowers or lilies are known from Obazine, Bonlieu, and Pontigny.

Among the fragments from Noirlac, c. 1185, are stylized flowers not blankglazed but set against a ground painted with crosshatching (see Plate V). Other Noirlac fragments present blankglazed interlace and also interlace which, like the flowers, is set against a crosshatched background (Zakin, plates 62, 65). We are so accustomed to crosshatched grounds, which become the unbroken rule in french grisaille by the mid-thirteenth-century, that the early Noirlac fragments seem routine. Not a bit of it! Crosshatching at that extremely early date may have appeared occasionally in minute decorative elements, but it was never used simply to 'identify' the ground. The Noirlac hatching, moreover, is large-scale and crude, not an accomplished technique but a hesitant experiment. If our assumptions above are correct concerning the significance of unimpeded (sun)light in cistercian blankglazing, why was this crosshatching added at Noirlac? And what does it achieve? The addition of crosshatching functions to distinguish the pattern from the ground, to set off the pattern and render it more legible. It follows, particularly in such an early and experimental example, that the pattern had great significance—as much significance as the sunlight. We are clearly not distorting the evidence in seeking twelfth-century cistercian texts to explain the meaning behind such floral patterns.[26]

Crosshatched grounds were adopted by the german-speaking Cistercians as early as the cloister of Heiligenkreuz (c. 1220–1250), and they appear among the motifs of the Reuner Musterbuch, a patternbook from the cistercian abbey of Reun dated to the early thirteenth century (Zakin, plates 155–57). By the mid-thirteenth century the crosshatched ground is the norm, and floral patterns begin to predominate in german cistercian windows.[27]

In England, thirteenth-century cistercian glass is known only from excavated fragments, discussed by Richard Marks in 1986.[28] Marks illustrates those of the Hailes refectory, c. 1250, and describes a great many others (Bordesley, Newminster, Warden, Kirkstall refectory, etc.) as similar in style: abstract foliage formed of stems and small stylized leaves or palmettes set against conventional crosshatched grounds. As he states, such grisaille is indistinguishable from coeval non-cistercian designs in England.

In France, the situation was probably similar. Zakin was unable to find evidence of cistercian glazing survivals between the last blankglazed patterns of around the mid-thirteenth century and the foliate designs on crosshatched grounds at La Chalade just after 1300.[29] The lacuna, however, may be filled by excavated fragments as in England. Those from Maubuisson (see Plate VI),[30] where the church was dedicated in 1244, are, like the english fragments cited by Marks, indistinguishable from general gothic grisaille of the mid-thirteenth century.

BERNARD THE MONK NE SAUGH NAT ALL, PARDEE!

Chaucer's proverb implies changing responses to changing times.[31] Scholars have traditionally criticized the confluence of cistercian and non-cistercian forms mentioned above as a degeneration, a failure on the part of the order to maintain its distinctive visual traditions. The confluence of forms is an art historical observation, but the moral judgment which seems to accompany it is inappropriate. A cistercian church of the late thirteenth century—Altenberg, for instance—was unquestionably distinctive from coeval ecclesiastical buildings. If we are correct in recognizing the specific cistercian significance of vegetal symbols in late twelfth-century cistercian glass, the adoption by the Cistercians of such imagery as it became current in mid-thirteenth-century gothic seems natural. In Lekai's study of 'The Challenge of Scholasticism', he outlined the order's impressive efforts under the extraordinary Stephen Lexington (d. 1255) to refurbish its response to the changing intellectual and cultural climate of Europe.[32] From around 1225 to his death, Stephen labored to remedy the Cistercians' '... crying need for educated monks'. Chief among the results of his labors was the establishment in Paris in 1245 of the College of Saint Bernard, which was to enjoy a century of expansion and prosperity slowed only by the Hundred Years War.

In the Paris of 1245, the theological climate was changing. Bickel has made reference to the teaching of Albertus Magnus (d. 1280) in Cologne, in discussing the magnificent naturalized foliage of the coeval grisailles of nearby Altenberg.[33] It is probably truer to see both Albertus and Altenberg as parts of a much larger picture. In 1984, I argued that the sea-change in the appearance of french gothic in the decades from 1240 to 1260 reflected the increasing criticism and condemnation of Erigena, a theological struggle of 'Augustine versus Dionysius', in Chenu's words.[34] In Paris two unrelated events played out at almost the same moment: the Ten Propositions of 1244 condemned pseudo-dionysian theology and aesthetics, and the great cistercian experiment at the College of Saint Bernard began. Lekai has referred to the testimony of Matthew Paris that '...the Cistercian students proved to be more popular with the university authorities than the Mendicants.' One can safely assume that they wholeheartedly supported the new theological climate of the 1240s, and its resultant new aesthetic, since its renewed emphasis on light melded so smoothly with cistercian traditions. No 'degeneration' is implied in the order's traditional ideal for an appropriate physical environment for contemplation.

Marks has noted that the last cistercian legislation to mention color was 1257, and that the Codifications of 1289 and 1316 only forbade 'superfluae novitates et notabiles curiositates'. Color, as mentioned above, was a distraction in Bernard's view, but to Augustine a positive element. It should hardly be surprising that the Cistercians, after the founding of the College of Saint Bernard, should have entertained an augustinian perspective. Nonetheless, except for nunneries[35]—where the rules were always applied 'with a difference'—color hardly plays a noticeable part in cistercian glazing through the end of the thirteenth century.

The introduction of figures is another matter. The earliest figures introduced into the glazing of cistercian monasteries seem to reflect donations: a secular woman (Queen Margarete of Denmark?) presenting a window at Doberan, recently dated by Christa Richter as c. 1270–1280; the Wettingen cloister of c. 1280, which includes a monk kneeling before the Virgin; perhaps the heraldic glass once at Tintern, c. 1288; and the Babenberg family in the Heiligenkreuz fountainhouse, c. 1290–1300.[36] References to donors—long standard in non-cistercian glazing—unquestionably would be among the distracting curiosities censured by Saint Bernard.

The real 'degeneration' of cistercian ideals after 1300 has been examined thoroughly by Lekai in 'The End of Prosperity'.[37] In the turbulent fourteenth century that produced the lay piety of the *devotio moderna*, the appearance in windows of worshippers and of holy figures is perhaps not surprising. What *is* surprising is the great white and gold window of the Altenberg façade, c. 1380, presented by a duke and duchess and filled with saints, and yet in its contemporary context undeniably a cistercian achievement.[38]

THE FORGOTTEN SYMBOLS OF GOD

Under this intriguing title, Patrik Reuterswärd has recently republished five essays written since 1982 investigating the significance, in medieval art, of forms and emblems that we customarily regard as functional or decorative only.[39] His first essay traces from early christian art into the twelfth and thirteenth centuries the significance of windows and groups of window openings as signifiers of the divine (*Ego sum lux*). Among his examples is the early twelfth-century cluniac priory of Berzé-la-Ville in Burgundy, where two frescoed angels flank, and clearly 'present' to the viewer, a round window.

Several of his subsequent studies establish the significance as divine signs, across the same centuries, of motifs like the circle, wheel, what he calls the 'compass rosette', whirl, tetragram (a four-looped figure forming an X-cross), 'improper' tetragram (that is, Solomon's knot), swastika, triquetra (trefoil), and also the lion, lily, and tree of life. The 'cosmic Paradise' theme he discusses is a combination of vegetal and geometric forms (see Plate VII)—which are, let us remind ourselves, the two types of cistercian blankglazing.

Reuterswärd (p. 109) allows that, 'Because of its strong inclination to figural images, the Romanesque period naturally did not leave much room for signs and emblems.' Even so, his vast accumulation of examples, from the twelfth century in context with previous works, presents a continuum of meaning that is completely convincing. Among the well-known romanesque sculptures to benefit from his illuminating study is the heavily figured Moissac portal, with its lintel of rosettes and trumeau of rosettes and lions.

Reuterswärd's work provides a most promising avenue for an understanding of cistercian art. Cistercian windows, and tiles, and sculpture, offer perfect examples of his emblems. Zakin (p. 198) had concluded that 'There seems to be little doubt that French Cistercian glass patterns are based on patterns taken primarily from French Romanesque sculpture.' Now Reuterswärd has amassed an impressive amount of evidence that such romanesque motifs, and those that preceded them, were not just decoration, but potent emblems of cosmic import, forgotten symbols of God.

From among Reuterswärd's vocabulary of motifs, one might remark that cistercian art was rather selective. Cistercian windows have lilies but not lions; cistercian geometric interlace includes interlocked circles, Solomon's knots, and 'tetragram' X-crosses, but not swastikas, whirls, or wheels. Leaving aside the lilies, for which Bernard's focal interest provides a basis, what did the forms of cistercian interlace signify to the monks? Following Zakin's suggestion (pp. 167–68) of metaphysical importance of measure, order, and form, Melczer and Soldwedel, in 1982, pointed out Bernard's condemnation of singularity and his emphasis on monastic simplicity and community, as well as the '... beautiful order established by divine providence'.[40]

Some cistercian window patterns, for example the 'box design' of La Bénissons-Dieu (Zakin, plate 16, also 44), are indeed extremely simple, neat, and orderly. Others, such as another window at the same church (see Plate VIII), present knots and interlace of such complexity as to appear disorderly—and not truly geometrically drawn in all details.

While knots and interlace have formed part of the decorative vocabulary in use since well before Christ, their appearance in christian art is constant and, in examples such as the Knotenkreuz (see Plate IX), seemingly meaningful.[41] The making of interlace and knots for use as apotropaic amulets was censured in penitentials, among them the widely diffused 'Corrector sive Medicus' of Burchard of Worms (1012–1023).[42] Magical symbols are normally those of recognized (orthodox) power, put to manipulative usage. Reuterswärd implies this in tracing his pre-medieval and medieval symbols to sixteenth- through eighteenth-century secular doorways and loft-doors.[43] Ernst Kitzinger has studied the use of Solomon knots (also X crosses and whirls) as apotropaic signs in early christian pavements, for example in Antioch (see Plate X).[44] He notes that a prohibition against the representation of the 'sign of Christ' on the floor was included in the Edict of 427 A.D. and reaffirmed as late as the Council of Trullo, 692 A.D., and he makes reference to 'the apotropaic use of knots [as] a recurrent phenomenon in the folklore of many centuries and periods.'[45] He concludes with a balanced statement that deserves a full quotation:

> It is not my intention... to open a floodgate of symbolic interpretations of innocent ornaments in late antique art. The perils are only too obvious. But one can err equally through an excess of skepticism. Certainly the... examples I have quoted are not the only ones... in which Solomon's knot was invested with a special meaning. I have chosen what I believe to be indisputable cases.... On the other hand, there are countless cases in which the motif clearly was used routinely and with little or no special purpose.... In surveying the material one soon becomes aware that a hard and fast determination is often impossible. Just as there were shades and degrees in the amount of emphasis which the motif received within a design, so there must have been shades and degrees in the amount of meaning that was attached to it in the designer's mind. Possibilities run the gamut from precise symbolism via the vaguely meaningful to the

purely ornamental. The notion of a 'semantic range' within which meaning is determined by context is familiar from modern linguistics. The principle has its application also in the visual arts. What precisely a motif signifies within a composition can depend on the context, in much the same way as does the meaning of a word in a sentence.

In short, I do not mean to imply that twelfth-century cistercian monks filled their church windows with apotropaic signs. I do mean to imply that it is not really so important 'whether the interlace and foliate motifs characteristic of later twelfth-century [cistercian] glass and tiles are a new development of that period or a continuation of earlier forms.'[46] I mean to imply that in the middle ages knots and interlace still signified—at the least—'power', and that within the semantic context of the cistercian church interior and monastic contemplation, the identity of that power was hardly in question.

NOTES

[1] Helen Jackson Zakin, *French Cistercian Grisaille Glass* (New York, 1979). Previous studies, such as those by Marcel Aubert, Hans Wentzel, and Eva Frödl-Kraft, had treated cistercian glass as a stylistically coherent art historical group, but without reference to any spiritual meaning or function. For their works see Zakin's bibliography.

[2] See Lillich, 'Monastic Stained Glass: Patronage and Style', in *Monasticism and the Arts*, ed. Timothy Verdon (Syracuse, 1984) p. 218 and n. 36. In Barcelona, in 1385, white and colored glass (except red) cost the same: Joan Ainaud i de Lasarte *et al.*, *Els Vitralls de la catedral de Girona*, Corpus Vitrearum Catalunya 2 (Barcelona, 1987) p. 35, Reg. 23. While early fourteenth-century documents from northern France indicate higher prices for colored glazing, a close reading suggests that workmanship (painting on the glass, elaborate leading) raised the price whether or not the glass was colored. See Lillich, 'Gothic Glaziers: Monks, Jews, Taxpayers, Bretons, Women', *Journal of Glass Studies* 27 (1985) 90 (C), where 'verre vigneté' (grisaille painted with foliage) cost more than plain white glass.

[3] Examples illustrated in Louis Lekai, *The Cistercians: Ideals and Reality* (Kent, Ohio: Kent State University Press, 1977): the fountainhouse of Maulbronn, façade of Chorin, south transept of Melrose (see pp. vi-vii). A sixth-century hymn specifies that the three windows of the apse of Edessa cathedral represented the Trinity: A. Dupont-Sommer, 'Une Hymne syriaque sur la cathédrale d'Édesse', *Cahiers archéologigues* 2 (1947) 31–32; André Grabar, 'Le Témoignage d'une hymne syriaque sur l'architecture de la cathédrale d'Édesse au VIe siècle et sur la symbolique de l'édifice chrétien', *Cahiers archéologique* 2 (1947) 41–67. In the Late Middle Ages the legend of Saint Barbara presents the same theme (see Caxton's version of the *Golden Legend*).

[4] *De consideratione* 5.13. See *Five Books on Consideration: Advice to a Pope*, trans. John D. Anderson and Elizabeth Kennan (Kalamazoo, 1976) p. 173f. Three and four are grouped in one of the early grisaille patterns, the 'box design' of La Bénissons-Dieu and Pontigny; see Lillich, 'Monastic Stained Glass', p. 222.

[5] *Parabola* 6, in *S. Bernardi Opera*, edd. Jean Leclercq and Henri Rochais (Rome, 1972) 6/2:292; Rochais, 'Enquête sur les sermons divers et les sentences de saint Bernard', *Analecta sacri ordinis cisterciensis* 28 (1962) 31–33, 42–43; Leclercq, 'Une Parabole restituée à saint Bernard', *Analecta sacri ordinis cisterciensis* 9 (1953) 135–36; Michael Casey, trans., 'The Story of the Ethiopian Woman Whom the King's Son Took as His Wife,' *Cistercian Studies* 11/2 (1986) 105. I am grateful to John Sommerfeldt, whose reference to this text in a 1989 paper at Kalamazoo alerted me to it, and who told me where to find it.

While windows were commonly compared to the five senses, the victorine texts relating five windows to five modes of contemplation and the fivefold dispensation of the incarnation appear to postdate Saint Bernard; see Carla Gottlieb, *The Window in Art* (New York, 1981) p. 221f.

⁶ The architectural iconography of Fontenay is discussed by Otto von Simson, *The Gothic Cathedral* (New York, 1956) p. 48f.

⁷ Christopher Norton and David Park (edd.), *Cistercian Art and Architecture in the British Isles* (Cambridge, 1986) p. 10. One might recall Schramm's characterization of a marxist history of Cluny: 'E. Werner speaks of spiritual and religious values as a blind man might speak of colors.' Robert Capaldi brought this quotation to my attention.

⁸ C. H. Talbot, 'The Cistercian Attitude Towards Art: The Literary Evidence', in Norton and Park, p. 64. See also Peter Fergusson, *Architecture of Solitude: Cistercian Abbeys in Twelfth-Century England* (Princeton, 1984) p. 64.

⁹ Conrad Rudolph, 'The "Principal Founders" and the Early Artistic Legislation of Cîteaux', in *Studies in Cistercian Art and Architecture*, 3, ed. Meredith Lillich (Kalamazoo, 1987) pp. 21–28; Christopher Holdsworth, 'The Chronology and Character of Early Cistercian Legislation on Art and Architecture', in Norton and Park, p. 54. See also the convenient chart presenting the cistercian statutes on art in the same volume: Table of Cistercian Legislation, p. 325. Holdsworth based his study on the work of Lekai, who, he states, '...of all modern Cistercian scholars has made contributions to the history of the Order which range over the greatest spans of times and space' (p. 43).

¹⁰ Richard Marks, 'Cistercian Window Glass in England and Wales', in Norton and Park, p. 213.

¹¹ Rudolph, p. 43, n. 66.

¹² Lekai, p. 262.

¹³ Emero Stiegman, 'The Aesthetics of Authenticity', in *Studies in Cistercian Art and Architecture*, 2, ed. Meredith Lillich (Kalamazoo, 1984) pp. 1–13.

¹⁴ Emero Stiegman, 'The Meaning of Light and Color in Cistercian Literature and Art', a paper presented at the Twenty-third International Congress on Medieval Studies, Kalamazoo 1988; summary reported by Terryl Kinder in *Cîteaux* 39 (1988) 168–69.

¹⁵ Elisabeth Melczer and Eileen Soldwedel, 'Monastic Goals in the Aesthetics of Saint Bernard', in *Studies in Cistercian Art and Architecture*, 1, ed. Meredith Lillich (Kalamazoo, 1982) pp. 35–39. See also Lillich, 'Monastic Stained Glass', p. 218; Lekai generously contributed to my work on that point.

¹⁶ Zakin, p. 76, citing *Annales archéologiques* 3 (1845) 226.

¹⁷ On dating, in addition to Zakin, pp. 83–84, see Catherine Brisac, 'Romanesque Grisailles from the Former Abbey Churches of Obazine and Bonlieu', in *Studies in Cistercian Art and Architecture*, 1:131. Namedy

is dated before 1250 by Wolfgang Bickel, 'Zur Glasmalerei im Cistercienserorden', in *Die Cistercienser, Geschichte, Geist, Kunst*, edd. Ambrosius Schneider et al. (2nd ed., Cologne, 1977) pp. 311, 315.

[18] Joan Vila-Grau, 'Cistercian Stained Glass Windows at Santes Creus', in *Studies in Cistercian Art and Architecture*, 4 (Kalamazoo, in press).

[19] Naomi Kline, *The Stained Glass of the Abbey Church at Orbais* (Diss. Boston University, 1983) pp. 42–47. The influence of Pontigny may have been significant. Virginia Jansen has posited such an influence (via the exiled english churchmen welcomed at Pontigny) on the basic development of english gothic architecture: 'Lambeth Palace Chapel, the Temple Choir, and Southern English Gothic Architecture of c. 1215–1240', in *England in the Thirteenth Century*, ed. W. M. Ormrod, Proceedings of the 1984 Harlaxton Symposium (Woodbridge, Suffolk, 1986) p. 99.

[20] Françoise Gatouillat, 'Vitreries de type cistercien dans l'Yonne', in *Actes du cinquante-sixième congrès, Association bourguignonne des sociétés savantes, Villeneuve-sur-Yonne* (31 May–2 June 1985) pp. 59–64; *Les Vitraux de Bourgogne, Franche-Comté et Rhône-Alpes*, Corpus Vitrearum France, Recensement III (Paris, 1986) pp. 138–39 and fig. 119, 204. The Hôtel-Dieu of Sens was discussed by Zakin under the name Saint-Jean (see Gatouillat, p. 204). I am grateful to Michael Cothren for telling me about the Gatouillat study.

[21] Michael Cothren, *The Thirteenth- and Fourteenth-Century Glazing in the Choir of the Cathedral of Beauvais* (Diss. Columbia University, 1980) pp. 172–74 (see, for example, plates 103, 105, 110, 111, 115 left).

[22] Wimpfen im Tal and the alsatian sites: Hans Wentzel, *Die Glasmalereien in Schwaben von 1200–1350*, Corpus Vitrearum Deutschland I (Berlin, 1958) pp. 248, 257, Abb. 556–57; also *Glasmalerei um 800–1900 in Hessischen Landesmuseum in Darmstadt* (Frankfurt, 1967) 1:58, nos. 60–63, 2: Abb. 48–49. Altenberg: Brigitte Lymant, *Die mittelalterlichen Glasmalerei der ehemaligen Zisterzienserkirche Altenberg* (Bergisch Gladbach, 1979) pp. 63–64, 101–103. On a similar panel in the Nuremberg museum showing Saint Mauritius, see Zakin, p. 193.

[23] Michel Hérold, 'Un Vitrail d'Hermann de Münster à la cathédrale de Toul', *Le Pays lorrain* 66 (1985) 35, 37–39. For a discussion of another example, in a now blinded lancet in the rural church of Écrouves near Toul: Lillich, *Rainbow like an Emerald: Stained Glass in Lorraine in the Thirteenth and Early Fourteenth Centuries* (University Park, Pennsylvania, 1991) Appendix VI.

[24] Zakin (p. 85, n. 2) pointed out that a pre-cistercian example, the reassembled floral design of (carolingian?) fragments from Séry-les-Mézières, is now suspect.

[25] Zakin, p. 157; *Sermones super cantica canticorum 36–38*; *S. Bernardi opera* 2:210.

26 The iconography of interlace—which also appears against cross-hatching at Noirlac—will be discussed at the conclusion of this paper. It is omitted here because geometric interlace becomes rare after the mid-thirteenth century.

27 For examples: Brigitte Lymant, 'Die Glasmalerei bei den Zisterziensern', in *Die Zistercienser*, catalog (Cologne, 1980) pp. 346–51, 537; Bickel, pp. 311, 314–15; *Mittelalterliche Glasmalerei in der Deutschen Demokratischen Republik*, catalog Erfurt (Berlin, 1989) nos. 7–10, 15–16.

28 Marks, pp. 215–17.

29 Zakin published two articles dating La Chalade, on heraldic evidence, between 1307 and 1314: 'Cistercian Glass at La Chalade (Meuse)', in *Studies in Cistercian Art and Architecture* 1:140–51; 'Recent Restorations of the La Chalade Glass', in *Mélanges à la mémoire du Père Anselme Dimier*, ed. Benoît Chauvin (Pupillin, 1982) 3/6:767–79.

30 I am grateful to Catherine Brisac for sending me photos in 1984. On the dating of Maubuisson: Terryl Kinder, 'Blanche of Castile and the Cistercians, an Architectural Re-evaluation of Maubuisson Abbey', *Cîteaux: Commentarii cistercienses* 3/4 (1976) 166–67.

31 'The Legend of Good Women', cited by Stiegman, *Studies in Cistercian Art and Architecture* 2:8 and n. 36.

32 Lekai, pp. 79–82. On the chapel constructed for the College of Saint Bernard, 'conjonction de deux natures, la cistercienne, rurale et spirituelle, et la parisienne, urbaine et universitaire', see the interesting study by Philippe Dautrey, 'L'Église de l'ancien collège des Bernardins de Paris et son image', in *Mélanges à la mémoire du Père Anselme Dimier* 3/6: 497–514 (quotation, p. 514).

33 Bickel, p. 309.

34 Lillich, 'Monastic Stained Glass', p. 225.

35 On Marks' list (pp. 217–18) of thirteenth-century sites where color and figures were introduced, the following were cistercian nunneries: Kirchheim in Ras, Wienhausen, Neukloster, Lichtental, Heiligenkreuztal. The lost (colored) glass of Schulpforta mentioned by Marks could not have been thirteenth-century, as Hayward has cogently argued: Jane Hayward, 'Glazed Cloisters and Their Development in the Houses of the Cistercian Order', *Gesta* 12 (1973) 95.

36 Doberan: Christa Richter, 'Die Grisaillemalerei im Doberaner Münster und ihre Stifterin', in *Neue Forschungen zur mittelalterlichen Glasmalerei in der Deutschen Demokratischen Republik* (Berlin, 1989) pp. 52–62; *Mittelalterliche Glasmalerei in der Deutschen Demokratischen Republik*, p. 21, no. 14 (color illustration). Wettingen: Hayward, p. 99. Tintern: Marks, p. 218. Heiligenkreuz fountainhouse glazing: P. Paulus Niemetz, *Die Babenberger-Scheiben im Heiligenkreuzer Brunnenhaus* (Heiligenkreuz, 1976); Eva Frödl-Kraft, *Die mittelalterlichen Glasgemälde in Niederösterreich* 1, Corpus Vitrearum Österreich 2 (Vienna, 1972) pp. 113–25.

[37] Lekai, p. 91ff.

[38] Lymant, *Altenberg*, p. 110ff.; Hayward, p. 104.

[39] Patrik Reuterswärd, *The Forgotten Symbols of God*, Stockholm Studies in History of Art, 35 (Uppsala, 1986). The articles first appeared in *Konsthistorisk Tidskrift*: 'Windows of Divine Light' (1982); 'The Forgotten Symbols of God' parts 1 (1982), 2, 3 (1985); 'The Lion, the Lily, and the Tree of Life' (1985). His specific references to cistercian art are in 'Forgotten Symbols' 3:91–101; see also the abstract of his paper 'An Overlooked Reserve in Cistercian Iconoclasm', in *L'Art et les révolutions*, 4, *XXVIIe Congrès international d'histoire de l'art* (Strasbourg, 1992) pp. 25–34.

[40] Melczer and Soldwedel, pp. 34–35, 39–40.

[41] On the Knotenkreuz, see K. H. Clasen, 'Die Überwindung des Bösen', in *Neue Beiträge Deutscher Forschung*, ed. E. Fidder, Festschrift W. Worringer (Königsberg, 1943) pp. 18–19. In addition to my Plate IX, he also illustrates the well-known image of Crucifixion in the Saint Gall Gospels (Saint Gall, Stiftsbibliothek, Codex 51, fol. 266r, ca. 750), in which Christ is swathed in interlace.

[42] Clasen, pp. 16–17. For Burchard of Worms: Cyrille Vogel, *Les 'Libri Paenitentiales'*, Typologie des sources du moyen âge occidental, fasc. 27 (Turnhout, Belgium, 1978) pp. 88–89, also 114–15.

[43] Reuterswärd, pp. 120–22. He notes about his symbols that 'their function today is hardly more than decorative, when they occur on chests and other furniture.' Americans would be reminded of the so-called 'hex signs' painted on Pennsylvania Dutch barns.

[44] Ernst Kitzinger, 'The Threshold of the Holy Shrine: Observations on Floor Mosaics at Antioch and Bethlehem', in *Kyriakon: Festschrift Johannes Quasten* (Berlin, 1970) 2:639–47 (quotations on pp. 642–44).

[45] In addition to Clasen, see Cyrus Lawrence Day, *Quipus and Witches' Knots* (Lawrence, Kansas, 1967), chap. 3. Both works are cited by Kitzinger, p. 642.

[46] See at n. 7 above.

Fontenay, 1139–1147. Interior view to the east. (photo: J. Feuillie, CNMHS/SPADEM/ARS, New York, 1990)

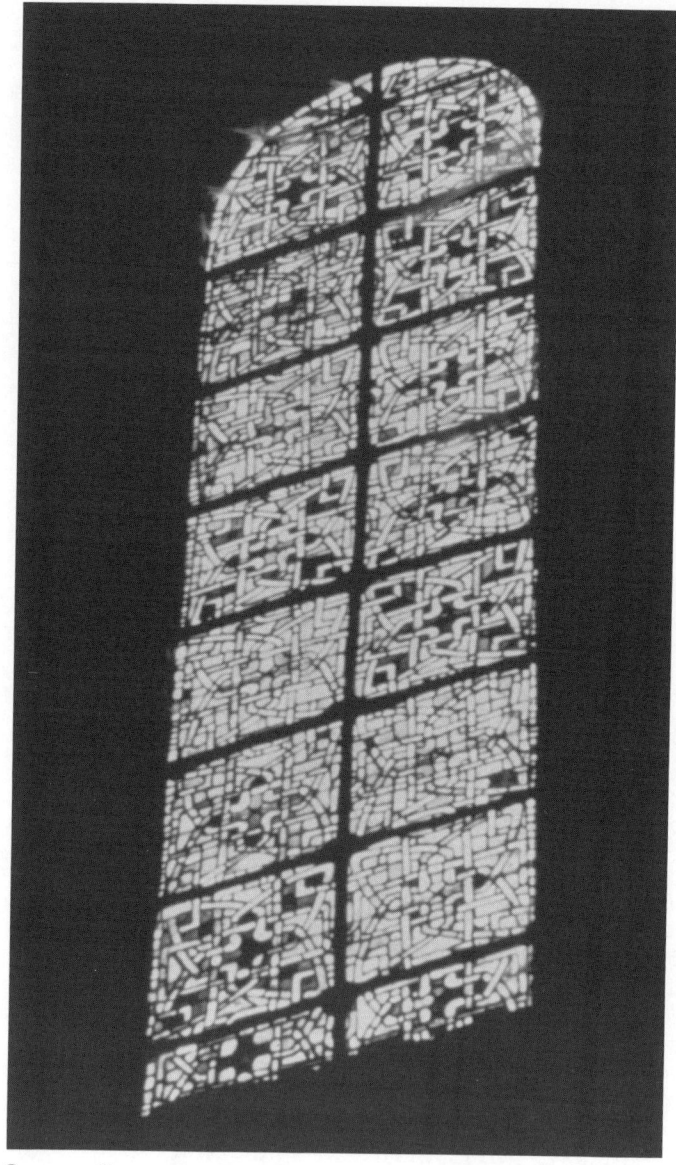

Santes Creus, east wall of north transept, bay T N II.
(photo: Roland Sanfaçon)

Santes Creus, west wall of north transept, bay T N V.
(photo: Roland Sanfaçon)

Sens Cathedral, upper bay of the north tower of the façade.
(photo: Françoise Gatouillat)

Noirlac, fragment now in private collection. (photo: Musées de la ville de Bourges)

Maubuisson, excavated fragments. (photo: courtesy of Catherine Brisac)

San Pietro, Spoleto, façade. The 'cosmic paradise', combining geometric motifs and vegetal ornament. (photo: Patrik Reuterswärd)

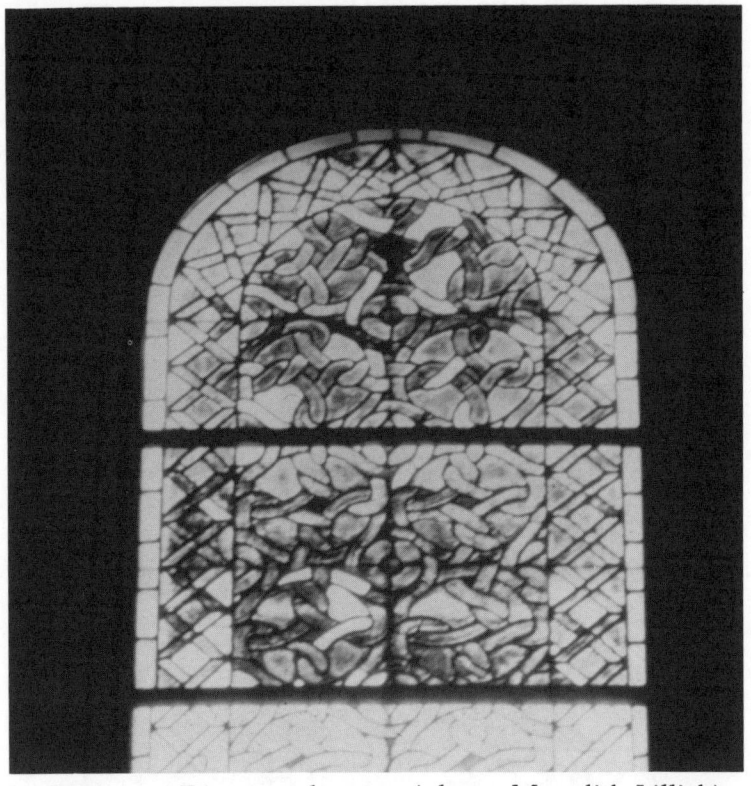

La Bénissons-Dieu, north nave. (photo: Meredith Lillich)

Knotenkreuz. Romanesque crucifix found in Bergen, Norway. Drawing by P. Blix (after Clasen).

Mosaic pavement, House of the Pheonix, Antioch. The three signs at the bottom are inserted into the border where it forms the threshold at the entrance. (photo: Department of Art and Archeology, Princeton University)

HISTORY:
THE BEARER OF CULTURE

John Lukacs
Chestnut Hill College

'HISTORY IS MORE OR LESS bunk. It's tradition. We don't want tradition. We want to live in the present and the only history worth a tinker's dam is the history we make today. I wouldn't give a nickel for all the history in the world. I don't want to live in the past. I want to live in the Now.'

'Tradition is the enemy of progress.'

'The past is a bucket of ashes.'

'The doctrine of original sin was a theory of human behavior adequate to the scientific knowledge of Saint Augustine's time, but overthrown by more recent research.'

Who said (or wrote) these things; and when? Surely they seem, and sound, like the ejaculations of american radicals, of intellectuals during the 'counterculture' of the 1960s. They are not. They were the expressions of american conservatives and populists. The first of these statements was made by Henry Ford; the second by Julius A. Klein, who was Herbert Hoover's Assistant Secretary of Commerce; the third by Carl Sandburg, the most vocal and popular admirer of Abraham Lincoln; the fourth by the Reverend Shailer Matthews, the dean of the Divinity

School of the University of Chicago. All of them date from the 1920s, from the decade that has been recently venerated by american conservatives of all stripes.

We must, therefore, consider two important conditions in the evolution of american history—at the core of which lies the history of american thinking about history. The first is that the anti-historical american idea of progress has had its own tradition, a longer and more deep-seated inclination than we are accustomed to think. The second is the, perhaps more promising, condition that at this time of writing, in 1988, these above cited statements, whether made in the 1960s or in the 1920s, have begun to seem outdated—not only to professional historians, not only to so-called conservatives, but to many Americans who, more or less consciously, are moving toward a different perspective of progress, and toward a different perspective of history.

The subject of this essay is history, rather than progress; but, at least in the beginning, these two subjects of thought are not really separable. So we must keep in mind that the very meaning, the very idea of progress has not been perennial: it has been the product of an age that began about five centuries ago, and many of the features of which are now passing. In the Middle Ages the word 'progress', in English, meant a movement in space, not in time. For the ancient Greeks 'barbarian' meant people who were outside (in space), not behind (in time) of Greece. A thoughtful student of the english language, Logan Pearsall Smith, once suggested that the appearance of the word 'primitive', around 1530, may have marked a profound mutation in the consciousness of our ancestors: the then emerging new meaning that some people were 'behind' others, historically, in time. (A glance at the present ungainly word 'underdeveloped' should reveal how our present concept of 'progress' remains essentially what it was centuries ago.)

But what happened during these centuries was the gradual separation of the idea of progress from an understanding of history. Progress has come to mean linear progress, the constant improvement of mankind which would be accomplished by the technical mastery of men themselves. Eventually this mastery included man's understanding of the universe and of life itself. The result was the theory of evolution, something that is fundamentally contrary to the idea of history, since evolution negates at least three fundamental historical truths: that human beings may change their circumstances but that human nature does not change; that, because of their spiritual and mental nature, that is, their consciousness, only human beings have a history, whereby they are unique among all living beings; and that, unlike mechanical or biological concepts of evolution, human beings make their own destinies, whereby they are responsible for themselves.

There were especial reasons for the american people to believe in progress, not in history. Their Republic was formed in the second half of the eighteenth century, at the zenith of the Modern Age. Moreover, the very idea of a New World suggested a drastic separation from the Old, a shedding of old dispensations, old orders, old societies, old sins: history. Whatever the mental qualities and the learning of the Founding Fathers were, for many Americans thereafter progress, and especially american progress, meant an escape from history—perhaps an escape forward but an escape nonetheless. It was not until the twentieth century, and not until the experience of two world wars, that these, now outdated, mental inclinations began to melt away in the consciousness of Americans. That this has been happening at a time when the more-or-less traditional teaching of history has been either abandoned or become corrupted and compromised in their schools and colleges and universities is lamentable; but it only proves that history is never of one piece, that there is something like a divine irony in history—or, as my favorite proverb says, from the Portuguese: 'God writes straight with crooked lines.' For—notwithstanding what happens in the schools, and notwithstanding the shallowness of political discourse—Americans in the last decades of the

twentieth century have become respectful of the past.*
Our task is to vitalize the consciousness of this condition: in other words, to remind—remind, even more than instruct—people of the inevitable connectedness, the dependence of the present on the past.

Keep in mind that everything that is human has its history—including history, including the past, including memory itself. Human nature does not change, but the operations of human minds change. There are many evidences that different people in different ages did not only see and hear different things but that their eyes and their ears functioned in ways that are different from ours. Their thinking and their consciousness of the past, too, was different from ours. It is thus that there is a glimmer of truth in the half-truth (even as half-truths are more destructive than outright lies) uttered by that man in Herbert Hoover's cabinet which I cited at the start of this essay, that 'tradition is the enemy of progress.' And this glimmer of truth is that people who are unwilling and unthinking captives of their customs and rituals are unable to reform or to change them—the condition expressed in George Santayana's famous aphorism: those who do not know the past are condemned to repeat it. The converse truth latent in this wisdom is that we can liberate ourselves and our minds from our—often self-imposed—burdens and habits of the past only by our conscious understanding and knowledge of it. It is not by some outside force, or fate, that we are condemned to repeat past mistakes; it is by not willing to face the past that we are condemning ourselves.

It is to these conditions of past-knowledge that this essay is directed. We must understand the great, but also inspiring, limitation of the human mind that C. S. Lewis (a thinker who, more than others, was profoundly aware of the changing conditions of human consciousness) expressed, when he once wrote that the past is all that human beings can know, understand, or even imagine. Human imagination is perhaps the most evident example of the supernatural existence of spirituality; it is *almost* limitless.

Almost, but not quite. The exception is the past. As C. S. Lewis reminds us: try to imagine a wholly new color, or a wholly new monster, or even a third sex. Nobody can. All we can do is to imagine a new combination of colors, a new combination of animal features, or a new combination of the two sexes that we already know. It is therefore that the past is real: not only tangible in all kinds of surviving objects but the inevitably central substance of our minds—as, indeed, memory is not merely one component of the human brain but inevitably and centrally involved in all of its functions.

The past is very large. As a matter of fact, it is getting larger every moment, every day—which is why, in an important sense, children are older than their parents: they have more past to look back on. People who lived at the time of Hitler or Stalin—and people who came into this world after Hitler and Stalin—know something that their ancestors did not know. They know more about tyrants and dictatorships, because—all similarities notwithstanding—Hitler was *not* Napoleon, and Stalin was *not* Ivan the Terrible. But our problem with history is that most people—including most historians—believe that history is that part of the past which is recorded. That is not sufficient. The recorded portion of the past is, of course, smaller than the entire past. The remembered past is larger than the recorded past but still smaller than the entire past. But we must accustom ourselves to the recognition that history is more than the recorded portion of the past; it is the recorded *and* the remembered past. There are dictionaries which will tell us—wrongly—that 'history' consists of those events and men and women of the past that were worth recording. This is not so. There is no difference between a person and a 'historical person', as there is no difference between a source and a historical source. That is not merely a democratic desideratum or a democratic statement. It is an evident reality in this age of bureaucracy into which our democracies are devolving, when a letter from one's grandmother may be *even more* of an authentic historical document than a letter or a speech or any other record of a president or of a public figure that has been thought up, drafted, written (and, in many instances, machine-signed) by someone else (perhaps by an anonymous bureaucrat).

But history is more than a compilation of surviving documents. It is not documents that make history; it is history that makes the documents. In the bibliographical remarks of one of my works I wrote:

> Living persons, all kinds of persons with all kinds of complexities and confused and ephemeral purposes, left us those residues in the form of records that are inevitably necessary for our reconstruction of the past. But it is experience and imagination that vitalize these residues. On the one hand, there may be more than one golden needle in the dustiest of bureaucratic haystacks. On the other hand, the historian must be honest enough to admit to himself that, in most cases, he knows what he is looking for; he re-searches the past rather than searches it; he knows what he wants to find.

During the last one hundred years the practices and the purposes of professional historianship have often led to a narrowness of perspectives—at the same time when the, often inchoate, appetite for history among previously untouched masses of people has grown. But the subject of this essay is not the history of professional historianship; it is the history of history, of historical thinking and of historical consciousness, of which the development of professional history has been only a part. (Few people know that history was not taught in the Middle Ages at all, that it was not a subject in any university until the eighteenth century, and that as late as one hundred years ago scholars and men of letters in England thought that to grant a Ph.D. degree in history was a slightly absurd idea.)

The history of history consists of three stages. From the very beginning of mankind living in history has been a fourth dimension of human life: among all living beings, historical existence is the patrimony of human beings alone, because of their conscious cognition of life and of time. The second stage came with the Greeks who, among other things, gave us the word 'history' (originally with the meaning of re-search). This was the achievement of historical thinking, a conscious and determined reconstruction of a certain portion of the past—as Thucydides said, for the purpose of reducing current untruths. During the following two thousand years there were all kinds of historical writers (and not only chroniclers); but the interesting thing is that—unlike, say, in medicine or mathematics or in most natural sciences—there was no further fundamental development in that regard. A few illustrations of this condition must suffice here. In Plutarch's great greek and roman historical portraits, for example, there is no account of the development of his subjects: he describes them as they were, not how they had developed through their lives. Again, the first autobiography, that is, the description of the developing life of a man, came less than five hundred years ago; its first practitioner may have been Benvenuto Cellini. Around that time emerged the last phase, that of historical consciousness. The very word, and meaning, of 'anachronism', for example, appears in England and Western Europe less than three hundred years ago. Before that, with all of his great interest in history, a Shakespeare, for example, presented Antony or Cleopatra in contemporary elizabethan costumes and settings, and a Titian or a Raphael would paint ancient and biblical people and settings in sixteenth-century italian clothes and with sixteenth-century houses and carriages in the background. By the eighteenth century all of this changed. Words such as 'century', 'decade', 'epoch' (and, as I mentioned earlier, 'progress' and 'primitive') had acquired a new meaning; and, for the first time in history, people began to distinguish between Ancient, Middle, and Modern Ages. I believe that this change represents, or at least reflects, a mutation of consciousness (at that time in the western world alone) that has been as important, and profound, as the contemporaneous scientific revolution, that is, a new way of thinking about man's place in the universe and about the so-called laws of nature—because the new scientific way of thinking involved principally men's relationship to things, whereas the emergence of historical consciousness involved their relationship to themselves.

What then happened during the last three hundred years may be summed up as follows. In the eighteenth century history was regarded as a—more and more interesting—branch of literature. In the nineteenth century history became seen as a science (in the then more spacious sense of the word 'science', as still exists in the german word *Wissenschaft*, encompassing both science and knowledge). About the twentieth century we cannot make such a general statement, because the evolution of historical consciousness in our times shows two different tendencies of thought. There are those (this applies, alas, to most professional historians) who are inclined to see history as a kind of social science, and there are those, including this writer, who recognize history as an increasingly spreading form of thought.

In any event, by the twentieth century it is history that has become the bearer of culture, because of the dominance of the historical form of thought, of which the above mentioned interest and respect for the past, the spreading popular appetite for history, is but a part, though one with protean and multiple manifestations. The word 'culture' was not known to the Greeks: but they knew that what we call culture, including art, consists of discrimination, and also comes from a kind of self-knowledge, which is what Socrates meant when he said that the unexamined life is not worth living.

History is the self-knowledge of mankind. In individual lives self-knowledge is usually the mark of a certain maturity. But, in spite of their many similarities, the history of humankind, and even the history of a nation, is not governed by the same conditions as govern the short life of a man. Self-knowledge itself has a history, as indeed everything that is human has a history—which may sum up the essence of history being a form of thought. Our self-knowledge is not quite the same as that of Socrates. His statement that 'know thyself' is the principal basis of all knowledge remains as inspiring and valid as it was two thousand and five hundred years ago, and so is Alexander Pope's statement of two hundred and fifty years ago, that 'the proper study of mankind is man.' Yet we have reached a stage in the evolution of our consciousness where 'know thyself' has come to mean: 'know thy past'. That historical consciousness and self-consciousness developed together may be seen, among other things, from the fact that, when new words and new meanings of words reflecting the former first emerged three or four hundred years ago, so had new words and new meanings involving the interior human condition—for example, new employments of the prefix 'self': 'self-pity', 'self-love', 'egotism', 'self-indulgence', etc. which were part of human nature ever since Adam and Eve; but the conscious recognition of their meaning began to occur only three or four hundred years ago, reflecting an increasing internalization of our consciousness.*

'Know thy past': by now we are not only aware that history (way beyond professional history) is *the*—and not only *a*—bearer of culture; we are also aware that only by knowing the past are we able to liberate ourselves from its burdens. In this sense the profound difference between physical evolution and history corresponds to the difference between fate and destiny, or between determinism and free will. The history of man's destiny has been marked by his struggle against the dumb determinism of things. Conversely, the more ignorant people are, the more determined their fate. And the main ingredient of that ignorance is, almost always, a willful and unthinking ignorance of the past.

NOTE

* There are innumerable—and concrete—evidences of this. Since I have often written about them, and since this is not the principal subject of this essay, I must restrict myself to only one example—which, at least to me, is very telling. In american English in the 1920s the word 'modern' was a positive adjective in all of its employments (in England *circa* 1925 a 'modern' girl was a fast girl; in America she was an all-american girl)—and 'old-fashioned' meant dusty, antiquated, weak (an 'old-fashioned' boy was a sissy). Now contrast this with what has been happening during the last twenty years, when 'modern' has lost all of its shine, while 'old-fashioned' has become an attractive term, used by all kinds of designers and advertisers and publicity men shamelessly.

THE CISTERCIAN NUNNERY OF SWINE PRIORY: ITS CHURCH AND CHOIR STALLS

John A. Nichols
Slippery Rock University

SWINE PRIORY was one of twenty-seven cistercian convents for women founded in England during the Middle Ages. The founder, Robert de Veri, settled on the site five miles north northwest of Kingston-upon-Hull in Yorkshire, the East Riding, at some date before 1153.[1] All that remains of the nunnery today (see Plate I) is the choir of the nuns' church which is used as the parish church for the village of Swine.[2]

Modern observers are perplexed by the size and beauty of the convent's only standing structure. The encyclopedic *Buildings of England* series by Nicholaus Pevsner, for example, has said: '... The present church was the east appendix to the nuns' church, although a remarkably lavish one. ...' And Arthur Mee, in *Yorkshire: East Riding with York*, calls the church '... a striking possession for... a priory of Cistercian nuns.'[3] Their surprise is justified since the current scholarship on medieval english nunneries is that nearly all convents were so poorly endowed that they were financially and administratively unable to build elaborate physical plants.[4] Moreover, as a house of the cistercian order, Swine should not have been 'lavish'.[5] To test the prevailing notions about medieval nunneries it is appropriate to examine the convent of Swine both as a house of women and as a monastery within the cistercian order.

Pevsner and Mee made their remarks about Swine Priory because its remains do not match their ideas of what a medieval cistercian nunnery should have looked like. Physical descriptions written by medieval observers of some cistercian sites have produced modern reconstructions of monastic plants. Esholt Priory, for example, located in Yorkshire, the West Riding, has had its ground plan reconstructed in a modern study because the convent was described by members of the suppression commission when a survey of the monastery was taken in 1539.[6]

Esholt nunnery is quite typically monastic, containing a small aisleless church on the north of the cloister, chapter house and parlor with dormitory built over the east range, kitchen and refectory on the south range, and servant and storage chambers on the west range. The same can be said of Kirklees Priory, also in Yorkshire, the West Riding, which was excavated in 1904–1905.[7] This cistercian nunnery, identified in a ballad as the place where Robin Hood died,[8] was quite simple and certainly very small, with the cloister only forty feet square. Based on descriptions such as these, it is easy to explain why students of the subject believe that cistercian nunneries were simple and unpretentious.

Swine, on the other hand, apparently differs from the norm. Based on documentary evidence, especially archbishop's visitation records, the suppression commission report of 1539, and the standing church in the village which was visited by me in 1979, I have constructed a diagram of what Swine's physical plant would have looked like in the fifteenth and sixteenth centuries (see Plate II). Using the measurements and language of the suppression commission report, the following is a physical description of the nunnery.

The church (see Plate III) was a single aisle nave that was seventy-six feet long and twenty-one feet wide. Its two-story stone walls were covered by painted boards which were protected by a lead roof. The choir was fifty-four feet long, and it contained thirty-six well-preserved wooden stalls of wainscot boards and timber on both sides of the church. One altar was in the choir, and two altars were in the body of the church. There were thirteen glazed windows containing 100 feet of glass by the commissioners' best estimation. The walls were covered by lead roofs, having windows all around, all glazed except one, with approximately 320 feet of glass. The chapter house was on the east part of the cloister and was thirty feet long and twenty-two feet wide; one window was found in it which contained twelve feet of glass. The dorter was over the chapter house and it was 100 feet in length and twenty-two feet in width, with a low roof covered with lead. The frater or refectory was on the south side, and it was sixty-eight feet long and twenty-four feet wide, with a high roof covered by lead and twelve little windows having thirty feet of glass in all. Two low cellars or rooms were under the frater. On the west range of the cloister were three chambers on the lower floor and three chambers above. This range was forty feet in length and eighteen feet in width, with a low roof covered by lead. The kitchen, thirty feet long and sixteen feet wide, had a good brick chimney. The infirmary was thirty-six feet long and eighteen feet wide; it was under one whole roof covered with tile and had two unglazed bay windows. There were small chambers under the infirmary for poultry and storage. A little sixteen feet by twelve feet house was at the east side of the infirmary, which was covered with a tile roof and had a brick chimney. The vicar's mansion had four priest chambers under one roof, with the cross end being forty feet in length and sixteen feet in width. It had timber walls which were covered with a tile roof.

In addition, a great number of outer buildings are mentioned, the location of which cannot be established with any degree of accuracy. Aerial photos (see Plate I) of the site show wall outlines in the turf west of the village, which must have been the servants' quarters, mill house, baker house, malt house, brew house, grain house, corn barn, cow barn, hay barn, ox house, stables, dove house, and kiln mentioned in the survey.[9] Parenthetically, a mound called Grant's Hill, located 300 yards due west of the church, was excavated in 1960–1961. The archaeologists found that a mound had been fashioned out of clay and peat sometime between 1350 and 1425. The mound was approximately eighty feet in diameter and fifteen feet high. It was neither a prehistoric nor a danish burial mound, as the excavators had hoped, nor a motte for military purposes. The mound contained forty-nine pieces of pottery and seven pieces of iron objects. All items correlated to previously identified pottery fired in the area in the fourteenth and fifteenth centuries. I have concluded that the religious at Swine were responsible for the mound, even though there is no record of a kiln at the nunnery.[10] The suppression commission's report proves that, indeed, there was one. In all there were seventeen outer buildings set apart from the cloister, some of which were in 'sore decay'. Collectively, the monastery with its buildings, grounds, orchards, and ponds covered a large area to the west of the village according to the best estimates of the commissioners.

The nuns' church (see Plate III) still extant in the village of Swine was started soon after the nunnery was founded in 1153 and was finished not later than 1189. The interior (see Plate IV) has four bays divided by round, stumpy piers that have multi-scalloped flat capitals which support an arcade of two steps, with pointed arches, two of which are adorned with norman zigzag designs. The ten clerestory windows, five on each side of the church, are small and pointed too. Clearly the church at this stage was transitional (1154–1189) since the pointed arches are in a building which is otherwise romanesque in character.[11] The exterior has a tower, which was built in 1787 to replace the medieval tower which preceded it. An engraving of the church from 1784 shows the nuns' tower before it was destroyed. There are lengths of string-course running north and south on the exterior of the church, and shallow buttresses can be found on the west and east walls.[12] The church can be entered through either the one doorway on the north side or the two doorways on the south side of the church.

A fire damaged the church and monastery at some time in 1308, according to a report entered in the archiepiscopal register concerning a dispute between the nuns and villagers of Swine. Repairs to the nunnery were ordered by Archbishop Melton in 1318. He told the prioress to act without delay in having the dormitory covered so that the nuns would be protected from storms; he ordered the roofs to other buildings repaired as soon as possible.[13] It was after these dates that the north and south aisles with 'decorated' tracery windows were added to the church. A north chapel was constructed between 1307 and 1377, with a window on the east wall containing five panels of glass. The final medieval phase in the remodeling of the church occurred between 1377 and 1485, when 'perpendicular' windows were added to the south wall over the sanctuary and an enormous eastern window was placed above the altar. Even today the large, clear glass east window of seven 'lights' (see Plate V) overwhelms the viewer because of its size and location at the end of the choir.

The nuns allowed generous benefactors to be buried in the church, and some fine alabaster monuments can be seen in the south aisle and north chapel. The earliest (see Plate VI) on the south wall dates from 1370 and has the effigies of an unknown knight and lady in a tomb with four shields in quatrefoils.[14] The easternmost tomb, which separates the sanctuary from the chapel, is of Sir Robert and Constance Hilton, who died around 1372. Their tomb (see Plate VII) has shields around the base. Today only a single kneeling mourner can be seen on the side, but the condition of the base makes it difficult to establish if there were accompanying mourners.[15] A memorial of a lone knight on the north wall of the chapel (see Plate VIII) is probably Peter de Bukton, who willed in 1413 that his '...body be buried in the Quire of the Church of the nuns of St. Mary of Swine.'[16] The last monuments are of Sir Robert and Joan Hilton, who died in 1431 and 1432 respectively. Their tombs (see Plate IX), which are embellished with a pair of angels holding shields, are also between the chapel and sanctuary in a line to the west of their ancestors. Collectively, the 'array of monuments [are] widely accepted as the finest collection of their kind in an East Riding Church.'[17] In addition to the alabaster tombs, windows, and architectural features, the church also has some wooden art which dates from the era of the nunnery. The most noticeable piece is an oak screen (see Plate X) which separates the north chapel from the aisle. It has linenfold panels and family shields, now gone, which were constructed in 1531 for Sir George Darcy in memory of his father, Lord Thomas, and other ancestors.[18] Of the thirty-six wooden wainscot stalls mentioned in the suppression commission survey of 1539,[19] nine can still be seen in the choir of the church, and it is these stalls or misericords which I shall discuss in further detail.

In the medieval church, the divine offices were said daily, and it was expected that the celebrant do so standing. Even when it became customary to kneel, sitting during the offices was canonically forbidden. As a concession to the old, infirm, or weak an act of mercy (*misericordia*) was extended by allowing wooden seats to be so constructed that persons could sit or lean against the seat when it was in an upright position, producing an appearance that the person was standing. The support on the underside of the seat was carved, and such a seat has come to be known as a misericord, thousands of which were created throughout Europe in the Middle Ages.[20]

In Great Britain nearly every extant misericord has a central figure carved under the ledge with wing supporters on the left and right which many times, but not always, relate to the subject in the center. Swine's misericords do not have supporters and in this way are more like continental seats which are also carved without supporters.[21] The subject matter sculpted in the carvings is incredibly varied, the artists taking their themes from book illustrations, stained glass figures, or daily life scenes. For this reason, one can find religious subject matter, domestic scenes, leisure pursuits, humor and satire, romance and popular tales, animals or creatures of fantasy installed side by side with little rhyme or documented reason for their locations. One should not find it surprising to see a carving of a beloved saint resting beside an obviously sexually suggestive scene.[22]

At Swine the current collection of misericords consists of five human heads or bodies and four creatures of fantasy or what are called grotesques, that is, representations of creatures which are abnormal or normally cannot exist. There are four misericords on the south side of the choir and four directly opposite on the right side.

The first misericord (see Plate XI) is of a woman, perhaps a prioress, in a wimple, who appears to be winking at the viewer. She is flanked by two tailless, hat-donning monkeys, one of whom has exceptionally long claws on talon-like feet. Medieval monkeys or apes always appear without tails (*cauda*) and were symbolically linked with evil or Satan, who had no Scripture (*caudex*).[23] By late medieval times the ape could imply a variety of meanings, and when associated with members of the church became a symbol of mocked piety.[24] Of the hundreds of misericords that I have seen or of which I have read descriptions, nothing is like this Swine stall, but a Haarlem, Netherlands, early sixteenth-century peasant's face, partly covered by a hood, shows a striking similarity.[25] Next to the 'winking prioress' is a seat (see Plate XII) with a delightful looking elf wearing a bishop's mitre. He has pointed ears, winged arms, and a corkscrew tail where his feet should be. The face is poutlike because the artist accented the cheek bones and carved the lips in a tightly closed frown. To the east and next in line is a carving of the head of a man whose face is swathed in foliage (see Plate XIII). Leaves spew out of his mouth and encircle his face. Such representations are called the 'Green Man' or 'Jack-in-the-Green' and have become the subject of at least one exhaustive scholarly study.[26] This motif dates from the prehistoric and pagan eras; the earliest extant leaf mask is from the second century A.D. in the Roman Empire. Its evolution can be followed continuously throughout the Middle Ages, and it is a popular image well suited for sculptural decoration. The meaning of the 'Green Man' is not altogether clear, but he seems to convey a sinister or demonic symbolism rather than a benevolent nature. Regardless of the meaning, the purely decorative aspect of the imagery is understandable.[27]

The last misericord (see Plate XIV) on the south side of the choir is the bust of a young woman with a head-dress dating from the second half of the fourteenth century. A fillet or metal band was used on the forehead to hold the veil or wimple in place during this time. The material hung loosely on either side of the face to give the wearer a square-looking appearance.[28] 'Fashionable ladies, from 1340 to 1400, often arranged their hair in vertical plaits which were passed straight down in front of the ears from the fillet to the angle of the jaw, and sometimes held in place by a net. The ends were turned up and hidden under the head-dress.'[29] The young woman at Swine has her hair concealed by her head-dress. The straight edge of the veil is next to her face, and the artist has ruffled the outer covering, giving it a more elaborate effect. Although the piece is relatively simple, the young woman's countenance is most attractive.

Opposite this stall is a misericord of a man in profile wearing a soft cloth hat and sporting a pointed beard (see Plate XV). The twisting lines in the elf's tail are repeated here by the sculptor in the man's beard. As with the dating of the woman's head-dress, both the style of the man's beard and cap date from the fourteenth century. Young men then wore short beards and had clean shaven cheeks. The close-fitting caul of linen, which enclosed the hair and ears and was tied under the chin, was called a coif.[30] It first appeared around 1200 and was worn by men well into the fourteenth century. Over the coif was normally worn a hat, and, starting around 1300, it was common for the brim to be peaked in front and turned up in back as seen in this Swine misericord.[31]

To the west in the next choir stall is a grotesque of a griffin which is standing on a foundation while at the same time biting its tail. Griffins are winged quadrupeds with the body and hind quarters of a lion and head and wings of an eagle. According to a twelfth-century bestiary, '... the griffin was vehemently hostile to hares and would tear to pieces any human being.' The motif is commonly found on misericords either alone, or in pairs, attacking other animals or humans who have the misfortune to be caught in their strong claws or beaks.[32] The Swine griffin has wings which are carved exactly like those found on the elf on the other side of the aisle, which gives evidence for the notion that the work was accomplished by a single artist-carver.

The next misericord (see Plate XVI) is the face of a man with hat, moustache, and beard. Short forked beards, generally twisted at the end, and moustaches were common for men in the fourteenth century. In the previous century full beards were normal in England, but during the fourteenth century the cheeks became clean shaven, and by the early fifteenth century it was standard for men to go beardless.[33] The hat worn by the man in the Swine misericord is one with a round crown and close, turned-up brim. Such hats were frequently in style in the fourteenth century, which suggests that the artist was drawing his inspiration from fashions of his contemporaries, for the vogue of the two other head-dresses also date from the fourteenth century.[34] In addition, the sculptor's carving style is most clearly shown in this seat. In all the human heads, the eyes have concave, carved pupils which give the subject an open-eyed stare. The hair and beard have a spiral, corkscrew effect, and the persons have some type of head covering, be it a hat, cap, or head-dress.

The eighth and last misericord (see Plate XVII) on the north side of the choir is of a hat-wearing nude man. He lies prostrate on his back while his bearded face peers between his legs which are held up in the air. Because the man is exposing himself to the viewer, a victorian vicar of the church had this misericord plastered over, so as not to offend the members of his congregation. The plaster was removed from the seat in this century, but the discoloration of its effect can still be seen. Sexually provocative subjects probably saved a great number of misericords, since the soldiers under Henry VIII's or Oliver Cromwell's orders were more interested in destroying religious scenes representing roman catholic beliefs and practices than 'secular ones'. But '... during the nineteenth century a number of misericords in Bristol Cathedral were considered so obscene that the dean had them destroyed, and exactly the same thing happened at Chester.'[35] Fortunately, at Swine the puritan morality of the vicar led him only to plaster over the work rather than destroy it.

The highly erotic or frankly sexual imagery found in the medieval churches of Europe has always attracted considerable academic curiosity.[36] Figures exposing their genitals, called in Irish 'sheela-na-gig', were mostly females who spread their legs and pulled apart their pudenda with their hands. They are found in the sculpture of churches and monasteries throughout the British Isles and France.[37] 'The exposure of the genitalia was supposed to be an evil-averting act, and it may be that this was the significance of these figures. Again, they may have formed part of the teaching of the Church against sensuality, but in this case such crude figuration would surely have been potentially dangerous in arousing, rather than repressing, such carnal feelings.'[38] In attempting to match the Swine figure to a similar male depiction, I found a roundel from a doorway decoration in Autun, France where the man does not have his feet in the air, but his legs are spread apart.[39] Another french scene, this time of a rear exposure, can be seen on a sixteenth-century misericord in the cathedral in Treguier.[40] And in England one can see another rear exposure, this time in a misericord in Magdalen College Chapel, Oxford.[41]

The last misericord (see Plate XVIII) at Swine is not in the choir, but rather it is nailed to the underside of a pulpit seat which was installed in 1619 in the nave of the Church:

> The head is crowned with curly hair and the face is bearded, the hair in both cases being depicted as long strands ending in curls. Two indentations are shown in the brow. The nose is a normal, human one. The ears are non-human, animal ears, probably cat's. The pupils of the almond-shaped eyes are carved out [like the others at Swine]. . . . The upper row of teeth are shown and between them and the lower lip protrudes a long narrow tongue which extends nearly as far as the tip of the beard. The upper lip of the mouth is extremely thick. The whole appearance of the face is crude and menacing, though not to the extent that is characteristic of some of the grotesque faces illustrated and discussed by Ronald Sheridan and Anne Ross in their book *Grotesque and Gargoyles*.[42]

A large number of monsters with protruding tongues can be seen in churches and cathedrals all over Europe. These monsters are particularly evident in bosses high overhead in the roof of the building.[43] Their grotesque faces, expressive eyes, sharp teeth, and extended tongues seem most menacing, and were intended to keep evil powers at bay while the services in the church were being conducted.[44]

In all, there are only nine misericords in the church at Swine, which reportedly had thirty-six in 1539. What happened to those missing twenty-seven has yet to be ascertained, although sixteen stalls were said to exist in the nineteenth century; yet no evidence is given to confirm that number.[45] In like manner, the date of the Swine misericords is most uncertain, with the earliest guess at around 1400 and the latest at 1531.[46] The only method used to date seats with some degree of success in the past has been to look at the shape of the ledge over the carved center piece.[47] The shape of the ledge at Swine matches the design for seats in the first half of the fourteenth century. In addition, the few english misericords without supporters date mostly from the late thirteenth or early fourteenth centuries.[48] The fact that the hair styles and head coverings on all human misericords corresponds to the fashions of fourteenth-century England offers further evidence that the Swine choir stalls were carved in that century. Since the priory is known to have had a fire around 1308, it seems safe to estimate that the misericords were made for the nunnery after that date, thus suggesting an earlier date than any given heretofore by experts on this matter.

As regards style, composition, and skill, I think that the misericords at Swine are not as elaborate or as intricate as ones carved in the fifteenth and sixteenth centuries, but there is a certain simplicity of line in the stalls which is attractive and pleasing to the eye. The artist's subject matter is consistent with the themes commonly found in the Middle Ages, and what was carved makes a statement about the nuns who commissioned the work. While we do not have all thirty-six misericords to judge, the remaining nine have a uniformity not only to one another but also complement the church for which they were built.

Now the discussion returns to the one first raised at the outset of this paper, namely, how does one account for a cistercian nunnery having the 'lavish church' which I have sketched in this article? The answer, quite frankly, is that Swine, like a great number of other twelfth-century english nunneries, was not founded in the same way as if it had been a monastery for cistercian monks. The reason for this is that the General Chapter, which consisted of the abbots from the cistercian houses, did not develop a uniform policy of incorporating nunneries into the order until the first quarter of the thirteenth century. I do not explain this development here, since my remarks on this matter have been presented elsewhere.[49] But clearly the order's policy not only had a profound effect on the spiritual and temporal life of the convents but also explains why the physical plants of the nunneries differed from houses of men.

We know a great deal about cistercian art because, over the past three decades, many studies have been written which not only analyze the architectural features of existing buildings but also enunciate what the early Cistercians themselves had to say on the subject—on how, for example, Bernard of Clairvaux's ideas became realities within the monasteries of the order and how the design, architecture, windows, and even floor tiles reflect the aesthetics of the founding fathers of Cîteaux. There was such a high degree of uniformity that it is quite proper to speak of a cistercian model for building a monastery.[50]

To explain this high degree of uniformity, it might be interesting to note how cistercian monasteries of men were founded. At Netley Abbey, its founder, Peter des Roches, bishop of Winchester, had his will written so that land and money were provided for the creation of a new house of male religious. He petitioned the General Chapter for approval, and an investigating commission consisting of two cistercian abbots, from Waverly and Quarr, were charged with finding an appropriate site, arranging for the physical plant to be built, and assigning an abbot, twelve monks, and three *conversi* from a mother house to take possession. If all went as planned, the General Chapter would officially incorporate the new monastery into the order at the next regularly scheduled meeting.[51] In theory, the monks were not sent to a new place without the prior construction of an oratory, refectory, dormitory, guest house, and gate-keeper's cell. The buildings, at first, did not have to be permanent stone structures, they could be temporary wooden buildings that would take less time for the founding religious to prepare. Once in operation, cistercian standards could be maintained by the visitation system and the disciplinary powers of the General Chapter.[52] In this way, one can see how uniformity could be controlled for the monks. In the case of nuns, however, no such uniformity was conceivable, since the same type of incorporation for the women was not possible in the twelfth century.

Since Swine's founder did not have the organizational structure of the Cistercians to supervise the foundation, he might have turned to the local bishop or a friendly abbot to aid with the establishment of a convent. Robert de Veri had some options available to him in 1153. With the approval of the bishop, the founder could request that the nunnery be subject to the *Rule* of Saint Benedict or the so-called *Rule* of Saint Augustine.[53] If the latter were chosen, the women were known as augustinian canonesses. If the former were selected, various interpretations of the *Rule* of Saint Benedict were possible. First, the house could be simply a regular benedictine monastery of nuns subject to the bishop, but the reforming zeal of the twelfth century made a foundation of this type less common. As a consequence, the founder was more likely to have the convent follow a rule as it was used and interpreted at the monasteries of Fontevault, Prémontré, or Sempringham. These famous mother houses which started new orders permitted convents of women to be affiliated with them, but in all cases canons or priests were attached to serve the nuns' spiritual needs and *conversi* to serve their temporal needs. In other words, the foundation of a nunnery along the new reforming lines of the twelfth century required the physical plant to have accommodations for not only the nuns but priests, 'lay' brothers, and 'lay' sisters as well.

A recent book on this subject has investigated the foundations of nunneries between the years 1130 and 1165 in the south of England compared with those in the north. The author has found that southern nunneries were made up exclusively of women, while northern houses combined nuns with canons, 'lay' brothers, and 'lay' sisters regardless of monastic affiliation. Her theory is that the difference derived from the fact that southern nunneries were founded with income-producing property that could be managed by nuns alone, while northern houses were given properties like churches and pasture land that required the use of men as priests for the former and 'lay' brothers for the latter. The syneisactism of the northern nunneries not only explains the reason for the male/female cooperation in the gilbertine order, but also clarifies why the cistercian nunneries had this type of male element as well.[54]

Instead of the nunneries having the relative uniformity of the cistercian houses of men, the physical plants could take on unusual characteristics, since separate areas had to be built for men as well as women. Evidence which I have gathered so far indicates that at least nine of the twenty-seven english cistercian nunneries were founded as 'double houses', and Swine Priory was different and elaborate because it was one of these nine.[55] In the future, when one writes about cistercian nunneries, it would be a mistake to assume that each convent was a scaled down version of a house of cistercian monks. When nunneries have artistic features which are at odds with cistercian aesthetics, it should alert one to the possibility that the convent of nuns had to make provision for personnel that made the buildings different from what had come to be accepted as normal in cistercian monasteries of men.

In approaching the subject of cistercian nuns, the investigator must not be satisfied merely to compare the houses of women to the houses of men. It is necessary to evaluate the women's monasteries on their own terms by looking into their history and not be disappointed if their features are 'uncistercian'. When such a study is accomplished, I think one will achieve a greater appreciation of the role women have played in the past. The impression that all english cistercian nunneries, for example, were simple, uninteresting structures can no longer be justified. The nuns of Swine made a contribution to their time and place in history; the remains of their church and choir stalls provide ample evidence of that fact.

NOTES

[1] David Knowles and R. Neville Hadcock (edd.), *Medieval Religious Houses: England and Wales* (New York: St. Martin's Press, 1971) pp. 272, 276. A short and entirely inadequate history of the nunnery can be found in T. M. Fallows, *Victoria County History* [hereafter VCH]: *York* (London: Archibald, 3 vols., 1913) 3:178–82.

[2] Aerial photography courtesy and permission of Cambridge University, Department of Aerial Photography, FU 47 (June 17, 1951).

[3] Nikolaus Pevsner, *The Buildings of England: Yorkshire East Riding* (Baltimore: Penguin, 1972) p. 353; and Arthur Mee, *Yorkshire: East Riding with York*, ed. C.L.S. Linnell (London: Hodden and Stoughton, 1964) p. 232.

[4] For example, see Eileen Power, *Medieval English Nunneries* (New York: Biblio, 1922) and the appropriate volumes in VCH. Sharon K. Elkins, *Holy Women of Twelfth-Century England* (Chapel Hill: University of North Carolina Press, 1988) makes the point that houses founded in the twelfth and later centuries were frequently poorly endowed, especially in the north of England where Swine is located.

[5] The spartan, yet harmonious features of the cistercian monasteries, especially in the twelfth and early thirteenth centuries, are well documented. See, for example, Benoit Chauvin (ed.), *Mélanges a la Mèmoire du Père Anselme Dimier: Architecture Cistercienne* (Arbois: Pupillin, 1982) vol. 3; and Louis J. Lekai, *The Cistercians: Ideals and Reality* (Kent, Ohio: Kent State University Press, 1977) pp. 261–81 for his chapter on art, and pp. 428–29 for the annotated bibliography. Also recommended is Lionel H. Butler and Chris Given-Wilson, *Medieval Monasteries of Great Britain* (London: Michael Joseph, 1979), which is an excellent comparative study of eighty houses (unfortunately, not one nunnery) of all the major orders. There are only a few articles on the architecture of cistercian convents: Anselm Dimier, 'L'architecture des églises de moniales cisterciennes', *Cîteaux: Commentarii cistercienses* 25 (1974) 8–23; John A. Nichols, 'The Medieval Remains of Sinningthwaite Nunnery', in *Studies in Cistercian Art and Architecture*, ed. Meredith P. Lillich (Kalamazoo: Cistercian Publications, 1982) 1:49–52, figs. 1–6; and John A. Nichols, 'Medieval English Cistercian Nunneries: Their Art and Physical Remains', in *Mélanges Anselme Dimier*, 3:151–76.

[6] H. E. Bell, 'Esholt Priory', *Yorkshire Archaeological Journal* [hereafter YAJ] 33 (1936–1938) 4–33, whose reconstruction was from an article by William Brown (ed.), 'Description of the Buildings of Twelve Small Yorkshire Priories at the Time of the Reformation', YAJ 9 (1886) 197–215, 321–33. His source was London: Public Records Office, SP 5/2/25–47.

[7] George Armytage, 'Kirklees Priory', YAJ 20 (1908–1909) 24–32.

[8] For a good article on the relationships between the priory and the legend of Robin Hood, see J. W. Walker, 'Robin Hood Identified', YAJ

36 (1944–1947) 4–46. Also read J. C. Holt, *Robin Hood* (London: Thames and Hudson, 1982).

[9] Brown, 'Description', pp. 328–30.

[10] W. J. Varley, 'Giant's Hill, Swine: The Excavations, 1960–61', YAJ 45 (1973), 142–48.

[11] Pevsner, *Buildings in England*, p. 353. For dating of English architecture, my source is the eighteenth edition of Sir Banister Flectcher's *A History of Architecture*, ed. J. C. Palmes (New York: Charles Scribner's and Sons, 1975) pp. 624–25.

[12] John Murray, *Handbook for Travellers in Yorkshire* (3rd ed., London, 1882) p. 122.

[13] William Dugdale (ed.), *Monasticon Anglicanum*, edd. John Caley et al. (London, 8 vols., 1817–1830; rpt. Westmead, England, 1970) 5:493; and T. M. Fallow, VCH:York, p. 181.

[14] Pevsner, *Buildings of England*, p. 354. While it is impossible to say who is buried in these tombs, it seems likely that they were from the local aristocratic families of the area. See Barbara English, *The Lords of Holderness 1086–1260* (Oxford: Oxford University Press, 1979), which details the early history of these families.

[15] J. M. Raines, *A Short History of the Church of St. Mary the Virgin Swine* (Beverly: Wright and Hoggard Ltd, n.d.), a pamphlet, unpaginated.

[16] Thomas Thompson, *The History of the Church and Priory of Swine in Holderness* (Hall: Thomas Topping, 1894) pp. 46–47; and Fred H. Crossley, *English Church Monuments A.D. 1150–1550: An Introduction to the Study of Tombs and Effigies of the Medieval Period* (London: B. T. Batsford, 1921) p. 216 (references to Swine, pp. 79, 129, 235, 240; illus. 21, 216, 223).

[17] Mee, *Yorkshire*, p. 233.

[18] Rainies, *Short History*.

[19] Brown, 'Description', pp. 328–30.

[20] G. F. Remnant, *A Catalogue of Misericords in Great Britain* (Oxford: Clarendon Press, 1969) p. xvii; and Dorothy and Henry Kraus, *The Hidden World of Misericords* (New York: George Braziller, 1975) pp. ix, 171–74.

[21] *Ibid.* and George C. Druce, 'Misericords: Their Form and Decoration', *British Archaeological Association Journal* 36, pt. 2, n.s. (June 1931) 244–64.

[22] A good treatment of subject matter can be found in J.C.D. Smith, *A Guide to Church Wood-Carvings: Misericords and Bench-Ends* (Newton Abbot, England: David and Charles, 1974).

[23] T. H. White, *The Bestiary: A Book of Beasts being a Translation from a Latin Bestiary of the Twelfth Century* (New York: Capricorn Books, 1960) pp. 34–35.

24 White, pp. 34–35.

25 D. Beerens de Haan, *Het Houtsnijweck in Nederland* (The Hague: Martinus Nijhoff, 1977) pp. 51–53, pl. 50.

26 Kathleen Basford, *The Green Man* (Ipswick, England: D. S. Brewer, Ltd., 1978).

27 Basford, pp. 9–14, pl. 252, 682. Basford is not very helpful on the meaning of the Green Man, for on p. 14 she says: 'Their meaning is quite clear: they are demons and spectres of the demon wood', and on p. 19: 'The idea of the revival of nature in springtime...imagery can be ambivalent...both beautiful and sinister.' On p. 20: '...very unlikely that he was revered as a symbol of the renewal of life in springtime.'

28 Frances M. Kelley and Randolph Schwabe, *A Short History of Costume and Armour, Chiefly in England, 1066–1485* (New York: Benjamin Blom, Inc., 1931) 1:23–24; Mary G. Houston, *Medieval Costume in England and France* (London: Adam and Charles Block, 1939) p. 86; R. Turner Wilcox, *The Mode in Hats and Headdress* (New York: Charles Scribner's Sons, 1959) p. 50; and Iris Brooke, *English Costume of the Later Middle Ages, the Fourteenth and Fifteenth Centuries* (New York: Barnes and Noble, 1935) p. 29.

29 C. Willett and Phillis Cunnington, *Handbook of English Medieval Costume* (Boston: Plays Inc., 1969) p. 97.

30 Kelly and Schwabe, *Short History*, pp. 19–20.

31 Cunnington, *Handbook*, pp. 64–65.

32 Remnant, *Catalogue*, pl. 442; Smith, *Church Wood Carvings*, pp. 77, 89–90; and White, *Bestiary*, pp. 22–24.

33 Cunnington, *Handbook*, pp. 65, 117–18; see also Richard Corson, *Fashion in Hair* (New York: Hastings House, 1965).

34 Kelly and Schwabe, *Short History*, pl. XII, c, pp. 19–20; and Cunnington, *Handbook*, pp. 65, 115.

35 Smith, *Church Wood*, pp. 18–19.

36 See John A. Nichols, 'Female Nudity and Sexuality in Medieval Art', in *New Images of Medieval Women: Essays toward a Cultural Anthropology*, ed. Edelgard E. DuBruck (Lewiston, New York: Edwin Mellon Press, 1988) pp. 165–206.

37 Jorgen Andersen, *The Witch on the Wall*, pp. 128–29, 138, 155–56.

38 Ronald Sheridan and Anne Ross, *Gargoyles and Grotesque: Paganism in the Medieval Church* (Boston: New York Graphic Society, 1975) p. 64.

39 Sheridan and Ross, p. 67.

40 Kraus, *Hidden World*, pl. 78.

41 Remnant, *Catalogue*, p. 129, although he mistakes the subject as a tumbler. The seat's location is on the north side, no. 8.

42 R. Williamson, 'A Note on the Hidden Misericord of Swine', YAJ 51 (1979) 153–54.

⁴³ Basford, *Green Man*, pl. 87a.
⁴⁴ Sheridan, *Gargoyles*, pp. 54–55.
⁴⁵ J. Rilson, *East Riding Antiquarian Societies Transactions*, IV, p. xx f.
⁴⁶ Francis Bond, *Wood Carvings in English Churches*, I, *Misericords* (London: Oxford University Press, 1910) p. 226, says 1400, citing Cox and Harvey, *English Church Furniture*. Remnant, *Catalogue*, pp. 184–85, says probably 1500 and cites G. Paulson, *History and Antiquities of...Holderness* (Hull, 1841) p. 211, who suggests similar to Beverley Minister (1520), and J. E. Morris, *East Riding, Yorkshire* (2nd ed., 1919) p. 311, who suggests the same date as the screen in the north aisle (1531).
⁴⁷ George C. Druce, 'Misericords: Their Form and Decoration', *British Archaeological Association Journal* 36, pt. 2, N.S. (June 1931) 244–64.
⁴⁸ Druce, pp. 245, 247. The earlier fourteenth-century misericords have a wide front and flat top as compared to those of the thirteenth century which are thin and narrow. Late fourteenth- and fifteenth-century ledges became very decorative with moldings (pp. 248–49).
⁴⁹ John A. Nichols, 'The Manner and Consequence of Monastic Filiation for English Cistercian Nunneries' (Kalamazoo paper, 1977). See also Sally Thompson, 'The Problem of the Cistercian Nuns in the Twelfth and Early Thirteenth Centuries', in *Medieval Women*, ed. Derek Baker (Oxford: Basil Blackwell, 1978) pp. 227–52; and Coburn V. Graves, 'English Cistercian Nuns in Lincolnshire', *Speculum* 54 (1979) 492–99.
⁵⁰ For a bibliography on cistercian art, see Lekai, *The Cistercians*, pp. 261–81; and John Bilson, 'The Architecture of the Cistercians with Special Reference to Some of their Earlier Churches in England', *Archaeological Journal* 64 (1909) 185–280.
⁵¹ C.A.F. Meekings, 'The Early Years of Netley Abbey', ed. R. F. Hunnisett, *The Journal of Ecclesiastial History* 30 (1979) 1–37; information on the foundation, pp. 1–2.
⁵² From the *Exordium Cistercii Summa Cartae Caritatis et Capitula*, printed in Lekai, *Cistercians*, p. 448.
⁵³ Brenda M. Bolton, 'Mulieres Sanctae', in *Women in Medieval Society*, ed. Susan M. Stuard (Philadelphia: University of Pennsylvania Press, 1976) p. 142.
⁵⁴ Elkins, *Holy Women*, pp. 76–101.
⁵⁵ David Knowles, *The Monastic Order in England* (2nd ed., Cambridge University Press, 1963) pp. 204–207; H. M. Calvin, *The White Canons in England* (Oxford: Clarendon Press, 1951) pp. 327–36 (built churches, cloister, buildings separate but side by side, p. 327); and Rose Graham, *St. Gilbert of Sempringham and the Gilbertines* (London: Elloit and Store, 1901) pp. 10–14, 48–77.

Aerial photograph reproduced by permission of Cambridge University: Department of Aerial Photography, FU 47.

The Nunnery of Swine Priory 293

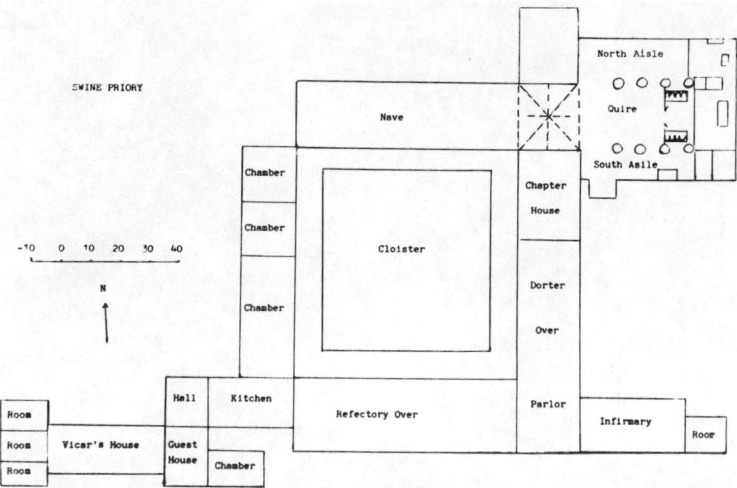

Diagram of Swine Priory, drawn by John A. Nichols based on physical descriptions of the nunnery in the fifteenth and sixteenth centuries and contemporary remains.

External view of Swine parish church showing the east end. This and all other photographs, unless otherwise noted, are the author's own.

Interior photo of Swine Church.

East Perpendicular window over the altar.

Poulson, *History*, 2:49.

Robert and Constance Hilton memorial.

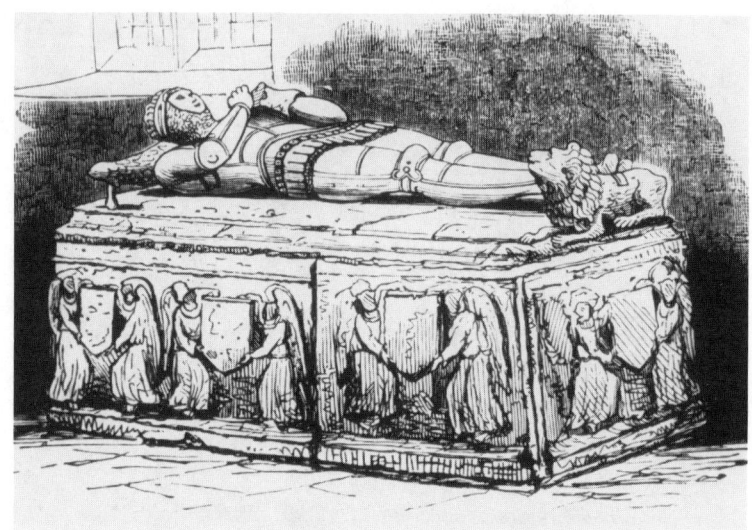

Poulson, *History*, 1:489.

Detail of Robert and Joan Hilton memorial.

Detail of linenfold wooden panel.

Misericord of prioress and monkeys.

Misericord of mitre-hatted elf.

Misericord of a foliated man.

Misericord of a young woman.

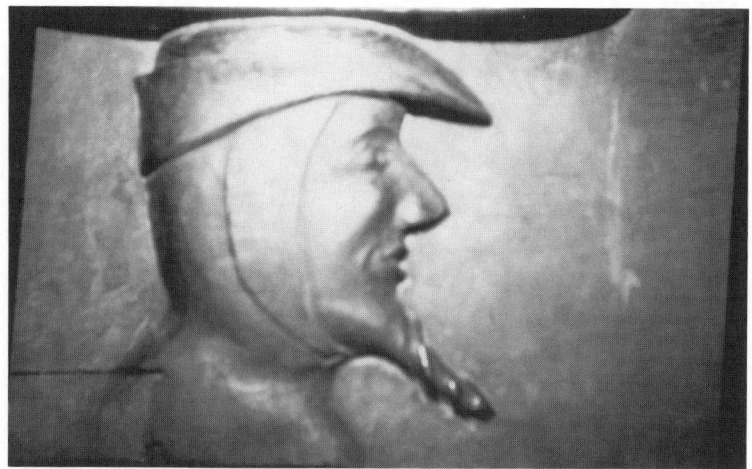
Misericord of bearded man with pointed hat.

Misericord of bearded man.

The Nunnery of Swine Priory

Misericord of man exposing himself.

Misericord of a beastly face.

FATHER LOUIS' FIRST BOOK: *THE SPIRIT OF SIMPLICITY*

M. Basil Pennington, OCSO
St Joseph's Abbey

THE FATHER LOUIS we speak of here is Father Louis Merton, OCSO, not Father Louis Lekai, O. Cist., in whose honor this volume is published. Like Father Lekai, when the young Thomas Merton entered the monastery, he received as his patron King Saint Louis of France. Both Father Louis published works on the history of the Cistercians, though their approaches and purposes were quite different.[1] Lekai saw Merton as an intellectual and spiritual man, '...a guide and model to his devout readers ...', possessing '...a highly receptive mind open to changes and a variety of new approaches to contemporary monasticism.' He judged that Merton's '...broad influence certainly contributed to the strength of reforming endeavors.'[2]

It could be questioned whether Merton can be properly called the 'author' of *The Spirit of Simplicity*.[3] A large part of the book is translation and part of it is compilation. Nonetheless, it is the compilation and commentary of Father Louis that turns a significant Chapter report into a more significant volume of formative theology.[4]

Although Thomas Merton's name never appears in the

volume, it opens with a six-page foreword by this 'Cistercian Monk of Our Lady of Gethsemani'. Then there is Merton's translation of the report of the 1925 General Chapter of the Order of Cistercians of the Stricter Observance: 'The Spirit of Simplicity: Characteristic of the Cistercian Order.'[5] There is inserted within the text of the report eleven plates of twelfth-century cistercian monasteries and the 'Plan of a Typical Cistercian Abbey of the 12th Century'. Part Two begins on page seventy-six and is entitled: 'St. Bernard on Interior Simplicity'. In the course of the following sixty pages Merton presents a number of texts of Saint Bernard concerning simplicity in a fuller theological sense and amply comments on them. He closes his volume with a three-page 'Conclusion'.

THE FOREWORD

After seeking to dispel some of the more superficial and popular understandings of the concept of simplicity, Merton notes that '...entering into the fundamentals of our Rule, our usages, our ascetic practices, our traditions, and the teachings of our Fathers we find that the deeper we go the deeper and more significant concept of simplicity do we obtain: and this concept is always more and more intimately bound up with the very essence of Cistercian spirituality.' Because the report itself '...deals principally with external simplicity...', Merton '...considered it worth while...' to add a second part on the teaching of Saint Bernard in regard to interior simplicity. This is typical of Merton, to want to get to the heart of the matter, to the inner vitalizing core that gives life to the externals, calls them forth, and justifies their existence. Merton identifies the mind of Saint Bernard with that of the cistercian founders as it is expressed in the *Little Exordium* and sums it up this way: '...*getting rid of everything that did not help the monk to arrive at union with God by the shortest possible way.*'[6] For Merton this meant not just getting rid of sin and '...all the pleasures, vanities and useless occupations of the world...' but even '... the *discarding of means of getting* *to God that were less direct.'*⁷ Merton sees a good witness to this in the architecture of the twelfth-century Cistercians. Thus he includes in his volume some pictures of the better remaining examples. Still, Merton notes that his definition '... leaves out one most important point, which is the fact that all this takes place because the intellect and the will of the monk seek one object alone, God as He is in Himself, not merely as reflected in His creatures or in His gifts.'⁸

Father Louis dedicated this little volume '... to the memory of a great Cistercian, one of the saints and mystical theologians of the Golden Age, Bl. William of St. Thierry, on the eight hundredth anniversary of his death' (September 8, 1948). In closing his Foreword, Merton brings forth a quotation from William's *Golden Epistle* which gives two definitions of simplicity: '... Simplicity may be defined as a *constant and unchanging desire for one object and Him alone;* ... simplicity is the perfect conversion of the will to God, asking one thing of God, and desiring that alone....'⁹

PART ONE: THE SPIRIT OF SIMPLICITY

The first part of the volume is made up of the Chapter document. This, of course, was not written by Merton, only translated. However, he does add a number of footnotes. These sometimes explain terms which might be unfamiliar to the general reader. Sometimes they explain how monks observed certain points at the time Merton worked on this text. (In some instances practices have changed considerably since the forties.) At times Merton indicates some later studies on the matter at hand. A few times Merton makes his own comment, usually in favor of good taste. The notes give evidence of a certain amount of naïveté on the part of the young monk. I have little doubt that a more mature Merton would have at least been tempted to make many more comments on the text. The document as it stands serves as a basis for the more positive theological contribution Merton makes in the second part of the book.

The report is composed of a brief introduction and five sections. The first section, quite short, speaks of 'Interior

Simplicity'. Exterior simplicity has to find its true source in interior simplicity, which the document sums up in Saint Benedict's fundamental phrase: '... vere Deum quaerit.'[10] The document sees this tied in with the act of contemplation in a way that might surprise some today: 'Grace will make every monk, who does not stop somewhere along the road in his quest for God, a *contemplative*.... Contemplation: that is to say, a *simple* gazing upon God, a gaze that is fused with love, and which is the prelude to that *consummation in unity* and, therefore, perfect simplicity which is the beatific vision.'[11] The monk seeks to be free for this contemplation; he '... works to remove every obstacle that stands in the way of his progress in union with God.'[12] One of the direct consequences of this is exterior simplicity.

Section two, which is also quite short, is an appeal to the monks to be true to their founders: 'Let Us Be True to the Ideal of Our Founders'. It leads into the next section which forms the bulk of the report. 'Simplicity in the *Little Exordium*' explores at length the provisions or institutes of this early document as a witness to the aims of the founders of Cîteaux. This reflects the purpose of the report: 'All the General Chapter requires is that we make use of the *Little Exordium* and other material of St. Bernard's time in order to show in a few pages calculated to be of service to the monasteries of our Order, what great importance our first Fathers attached to the *Spirit of Simplicity*....[13] The aim of this third section was to show that a jealous love of simplicity sums up the reasons why Cîteaux was founded.'[14] The *Little Exordium* has little to say about architecture as such, so the document appeals to Saint Bernard, especially to his *Apologia*, as well as to the appraisals of some modern scholars and architects. This material occasions Merton's inclusion of the photographs of a number of twelfth-century cistercian monasteries.

The fourth section, 'Anxiety of the General Chapters to Preserve the Spirit of Simplicity', traces their activity through the Golden Age (1098–1256) and the Silver Age (the next hundred years) to the period of decline. The frequency of chapters greatly decreased while Christendom struggled with the Black Death, incessant wars, the *commendam*, and the beginnings of Protestantism. 'But the chief thing was that the Order was less and less prepared to defend itself against these external enemies and against the general environment of a Christianity that was worse then tepid. This helplessness was due, in large part, to the loss of the spirit of simplicity.'[15]

The hortatory concluding chapter picks up the story with the establishment of the Order of Cistercians of the Stricter Observance in 1892 as a result of the activity of Pope Leo XIII. The report sees the establishment of what was called at the time the Order of Reformed Cistercians as a moment of renewal which sent the newly formed order to its ancient sources: the cistercian fathers, Saint Benedict, and back to the monastic fathers of the East: Climacus, Chrysostom, Basil, and others. The emphasis again is on interior simplicity. And thus the report concludes with the then latest word from the papal throne. In the year just prior to the writing of this report, Pope Pius XI approved the revised constitutions of the order, and in his Brief, *Monachorum vita*, he gave his own expression of the simplicity characteristic of the Cistercians: 'Their purpose in this is to devote themselves exclusively to contemplation: . ..*ut ad caelestia unice intenderent animum.* . . .'[16]

This report, attributed to the 1925 General Chapter, certainly lacks the logical order that might give it more strength. It reveals a certain naïveté and lack of historical criticism. But it would be wrong to fault something that was written in 1925 and commented on by a young monk in 1948 because it did not incorporate the insights we have as a result of the many excellent studies that have been made in more recent years. There is a certain polemic in the text, albeit clothed in a pastoral alb. The many texts from the Fathers make it a fruitful document for *lectio*. It presents a valid thesis and challenge. It challenged Merton. Let us explore his response.

SAINT BERNARD ON INTERIOR SIMPLICITY

In this second part, which he calls an 'appendix' to the report, Merton does not use any of the texts of Saint Bernard which were quoted in the report itself. His choices show how wide was his familiarity with the writings of the saint. He chooses what he considers to be a '...few extremely important quotations...' from Saint Bernard's writing, mostly his classic work on the *Song of Songs*, along with supporting texts from such lesser known sources as the *Sermons for Easter* and *Sermons for the Feast of Saint Michael and the Angels*, which do more than just throw light on what is in the report. Rather, as Merton sees it, they '...give us the massive dogmatic foundation upon which the Cistercian doctrine of simplicity is built as upon granite.'[17] Unlike the report, then, which narrows down its considerations in part to the more specific tradition of the Stricter Observance, what Merton has to offer here, an articulation of some of the foundational teaching of Saint Bernard, is applicable to and can be fruitful for all Cistercians and, indeed, for all Christians.

Before setting forth his chosen texts and commenting on them, Merton offers in his brief introductory section a very concise presentation of what he considers '...the key to the whole mystical theology of St. Bernard.' We were first made in the image and likeness of God. We were made not the very image of God as is the Son, but to the image of God, dependently participating in the divinity. When we sought in our primogenitor to be like God in our own right, we lost, not the indelible image of God that is of our very nature, but our likeness to him, our rectitude. The tragedy, our unhappiness, lies in this: the image within us, which consists in simplicity, immortality, and freedom of will, is constantly confronted with the disfigurement of our duplicity and our servitude to sin and death.

The whole aim of the cistercian life is to set us apart from the world with its doings and ambitions so that we may be purified and be brought to perfect union with God by the recovery of our lost likeness to him. The many exercises and observances of the life are to make us keenly aware of our miserable state of division and lead us to prayer and to open ourselves to the mercy of God. As we are healed by his grace and freed from our unlikeness and all the fear that goes with it, confidence and love grow, the image is more and more fully restored. Merton concludes: 'St. Bernard does not hesitate to promise, as the *normal* term of the Cistercian life of simplicity, a perfect union of wills with God, by love, which he calls the Mystical Marriage.'[18]

In the following pages Merton sets forth four basic texts. But he divides his treatment into five sections.

The first section, 'Man's Original Simplicity', uses *Sermons 81* and *82 on the Song of Songs*. It is a concise presentation of Saint Bernard's anthropology, much of which Merton already set forth in his introduction to Part Two. The human person is made in the resemblance of God but is not equal to God. For God, to be (*esse*) is to live happily (*beatum vivere*)—the highest and most pure simplicity. The second is like unto this: for the human to be (*esse*) is to live (*vivere*). And this makes it possible for the human to ascend, by God's grace, to participate in the divine *beatum vivere*.

In the Fall, this simplicity of the human soul remains truly unimpaired in its essence. It is only covered over by duplicity, deceit, simulation, and hypocrisy. The resulting contradiction between our essential simplicity and the duplicity engendered by sin confront each other, causing confusion and pain. Desire for the earthy, rather than the immortal, makes us like that which we desire: darksome and unstable. We have put on the mortality of sin and death.

What we desire to possess, we fear to lose. This fear has 'discolored' our liberty, covered it over, and concealed it. Our liberty is held in the bonds of our fear. If we desired nothing—simply loved God whom we possess—we would fear nothing, we would be filled with confidence and remain free, strong, and beautiful.

Everything has been 'reduplicated': our simplicity by duplicity, our immortality by the death of sin and of the body, our freedom by the desire of material concerns, our likeness to God by unlikeness. Our essential goodness has been defiled, but not destroyed, by accidentals, making us not only unlike God but unlike our true selves. We have become like the beasts. Merton notes here how in this Saint Bernard vindicates the goodness of human nature. The first step in our ascent to God is to know ourselves, and the labor of our lives is to be our true selves, returning to the simplicity, immortality, and freedom that belong to us. 'The whole of Cistercian simplicity can be summed up in this', says Merton. He goes on to develop the steps: first we come to know the truth abut ourselves—sincerity; then we accept it—meekness, self-effacement, humility; then we rid ourselves of all that is useless—mortification: mortification of the lower appetites through external simplicity; of the internal sense and intellect through devotion, study, and methods of prayer; and of the will (which is most important) through obedience. The document of the Chapter has spoken at length about the first means of mortification, so Merton goes on in the following sections to bring forth Saint Bernard's teaching on the latter two.

Merton's second section, on 'Intellectual Simplicity', uses primarily *Sermons 35* and *36 on the Song of Songs*, but also *31, 37*, and *38*, along with references to the fourth of the *Sermons on Various Subjects* and the treatises on *The Steps of Humility and Pride, On Consideration,* and *On the Love of God*.

We are capable of a twofold ignorance: of ourselves and of God. If we truly know ourselves, we will be humble and fear God; this is the beginning of wisdom and the opposite of pride. If we know God, we will be filled with love and hope, possess him, and come to the perfection of wisdom. Without this knowledge of God, in knowing ourselves we could despair. Intellectual simplicity allows us to be taught by God's love. Contemplation is the '... extreme simplicity of an intuition', beyond all concepts, images and pictures, phantasms and discursive acts of the mind. There is no figure; there is the direct contact of love, the created effect of love: *facies formans*. The fact that intellectual simplicity is brought to its fullness through the unity brought about by love leads naturally to the next section: 'The Simplification of the Will'.

Saint Bernard, in his third *Sermon for the Feast of the Resurrection*, notes that there is a twofold leprosy that can infect the human heart: attachment to one's own will and attachment to one's own judgment. In the light of this, Merton divides his third section into two parts to consider each of these.

There can be, should be, a good self love which seeks one's own perfection according to the will of God. The self will that is leprous is the intention to please self, intention here understood as the actual movement of the will toward the object of its selfish desires. This self will is destroyed by obedience that is subordinated to charity and integrated with the communal life. Such obedience seeks *nihil plus, nihil minus, nihil aliter quam imperatum*, nothing more, nothing less, nothing other than what is commanded by the superiors, the *Rule*, and the brethren. It abandons all internal argument. Our will becomes one with the common will.

Attachment to our own judgment is more pernicious. The more strongly we are so attached, the more we are deceived, setting up our own standard and unable to see our self-deception. We are freed from this by following the example of Christ, who submitted himself to Mary and Joseph, who submitted his human will, however good it be, to the will of his Father. For Saint Bernard, the will is the highest faculty; hence unity of wills, charity, produces the highest and most perfect simplicity. It is the work of the Holy Spirit, and it will be realized perfectly only in heaven.

Suddenly Merton becomes universal and eschatological: 'Indeed the whole work of achieving this final magnificent and universal simplicity of all men made one in Christ will be His eventual triumph at the last day.'[19] And he goes on to say with emphasis: '*Hence we see that the very essence of Cistercian simplicity is the practice of charity and loving obedience and mutual patience and forbearance in the community life which should be on earth an image of the simplicity of heaven.* We begin to see something of the depth of this beautiful Cistercian ideal!'[20]

Merton goes on to develop a line of thought here that is perhaps key to his own future development. I shall quote the entire paragraph here, because it sums up much of what he has been saying all along but also opens up this new vista:

> Cistercian simplicity, then, begins in humility and self-distrust, and climbs through obedience to the perfection of fraternal charity to produce that unity and peace by which the Holy and Undivided Trinity is reflected not only in the individual soul but in the community, in the Order, in the Church of God. Once a certain degree of perfection in this social simplicity is arrived at on earth, God is pleased to bend down and raise up the individuals who most further this unity by their humility and love to a closer and far more intimate union with Him by mystical prayer, mystical union.[21]

From the time he first consciously set forth on the spiritual journey, Merton was always keenly interested in the mystical dimension of the christian life, keenly desirous of mystical prayer, mystical union with God. In this little book he will go on to teach that such union is the expected outcome of following the cistercian way of simplicity. Here Merton shares a certain insight. He perceives that the ones on whom God bestows such grace are those individuals who most further social simplicity, most further unity and peace. Perhaps we have here the key as to why Merton began to be very sensitive to social issues and was as actively involved in the peace movement and in the questions of racial integration as his contemplative vocation and the demands of his vows would allow. A deep and sincere loving concern for peace and unity would dispose him to receive the mystical graces of union for which he so longed. Merton goes on here to say (summing up his whole next section in so doing):

> The culmination of Cistercian simplicity is the mystical marriage of the soul with God, which is nothing else but the perfect union of our will with God's will, made possible by the complete purification of all the duplicity of error and sin. This purification is the work of love and particularly of the love of God in our neighbor. Hence it is inseparable from that social simplicity which consists in living out the *voluntas communis* in actual practice.[22]

Sanctified by participation in the common will, which is God himself working in us and in the Church, the individual is prepared for the graces of infused contemplation.

As we have already stated, the fifth section, 'Perfect Simplicity, Unity of Spirit with God', was essentially summed up by Merton in the quotation above. To develop his teaching more concretely, Merton brings forth a text from Saint Bernard's treatise *On the Love of God* concerning the fourth degree of love. According to Saint Bernard we are first caught up in self love. Then we begin to love God because we perceive how good he is to us. As we become more and more aware of his goodness, we begin to love him in himself. Finally, we come to be so one with God in love, that we love even ourselves only because he loves us. This complete unity of will with God is the consummation of simplicity.

It may seem a bit paradoxical that we attain a more perfect simplicity when we are more fully absorbed in this union. But the essence of the human soul is to be like God. We are most truly ourselves when we are identified with him, when we lose our own will and are one will, one spirit with him. We come to forget ourselves, all our own wishes and desires, and come to have only the wishes and desires of God. 'This, then, is the ultimate limit of Cistercian simplicity: the simplicity of God Himself, belonging to the soul, purified of all admixture of self-love, admitted to a participation in the Divine Nature, and becoming one Spirit with the God of infinite love.'[23]

Merton's 'Conclusion' is brief: three pages. He begins by noting that when a person has been sanctified and has come to be closely united to God, there is a certain beauty about him. The soul communicates even to the flesh which it informs something of its own peace and supernatural radiance. The whole bearing of the person is so marked. So, too, the inner simplicity of cistercian communities gave expression to the expansive, simple beauty we see in their buildings and (a great literator like Merton would note this) in their writings. If these things are the natural expression of an interior simplicity, it is also true that their simplicity can in turn foster interior simplicity. Hence the exhortations of the General Chapter, to which Merton joins his voice in practical ways, to foster simplicity in our lives and in our buildings. Merton urges his readers to turn to the literature of the early Cistercians.[24] 'We can never hope to acquire the spirit of simplicity characteristic of our Order if we never enter into contact, directly or at least indirectly, with the sources from which it flowed.'[25] Nevertheless, he notes that study is not enough. We need to practice all that Saint Bernard has set forth and to devote ourselves to fervent prayer to the Holy Spirit.

This little book, quietly published on the eve of Merton's monumental best-selling autobiography, ended his career as an obedient translator. I do not think the new demand for his writings was the only reason why Merton moved on in his literary career. When he undertook this third volume in 'The Cistercian Library', Merton moved beyond mere translation to begin to share something of the rich spiritual insight he himself had attained through his contact with the 'sources'. He had found in Saint Bernard an anthropology that imperiously demanded that one be all that he can be and a solid dogmatic foundation, solid as granite, on which to build an integrated spiritual theology that can be universal, immanent, and eschatological. He was ready for the great literary vocation that lay ahead of him.

NOTES

[1] To achieve a graphic sense of the differences in their outlook, one has only to compare the plates Merton included in *The Spirit of Simplicity* with those that Lekai included at the end of *The White Monks*.

A strictly historical work, one which Father Lekai characterized as 'misleading... presented in amateurish fashion', *Compendium of the History of the Cistercian Order* by 'A Father of the Abbey of Gethsemani', has sometimes mistakenly been attributed to Thomas Merton. The author, Father Alberic Wulf, could not have known, when his volume was published in 1944, that the young Frater Louis, who was making profession that year, would five years later be a best-selling author under the name of Thomas Merton, so he did not hesitate to sign his 'Author's Note' with his laundry mark, 'T'. In our volume (p. 137, n. 10) Merton especially recommends his brother monk's volume.

Lekai does not mention Merton's *The Waters of Siloe* (New York: Harcourt, 1949), which was published four years before *The White Monks*, in his Bibliographical Notes in that volume. But he will note it (and omit notice of Wulf's work) when he revises and updates the Notes in *The Cistercians*.

[2] Louis J. Lekai, *The Cistercians: Ideals and Reality* ([Kent, Ohio]: Kent State University Press, [1977]) p. 213.

[3] Trappist, Kentucky: The Abbey of Gethsemani, 1948. Hereafter referred to as SoS.

[4] It could also be argued whether this is properly speaking Merton's 'first book'. His work on Jean-Marie Chautard's *The Soul of the Apostolate* was quite simply a work of translation as far as Merton was concerned. The twenty-eight-page *Thirty Poems*, published by New Directions in 1944, can hardly be considered a book.

[5] Merton's statement, 'the General Chapter of 1925 suggested and approved the official report', might be a bit misleading. That Chapter had unanimously approved the proposal that the preparatory work done by Dom Jean-Marie Chautard of Sept Fons be published in a brochure for the edification of the communities; *Actes XXVIIe Chapitre General: 1925* (Westmalle: Typographie de l'Ordre) p. 18. The following year, during the Chapter, the Abbot General urged Dom Chautard to publish as soon as possible '... le remarquable travail dont il nous a donné les lignes principales l'an dernier'; *Actes XXVIIIe Chapitre General: 1926* (Westmalle: Typographie de l'Ordre) p. 18. Thus it is clear that the report as such is the work of one man and was approved by the Chapter only according to its principal or general lines.

[6] SoS, p. iii. Italics Merton's.

[7] SoS, pp. iii-iv. Italics Merton's.

[8] SoS, pp. iv-v.

[9] SoS, pp. v-vi. Italics Merton's.

The Spirit of Simplicity

10 '...He truly seeks God.' Saint Benedict, *Rule for Monasteries*, ch. 58.

11 SoS, pp. 6–7. Italics theirs.

12 SoS, p. 10.

13 SoS, p. 22. Italics theirs.

14 SoS, p. 51.

15 SoS, p. 60.

16 SoS, p. 74.

17 SoS, p. 76.

18 SoS, p. 80. Italics Merton's.

19 SoS, p. 126. Merton, writing almost a half century ago, does not hesitate to use the masculine form in a generic sense. I am sure if he lived today he would be most sensitive to the issues involved in this.

20 SoS, p. 126. Italics Merton's.

21 SoS, p. 126f.

22 SoS, p. 127.

23 SoS, p. 135.

24 Merton laments that so little is available in the english language. This lack he greatly helped remedy, not only by his own copious writings but by the role he played in helping to establish Cistercian Publications just prior to his untimely death. We also owe an enormous debt of gratitude to Louis Lekai for participation in Cistercian Publications and for his own very significant literary output.

25 SoS, p. 138.

CISTERCIANS AND BETHLEHEM: A HISTORICAL VIEW

Thomas Renna
Saginaw Valley State University

MONKS IN THE TWELFTH CENTURY, as in other centuries, used biblical images to express the operations of their interior lives. Occasionally they chose place-names to suggest some aspect of this experience. Babylon, Megiddo, Bethlehem, Nazareth, Bethany, and Cana, among other towns, provided abundant material for the commentator or preacher. Perhaps no biblical city appears more frequently in medieval biblical commentaries, sermons, and the liturgy than does Jerusalem, a figure of heaven and, especially for monastic writers, a foretaste of the Jerusalem above. The manner in which monastic authors handle these places can reveal much about their monastic ideals. For the modern historian it is always significant when the monastic commentator alters the conventional meanings given to a biblical name. Scholars have not noticed that the image of Bethlehem changed direction in twelfth-century monastic writings. It will be argued here that some early Cistercians employed the image of Bethlehem less as a theological statement (as did many of the Church Fathers) than as a phase in the spiritual development of monks.

In the New Testament, Bethlehem is the place where Jesus was born in fulfillment of Micah's prophecy (Micah 5:2; Matthew 2; Luke 2; John 7:42). Paul does not assign to Bethlehem any allegorical significance, as he does, say, to Jerusalem (Galatians 4:25–26). In post-apostolic centuries, greek and latin writers often repeat the gospel references to Bethlehem, where the Nativity and related events occurred. The town came to suggest the doctrine of the Incarnation. Perhaps some of the Fathers alluded to Christ's birth partially in response to doctrines which they opposed, especially gnosticism and monophysitism. The Incarnation was taken to be proof that Christ was man as well as God. The medieval exegetical commonplace of Bethlehem as the 'house of bread' perhaps derives chiefly from Jerome, who reminded his readers of the original hebrew meaning. In Letter 108, Jerome refers to the Bethlehem of Matthew 2:14 as the *domus panis*.[1] Also influential in medieval exegesis was Jerome's allusion to 'Bethlehem Iudae' (Matthew 2). He associates Juda with Rachael, who died and was buried at Bethlehem (Genesis 35:18–19), to show how the coming of Christ fulfilled the hebrew prophecies.[2]

Commenting on Luke 2:16–17, Ambrose associates the gates of Bethlehem with the 'virginal beauty of the Catholic Church' and its doctors.[3] The manger represents the humility of the Savior. Ambrose's brief remarks are typical of the Latin Fathers, who saw in the New Testament accounts of the Nativity the fulfillment of the hebrew scriptures and also a proof-text of certain theological doctrines, especially the Incarnation.

Augustine's numerous sermons on Christmas illustrate the late patristic approach to the image of Bethlehem. The bishop of Hippo uses the Nativity to demonstrate Christ's genealogy and its hidden meanings. Two themes are paramount in Augustine's sermons: the Church and the Incarnation. Since these are sermons and not learned treatises, Augustine's allusions to *ecclesia* are direct and simple. The virgin birth represents the various states of life within the Church universal: virgins, widows, and married.[4] As in his other works, Augustine is quick to praise the virtues of widowhood and the married state,[5] perhaps as a corrective to other authors, such as Jerome, who elevated the status of virginity. The Church itself is both 'virgin and mother'.[6] When God became man, moreover, he set an example for the practice of humility.[7] An ecclesiological theme, which Augustine expanded in his sermons on the Epiphany, is the union of Jews and Gentiles, the two parts of the family of God.[8] The hebrew scriptures stand as a witness to the truth of the Gospel.[9] Augustine hopes that Jews and Gentiles will eventually be reunited in a single Church.

But certainly the leitmotif of Augustine's Christmas sermons is the Incarnation, the 'double birth' of Christ, who had a divine Father and a human mother.[10] Although Augustine had pastoral aims for these sermons (to lead his audience to imitate Christ's humility, Mary's virginity, Mary's hope of salvation), his theological concerns are also evident. He places less stress on Christ as a model of virtue than on the awe with which we should consider the Incarnation. These sermons read like a primer on the Incarnation. Indeed, Mary is perhaps more prominent than Christ as the prototype of virtue.[11] Specific references to Bethlehem are infrequent; the town of Christ's birth is given no symbolic importance.

It may be asked if the liturgy of Advent and Christmas influenced the meanings attached to Bethlehem in latin sermons and biblical commentaries. Or is the reverse the case: did the patristic writers influence liturgical practices? Unfortunately, we know too little about the latin liturgy during the later roman empire to be able to answer this question satisfactorily. Surviving church decorations in Rome from the late fourth to the early sixth centuries suggest that the visual representation of the town was indeed prominent. In several apse mosaics in Rome, pictures of Bethlehem and Jerusalem flank Christ.[12] It is unfortunate that no contemporary manuscripts explain the meaning of these opposing cities. There is probably some connection between the cities and the *traditio legis*, the transmission of the two laws, the old and the new.[13] On the basis of the apse mosaics of Santa Sabina and Santa Pudenziana, most art historians argue that the two cities represent the two parts of the Church universal.[14] According to this view, Bethlehem stands for the Church of the Gentiles, and Jerusalem represents the Church of the circumcision. The two cities signify not only the double origin of the *ecclesia*, but also the Church at the end-time, when the Jews (Jerusalem) will return to the true Church. The use of Bethlehem as part of this twin-cities portrait did not, however, continue in the Middle Ages. Certainly the *ecclesia-synagoga* dualism remained popular in medieval sculpture and painting—as well as biblical exegesis. But the emphasis in the Church-Synagogue figures is *not* on the two halves of the Church, but rather on the Church as the fulfillment and completion (and, to a point, rejection) of the Old Law. For whatever reason, the image of Bethlehem as the Church of the Gentiles does not appear to have interested medieval people.

Pilgrims who actually visited Bethlehem (or claimed they did) sometimes refer to the city in terms of its liturgical usage, often as part of a processional route. Writing in the late fourth century, Egeria mentions the vigil service held at Bethlehem.[15] Some fifty years prior, the Bordeaux Pilgrim refers to 'Bethlehem, where the Lord Jesus Christ was born, and where a basilica has been built by... Constantine.'[16] Neither pilgrim attaches any symbolic importance to Bethlehem, even though Bethlehem was, by as least the time of Egeria, included in the liturgical festivals of Jerusalem.

Medieval *itineraria* to the Holy Land often describe Bethlehem, as might be expected. Placantius marveled at the splendor of the church at Bethlehem. He notes that the cave and tomb of Jerome are nearby.[17] Monks, moreover, dwell in the vicinity.[18] Theodorich (c. 1172) gives some details about the Bethlehem church, manger, crypt, and the tombs of Jerome and Joseph of Arimathea.[19] Pilgrims in the fourteenth and fifteenth centuries sometimes describe the church of the Nativity in some detail, as well the environs of the city.[20] One might expect that franciscan travelers in particular, given their devotion to the infant Jesus and their long tradition as tour guides at the holy places, would see something more in the town of Bethlehem, but in fact they do not. Even those who complain that 'so devout a place should be in the care of the Saracens'[21] can think of no more to say. In short, the Bethlehem of the *itineraria* is a town important mainly for the cave and the church of the Nativity. The physical aspects of these places are described matter-of-factly and without interpretation.[22]

Latin authors who immediately followed Augustine generally repeat patristic exegesis. For Pope Gregory the Great, the imperial enrollment just prior to the Lord's birth signifies God's will to register his elect in eternity.[23] Bethlehem, the house of bread, is the living bread (John 6:51), presumably the Eucharist, which nourishes our hearts.[24] The manger reminds us of heavenly knowledge as opposed to earthly pleasures.[25] There is nothing in Gregory's homilies on Christmas which cannot be found in Augustine. But there is a dual emphasis which is characteristic of Gregory: Christ as the model of other-worldliness, and the Jews' prefiguration of the coming of Christ.[26] Gregory's approach to the Nativity is generally less speculative than that of Augustine; the pope prefers to focus on simple moral lessons involving repentance for sin and the desire to seek the things of heaven.

The Venerable Bede's influential commentary (and sermons) on the Nativity section in Luke relies heavily on Jerome, Ambrose, and Pope Gregory the Great. Bethlehem as the *domus panis* descends daily to the souls of the faithful.[27] Daily the Church praises the eternal King.[28] David prefigured Christ, the true pastor of sheep, the *rector animarum*.[29] Frequent references to the *ecclesiae pastores* are typical of Bede.[30]

Carolingian commentaries on Luke and Matthew echo the received tradition of Bethlehem. After the usual references to Bethlehem as the *domus panis*, Christian of Stavelot notes that the true meaning of *domus* is *ecclesia*.³¹ The Church is the 'verus panis, et satietas aeterna reperitur ab omnibus in veritate quaerentibus.'³² In a homily on Matthew 2:1, Remigius of Auxerre follows Jerome's remarks on 'Juda not Judaea'. Jesus is the *panis vivus* of the *domus panis*.³³ The house of bread is also the Church, 'in qua quotidie notitia Christi invenitur.'³⁴ In the moral sense, Bethlehem is the faithful soul. Paschasius Radbertus is more verbose in his commentary on Matthew 1 and 2. He repeatedly links Bethlehem with the *ecclesia Christianorum* and the body of Christ.³⁵ Rhabanus Maurus adds nothing to Matthew 2, giving his readers what is largely a catena from patristic texts.³⁶

If there is any significant emphasis in carolingian commentaries, it is the explicit allusions to Bethlehem as *ecclesia*, and the 'daily' descent of Christ, that is, the continuous spiritual nourishment brought to Christians by the Church and its sacraments. Little is original in the eleventh-century commentaries, such as Rubert of Deutz's lengthy exegesis of Matthew.³⁷

Surprisingly, the *Glossa ordinaria*, a work widely consulted by twelfth-century monks, gives sparse attention to Bethlehem. To be sure, Bethlehem is the *panis vivus* as both Christ and the Church.³⁸ But the *Glossa ordinaria* on Matthew does not elaborate further. The Gloss' comments on Luke 2 are largely quotations from Bede.³⁹

However, it is in the twelfth century that the image of Bethlehem undergoes a charge in emphasis. Monastic authors internalize the town of Christ's birth. In his sermons on Christmas, the scottish Carthusian, Adam of Dryburgh (d. 1212), strenuously tries to give Bethlehem a 'monastic' content by relating the town to the various stages in the spiritual life. His audience is the 'elect',⁴⁰ presumably his carthusian listeners. Adam of Dryburgh's central message is that the holy soul performs good actions from the right intention. A person progresses from Nazareth to Bethlehem (not the other way around, as one might expect), that is, from external works to 'internal intention'.⁴¹ Bethlehem stands for both profession and internal intention. Why does Adam place intention *after* action, which would seem the reverse of the proper sequence? Was Adam boxed in by his own choice of metaphors? He could not, after all, escape the time-honored exegesis of Nazareth as flower (that is, the practice of the virtues) and of Bethlehem as profession. But since Adam's repetition of this Nazareth-to-Bethlehem process is the basis of all six Christmas sermons,[42] it seems more likely that his designation of right intention following virtue was indeed deliberate. It is clear that he meant the sequence to be chronological, and not simply to be a treatment of two aspects of the spiritual life (faith and virtue). He implies that the acquisition of right intention is a gradual process, following long periods of external practices. In this sense Adam's view of 'intention' is the classic monastic conception of external works as a *preparation* for the contemplative life. The active life of beginners is followed by the contemplative life of more advanced ascetics.

Adam's treatment of Nazareth-Bethlehem is full of difficulties. His listeners must have been confused by at least the third sermon. Monastic preachers certainly permitted themselves to give various layers of meaning to a single literary image, often in no discernible order. But Adam's decision to retain the intention meaning of Bethlehem makes his description of the soul's ascent hard to follow. In the first place, Adam is aware that right intention does indeed precede action, even if the latter also prepares the way for right intention. So too, confession precedes faith. The consistency of the Nazareth-Bethlehem imagery breaks down when Adam refers to Bethlehem also as virtue and growth in love.[43] Indeed, Bethlehem the 'holy city' sometimes sounds like a metaphor for heaven![44] Bethlehem as confession is a kind of anticipation of the heavenly Jerusalem, where the praise of God is eternal. Adam hints that the proper progression for the soul is from Nazareth to Bethlehem to Jerusalem. This triad, however, remains undeveloped in Adam's sermons.

It would be unreasonable to demand of Adam too rigorous a logic in his use of Bethlehem as a facet of the monk's spiritual development. Monastic sermons are not scholastic treatises. Perhaps his aim was simply to stimulate some prayerful reflection on virtuous living, particularly humility. His images are indeed striking and sometimes original. For our purposes, however, the importance of Adam's sermons lies in the portrayal of Bethlehem as: 1) a phase in the monk's spiritual life, 2) an idea set against the image of Jerusalem, and 3) an image, however ill-defined, of the *vita contemplativa*.

It could be argued that Adam's Bethlehem ultimately fails as an effective short-hand description of the monastic way because this town's counter-image (Nazareth) can also apply to non-monks, namely, anyone who engages in active charity. While Adam refers to the 'elect' (a term the patristic authors usually reserved for the blessed in heaven) and to Bethlehem as 'profession'[45] (perhaps an intimation of the monastic profession), the bond to the monastic life *per se* is never made explicit. Neither the good works nor the confession/intention duality are related directly to the *vita monastica*. To be sure, Adam's Bethlehem is pregnant with possible monastic concepts, but the city never quite becomes a bona fide monastic symbol.

The Cistercians make explicit what is implicit in Adam of Dryburgh. Two of the best-known Cistercians of the early twelfth century, Aelred and Bernard, transform Bethlehem into a veritable *civitas monastica*. Aelred of Rievaulx solves the ambiguity of Nazareth (as virtue) and Bethlehem (intention/profession) by a single brilliant stroke: the two cities are the first two phases in the formation of the contemplative monk. Bethlehem is the beginning of the good life, repentance, blind obedience, commitment to the spiritual life, the start of the desire for God; it is the 'purgative way' (to use a later term) which precedes the quest for perfection.[46] Nazareth is the practice of the virtues, the 'illuminative way', the growth in love and meditation on God's wisdom.[47] Finally, Jerusalem is the direct experience of God, the sweetness of contemplation, a prelude of the vision of God in the hereafter.[48] This last city is not simply an image of heaven; it is also a symbol of the *vita contemplativa* here below. Thus the three cities are fixed firmly within the experience of the soul's spiritual development in the present life. Aelred's tripartite frame is simple, compelling, and consistent.

Bernard of Clairvaux continued this line of 'monastic' reasoning about Bethlehem. In his Christmas sermons Bernard repeats many of the patristic commonplaces, with emphasis on Bethlehem as a sign of poverty and humility (two of Bernard's favorite virtues).[49] His images often come in threes. The Nativity suggests three degrees of knowledge: penitence, amendment of life, spiritual joy.[50] Monks are exposed to three 'winds' (temptations): the world, the flesh, and the devil.[51] One must keep three 'watches': on one's exterior conduct, one's purity of intention, and the preservation of concord and unity (presumably a reference to the spirit of fraternal charity which should characterize the monastic community).[52] The first two watches are reminiscent of the action-intention duality of Adam of Dryburgh. The Incarnation, moreover, effected three unions: the divine nature was united to the human, virginity to motherhood, and faith to the human heart.[53] God willed the first two of these three unions for the benefit of fallen man. Bernard introduces many images of this type throughout his sermons on Christmas eve and Christmas.

What is distinctive, however, about Bernard's treatment of Bethlehem is his radical internalization of this city. Monks 'become' Bethlehem. When this happens, Christ is 'born' in their souls.[54] Significantly, Bernard reserves this view of Bethlehem for the later sermons in this series because he wishes to place Bethlehem (here the act of contemplation) as part of the progress of the spiritual ascent. In other words, contemplation follows certain preparations: ascetic exercises and meditation. To become a 'Bethlehem' is a *process* which involves the monk's entire inner development. But the idea of Bethlehem is also the end of this process, an advanced state in the spiritual life.

Normally, Bethlehem precedes Jerusalem, a more sublime stage. Drawing on Jerome's use of Jerusalem as 'confession', the 'true Jew' confesses his sins and at the same time 'confesses' (that is, praises) God.[55] Once the soul has succeeded in attaining a high degree of repentance, it is ready to proceed to some experience, however limited, of the *visio pacis*, Jerusalem.[56] In order not to confuse Jerusalem with Bethlehem, Bernard does not follow up on this allusion to Jerusalem, a term he usually restricts to heaven or the desire for heaven. To keep the two cities distinct, Bernard does not equate Bethlehem with the celestial vision of peace. His point is subtle: Bethlehem is the beginning of the more advanced stages of *contemplatio*. When we become a Bethlehem of Juda we prepare ourselves for the contemplative experience. The bread (of the house of bread) strengthens the heart as it makes itself deserving—with the aid of grace—of Christ's birth within the soul. Bernard links Bethlehem with Jerusalem in an indirect way: 'Juda' (confession of praise) implies 'spiritual Jews' who confess and praise the Lord.

It should be emphasized that Bernard's use of Bethlehem as an interior state is not at all like Eckhart's birth of Christ in the soul.[57] Bernard's does not conceive of the Nativity as the holy soul's vision of peace. Bethlehem lies halfway between the ascetic, preparatory phases and the highest experiences of contemplation. Bernard describes the Bethlehem stage in personal terms, not in the speculative language of some late medieval mystics. Bethlehem is still closely associated with the conventional Nativity virtues of poverty and humility. It should be added that Bernard's treatment of true Jews and Bethlehemites is not always chronological, in the sense of a linear process from one to the other. In the same sermons he also places true Jews and Jerusalem *after* the preparatory stages of Bethlehem.[58]

Clearly he wants his monastic audience to envision Bethlehem and Jerusalem as two aspects of the spiritual life; they are present simultaneously (as well as in sequence). This method of dealing with two facets of the spiritual life alternatively in both chronological and qualitative, descriptive senses is common in his writings. The historian cannot demand, then, too much precision and system in Bernard's homiletic discussion of the city of Christ's birth.

What is important here is not the exact order of the spiritual levels but the essential meaning attributed to Bethlehem. Bernard turns the historical event of Christ's birth into an ever-present reality. The Nativity is a 'daily' occurrence, not just in the *panis vivus* (as the Eucharist) but also in the normal activities of the monk.[59] Bethlehem is a metaphor for the spiritual life. Specifically, it is the ongoing sanctification of the monk's efforts (interior and exterior). Bethlehem is the union of the soul and Christ as the soul advances in holiness. Unlike the later rhineland mystics' use of the birth of God in the soul, Bernard's use of the Bethlehem image is thoroughly monastic. All the virtues and types of prayer are conceived entirely in a monastic context. Bernard seems uninterested in the Bethlehem-as-Church notion of the early medieval commentaries. Perhaps he thought his peculiar rendering of Bethlehem did not contradict this exegetical tradition, since the monk and the monastic community are themselves a kind of Church in microcosm. The monk's holiness places him at the center of what might be called the 'charismatic Church'.

The patristic propensity to refer to Bethlehem as an image of the Incarnation could be taken to imply the life of God in the individual soul. If God became man, it would not be too much an exaggeration to say that the human soul in some sense 'becomes' God, who after all infuses the soul with grace. So too, the carolingian tendency to equate Bethlehem with the Church implies that the Christian receives Christ (as the Mystical Body) in his soul. No doubt the twelfth-century monks who internalized Bethlehem believed they were simply drawing out the implications of previous scriptural commentaries. It is possible that this kind of extreme spiritualization of certain biblical places would not have occurred were it not for the monastic context in which this exegesis was developed. Medieval monastic culture provided a laboratory for this kind of probing of the deeper senses of biblical commonplace terms. Cistercian and other monks gave nuances of meanings—firmly rooted in patristic interpretations—which enriched their vocabulary of the spiritual life. They had mastered the art of reading the Bible as a veritable instruction manual for monks.

It might be noted that the famous doctrine of the birth of God in the soul of the late medieval mystics was developed outside of the twelfth-century monastic framework. To be sure, there may have been some direct influence of some medieval writers, particularly the Victorines and the Cistercians, on the mystics of the Low Countries. Indeed, it could be argued that the Cistercians prepared the path for Eckhart by demonstrating how to internalize the images of Bethlehem and the Nativity. But the influence may also have been negative: Eckhart consciously rejects the monastic setting of the birth of God idea, and develops further the notion of divinity in the soul without reference to monastic qualifiers. Eckhart's determination to focus on the divine birth apart from the ascetic life illustrates the decline in influence of monastic spirituality on late medieval mysticism. The twelfth-century monastery could easily accommodate Bethlehem, the prototype of Clairvaux. Later, in the Rhineland, Jesus was born again in a beguinage, for there was no room for him in the cloister.

NOTES

[1] *Epistola* 108.10; *Corpus Scriptorum Ecclesiasticorum Latinorum* [hereafter CSEL] 55:516–18.

[2] Commentary on Matthew; J.-P. Migne (ed.) *Patrologia Latina* [PL] 26:26–27; *Corpus Christianorum, series latina* [CCSL] 77:13. See Commentary on Luke; PL 29:647–48.

[3] Ambrose, Commentary on Luke; CCSL 14:7, 104, and 33, 53; see John Chrysostom's Commentary on Matthew; *Nicene and Post-Nicene Fathers* 10:39, 47.

[4] Sermon 192; PL 38:1011–13 (listed as Sermon 10 in T. Lawler [trans.], *St. Augustine: Sermons for Christmas and Epiphany*, Westminster, Md., 1952), and Sermon 14; PL 38:1019–21 (Sermon 14 in Lawler).

[5] Such as *De bono viduitatis, De bono coniugali, De sancta virginitate*, all in CSEL 41.

[6] Sermons 191, 192; PL 38:1009–1013.

[7] Sermon 192; PL 38:1012; and Sermon 191; PL 38:1010.

[8] Sermons 199–204; PL 38:1026–39 (Sermons 18–23, in Lawler). This theme of *Christus Judaeis et Gentibus adunandis angularis* (PL 38:1037) appears prominently in Gregory the Great's *Moralia in Job*, particularly in the final chapters.

[9] Sermon 201; PL 38:1031–33. This motif is continued in Augustine's *Adversus Iudaeos*.

[10] Sermons 189, 190, 195, 196; PL 38:1005–1009, 1017–21.

[11] Sermons 189, 191; PL 38:1005–1007, 1009–1012.

[12] The most important are in Santa Pudenziana, Santa Sabina, Santa Maria Maggiore, San Prassede, San Clemente, San Marco, San Lorenzo (outside the walls), Santa Maria in Trastevere, Santa Cecelia, SS. Cosma e Damiano. There is not much variation in the way Bethlehem is portrayed. The sheep which are emerging from the city probably represent those apostles who themselves stand for the gentile Church. It is unlikely, in my view, that Bethlehem and Jerusalem signify the historical places associated with Jesus.

[13] See Y. Congar, 'Le thème du "don de la loi" dans l'art chrétien', *Nouvelle revue théologique* 85 (1962) 319–99; W. Schumacher, 'Dominus legem dat', *Römische Quartelschrift* 54 (1959) 1–39. There is apparently no suggestion of Bethlehem in Santa Costanza, which contains the most important representations of the transmission of the laws.

[14] See M. L. Thérel, *Les symboles de l'"ecclesia' dans la création iconographique de l'art chrétien du IIIe au VIe siècle* (Rome, 1973) pp. 72–125.

[15] *Itineraria*; CCSL 175:96–97; J. Wilkinson (trans.), *Egeria's Travels to the Holy Land* (rev. ed., Jerusalem, 1981) pp. 46–48, 78–82, 127–28, 262. See E. Hunt, *Holy Land Pilgrimage in the Later Roman Empire, A.D. 312–460* (Oxford, 1982) pp. 15, 18, 85, 87.

[16] *Itinera Hierosolymitana*; CSEL 39:25; and *Itineraria et alia geographica*; CCSL 175:19–20. See 'Bethlehem' in *Lexikon für Theologie und Kirche* (Freiburg im Breisgau, 1958) 2:311.

[17] *Itinera Hierosolymitana*; CSEL 39:178; and *Itineraria*; CCSL 175:143f.

[18] *Itineraria* 19–20; CCSL 175:144.

[19] *Itineraria*; CCSL 175:124; and Theodorich, *Guide to the Holy Land* 33, trans. A. Stewart (New York, 1986) pp. 51–52. See also Burcard (1283) and Anonymous, *De civitatibus terrae sanctae* (thirteenth-century) in S. de Sandoli (ed.), *Itinera Hierosolymitana Crucesignatorum (Saec. XII-XIII)* (Jerusalem, 1984) 4:197, 359. Other examples for itineraria, A.D. 1100–1300, are in vol. 2 of this series (Jerusalem, 1980) pp. 23, 39, 47, 49, 77, 99, 107, 135, 145, 163, 181, 183, 191, 219, 235, 277, 279, 305, 365. Over twenty more citations in vol. 3 (1983).

[20] For example, Niccolò of Poggibonsi, *A Voyage Beyond the Seas (1346–1350)* (Jerusalem, 1945) pp. 50–57. As is typical of late medieval pilgrims to Palestine, Niccolò mentions the ecclesiastical indulgence associated with many sacred sites.

[21] E. Hoade, *Western Pilgrims* (Jerusalem, 1952) p. 73; see Thomas Brygg in this same volume, p. 80. I might add that, even in franciscan sermons on the Nativity, there are little more than the expected commonplaces on Bethlehem. See, for example, the Christmas sermons of Bonaventure; *Omnia opera* (Quaracchi, 1882) 9:102–106.

[22] See D. Baldi (ed.), *Enchiridion Locorum Sanctorum Documenta S. Evangelii Loca Respicientia* (2nd ed., Jerusalem, 1982) pp. 82–165, which lists some sixty-nine annotated texts in Latin, Greek, and Arabic relating to Bethlehem, dating from the second to the seventeenth century.

[23] Homily 8 on Luke 2; PL 76:1103D; listed as Homily 7 in D. Hurst (trans.), *Gregory the Great: Forty Gospel Homilies*, Cistercian Studies 123 (Kalamazoo, Michigan, 1990) pp. 50–53. Bede uses these lines in his own Commentary on Luke (CCSL 120:48 and 50).

[24] PL 76:1104A.

[25] PL 76:1104B.

[26] Homily 10 on Matthew 2:1–12; PL 76:1110–14; as Homily 8 in Hurst, pp. 54–61.

[27] Commentary on Luke 2; CCSL 120:48; see PL 92:327–34.

[28] Commentary on Luke 2; CCSL 120:1165–69.

[29] Commentary on Luke 2; CCSL 120:1137–40.

[30] See Commentary on Matthew 2, 'Bethlehem Iudae' (PL 92:13–15); Homily 6 on Luke 2:1–14 (CCSL 122:37–45); and Homily 7 on Luke 2:15–20 (CCSL 122:46–51). See also Bethlehem in Bede's *Itinerarium*; CCSL 175:264–65; and compare Adamnus, *De locis sanctis*, *Itineraria*; CCSL 175:206.

31 Commentary on Matthew 2; PL 106:1280D. Compare *Expositio in Lucam*; PL 106:1506B.

32 PL 106:1280D.

33 Homily 7 on Matthew; PL 131:900A. Compare Peter of Blois, *In nativitate Domini, sermo 6*; PL 207:582.

34 PL 131:903A. Compare Pseudo-Bede (750–800) on Matthew 2; PL 92:12–14.

35 PL 120:132–35, *passim*; *Corpus Christianorum, Continuatio Medievals* [CCCM] 56:148–52. The *domus panis* nourishes believers daily and also represents the *ecclesia Christianorum*; PL 120:134, CCCM 56:148.

36 Commentary on Matthew 2; PL 107:754–55.

37 Commentary on Matthew 2; PL 168:1333–49; CCCM 29:35–52.

38 Commentary on Matthew 2; PL 114:72–78.

39 PL 114:251–52. Compare Bruno of Asto, Commentary on Luke; PL 165:354–55.

40 The title of Sermon 23 is: 'De sublimitate incarnationis Christi, et de spirituali electorum profectu'; PL 198:219A. Adam of Dryburgh's carthusian audience are the 'elect'; PL 198:229A; M. Hamilton (trans.), *Adam of Dryburgh: Six Christmas Sermons* (Salzburg, 1974) pp. 164–65.

41 'Ideo quoque a sanctitate bonae actionis, quam exterius proximis ad utilitatem'; Sermon 24; PL 198:229C. Historically, the proper sequence should be from Bethlehem to Nazareth.

42 PL 198:219–65.

43 Sermon 24; PL 198:229.

44 Sermon 25; PL 198:243.

45 Sermon 23; PL 198:225, *passim*.

46 A. Hoste and C. Talbot (edd.), *De Iesu puero* 19; CCCM 1:266; PL 184:861–62; T. Berkeley (trans.), 'Jesus at the Age of Twelve', in *Aelred of Rievaulx: Treatises*, Cistercian Fathers 2 (Spencer, Massachusetts, 1971) pars. 19–20, pp. 25–28.

47 Aelred's three stages (Bethlehem-Nazareth-Jerusalem) are modelled after the progressions of the 'allegorical sense'. *De Iesu puero* 11–18; CCCM 1:258–65.

48 CCCM 1:266–78.

49 *In vigilia nativitatis*, [V Nat] 1; in J. Leclercq et al. (edd.), *Sancti Bernardi opera* [SBOp] (Rome, 1957–1977) 4:201. See also *In Epiphania, sermo 1*; SBOp 4:297.

50 V Nat 3; SBOp 4:214.

51 V Nat 3; SBOp 4:215.

52 V Nat 3; SBOp 4:216.

53 V Nat 3; SBOp 4:216–17. Compare Nicholas of Clairvaux's three Christmas sermons; PL 184:827–50.

54 V Nat 6; SBOp 4:242–44.

55 V Nat 1; SBOp 4:201–202. Compare Bede (CCSL 122:47); Jerome,

In Zachariam (CCSL 76A:876, 899, 923); and *Liber interpretationis hebraicorum nominum* (CCSL 72:67).

[56] V Nat 2; SBOp 4:204. As 'true Jews', monks should aspire to be 'Jerusalem', the anticipation of the final *visio pacis*. See also Bernard's V Nat 5; SBOp 4:189f.

[57] See Meister Eckhart, *Sermon 9*, and *Tract 8*, in F. Pfeiffer and C. Evans (trans.), *Meister Eckhart* (London, 1924) 1:20–25, 336–40; M. Fox, *Breakthrough: Meister Eckhart's Creation Spirituality* (Garden City, New York, 1980), sermons 21, 22; E. Colledge and B. McGinn (trans.), *Meister Eckhart* (New York, 1981) german sermon 6 (see also pp. 50–57). Eckhart, and other late medieval mystics such as Julian of Norwich, refer to the soul as the 'city', but without specifically naming Bethlehem; M. O'C. Walshe (trans.), *Meister Eckhart* (London, 1981), sermon 64, pp. 123–29.

[58] The first sermon for Christmas eve is about the soul as Bethlehem. The second treats the soul as Jerusalem.

[59] This is the main theme of all six sermons for Christmas eve. Compare Guerric of Igny, *De nativitate Domini, sermo 4*; PL 185:42.

THE PAPACY AND THE REFORM OF THE CISTERCIAN ORDER IN THE LATE MIDDLE AGES*

Bernhard Schimmelpfennig
Universität Augsburg

SCHOLARSHIP ON MEDIEVAL cistercian history has centered on Bernard of Clairvaux and the springtime of the order in the twelfth century, both so important for the whole of western Europe. Scholars pay less attention to the thirteenth century, and the Late Middle Ages are virtually ignored. This emphasis—or lack thereof—is the case with almost all of the monastic reform centers which grew out of the reforms of the High Middle Ages. Once their original élan disappeared, once monastic life became 'normal' within them, the interest of many historians diminishes. To cite only a few examples, whom does Cluny, Vallombrosa, or Camaldoli interest after the splendor of their early period was extinguished? Quite apart from a descent into normality or even into decline, the disinterest of historians may very well be based on the fact that, in the later Middle Ages, many monasteries no longer determined their own direction but were increasingly regulated by other authorities. These authorities included bishops opposed to monastic exemption, popes, and, more and more, the temporal authorities. The Cistercians too did not escape this fate; most important for them, the papacy gained increasing power over them.

Just as in the twelfth and thirteenth centuries, the Late Middle Ages saw a host of papal privileges and mandates, mostly about matters concerning a few cistercian houses. They were usually responses to the requests of those who received them and followed the appropriate formulaic patterns of the papal chancellery. As a result, these privileges usually suited the purposes of the receivers, only rarely those of the popes who granted them.

My intention here is to investigate whether and to what extent individual popes of the fourteenth and fifteenth centuries actively promoted the reform of the order. This purpose is best accomplished methodologically by a study of the papal receipts received by the order's leadership and intended for dissemination throughout the order. For that reason, I shall concentrate on an evaluation of the resolutions of the Chapter General.

In September 1486, the Chapter General set forth, with rather overstated self-praise '... that the constitution... of Benedict XII, which began *Fulgens quasi* [*sicut*] *stella*, and the other constitutions on the reform of our order... have been observed to our day by the order and its members.'[1] In fact, at least some of the provisions of the so-called *Benedictina* were repeatedly strengthened by the Chapter General and cited as the basis for new resolutions. Therefore, I should like to begin with Benedict XII.

THE *BENEDICTINA*

It is surely well known that, from the first days of his pontificate, Benedict XII sought to reform the Church which had been entrusted to him.[2] For that reason, he concerned himself in an especially intensive way with the dissemination of reform constitutions for the individual orders. There were several reasons why he began his series of reform laws with the Cistercians. He was himself a Cistercian. He had learned of the need for reform in the southern french monasteries at the time of his studies at Paris and, later, as cardinal-protector of the order. The first stimulus to the specifics of his reform he received from his uncle, Cardinal Arnaud Nouvel, who, in 1316–1317, under Pope John XXII, had striven in vain for a papal initiative in reform. Moreover, it must have seemed opportune to Benedict to begin with a reform of his own order, to combat better the expected resistance from other orders. His purpose was facilitated by the fact that four of the five protoabbots—the abbots of Cîteaux, Clairvaux, La Ferté, and Morimond—had set out for Avignon, at the beginning of 1335, to hail the election of their confrère.[3] And it is precisely these four abbots whom the constitution designates as co-sponsors.[4] The pope's first draft shows a desire to do more than he succeeded in accomplishing, and this is due to the fact that a contradictory position was advocated by these same four abbots.[5] In spite of this resistance, the final form was achieved and issued only a half year after the papal coronation, on 12 July 1335.

In his later constitutions, the pope formulated his relationship to the contemporary orders in stock rhetorical phrases.[6] But, in this constitution, he praised the performance of his own order with words that seem rather exaggerated, given the actual condition of the order and the regulations he attached to reform it. The constitution begins:

> Shining through the mist like the morning star, the holy cistercian order fights in the Church militant by work and example. By the exercise of holy contemplation and the merit of innocent life, it fervently strives to scale the heights with Mary. It strives to conform itself to the work of the anxious Martha through the exercise of praiseworthy deeds and assiduous concern for pious works.[7]

Then follows praise of the order for its liturgical practice and mastery of Scripture. The constitution's provisions show that this praise too was not altogether justified.

Unfortunately, Benedict did not explain what he meant by reform and to what goals that reform should lead. Still, this deficiency can be largely overcome by an analysis of the constitution's fifty-seven paragraphs. According to Louis Lekai, to whom this volume is dedicated, the *Benedictina* '... was basically a reform of fiscal administration.'[8] Despite the well-known fiscal interests of the Avignon popes, I consider this description somewhat one-sided. Pope Benedict did indeed place great value on the good financial condition and the effective administration of the monasteries and other institutions. But these measures were only to serve as the basis for the greater effectiveness of the Chapter General and the visitors, and also for the improvement of scholarly formation. The chief goal of the reforms was to allow monastic life to reflect the order's original ideals—or, rather, the notion of the early period of the order as Pope Benedict understood it.

We begin with the regulations on life in the monasteries.[9] These prescriptions and prohibitions show what improprieties the pope wished to remove. That only those be admitted as monks or *conversi* who demonstrated a suitable conversion of life seems a comparatively harmless and understandable injunction—at least as far as concerns the financial conditions of the contemporary monasteries. Their members should simply live a life reflecting the order's original ideals. To that end the pope forbade any luxury in clothing or customary usages. The abbots' retinues were limited to one mounted companion; only the five protoabbots were allowed larger retinues. Simple monks or *conversi* were not allowed to ride; monastery officials were allowed only one horse—if the abbot permitted. The pope formulated more precisely the standard prohibition against the eating of meat, which earlier papal dispensations and privileges had revoked. The seriously ill or worthy retired abbots (*benemeriti*), the reigning abbot and one monk invited by him, and *notabiles persone* on trips were exempted from this prohibition. Benedict strictly forbade the building of cells in common dormitories. With the exception of the abbot, who possessed a separate dwelling, only the prior and subprior (according to Cocquelines: *superiores*) might have their own cell in the dormitory—if the abbot allowed. Concerning the usages of the common life were prohibitions against monks possessing individual *portiones* of food or money, against abbot and community dividing up the monastery property, and against conducting unilateral monetary transactions.

In order that these regulations on the common life might be realized, every abbot was to manage carefully the goods of his monastery. As a consequence, the alienation of monastic property was generally forbidden. Exceptions were precisely regulated, and in no case could the abbot act arbitrarily. The provisions which followed concerned relations between abbot and community, but through their formulation as law they diminished the previously prevailing authority of the abbot in favor of the community. Henceforth, abbot and community—like bishop and cathedral chapter—would constitute two separate partners. This followed from the regulation that each community should possess its own seal. The community was to agree to all property transactions. A protocol was to be prepared governing the relations between abbot and community, and both partners were to attach their seals to it. Moreover, the sale of property required the consultation of two neighboring abbots, designated by the Chapter General and required to report to it. In the case of a proposed alienation of a monastery or a monastic estate—a *castrum, villa,* grange, or other *res multum notabilis*—the Chapter General could permit this only if the pope had previously agreed. Procedures for the transference of rights and revenues, for relocations, and exchanges were similarly regulated. These regulations show clearly how much reform of the order could increase the possibility of interference by the papacy in the life of each individual cistercian house as the reform was realized.

For all administration of funds, two bursars were to be appointed by the abbot with the approval of the *seniores de conventu*. These bursars were to give an account four times a year to the abbot and *seniores*. The abbots were required to give over to these bursars all monies received from outside the monastery and give an account of this income to the bursars and *seniores*. The money gained from property transactions was to be kept in boxes with four locks, the keys to which were to be held by the abbot, one bursar, the prior, and one monk elected by the community. The result of these regulations was the strict control of the abbot by the community. This control Benedict wished to extend still farther by requiring that—following the practice in the Order of Preachers—each community send to the Chapter General an elected delegate in addition to the abbot. This plan was frustrated by the opposition of the four protoabbots present at Avignon.

Just as the abbot's power was to be checked from below by the community, so he was to be controlled, more than had been the case, by the institutional representative of the whole order, the Chapter General. This control presupposed, however, that all abbots would attend the Chapter General. To ensure their attendance, the pope decreed that every abbot absent from the Chapter General without sufficient reason would have to pay as penalty twice the estimated cost of the journey. The customary contributions for the support of the abbot of Cîteaux and the Chapter General were to be collected and accounted for by three abbots chosen and sworn by the Chapter General or its definitors. The *litere solutionis* written for this purpose were to be sealed. The seal's storage place could only be opened by three keys kept by the three abbots or their delegates. The principle of mutual control was here again operative. And, so that the abbots assembling for the General Chapter would not be too long on their journey, their stay in the monasteries serving as stopping places was limited to a maximum of two days.

In the same way, the visitors' stay in their daughter houses was limited. Visitors could remain only three days unless the condition of the daughter house demanded a longer visitation. In monasteries which did not belong to their visitation circuit, they could receive no fees; in these they could receive only the food and lodging due to any other member of the order. Only in the most pressing cases—the deposition of an abbot, for example —could the visitors call in other abbots. Even so, it was forbidden the abbots to realize their own purposes through attaching themselves to visitors. And, as in ecclesiastical inquisitorial processes, the visitors were not to make known the names of those who entrusted them with secret information, even if the informer had been guilty of some sort of transgression. With regard to the Chapter General and the visitors, Lekai's characterization of the *Benedictina* proves correct, at least to some degree. But even here the intention of the legislation went farther: through the regulations and sanctions the functioning of the leadership and control agencies of the whole order was to be guaranteed, and the independence of individual monasteries was to be diminished through these agencies.

Almost a third of the entire constitution concerned regulation of the studies of the order's members. As before, studies were limited to theology. The monasteries were assigned to fixed regional study centers, of which the french centers were undoubtedly most prized. The College of Saint Bernard in Paris served as the study center, not only for the northern french monasteries, but for the most qualified members of all monasteries. Every monastery with more than twenty-nine monks was required to send one or two monks there. The preeminence of Paris is shown by the fact that the stipends of the professors and students there were higher than in the other study centers. The other centers included Toulouse and Montpellier—not only for the southern french monasteries, but also for those in the kingdoms of Navarre and Aragon. As a result, advanced studies at Salamanca (succeeding Estella in Navarre) were restricted to the monasteries of Castile and Portugal. Oxford was the center for the British Isles, Bologna for Italy. The obligations of the other monasteries were formulated vaguely. To be sure, a study center was to be organized at Metz. But only the *scientie primitive* were to be taught there, and only to the *Alemanni* and to members of monasteries belonging to the Morimond filiation east of the Rhine. As a result, Paris was the only study center designated for the monasteries in middle, northern, and eastern Europe. Benedict regulated in great detail the student quota, the stipends, the range of tasks for teachers and officials, the length of study, and the expenditures for celebrations following successful examinations. Just as in the case of failing to appear at the Chapter General, the abbot was to pay twice the cost if he failed to send students or did not forward tuition money to his students.

Seen as a whole, the *Benedictina* did not contain much that was new—except for the means of enforcement. Still, for the first time it regulated usages which had emerged after the foundation period and after the so-called *Clementina* of 1265—above all concerning studies and contributions. And, after the *Carta caritatis* and the *Rule* of Benedict itself, it created the future legal basis for the statutes of the Chapter General, for the activity of the visitors, for the regulation of monastic life, and for studies within the order. Of course this does not prove that the constitution was observed always and in every respect—as the participants in the Chapter General of 1486 were to indicate.

THE IMPACT OF THE *BENEDICTINA*

To carry out his constitution, Benedict ordered its text read at every Chapter General and, likewise, once a year in every monastery chapter. Following this instruction, the Chapter General, which met two months after the publication of the *Benedictina*, ordered the preparation, within three months, of a copy for each monastery.[10] It is true that this regulation was not everywhere observed. For that reason, the next Chapter General, of 1336, once more ordered the copies published and, at the same time, attached to it the *Libellus definitionum* and the *Rule* of Saint Benedict.[11] Abbots who resisted were to be deposed. From this year forward, we can presume a knowledge of the *Benedictina* in most monasteries. And, from 1335, certain measures were taken by the Chapter General with reference to the text of the *Benedictina*. Among these were regulations for the reform of studies at Paris,[12] statutes requiring the preparation of monastery seals[13] and their preservation,[14] prohibitions of meat consumption,[15] and a supervision of each filiation with regard to attendance at the Chapter General.[16]

Nevertheless, it would be rash to assume a universal acceptance of the *Benedictina*. Scarcely any abbot from the territory ruled by Louis the Bavarian could have attended the Chapter General. In the same way, the 'french' papacy was not popular in the England of Edward III. One may doubt, on these grounds, that the constitution was universally known or accepted in these lands. The Hundred Years War soon broke out, as did the Black Death which decimated monks as well as everyone else. These events caused monastic morale and economics to decline and prevented attendance at the Chapter General.[17]

More a reaction to the actual conditions than an observance of the *Benedictina* appears in a order of the Chapter General dating from about 1354/1355. At that time, the plan for a register of contributions was ordered; this has been preserved in a copy of 1460.[18] Modeled on the collections system of the apostolic camera, receipts were arranged according to ecclesiastical province, even though the accounts of the individual houses were reckoned according to filiation. There were four classes of contributions arranged according to the total amount desired by the Chapter General: the *contributio moderata* (9,000 *livres* of Tours), *mediocris* (12,000 *livres* of Tours), *duplex* (18,000 *livres* of Tours), and *excessiva* (24,000 *livres* of Tours). The monasteries were thus classified and, accordingly, the amounts they were to pay. Women's monasteries were seldom named, since they had been freed from payment since 1339. With regard to the men's monasteries, the register offers a revealing picture of the size of the order (about 650 houses) and the various and regionally differentiated financial strengths of the houses. To be sure, the evidence offered by the register is limited: not all houses are listed. Moreover, the register's compiler used several old lists from the thirteenth and fourteenth centuries, so that monasteries were included which had already been abandoned in the thirteenth century. As a result, it is problematic whether one can regard all the numbers as reflective of the situation in the middle of the fourteenth century. And the economic ranking cannot be accurately reproduced, since several houses either paid yearly the amounts assessed by the Chapter General or relatively meager contributions resulting from successful 'persuasion' by the collectors. As is well known, caution is advisable when dealing with most medieval fiscal texts.

Distress was magnified during the Great Schism, for the order was now split by the two obediences. The Chapter General did indeed affirm several regulations of the *Benedictina*—the payment of contributions,[19] attendance at the study centers,[20] the administration of monastery funds[21]—but the separation by obediences resulted in little response. The abbots of the Chapter General themselves testified that they could not continue to observe all the regulations. Thus, in 1390, the Chapter General allowed as visitors not only abbots and theologians, but also canonists.[22] That presupposes that at least some monks had studied canon law—and had even taught it. And, a few decades later, allegations from roman law excited no protest at the Chapter General of 1438.[23]

After the end of the Schism, the *Benedictina* was often cited at the Chapter General; the number of topics also increased. Together they served as the basis for visitations.[24] The regulations were affirmed on the alienation of monastery property,[25] on contributions,[26] on studies in the order,[27] on the prohibition of meat,[28] on the prohibition of separate incomes for monks,[29] on the prohibition of cells in dormitories,[30] on simple clothing,[31] and on attendance at the Chapter General.[32] The rules on the admittance of monks and *conversi* were made stricter; illegitimate children were forbidden entrance into the order.[33] But the very frequency of references and their frequent repetition—

for example, on studies—shows that the real situation was usually at odds with the regulations of Benedict's constitution. But these limitations can not lessen the contributions of this pope. He was the first, and remained the only, pope who attempted to reform the order on his own initiative. The fact that his constitution was cited by the Chapter General more often than any other papal text shows, moreover, how much the *Benedictina* served at least as the guideline for life within the order.

THE POPES AFTER BENEDICT XII

After Benedict XII, the popes interfered only rarely with the important affairs of the order. The first to do so was the aragonese pope, Benedict XIII. At his direction,[34] the Chapter General of his obedience decided, in 1405, to commission the abbot of Cîteaux or another protoabbot to undertake a reform of the monasteries in the kingdoms of the iberian peninsula and in its neighboring regions— that is, in southern France. For this purpose, the abbot was to hold a meeting at which irregularities would be identified and corrected. I do not believe that this pope initiated the future development of the spanish cistercian congregation, for the regions named in the resolution constituted the major part of the obedience remaining to him. Yet the establishment of the resolutions through the Chapter General is important. This action occurred to satisfy the pope, '... et domini temporales in tali reformatione laetentur.' With it a tendency was acknowledged by the Chapter General itself—a tendency which had shown itself especially since the beginning of the Schism and which, from that time on, proved decisive for the cistercian order as well—the participation of the territorial lords in reform. By this, the initiatives of the Chapter General, as those of the pope, were first made contingent and, after the second half of the fifteenth century, reduced more and more to a subsidiary role.

This development was already apparent under the first pope of the reunited Church, Martin V. In my opinion, this pope instituted church reform only to the extent that he had promised on the occasion of his election by the Council of Constance.[35] The restoration of papal power and of the papal states was his primary concern. For that reason, he did not take the initiative on matters, such as the reform of the Cistercians, which the Council of Constance had not specifically ordered. On 23 April 1424, he confirmed the order's exemption from tithes;[36] after 1425, he supported the efforts of Martin de Vargas toward the formation of a reform congregation in Castile.[37] The bulls he issued were rescripts which were based on the interests of the suppliants. In 1424—analogously to the situation of 1405—he mentioned among the supplications those *nonnullorum regum et principum.*

Martin's successor, Eugenius IV, followed the same approach. He did direct a letter of 16 March 1444 to the next Chapter General. In the letter, he exhorted the Chapter General to hold to the customs of the order and to observe the order's statutes and papal constitutions. Above all, this was to combat *sinistrae opiniones* in the order and edify the laity through reform.[38] On the basis of these admonitions, one might suppose that the pope was acting on his own initiative. He did, however, give further instructions—either orally or formulated in a *littera clausa*—to the order's procurator, Abbot John of Oliva. On the basis of this, one might conclude that the pope's action may have been based on John's initiative or on that of some group which had not as yet prevailed completely in the Chapter General. The other documents of this pope concerning things of importance to the Cistercians were like those of his papal predecessors—simply rescripts based on the requests of supplicants.[39] Unlike Eugenius' support of benedictine reform congregations, there was no equivalent papal initiative in the reform of the Cistercians.

Eugenius' successors—Nicholas V, Pius II, Paul II, and Sixtus IV—also customarily reacted to initiatives of the order's members, initiatives sometimes demanded by temporal princes.[40] In the case of Paul II, it has been said that he did not grant the order any privileges because he called the monks *fraticelli* and gave over many monasteries to commendatory abbots.[41]

With this statement we call attention to a phenomenon which contributed considerably to the decline of the order: commendation. Since the middle of the thirteenth century at least, church offices had been increasingly viewed as benefices. The enjoyment of the incomes—even the form of granting the benefices, as commendations—had thrust the observance of the associated obligations into the background and had made them attractive to the upper levels of the clergy and laity.[42] It is, therefore, understandable that Benedict XII had drastically curtailed the granting of commendations in pursuit of his reforms.[43] It is true that, at that time, the institution of commendation could still be used as a means of reform. For example, in 1342, Clement VI granted, for the purpose of reform, the southern italian, cistercian monastery of S. Giovanni in Lamis—at the instigation of its prior—to Guillaume Court, the so-called *Cardinalis Albus*, one of the closest colleagues of Benedict XII.[44] Something similar happened to the Benedictines of S. Giustina in Padua at the beginning of the fifteenth century.[45]

Still, since the middle of the fifteenth century at the latest, cistercian monasteries were more and more granted *in commendam* by the popes for the benefit of cardinals and territorial rulers. Considering the financial advantages which the popes reaped from commendation, considering too the ecclesiastical politics of the time, papal support for the elimination of this bad practice or for other reform attempts was out of the question. Now, in fact, the financial advantages of granting or refusing privileges and reform bulls came to the fore for the popes. This is shown quite clearly in a report by Jean de Cirey, abbot of Balerne, about a delegation sent to the papal curia by the Chapter General of 1475.[46] This report is conclusive for the position of the Chapter General as well as for the way business was now being conducted at the curia. The order's representatives paid considerable *propine* to the cardinals, to the curialists, and to to the pope himself. Horses were also given, since horses and ducats were considered the 'gods of the curia'. Still, for some 6000 ducats only a rather meager rescript was issued.[47]

But Jean de Cirey did not lose heart. For a great deal of money—for which, in addition to contributions, subsidies also must have been demanded—Jean, now the abbot of Cîteaux (1476–1501),[48] obtained various privileges from Innocent VIII.[49] For these, the grateful Chapter General of 1489 praised the 'dear' pope as *nostri Cisterciensis Ordinis zelator, reformator, restaurator et defensor clementissimus*.[50] It is true that the privileges obtained accomplished nothing. The pope's support was costly but no longer carried much weight.

To the cause of reform, the Chapter General itself could contribute little more than pious formulae. The Chapter General was attended almost exclusively by french abbots. On the initiative of Jean de Cirey, it issued the 'Articles of Paris' in 1494.[51] In these articles, the Chapter General defined its understanding of reform: 'We know that reform must not concern itself with the introduction of novel inventions; it must, rather, evidence a return to the life, liturgy, and organization of the holy fathers.'[52] With this orientation toward the past, the abbots of the Chapter General themselves erected a barrier to a new flourishing of the order.

As long as the popes remained primarily concerned with the Papal States and its princely court—as well as with the fiscal side of ecclesiastical institutions—they could contribute nothing to the reform of the order. The Chapter General scarcely possessed the power to initiate a reform of the whole order. It consisted almost exclusively of french abbots and, after the later days of Charles VII's reign, fell increasingly under the influence of the french crown. And elsewhere—in Castile, for example—the reformers had the prospect of success only when they were useful to the rulers of the newly emerging national states. Movements for reform could only come—when at all—from individual territorial princes or from bishops, regional congregations, or local reform groups. The central institutions of the Middle Ages had no opportunity to envision a reform—to say nothing of carrying it out. As at the beginning of the order, the initiative once more lay with individual monasteries or regional groupings. The modern world would show whether and how they realized their opportunities.

NOTES

* A shorter version of this paper has been published in K. Elm (ed.), *Reformbemühungen und Observanzbestrebungen im spätmittelalterlichen Ordenswesen*, Berliner Historische Studien 14, Ordenstudien VI (Berlin, 1989) pp. 399–410.

[1] J.-M. Canivez, *Statuta capitulorum generalium ordinis cisterciensis* (Louvain, 8 vols. [organized chronologically], 1933–1941) 1486:100: 'Praesens generale Capitulum... notificat per presentes, quod constitutio felicis recordationis domini Benedicti Papae XII, quae incipit "Fulgens quasi stella", necnon et aliae eiusdem constitutiones super reformatione Ordinis nostri Cisterciensis editae... ab ipso Ordine eiusque personis usque hodie observatae....' In the notes which follow, the statutes of the Chapter General will be cited by year, not by volume and page number.

[2] See, especially, the following: B. Schimmelpfennig, 'Zisterzienserideal und Kirchenreform: Benedikt XII. (1334–42) als Reformpapst', in *Zisterzienser-Studien 3* (Berlin, 1976) pp. 11–43; L. Böhm, 'Papst Benedikt XII. (1334–1342) als Förderer der Ordenstudien: Restaurator—Reformator—oder Deformator regularer Lebensform?', in G. Melville (ed.), *Secundum regulam vivere: Festschrift Norbert Backmund* (Windberg, 1978) pp. 281–310. For the relations between the papacy and the Cistercians, see B. Schimmelpfennig, 'Zisterzienser, Papsttum und Episkopat im Mittelalter', in K. Elm et al. (edd.), *Die Zisterzienser: Ordensleben zwischen Ideal und Wirklichkeit*, Schriften des Rheinischen Museumsamtes 10 (Bonn, 1980) pp. 69–85.

[3] See the compensation for the costs of their journey in *Statuta* 1335:6.

[4] C. Coquelines (ed.), *Magnum bullarium Romanum* 3/2 (Rome, 1741) p. 204a:2. The Turin edition of the *Bullarium* was not available during the preparation of this article.

[5] J.-B. Mahn, *Le pape Benoît XII et les Cisterciens*, Bibliothèque de l'École des Hautes-Études 295 (Paris, [1949]) appendix, pp. 85–135.

[6] See Cocquelines, pp. 214b–15a, 242b–43a, and 264ab.

[7] Cocquelines, p. 203b prooemium: 'Fulgens sicut stella matutina in medio nebulae, sacer Cisterciensis Ordo in ecclesia militante militat operibus et exemplis, fervideque satagit per sanctae contemplationis applausum et innocentis vitae meritum montana scandere cum Maria seque per exercitium laudabilium actionum et pensum piorum operum curiosum Marthae satagentis officio conformare.'

[8] L. J. Lekai, *The Cistercians: Ideals and Reality* ([Kent, Ohio, 1977]) p. 72.

[9] For the following, see Cocquelines, pp. 203b–213b; *Statuta* 1335: Constitutio 'Fulgens'.

[10] *Statuta* 1335:4.

[11] *Statuta* 1336:4.
[12] *Statuta* 1335:13.
[13] *Statuta* 1335:2.
[14] *Statuta* 1336:1.
[15] *Statuta* 1336:3.
[16] *Statuta* 1337:3.
[17] See Lekai, pp. 96–101.
[18] A. O. Johnson and P. King (edd.), *The Tax Book of the Cistercian Order*, Det Norske Videnskaps-Okademi, 2, Hist.-Filos. Klasse, Avhandlinger, Ny serie No. 16 (Oslo etc., 1979).
[19] *Statuta* 1390:6f., 1406:6, 1407:6.
[20] *Statuta* 1390:14, 1394:8, 1405:1.
[21] *Statuta* 1402:9.
[22] *Statuta* 1390:8.
[23] *Statuta* 1438:58. See, for the above, P. Feige, 'Filiation und Landeshoheit: Die Entstehung der Zisterzienserkongregationen auf der Iberischen Halbinsel', in *Zisterzienser-Studien 1* (Berlin, 1975) p. 56. For studies, see Böhm, *passim*; J. A. Brundage, 'The Monk as Lawyer', *The Jurist* 39 (1979) 423–36; and L. J. Lekai, 'Studien, Studiensystem und Lehrtätigkeit der Zistenzienser', in *Die Zisterzienser*, pp. 165–70.
[24] *Statuta* 1451:57, 1486:45.
[25] *Statuta* 1486:100, 1520:10, 47, 52, 53.
[26] *Statuta* 1490:6, 1496:46.
[27] *Statuta* 1423:47, 1425:12 and 14, 1427:30, 1437:55, 1438:59, 1439:92, 1445:9, 1454:98, 1456:115, 1460:19, 1461:36, 1464:37, 1490:33, 1492:63, 1503:10.
[28] *Statuta* 1430:60, 1437:44, 1439:96 (dispensation), 1465:11, 1481:61 (dispensation), 1494:43.
[29] *Statuta* 1433:32, 1461:33, 1494:43.
[30] *Statuta* 1439:96, 1494:45.
[31] *Statuta* 1494:45.
[32] *Statuta* 1496:45f., 1504:7, 1535:11.
[33] *Statuta* 1445:30.
[34] *Statuta* 1405:15. See also Feige, p. 51.
[35] See, for example, K. A. Fink, 'Papsttum und Kirchenreform nach dem Grossen Schisma', *Theologische Quartalschrift* 126 (1946) 110–22; Fink, 'Die konziliare Idee im späten Mittelalter', in *Die Welt zur Zeit des Konstanzer Konzils*, Vorträge und Forschungen 9 (Konstanz, 1964) pp. 119–34. Fink evaluates more positively the position on reform of Martin V.
[36] Cocquelines, III/2: 446b: *Militanti ecclesie*.
[37] Feige, pp. 52–55.
[38] *Statuta* 1444: brief *Inter ceteros*.

[39] *Statuta* 1438:59; Cocquelines, III/3: 21ab: *Ad universalis ecclesie regimen* (8 December 1438), and pp. 24b–25a: *Regularem vitam professis* (14 February 1439). The initiative for reform became stronger under Eugenius IV and other popes, as emphasized by K. Walsh, 'Papsttum und Ordensreform in Spätmittelalter und Renaissance: Zur Wechselwirkung von Zentralgewalt und lokaler Initiative', in Elm (ed.), *Reformbemühungen*, pp. 411–30.

[40] See *Statuta* 1448: brief *Etsi omnes* (14 July 1448), 1448:27, 1486:12 and 74. See also Cocquelines, III/3: 145a–46a: *Etsi cunctis* (13 December 1475). See, too, the more frequent mention of the *Piina* and *Sixtina* about the accounting of contributions. These are not reproduced in the *Statuta* or Cocquelines—for example, in *Statuta* 1478:35, 1492:34.

[41] *Statuta*, vol. 5, appendix, p. 761.

[42] With regard to the Cistercians, see Lekai, p. 101ff. See also W. J. Telesca, 'The Cistercian Dilemma at the Close of the Middle Ages: Gallicanism or Rome', in *Studies in Medieval Cistercian History Presented to Jeremiah F. O'Sullivan*, Cistercian Studies 13 (Spencer, Massachusetts, 1971) pp. 163–85, where the influence of the french crown on the cistercian order is discussed.

[43] Schimmelpfennig, 'Zisterzienserideal', pp. 24–26.

[44] T. Gasparrini Leporace (ed.), *Le suppliche di Clemente VI*, no. 17 (23 May 1342) p. 7f. On Guillaume Court, see Schimmelpfennig, 'Zisterzienserideal', p. 40f.

[45] See, for example, P. Schmitz, *Geschichte der Benediktinerordens*, 3 (Einsiedeln, Zürich, 1955) p. 151ff.

[46] *Statuta*, vol. 5, appendix, pp. 761–65. See also Lekai, p. 105.

[47] *Statuta* 1489: brief *Accepimus litteras vestras* and 9, 1492:33ff.; Cocquelines 3/3:209a–210a.

[48] On this, see also Lekai, pp. 105f., 110–12.

[49] *Statuta* 1487: brief *Meditatio cordis nostri*, 7, 23, 35, 54; 1489: bull *Ad sacrum apostolatus ministerium* and brief *Accepimus litteras vestras*, 9, 13–15; 1492:33f.; 1494:38. Cocquelines, III/3: 209a–210a: *Ad romani pontificis* (30 August 1486). On the following, see also Telesca, *passim*.

[50] *Statuta* 1489:14.

[51] *Statuta* 1494. See also Lekai, pp. 111–13.

[52] *Statuta* 1494:38: '. . . scientes reformationem non novarum quidem adinventionum introductionem, sed potius ad sanctorum patrum vitam, caerimonias pariter et instituta reductionem respicere. . . .'

BERNARD OF CLAIRVAUX'S ABBOT: BOTH DANIEL AND NOAH

John R. Sommerfeldt
The University of Dallas

BERNARD'S TEACHING ON HUMAN life is a dynamic one, and he offers a dynamic image of that life. The image which Bernard employs to convey that dynamism is the sea; human life is the crossing of that sea. But that sea is crossed by more than one means and by more than one sort of person:

> My brothers, this extensive sea [Psalm 103:2]...
> is traversed by three classes of persons, each crossing safely in its own way—so that they may pass over to deliverance [Isaiah 51:10]. The three are [typified by] Noah, Daniel, and Job [Ezekiel 14:14], of whom the first crossed by ship, the second by a bridge, the third by a ford. These three men signify the three orders of the Church. Noah guided the ark, in which I perceive immediately the form of the Church of the just, so that it did not perish in the flood [Genesis 7:7]. Daniel, a man of longings [Daniel 9:23], dedicated himself to abstinence and chastity [Daniel 1:8]; this is the order of penance and continence which free one for God alone. Job, too, dispensing well the

goods of this world [Job 1:3; 1 John 3:17] in the married state, signifies the faithful [laity] rightly possessing the goods of this world.[1]

The path to perfection which Bernard himself follows is, of course, that of the monk. His path is the way of Daniel.

But Bernard is also an abbot, and that means to him that he is not only a Daniel but also a Noah. Addressing abbots and monks, Bernard writes:

> I propose to speak of the first and second orders [of prelates and monks] because there are present my venerable brothers and fellow-abbots of the order of prelates, as well as monks of the order of penitence. However, we abbots may not think ourselves outside this second order, unless—God forbid—we are unmindful of our profession because of the office we hold.[2]

The abbot, though elected a prelate, remains a monk.[3] His duties, however, are those of a prelate. The abbot ministers to the needs of those for whom he is responsible:

> The prelate should possess a pure heart [1 Timothy 1:5] if he desires to do good rather than merely rule. He must not seek his own interests or worldly honor—or any thing other than what is pleasing to God and serves the salvation of souls. But, with a pure intention and an irreproachable life, he must be a model for the flock [1 Peter 5:3] and begin to do and teach [Acts 1:1]. As the *Rule* of our teacher [Benedict] enjoins: 'By his deeds he must make it clear that nothing may be done which he has taught his disciples is forbidden' [*Rule* 2]. Otherwise, a brother whom he corrects may murmur quietly: 'Physician, heal yourself' [Luke 4:23].[4]

The abbot must live for the welfare of his monks, for their happiness.[5]

The abbot must be a model for his monks. He must also be a teacher, ready with 'useful teaching' for his sons.[6] But to preach and teach as he must, the abbot must also be a bride, a bride who receives the ecstatic embrace of the Bridegroom and thus begets and nurses her offspring:

> See how she [the bride] yearns for one thing and receives another. In spite of her longing for contemplation, she is burdened with the task of preaching. Despite her desire to bask in the Bridegroom's presence, she is entrusted with the cares of begetting and rearing children. Nor is this the only time she has been so treated. As you may remember, once before, when she had sighed for the Bridegroom's embrace and kiss, his response to her was: 'Your breasts are better than wine' [Song of Songs 1:1]. And this made her realize that she was a mother, that her duty was to suckle her babes, to provide food for her children. . . . So now too, the bride, desiring and enquiring about the place where her beloved pastures his flock and rests at noon [Song of Songs 1:6], is given instead ornaments of gold studded with silver [Song of Songs 1:10], wisdom with eloquence, and committed to the work of preaching.[7]

But preaching is not the only task of the abbot. He must act both as apostle and prophet, both in preaching and in providing guidance:

> I am neither prophet nor apostle, but, I must say, I act the role of both prophet and apostle. Though far beneath them in merit, I am caught up in similar cares. Even though it be a great embarrassment, though it puts me at serious risk, I am seated on the chair of Moses [Matthew 23:2], to whose quality of life I do not lay claim and whose gifts I do not experience. But, then, should

one withhold respect for the chair because the one sitting there is unworthy? Even though the Scribes and Pharisees sit on it, Christ has said: 'Do what they tell you' [Matthew 23:3].[8]

The tasks of preaching and guidance require spiritual maturity, the maturity of a bride and mother:

> With the wisdom of Paul [in Romans 12:15], I shall assign these two affections to the bride's two breasts, compassion to one and congratulation to the other. She is but a girl too immature to marry and with breasts still underdeveloped if she is not prompted to congratulation, prone to condolence. If such a one should assume the governance of souls or the office of preaching, she would do no good for others and great harm to herself.[9]

In preaching and giving counsel to those entrusted to him, the abbot must practice great discernment:

> We must return to the breasts of the bride and show how both they and their milk differ. Congratulation yields the milk of encouragement, compassion that of consolation. As often as the spiritual mother receives the kiss [of the Bridegroom], she feels both breasts flowing with heavenly milk. You may see her nourishing her babes, suckling them with full breasts, from one the milk of consolation, from the other the milk of encouragement, according as she sees is the need of each.[10]

The abbot's wise discernment is especially needed in ascertaining motivation. Bernard writes to a nun seeking to leave her monastery for the eremetical life:

> You would have done better to choose someone more learned than I to counsel you on this matter, but, as you have seen fit to do so, I shall not

> hide what seems better to me. I have thought and rethought the plan you have presented, but I do not dare to give an easy response. You could have zeal for God in mind, in which case your motivation is excusable....[11]

But whether preaching or discerning or giving counsel, the abbot is always to keep in mind his service to those who need it most:

> You must see yourself the abbot and father of those whom you find sad, faint-hearted, and discontented. It is by consoling, encouraging, and admonishing that you do your duty, that you bear your burden. And by bearing that burden, you carry to health those who need healing.[12]

The burdens of the abbot are onerous indeed. Bernard's response to the burdens of counselling his brethren are mixed. He regrets the loss of leisure for meditation, but still feels impelled by love to spend himself on the needs of his monks:

> There are some sitting here [Matthew 16:28] whom I wish... might begin to spare me a little bit more than in the past and not intrude rudely and irresponsibly on my leisure.... I make this complaint reluctantly, however, for some timid persons might conceal their needs and overtax their powers of endurance through fear of disturbing me.... They will spare me by not sparing me, and I shall rest more in knowing they are not afraid to trouble me about their needs. I shall accommodate myself to them as far as I can [Psalm 145:2]. As long as I shall live I shall serve God in them, in unfeigned love [2 Corinthians 6:6].[13]

Responding to requests for guidance is burdensome, but Bernard is diligent in responding.[14]

Preaching is a continuing burden, for '...no small effort and fatigue are involved in going out day by day to draw waters from the open streams of the Scriptures and providing for the needs of each of you....'[15] The burden is great, for it is a distraction from the meditation in which Bernard finds his greatest joy:

> How I wish that all had the gift of teaching! I should be rid of the need to preach these sermons! It is a burden I should like to transfer to another. Or, rather, I should prefer that none of you would need to exercise it and that all would be taught by God [John 6:45]. Then I should have leisure to contemplate God's beauty [Psalm 45:11].[16]

Bernard also fears the potential damage to his spiritual life in his assumption of the office of preacher; yet he must be of service to his monks: 'If I spoke with profit about humility, I feared I might be found lacking in it. If humility kept me silent, I should be good for nothing.'[17]

Bernard sees the conflict resolved in himself and, he counsels, in all abbots by an assessment of the motives behind both the leisure of meditation and the intense activity of preaching and guidance. Love must motivate both, and in that love action and contemplation become one.[18] Bernard addresses the question through the speech of the bride to her bridesmaids:

> She speaks to them this way: 'Be happy, be confident, "the king has brought me into his bedroom" [Song of Songs 1:3]. You may view yourselves brought in too. Even though I alone seem to have been brought in, that is not for my advantage alone. Every gift I enjoy is a joy for you. And with you I shall divide all that I merit over your measure.'[19]

The love of the Bridegroom for the bride overflows to all through the preaching and guidance of the abbot. The abbot's leisure for meditation is the source of his service to his monks. Like Paul, Bernard's abbot is compelled to share the fruits of his contemplation.[20] The bride, fresh from her bed of contemplative union with her Spouse, is sent out to bring forth fruit for him.[21] The wholehearted response of the abbot must be to serve his monks in love.

NOTES

[1] *Sermo ad abbates* [Abb] 1; SBOp 5:288–89. SBOp is the abbreviation for the critical edition *Sancti Bernardi opera*, edd. Jean Leclercq et al. (Rome: Editiones Cistercienses, 8 vols. in 9, 1957–1977). Bernard Jacqueline points out that Gregory the Great, following Origen and Augustine, makes the same distinction. See 'Saint Gregoire le Grand et l'ecclésiologie de saint Bernard', *Collectania cisterciensia* 36 (1974) 72.

[2] Abb 1; SBOp 5:289.

[3] *De moribus et officio episcoporum* [Mor] 9.33; SBOp 7:127–28. Though of the order of prelates, abbots must not '. . . claim the pontifical insignia for themselves, using miter, ring, and sandals.' Mor 9.36; SBOp 7:130.

[4] Abb 6, SBOp 5:292–93.

[5] *Sermo super cantica canticorum* [SC] 24.1; SBOp 1:151.

[6] SC 26.6; SBOp 1:174.

[7] SC 41.5; SBOp 2:31.

[8] SC 42.2; SBOp 2:34. See also SC 42.4–5; SBOp 2:35–36.

[9] SC 10.1; SBOp 1:47.

[10] SC 10.2; SBOp 1:47.

[11] *Epistola* [Ep] 115.1; SBOp 7:294.

[12] Ep 73.2; SBOp 1:180.

[13] SC 52.7; SBOp 2:94–95.

[14] See *Apologia ad Guillelmum abbatem* 30; SBOp 3:106–107.

[15] SC 22.2; SBOp 1:130.

[16] SC 22.3; SBOp 1:130–31. See also *De diligendo Deo* 27; SBOp 3:142–43.

[17] *De gradibus humilitatis et superbiae* [Hum], praef.; SBOp 3:16.

[18] What follows is a condensation of my treatment of the question in *The Spiritual Teachings of Bernard of Clairvaux*, An Intellectual History of the Early Cistercian Order [1], Cistercian Studies 125 (Kalamazoo, Michigan: Cistercian Publications, 1991) pp. 248–49. Some relevant passages not cited there include: SC 23.1 (SBOp 1:138–39); SC 41.6 (SBOp 2:32); SC 50.5 (SBOp 2:81); SC 60.9 (SBOp 2:147); Ep 82.1–2 (SBOp 7:214–16); Hum 10.29 (SBOp 3:39); and *De psalmo 'Qui habitat'*, sermo 11.11 (SBOp 4:456).

[19] SC 23.2; SBOp 1:139.

[20] *In solemnitate apostolorum Petri et Pauli*, sermo 1.2; SBOp 5:189. See also SC 8.7; SBOp 1:40.

[21] SC 58.1–2; SBOp 2:127–28.

A SAVIGNIAC FORGERY RECOVERED: LUCIUS II'S BULL *HABITANTES IN DOMO* OF DECEMBER 5, 1144

Francis R. Swietek
The University of Dallas
and
Terrence M. Deneen
Washington, D.C.

SOME YEARS AGO the present writers offered an investigation of the relationship of Pope Lucius II (1144–1145) to the norman monastery of Savigny, which, between its foundation in 1113 and its merger with the cistercian order in 1147, became the head of a congregation including more than thirty houses on the continent and in England.[1] Much of the study was devoted to an analysis of two bulls ostensibly issued by Lucius in favor of the abbey on December 5, 1144; these were distinguished by Dom Claude Auvry, the prior of Savigny between 1688 and 1712, who composed an account of the savigniac congregation which was finally edited and published in the nineteenth century.[2] The authenticity of the first letter, *Desiderium quod*, was demonstrated by its provenance, form, and content. The original remained at Savigny through the eighteenth century, when it was transcribed and analyzed by Auvry. Now deposited at the Archives nationales in Paris as series L 966, no. 5, it exhibits all the hallmarks of a product of the chancery under Pope Lucius.[3] Moreover, contemporary observers certainly accepted the privilege as genuine; the substantive portions of the letter were reiterated in a series of later twelfth-century papal privileges for the abbey, and it was copied in the thirteenth-century cartulary of Savigny, whose compiler endeavored, with some success, to exclude spurious title-deeds and confirmations.[4]

The contents of *Desiderium quod* are equally reassuring. The privilege is an unremarkable example of a conventional papal confirmation of the property holdings of a monastic house. The confirmatory portions of the letter follow the regular *ex dono* formula standardized by the chancery during the mid-twelfth century.[5] The abbey's possession of the numerous properties enumerated in the privilege is verified by contemporary confirmations and pancartes issued by local bishops and lay magnates.[6] Moreover, Lucius had granted very similar privileges in favor of other savigniac houses on the same day as the issuance of *Desiderium quod*.[7] Thus, the authenticity of the privilege is virtually unimpeachable.

The second bull discussed by Auvry, bearing the arenga *Quia igitur*, is an entirely different matter. Its original has not survived, it is not mentioned in any later papal letters, and it was not enrolled in the cartulary.[8] Until now, its text was known only from its inclusion in a body of charters appended to the foundation history of the savigniac abbey of Fontaines-les-Blanches written by Peregrinus, abbot of that house from 1188 to 1211. The background of Peregrinus' history is itself uncertain; no manuscript seems to have survived, and the only known witness to the text is a seventeenth-century edition by Luc D'Achery.[9]

The manner in which Auvry cited the letter is also disquieting. While the notes to his work obliquely suggest that he consulted the original (or a copy) of the privilege, the body of his *Histoire* states that he was following an 'extract', and a close scrutiny of his quotations indicates that he was in fact simply depending on the edition of D'Achery.[10]

The problematical textual history is reflected in the manner in which modern accounts have treated this second letter. Philip Jaffé and Samuel Loewenfeld regarded D'Achery's text and the *Desiderium quod* as a single document, and Marie-Anselme Dimier did the same, even though he recognized the significant variations between the letters.[11]

Even the limited evidence available in 1983 led us to suggest that the second letter was in all likelihood a forgery created between 1148 and 1153. We noted first that the printed editions of *Desiderium quod* were unsatisfactory, and that an accurate edition of its text established that this genuine letter and the *Quia igitur* were wholly different documents.[12] Next, we observed that two anomalies undercut the authenticity of the second letter.

First, the apparent dependence of the text in large measure on the bull *Habitantes in domo* issued by Pope Innocent II for Cîteaux in 1132 seemed peculiar in a savigniac document dated three years before the union of 1147. In addition, certain portions of the bull appeared to refer to concerns more appropriate to the seven years following the union rather than earlier.[13] The possibility that the document was a forgery was strengthened by the conclusion of other researchers that Savigny and some of her daughter-houses can be shown to have engaged in the occasional fabrication or amplification of documents.[14]

Now the recovery of virtually the complete text of the second bull of Lucius II makes possible a fuller analysis of its character. A copy of the text occurs in Paris, Bibliothèque nationale MS nouv. acq. lat. 2652, fol. 61r-v (see Plates I-II). The codex, which was acquired by the Bibliothèque nationale in 1971, consists for the most part of fragments of a latin Bible (fols. 1r–60v); the last folium, however, represents a copy of the second savigniac bull ascribed to Lucius II.[15] The copy, which can be securely dated to the second half of the twelfth century, is severely mutilated, but fortunately its text can be reconstructed almost fully by reference to the edition of D'Achery, to the demonstrably authentic bull of December 5, and to the sources on which it was apparently based. In the edition which follows, triangular brackets are used to indicate completions of the mutilated text from identified sources (the particular sources will be indicated in the accompanying commentary); square brackets represent editorial conjectures, emendations, and additions; and parentheses denote scriptural and other quotations. Parentheses accompanied by an asterisk are employed to indicate the thirteen sections into which, for convenience of reference in the commentary, the text has been divided.

THE TEXT

(*1) LUCIUS EPISCOPUS SERVUS SERVORUM DEI DILECTIS FILIIS SERLONI ABBATI SANCTE TRINITATIS S‹AVINGEIENSIS MONASTERII EJUSQUE SUCCESSORIBUS REGULARITER SUBSTITUENDIS IN PERPETUUM.› Habitantes in domo Domini in sinceritate caritatis unanimes conservant *unitatem sp‹iritus in vinculo pacis* (Eph 4:3). Pure namque mentis› religio indissolubili divini amoris glutino confirmata vultum clementissimi creatori‹s ut terrena celestibus coniungantur et ima superis› socientur mundis orationibus incessanter profusis inclinat. Quia igitur fratres Savigneiensis monasterii a cura secula‹ri liberos et divinis servitiis mancipatos› pie vivere ac religiose cognovimus, iccirco dilecte in Domino fili Serlo abbas, tuis iustis postulationibus du‹ximus annuendum (*2) et prefatum Savigneiense› monasterium cui Deo auctoritate presides cum omnibus suis pertinentiis sub beati Petri et nostra protectione s‹uscipimus et presentis scripti privilegio com›munimus. In primis siquidem statuentes ut ordinem monasticum secundum beati Benedicti regulam et in‹stituta regulae competentia inviolabiliter› observetis, nec a statu religionis qui per Dei gratiam in vestra congregatione vigere cognoscitur in posterum d[eclinetis sed]ᵃ in melius proficiendo in ordinis ac religionis augmento

---

ᵃ declinetis sed] *coniecimus*

proficere[b] studeatis. (*3) Si quis vero ex abbatibus, monachi‹s quoque vel conversis vestre congregationis a proposito et ordine› exorbitaverit, et secundo terciove commonitus incorrigibilis permanserit, abbate absque ulla contradictione re‹tento[c] iuxta providentiam› Savigneiensis abbatis qui pro tempore[d] fuerit,[e] loco ipsius [alius][f] idoneus substituatur, monachus vero si contumax fuerit re‹gulariter corrigatur. (*4) Prohibemus etiam ut nullus abbatum› in ordine vestro facere scisma presumat aut commissam sibi abbatiam vel quemlibet alium locum [absque assensu][g] communi a‹lterius ditioni tradere. (*5) In benedictione› vero abbatum vestrorum exactionem cape, vestimenti, pastus seu cuiuslibet terreni questus ab aliquo fieri omnino int‹erdicimus. (*6) Preterea quecumque possessiones› aut bona que ad eundem locum in presentiarum iuste et canonice pertinere noscuntur aut in futurum c‹oncessione pontificum, liberalitate› regum vel principum, oblatione fidelium seu aliis iustis modis auxiliante Domino ei conferri contig‹erit, firma tibi tuisque successoribus et› illibata permaneant. (*7) Quia vero Savigneiense monasterium huius religionis origo est atque principium, nostra concessione hac pre‹rogativa non immerito› gaudeat ut si quando fuerit pastore proprio viduatum, quemlibet abbatem de omnibus abbatibus vestri ordinis vel monachum sibi libere ‹preficiendum eligat› et absque aliqua contradictione[h] optineat. Ceteris vero vestri ordinis abbatiis que unam vel plures abbatias habent sibi subditas et ‹de sui corporis fructifera› copia derivatas, abbate suo rebus humanis exempto, eligendi quemcumque maluerint de sibi subditis abbatibus vel quemlib‹et mona›chum de omnibus [congregationibus

---

[b] proficere] profiscere MS
[c] re‹tento] in MS
[d] pro tempore] preter MS
[e] fuerit] furit MS
[f] alius] om. MS
[g] absque assensu] om. MS
[h] contradictione] contradicione MS

Savigneiensibus liberam concedimus facultatem. Illa autem abbatia que nullam habet sibi subditam, quemlibet monachum de omnibus]ⁱ prefate religionis congregationibus cum consilio et deliberatione Savigneiensis abbatis et illius qui eidem fratri eligendo prefuerit libere sibi in abbatem eligat et habeat. (*8) Et quoniam *ubi spiritus [Domini,]ʲ ibi libertas* (2 Co 3:17), ut liberius divinis famulatibus valeatis insistere et purgata mentis acie sincerius contemplationi vacare, prohibemus ne aliquis archiepiscopus aut episcopus te vel successores tuos seu aliquem abbatem Savigneiensis ordinis nisi pro certa et evidenti negociorum ecclesiasticorum causa vel culpa manifesta ad concilium vel sinodum venire compellat. (*9) Porr‹o› conversos vestros qui monachi non sunt post factam in vestris cenobiisᵏ professionem nullus archiepiscoporum, episcoporum vel abbatum sine vestra grata licentia ‹suscipere› aut susceptum retinere presumat. Verum, quoniam sicut beato Gregorio Augustinum Anglorum episcopum instruente (Beda, *Historia ecclesiastica* 1.27), didicimus *communi vita viventibus, iam de faciendis portionibus vel exhibenda hospitalitate et adimplenda misericordia nobis quid erit dicendum ? C‹um› omne quod superest in causis piis ac religiosis erogandum est, Domino magistro omnium dicente: quod superest date elemosinam ‹et ecce› omnia munda sunt vobis* (Lk 11:41), statuimus ut de laboribus quos vos et totius vestre congregationis fratres propriis manibus et sumptibus coli‹tis› et de animalibus vestris a vobis decimas expetere vel recipere nemo presumat. (*10) Nulli ergo hominum liceat idem monasterium temere perturbare aut eius possessiones aufferre vel ablatas retinere, minuere aut aliquibus molestiis fatigare, sed omnia integra conserventur vestris et aliorum pauperum Christi usibus profutura, salva apostolica sedis auctoritate. Si qua igitur in posterum ecclesiastica secularisve persona hanc nostre constitutionis

---

ⁱ congregationibus...de omnibus] *om.* MS
ʲ Domini] *om.* MS
ᵏ cenobiis] cecobiis MS

paginam sciens, contra eam temere venire temptaverit, secundo terciove commonita si non sat‹is›factione[l] congrua emendaverit, potestatis honorisque sui periculum patiatur et a sacratissimo corpore et sanguine Domini nostri Ihesu Christi aliena fiat, atque in extremo examine[m] districte ultioni subiaceat. (*11) Conservantibus vero eidem loco que sua sunt ‹sit pax Domini nostri Ihesu Christi, quatenus et› hic fructum bone actionis percipiant et apud districtum[n] iudicem premia eterne pacis inve‹niant. Amen.›

(*12) [*In Rota:*] Ostende nobis domine [misericordiam tuam Sanctus Petrus] Sanctus Paulus [Lu]cius [papa][o]II

Ego Lucius catholice ecclesie episcopus SS.

(*13) [Ego Conradus Sabiniensis episcopus.

Ego Gregorius diaconus cardinalis sanctorum Sergii et Bachi.

Ego Gregorius presbyter cardinalis tituli sancti Calixti.

Ego Petrus Albanensis episcopus.

Ego Guido diaconus cardinalis sanctorum Cosme et Damiani.

Ego Raynerius presbyter cardinalis sancte Prisce.

Ego Guido presbyter cardinalis sanctorum Laurentii et Damasi.

Ego Gregorius diaconus cardinalis sancti Angeli.

Datum Laterani, per manum Baronis sancte Romane ecclesie subdiaconi, nonis decembris, indictione VIII, incarnationis dominice anno MCXLIV, pontificatus vero domini Lucii secundi pape anno primo.][p]

COMMENTARY

(*1). The source of this section, of which D'Achery printed only a partial transcription of the salutation and

---

[l] sat‹is›factione] esat...factione MS
[m] examine] *corr. ex* exame MS
[n] districtum] districtem MS
[o] misericordiam...Petrus, Lu..., papa] *om.* MS
[p] Ego Conradus...anno primo] *omnia om.* MS

entirely omitted the section *Habitantes in domo . . . profusis inclinat*, is the bull *Habitantes* issued by Pope Innocent II for Cîteaux on February 10, 1132.[16] Apart from the necessary changes in the names of the recipients, Innocent's bull serves as the source for the completion of the text.

It is notable that *Habitantes in domo* is known to occur as an arenga in the letters of only two pontiffs, Honorius II (1124–1130) and Innocent II (1130–1143). Four of the former's extant bulls and six of the latter's employ the locution.[17] Significantly, this arenga is not found in other letters of Lucius II, or in any catalogued privilege of any other pontiff.[18]

(*2). This section of the text is original, and has been completed by reference to D'Achery's edition of Peregrinus.

The first portion of the section (*et prefatum . . . communimus*) is conventional. It may be compared to the analogous statement in the authentic bull of Lucius II for Savigny of December 5: 'et monasterium sancte Trinitatis cui, Deo auctore, preesse dinosceris sub beati Petri et nostra protectione suscipimus et presentis scripti privilegio communimus.'[19] Compare also the bull of Pope Eugenius III on behalf of Savigny dated January 20, 1148: 'et prefatum sancte Trinitatis monasterium, in quo divino mancipati satis obsequio, sub beati Petri et nostra protectione suscipimus et presentis scripti privilegio communimus.'[20]

The remainder of this section, which D'Achery gives only in part (*In primis . . . observetis*), and which can therefore be completed only conditionally, represents a version of what J. Dubois has identified as the *clause de régularité*.[21] Dubois concludes that the *clause* was instituted under Innocent II, but no version of it occurs in that pontiff's bull of 1132 for Cîteaux; the ordinary usage in cistercian bulls from his pontificate onward is said to be: '[In primis siquidem statuentes, ut] ordo monasticus, qui secundum Deum et beati Benedicti regulam et institutionem Cisterciensium fratrum [*or* institutionem Cisterciensis ordinis] in eodem monasterio institutus esse dinoscitur perpetuis ibidem temporibus inviolabiliter observetur.'[22] Insofar as Savigny is concerned, Dubois cites the bull of Anastasius IV of April 20, 1154,[23] but this document is dependent on one issued for the monastery by Eugenius III on April 10, 1148, where the *clause* reads: 'statuentes ut ordo monasticus secundum institutionem Cisterciensium fratrum, tam in prefato monasterio quam in his que sub eius potestate consistunt, futuris temporibus inviolabiliter conservetur.'[24]

The version in the present text obviously avoids the cistercian reference, and is considerably expanded as well. In particular it places emphasis on the preservation and strengthening of the *religio* existing within the savigniac congregation, which is to find expression in the expansion of the savigniac *ordo* ('in ordinis ac religionis augmento proficere studeatis').

This emphasis might well be explained by a desire to insure the preservation of a savigniac 'identity' after the union of 1147, and especially to justify the continued expansion of the congregation within the cistercian order at that time. This was not a matter of purely academic interest. There was a growing movement among the Cistercians after 1147 to cap the hitherto unlimited growth of the order—a movement which culminated, in 1152, with a prohibition by the General Chapter against the foundation or incorporation of new houses.[25] In such circumstances it is entirely plausible that Savigny should have taken steps to provide a 'legal' basis for the continued growth of its congregation, which, in the period between the union in 1147 and the resignation of Abbot Serlo in 1152/1153, involved the addition of some eight houses.[26]

In this connection it is to be noted that Savigny apparently took pains to secure papal recognition of her headship of the congregation during this period. In Eugenius III's bull of April 10, 1148, for example, abbeys permanently subject to Savigny were enumerated, but the list was limited to the thirteen english savigniac houses.[27] When restatements of Eugenius' bull were secured in 1154 from both Anastasius IV and Adrian IV, however, all of the savigniac houses, including earlier continental foundations and the most recent additions on both sides of the channel, were specifically named.[28] At a time when a strong movement had developed among the Cistercians to limit the expansion of the order, Savigny seems to have been concerned to establish papal recognition of the identity of her congregation within the order, and by implication the propriety of her most recent additions. The expansion of the *clause de régularité* in the present text would thus seem appropriate to the circumstances of 1147–1154, since it would provide a more general approbation of the savigniac congregation as a whole and, in more specific terms, offer clear papal encouragement of further savigniac growth.

(*3) This section of the text is original, and is completed by reference to the edition of Peregrinus by D'Achery. The greater portion of it is clearly derived from the stipulations of the *Regula Benedicti* on the correction of monks.[29] What is distinctive, however, is the extraordinary authority granted to the abbot of Savigny over the other abbots of the congregation. He could peremptorily remove any recalcitrant abbot from office, and replace him with someone more suitable; there was no appeal from his decision.

This remarkable stipulation does not seem unrelated to an episode which followed the union of 1147. Peter of York, the abbot of the english savigniac house of Furness, objected to the subjection of his community to cistercian discipline. According to the traditions of Furness, he went so far as to approach Pope Eugenius III to request an exception for Furness from the effects of the union. On his return from Rome, however, he was said to have been seized by monks of Savigny, taken to the mother-house, and compelled to resign his abbacy and submit to the cistercian order.[30]

The Furness account is much oversimplified. Eugenius III did not, as this tradition asserts, guarantee Peter that his house would remain of the order in which it had been founded. Instead, the pontiff referred the matter to bishops Hugh of Rouen and Arnulf of Lisieux, instructing them to judge the case. There survive three episcopal letters detailing the result.[31] The court was originally scheduled to meet at Michaelmas, but Peter requested, and won, a six-week postponement until Martinmas. He failed to appear as scheduled, however, and so the judges-delegate simply heard the presentation of Savigny's evidence and decided in her favor. Peter arrived after the case had been concluded and was ordered to submit to the court's determination.

It is to be noted that the episcopal letters make no mention of Peter's having been 'captured' by monks of Savigny, as the Furness tradition maintains. There are certain aspects of the three epistles, however, that suggest that the Furness account might have some basis in fact. To begin, it should be observed that the three letters derive from distinctly different moments in the episode. The first of them is addressed by both Hugh and Arnulf to Peter and the Furness community, and recounts events through the hearing at Martinmas, ordering immediate submission to their decision; clearly it was written prior to the tardy appearance of Peter at the court.[32] The second letter, addressed by Hugh alone to the community of Furness, notes that Peter had submitted to their decision and returned to the obedience of Savigny; it obviously followed Peter's late arrival, and was designed to compel his community to follow his example.[33] The third letter, addressed by Hugh to Archbishop Henry Murdac of York, rehearsed the details of the case, and notes specifically how Peter attempted to have the case reopened after his arrival, but submitted unconditionally under threat of papal excommunication.[34]

What is curious about these letters is that nowhere in them is Peter, in the later stages of the case, specifically identified as abbot of Furness. In the first he is addressed simply as *frater*. The mode of reference in the second letter is even stranger; the case, the community of Furness is told, was 'inter abbatem Saviniacensem et fratrem Petrum qui vobis praefuit.' In the third letter Hugh writes that the original dispute was 'inter abbatam Savigniacensem et abbatem Furnesiensem', but subsequently he refers to Peter simply as 'Petrus Furnesiensis', without mention of his office.

This vagary of identification might, of course, be entirely accidental and devoid of deeper meaning. But it may be noted that in the first of the letters it is specifically stated that when Peter was granted a delay in the hearing of the case, notice of the postponement was to be carried to Savigny by Peter himself.[35] Is it possible that while he was at Savigny he was stripped of his abbatial dignity? It is known that eventually he was replaced by Richard of Bayeux, a monk of Savigny, but the precise timing and circumstances of the change are not clear.[36] The modes of reference to Peter in Hugh's two letters, however, might mean that, while still allowed to act on behalf of his community's legal rights, he was no longer to be treated as abbot. One might even postulate a transitional period during which the abbacy of Furness was regarded as effectively vacant until the situation was finally settled. Such a confused and difficult situation might easily have been exaggerated in the Furness record into an account of Peter's being seized and forced to resign.

The evidence is hardly sufficient to reach a conclusive understanding of this episode, but it is enough to indicate that, between 1148 and 1150,[37] the abbot of a savigniac house was in effect removed and replaced in extraordinary circumstances. It is in connection with such an event that this section of the present text would have had significance, and it is possible that it was created *post factum* in an attempt to justify an action which might arguably have exceeded the authority of the abbot of Savigny.

(*4) This section of the bull is original, and is completed by reference to D'Achery's edition of Peregrinus. Once again, it seems to relate to the dispute with Furness between 1148 and 1150. Of particular interest is its distinct similarity to a portion of the letter addressed by Hugh of Rouen and Arnulf of Lisieux to Peter of Furness and his community regarding the dispute: 'mandamus atque precipimus quatinus abbati Saviniacensi et ecclesie sue amodo obediatis et ab invasione et presumptione et rebellione vestra, visis litteris ipsis, omnino desistatis, atque liberam facultatem disponendi de rebus et possessionibus Furnesii, pro voluntate et arbitrio suo, eidem abbati Saviniacensi habere permittas.'[38] In both instances the concern seems to focus on the maintenance of Savigny's power to dispose of the properties of her daughter houses without interference.

(*5) Once again, this portion of the document is original, and is completed by reference to D'Achery's edition of Peregrinus. It represents a general prohibition of temporal exactions from savigniac abbots at the time of their benedictions. In its emphasis on purely material exactions, the section is unlike any stipulation to be found in twelfth-century cistercian documents, which were concerned almost exclusively with episcopal attempts to interfere in abbatial elections in contravention of the order's statutes.[39] By comparison the claims of the present clause are exceedingly modest, since they simply seem directed against a bishop's (or secular lord's) demand for gifts at an abbatial benediction.

No details are known about the benedictions of the first four abbots of Savigny, but it is possible that, prior to the union of 1147, the bishop of Avranches did in fact expect some symbol of deference to be provided him in the course of the ceremony. In a surviving notice dating from the last quarter of the twelfth century, a careful inventory is made of the obligations of the various religious establishments in the diocese to the episcopal authority.[40] The listing specifically states that the abbot of Savigny was to be blessed by the bishop in the cathedral of Avranches, and was publicly to swear canonical obedience to him.[41] There is no mention of any customary temporal exactions, but if any had once existed, they would certainly have been rendered obsolete by the more general privileges accorded to the Cistercians regarding abbatial elections and benedictions by Pope Alexander III in 1165 and 1169.[42]

It should further be noted that issues surrounding abbatial benediction would also have been matters of concern to Savigny following the union of 1147. Abbot Serlo of Vaubadon, who effected the merger with Cîteaux, was moved to tender his resignation after the event; he did so at Clairvaux following the cistercian General Chapter of 1152. The reluctance of the community of Savigny and of the other abbots of the congregation delayed acceptance of the resignation until at least 1153, but it is surely possible that indications of Serlo's intentions might have existed for some years.[43] Thus, as in the case of its clauses regarding the expansion of the congregation and the removal of obstreperous savigniac abbots, the document here points to considerations that would have been acute in the early 1150s.

(*6) This represents a conventional property confirmation, similar to that found in the demonstrably authentic bull of Lucius II for Savigny.[44] The wording, however, is derived from the bull of Innocent II for Cîteaux of 1132,[45] and the completion of the text is based on that document, as altered in its introduction (*Preterea* for *Statuimus ut*) by Peregrinus in the edition of D'Achery.

(*7) This section, dealing with abbatial elections in the savigniac congregation, is derived, with the necessary scribal changes in proper names, from the 1132 bull of Innocent II for Cîteaux, on the basis of which the text has been completed. The scribe, however, dropped seventeen words of text as a result of a copying error *saut du même au même*; we have restored these using Innocent's bull as exemplar. On the other hand, there is a second omission, of the words *salva nimirum Sedis apostolice reverentia*, in the first line, immediately after the words *de omnibus abbatibus vestri ordinis vel monachum*. As there is no obvious copying difficulty which might have caused this omission, this deletion is presumed to have been a deliberate scribal decision.

This section of the document might also have been especially applicable to the early 1150s. At that time it would have been useful both in preserving the identity of the savigniac congregation (as with *2 above) and in trying to insure that, if Abbot Serlo did in fact resign, a successor from outside the savigniac congregation would not be imposed on the house. (Indeed, the deletion of the words pertaining to the papacy might have been intended to hinder the possible intervention of Pope Eugenius III, a Cistercian who seems to have been deeply interested in facilitating the merger of 1147, in the selection process.[46]) In the event Serlo was followed as abbot by Richard of Courcy, a monk of Savigny who had served as prior of the community.[47]

(*8) This section is also based on Innocent II's bull of 1132 for Cîteaux, but it is significantly altered. In the Cîteaux privilege, archbishops and bishops are prohibited from compelling the attendance of cistercian abbots at councils or synods *nisi pro fide*.[48] Here the clause reads *nisi pro certa et evidenti negociorum ecclesiasticorum causa vel culpa manifesta*. The purpose behind the alteration is not clear. On the one hand, the new wording seems to transfer the emphasis from doctrinal considerations to legalistic ones. In addition, it seems to mandate the presentation of a compelling case for the attendance of an abbot at a council for any summons to be effective. As such it might have been directed against the possibility that Savigniacs might be brought routinely under episcopal jurisdiction for purposes of ordinary litigation.

(*9) This section of the document is based *verbatim* on the 1132 bull of Innocent II for Cîteaux, from which the text is completed. It protects the *conversi* of the congregation from external ecclesiastical authorities and prohibits the exaction of tithes from savigniac houses.

(*10) This final sanction is the same as that found in both Innocent's bull for Cîteaux and the authentic bull of Lucius II for Savigny, but the latter shares one noteworthy variant with the present text. In both instances, the decretum forbids any infringement or modification to the abbey's immunities *salva apostolice sedis auctoritate*. It was once commonly accepted that this formula acted to confer episcopal exemption on the recipient's monastery.[49] As a result, a number of scholars have suggested that Lucius had, by using it here, granted Savigny an exemption from diocesan jurisdiction.[50] This hypothesis, however, probably misconstrues the juridic effect of the formula.[51] Moreover, other evidence indicates that any savigniac claim to episcopal exemption was at best questionable.[52]

(*11) The wording of the conclusion is identical to that found in the 1132 bull of Innocent II for Cîteaux, from which the text has been completed. Virtually identical wording is included in the securely authentic 1144 bull of Lucius II for Savigny.

(*12) The *rota* is only partially finished by the scribe; the entire circle is given, but only half the text has been inserted within it. The remainder is completed by reference to the authentic 1144 bull of Lucius II for Savigny.

(*13) The text of the document breaks off after the subscription of Lucius II, but the remaining signatories are added here as given in the edition of Peregrinus by D'Achery. The names are the same as those found in the demonstrably authentic 1144 bull of Lucius for Savigny, but the order is different. The final notarial *Datum*, identical to that found in the authentic bull, is also added from D'Achery's edition of Peregrinus.

CONCLUSION

The document edited here is clearly based on two fundamental sources: Pope Innocent II's bull *Habitantes in domo* of February 1132, for Cîteaux, and, to a lesser but still very significant extent, the bull *Desiderium quod* issued by Pope Lucius II for Savigny on December 5, 1144. Of the thirteen sections into which the text has been divided above, nine are derived directly from them, although in some cases there are important changes which might have been considered especially useful to Savigny.

The four sections of the document not traceable to either of these sources occur in a cluster toward the beginning of the text (*2–5 above). As the commentary has disclosed, each seems related to an issue of obvious concern to Savigny not in 1144, the purported date of the bull, but in the five-year period following the union with Cîteaux, roughly 1148–1153. These unusual items, each of which poses substantial difficulties, occur within a larger text which seems to represent little more than a pastiche of two other, clearly authentic bulls—one contributing content, the other largely supportive detail. A thorough study of the reconstructed text, therefore, strongly supports the suggestion, originally made in 1983, that the document is a forgery dating from the late 1140s or early 1150s.

As to what is now fol. 61r-v of Bibliothèque nationale MS nouv. acq. lat. 2652, there are two possibilities. On the one hand, it might represent a poor copy of a forged bull previously prepared at Savigny, which would have also been the source of the fuller text (including complete subscriptions and *Datum*, for example) found in Peregrinus' *Historia*; this might explain its numerous textual imperfections.

On the other hand, it is difficult to imagine why a simple copy should have been prepared as this one was—why, for instance, an effort should have been made to duplicate the *rota*. Even more, it is difficult to understand why such an attempt, once begun, should have abruptly been broken off.

It seems more plausible to argue that the Paris folium represents a first draft of the forgery. When the scribe found the text spilling over onto the verso of the leaf—a circumstance that could not have applied to an authentic papal bull—or when he noticed his mistake in abbreviating the section of the text dealing with savigniac abbatial elections, he simply decided to stop writing. He would then have used the draft to prepare a more careful version, more visually convincing and without the verbal errors, which would later have served as the source for such complete texts as that found in the *Historia* of Peregrinus.

If this supposition is correct, the present edition represents not only a reconstruction of an important savigniac forgery, but a unique glimpse into the savigniac *scriptorium*—an opportunity to examine a forgery-in-progress.

NOTES

[1] Francis R. Swietek and Terrence M. Deneen, 'Pope Lucius II and Savigny', *Analecta Cisterciensia* 39 (1983) 3–26. The major primary and secondary sources dealing with the foundation of the monastery and the growth of the savigniac congregation are catalogued in that study at p. 3, nn. 1–2; to the items listed there should now be added Jacob Johannes van Moolenbroek, *Vitalis van Savigny (+1122) : Bronnen en vroege Cultus* (Amsterdam, 1982); Francis R. Swietek, 'Savigny', in *Dizionario degli istituti di perfezione* 8 (Rome, 1988) 991–94; and Jaap van Moolenbroek, *Vital l'eremite, prédicateur itinérant, fondateur de l'abbaye normande de Savigny* (Assen, Maastricht, 1990).

[2] Claude Auvry, *Histoire de la congrégation de Savigny*, ed. A. Laveille, Société de l'histoire de Normandie 30 (Rouen, 1896–1899) 2:340–43. An analysis of the printed works cited in the *Histoire* suggests that Auvry wrote his account sometime between 1707 and 1712.

[3] The bull is analyzed in Swietek and Deneen, 'Pope Lucius II', pp. 8–11, and edited there as Appendix I (pp. 20–23).

[4] The cartulary does not itself survive, but a catalogue of its contents, prepared in the nineteenth century by Léopold Delisle, is now MS nouv. acq. lat. 1022 of the Bibliothèque nationale (Paris). The prologue to the cartulary is printed from Delisle's transcription by Swietek and Deneen, 'Pope Lucius II', pp. 25–26 (as Appendix II).

[5] There is a very full discussion of the formula in Dietrich Lohrmann, *Kirchengut im nördlichen Frankreich: Besitz, Verfassung und Wirtschaft in Spiegel der Papsturkunden des 11.–12. Jahrhunderts*, Pariser historische Studien 20 (Bonn, 1983).

[6] For such confirmations see, among others, Paris, Archives nationales L 968, no. 206 (a charter of Henry of Fougères dated 1150); Léopold Delisle and Elie Berger, *Recueil des actes de Henri II, roi d'Angleterre et duc de Normandie* 1 (Paris, 1916) pp. 184–88 (a confirmation of King Henry II issued between 1156 and 1158); and Paris, Archives nationales L 968, no. 207 (a general confirmation issued by Bishop Alan of Rennes in 1158).

[7] There are surviving privileges for the norman savigniac houses at Foucarmont and Saint André-en-Gouffern; see Swietek and Deneen, 'Pope Lucius II', p. 11. In addition, Vivian Galbraith, 'Monastic Confirmation Charters', *Cambridge Historical Journal* 4 (1934) 215, n. 38, has drawn attention to an abstract of an *ex dono* confirmation issued by Lucius for the savigniac abbey of Quarr on the Isle of Wight.

[8] Its absence from the now-lost cartulary is demonstrated by reference to the nineteenth-century catalogue of Delisle noted above, n. 4.

[9] Peregrinus of Vendôme, *Historia praelatorum et possessionum ecclesiae B. Mariae de Fontanis*, in Luc D'Achery (ed.), *Spicilegium sive collectio veterum aliquot scriptorum* (Paris, 1671) 11:378, and (2nd ed., Paris, 1723)

2:578, reprinted in André Salmon, *Recueil de chroniques de Touraine* (Tours, 1854) pp. 277–78, who notes (at p. lxxxvi) the lack of any manuscript of Peregrinus' work.

[10] A close reading of Auvry's french version of the *Quia igitur* (Auvry 2:342–43) demonstrates that he was relying on D'Achery's misleadingly abbreviated edition of the document; his translation shows the same omissions and paraphrases as occur in the latin edition of D'Achery. Auvry's citations to Peregrinus' *Historia* (for example, Auvry 2:53 and 2:209), moreover, reflect his access to the first edition of D'Achery's *Spicilegium*.

[11] Philip Jaffé, *Regesta pontificum Romanorum ab condita ecclesia ad annum post Christum natum MCXCVIII*, corr. et auct. W. Wattenbach, S. Loewenfeld, *et al.* (Leipzig, 1885–1888) [hereafter cited as JL] no. 8673 (6104), lists both documents as one. Marie-Anselme Dimier, 'Savigny et son affiliation à l'ordre de Cîteaux,' *Collectanea ordinis Cisterciensis reformatorum* 9 (1947) 355, n. 15, while recognizing the variants between the texts, appears to consider them versions of a single original.

[12] Swietek and Deneen, 'Pope Lucius II', p. 10.

[13] Swietek and Deneen, 'Pope Lucius II', pp. 12–19.

[14] Léopold Delisle, *Recueil des actes de Henri II, roi d'Angleterre et duc de Normandie*, Introduction (Paris, 1909) pp. 303–306, 316, and 326–29; Joseph R. Strayer, 'A Forged Charter of Henry II for Bival', *Speculum* 34 (1959) 230–37; Mary Suydam, 'Origins of the Savignac Order: Savigny's Role Within Twelfth-Century Monasticism', *Revue Bénédictine* 86 (1976) 94–108.

[15] Brief descriptions of the codex are found in Marcel Thomas, 'Novelles acquisitions latines et françaises du département des manuscripts de la Bibliothèque Nationale pendant les années 1969-1971', *Bibliothèque de l'Ecole des Chartes* 130 (1972) 512–13, and Bibliothèque Nationale, *Enrichissements 1961–1973* (Paris, 1974) p. 88 (no. 635). The latter description suggests that the presence of Lucius' bull indicates that the manuscript might have originated at Savigny or one of the other houses of its congregation. We are indebted to the Institut de Recherche et d'Histoire des Textes, and particularly to Annie Dufour of its Section des Sources documentaires, for providing us with photocopies of these descriptions.

[16] JL 7537 (5399). The edition used is that of J. Marilier, *Chartes et documents concernant l'abbaye de Cîteaux 1098–1182* (Rome, 1961) pp. 92–93 (no. 90), where manuscripts and previous editions are cited.

[17] Honorius II: JL 7255, 7286, 7318 (5272), and 7387 (5307). Innocent II: JL 7537 (5399), 7749 (5531), and 8259 (5871); Johannes Ramackers, *Papsturkunden in Frankreich*, Neue Folge 5, *Touraine, Anjou, Maine und Bretagne*, Abhandlungen der Gesellschaft der Wissenschaften zu Göttingen, philologisch-historische Klasse, Dritte Folge 35 (Göttingen,

1956) no. 37; Dietrich Lohrmann, *Papsturkunden in Frankreich*, Neue Folge 7, *Nordliche Ile-de-France und Vermandois*, Abhandlungen der Gesellschaft der Wissenschaften zu Göttingen, philogisch-historische Klasse, Dritte Folge 95 (Göttingen, 1976) no. 52; and Carolus Le Couteulx, *Annales Ordinis Carthusiensis* (Montreuil, 1887) 1:399.

[18] Jaffé in JL 2:792, and Rudolf Hiestand, *Initienverzeichnis und chronologisches Verzeichnis zu den Archiveberichten und Vorarbeiten der Regesta pontificum Romanorum*, Monumenta Germaniae historica, Hilfsmittel 7 (Munich, 1983) p. 41.

[19] Swietek and Deneen, 'Pope Lucius II', p. 20.

[20] JL 9175. The text is edited in Johannes Ramackers (ed.), *Papsturkunden in Frankreich*, Neue Folge 2, *Normandie*, Abhandlungen der Gesellschaft der Wissenschaften zu Göttingen, philologisch-historische Klasse, Dritte Folge 21 (Göttingen, 1937) pp. 125–126 (no. 55).

[21] J. Dubois, 'Les ordres religieux au XIIe siècle selon la curie romaine', *Revue Bénédictine* 78 (1968) 283–309.

[22] Dubois, pp. 285, 293.

[23] Dubois, p. 293. The text, JL 9867 (6793), is edited in Edmund Martène and Ursin Durand, *Thesaurus novus anecdotorum* 1 (Paris, 1717) pp. 433–34, reprinted in Migne, *Patrologia latina* [hereafter cited as PL] 188:1054–55, and in Maurice P. Sheehy, *Pontificia Hibernica: Medieval Papal Chancery Documents Concerning Ireland, 640–1261* 2 (Dublin, 1965) pp. 11–12 (no. 3).

[24] JL 9235 (6418). The text is found in Martène and Durand, *Thesaurus* 1:404–406; Victor De Buck, 'De BB. Gaufrido et Serlone, abbatibus, Guilemo, novitio, et Adelina abbatissa, Saviniaci in Normannia', *Acta sanctorum* October 8 (Brussels, 1853) pp. 1018–19; and Léon Guilloreau, 'Le démêlé entre Serlon, abbé de Savigny, et Pierre d'York, abbé de Furness, 1147–1150', *Revue catholique d'histoire, d'archéologie et de litterature de Normandie* 25 (1916) 130.

[25] Joseph-Marie Canivez, *Statuta capitulorum generalium ordinis Cisterciensis ab anno 1116 ad annum 1786* 1, Bibliothèque de la Revue d'Histoire ecclésiastique 9 (Louvain, 1933) p. 45: 'Anno ab Incarnatione Domini MCLII°, statutum est in Capitulo generali abbatum, ne ulterius alicubi construatur nova abbatia nostri ordinis, neque aliquis locus alterius religionis per subiectionem nostri ordinis societur.' See also Louis J. Lekai, *The Cistercians: Ideals and Reality* (Kent, Ohio, 1977) p. 48.

[26] De Buck, pp. 1032–34.

[27] See n. 24 above.

[28] Anastasius IV: see n. 23 above; Adrian IV: JL 9962, edited in Ramackers 2:165–66 (no. 80).

[29] *Regula Benedicti* 23.

[30] J. C. Atkinson (ed.), *The Coucher Book of Furness Abbey*, Remains Historical and Literary Connected with the Palatine Counties of Lancaster and Chester n.s. 9/1 (Manchester, 1886) p. 9: 'a qua redditione

praed. Petrus Abbas, cum Conventu suo, ad summum Pontificem et Sanctam Sedem Apostolicam appellavit. Ad quem Sedem personaliter accedens impetravit a Domino Eugenio Papa iii° confirmationem ut Monasterium suum Furnesii remaneret imperpetuum de eodem ordine de quo primo fundatum erat, non obstante redditione praedicta. Sed in reditu suo a Curia Romana captus est in itinere per monachos Savigniacenses et ductus ad Savigniacum. Ibi cessit officio Abbatiali, et factus est ibidem monachus probatissimus, discens Ordinem Cisterciensem.' This account is discussed by F. M. Powicke, 'The Abbey of Furness', in *The Victoria County History of the County of Lancaster*, edd. William Farrer and J. Brownbill, 2 (London, 1908) p. 115.

[31] The letters are edited by Léopold Delisle, 'Documents Relative to the Abbey of Furness, Extracted from the Archives of the Abbey of Savigny', *Journal of the British Archaeological Association* 6 (1851) 420–23 (nos. 2–4), and by Guilloreau, pp. 138–41 (nos. 3–5).

[32] Delisle, 'Documents', pp. 420–21 (no. 2) and Guilloreau, pp. 138–39 (no. 3).

[33] Delisle, 'Documents', pp. 421–22 (no. 3) and Guilloreau, p. 140 (no. 4).

[34] Delisle, 'Documents', pp. 422–23 (no. 4) and Guilloreau, pp. 140–41 (no. 5).

[35] Delisle, 'Documents', p. 420, and Guilloreau, p. 139: 'ut requisisti, prefatum terminum usque in festum beati Martini prolongavimus, atque litteras nostras inde abbati Saviniacensi per te ipsum transmisimus.'

[36] Auvry 3:17.

[37] The letters of the papal judges-delegate are not dated, and thus it cannot be absolutely determined whether their decisive hearing occurred in 1149 or 1150.

[38] Delisle, 'Documents', p. 421 (no. 2) and Guilloreau, p. 139 (no. 3). This phraseology seems ultimately to depend on Pope Eugenius III's bull of October 21, 1149, to Abbot Serlo of Savigny—JL 9351 (6495), edited in Edmund Martène and Ursin Durand, *Veterum scriptorum et monumentorum historicorum, dogmaticorum, moralium amplissima collectio* 1 (Paris, 1724) p. 813, reprinted in PL 180:1398: 'statuimus ut in omnibus monasteriis quae de monasterio cui praesides, sunt egressa, et in his quae de egressis ab eodem monasterio prodierint, tam de ipsis personis quam de rebus monasteriorum, juxta Cisterciensium fratrum institutionem, disponendi et ordinandi liberam habeas facultatem.'

[39] See the discussion in Jean-Berthold Mahn, *L'ordre cistercien et son gouvernement des origines au milieu du XIIIe siècle (1098–1265)* (Paris, 1945) pp. 73–81.

[40] The text is printed by Charles Homer Haskins, *Norman Institutions* (Cambridge, 1918) pp. 340–43.

[41] Haskins, p. 340: 'Abbatia Savigneii in episcopatu Abrincensi sita debet...tam episcopo quam ecclesie Abrincensi canonicam obedien-

tiam, quam abbas cum benedicendus est in ecclesia Abrincensi publice profitetur.'

[42] JL 11226 (7493) of August 5, 1165, printed in PL 200:390–94, and JL 11632 (7767) of July 4, 1169, newly edited in Jean Waquet, *Recueil des chartes de l'abbaye de Clairvaux, XIIe siècle* 2, pub. Jean-Marc Roger and Philippe Grand (Troyes, 1982) pp. 142–43 (no. 133).

[43] *Auctarium Savigniacense*, in Léopold Delisle (ed.), *Chronique de Robert de Torigni*, Société de L'histoire de Normandie (Rouen, 1872–1873) 2:162–163.

[44] Swietek and Deneen, 'Pope Lucius II', p. 20.

[45] Marilier, p. 92.

[46] The place of Eugenius in the merger of 1147 is newly examined in Francis R. Swietek, 'The Role of Bernard of Clairvaux in the Union of Savigny with Cîteaux: A Reconsideration' in John R. Sommerfeldt (ed.), *Bernardus Magister. Papers Presented at the Nonacenterary Celebration of the Birth of Saint Bernard of Clairvaux, Kalamazoo, Michigan, Sponsored by The Institute of Cistercian Studies, Western Michigan University, 10–13 May 1990*, Cistercian Studies 135 (Kalamazoo: Cistercian Publications—Saint-Nicholas-lès Cîteaux: *Cîteaux: Commentarii Cistercienses*, 1993) 289–302.

[47] *Auctarium Savigniacense*, in Delisle (ed.), *Chronique*, 2:163, and Auvry 3:65.

[48] Marilier, p. 92. This provision is placed within the context of early cistercian attitudes regarding attendance at diocesan synods by Georg Schreiber, *Kurie und Kloster im 12. Jahrhundert: Studien zur Privilegierung, Verfassung und besonders zum Eigenkirchenwesen der vorfranziskanischen Orden vornehmlich auf Grund der Papsturkunden von Paschalis II bis auf Lucius III (1099–1181)*, ed. Ulrich Stutz, Kirchenrechtliche Abhandlungen 65–68 (Stuttgart, 1910) 1:221–24, and by Friedrich Pfurtscheller, *Die Privilegierung des Zisterzienser-ordens im Rahmen der allgemeinen Schutz- und Exemtionsgeschichte vom Anfang bis zur Bulle 'Parvus Fons' (1265): Ein Überblick unter besonderer Berücksichtigung von Schreibers 'Kurie und Kloster im 12. Jahrhundert'* (Bern, 1972) pp. 98–99.

[49] Schreiber, *Kurie und Kloster*, 1:50–58 and 1:91.

[50] Jacqueline Buhot, 'L'abbaye normande de Savigny, chef d'ordre et fille de Cîteaux', *Le moyen âge* 46 (1936) 107; and Bennett D. Hill, *English Cistercian Monasteries and their Patrons in the Twelfth Century* (Urbana, 1968) pp. 92–93.

[51] The formula first appears in letters of Gregory VII, and reflects the pope's right to modify or revoke privileges: C. Lefebvre and J. Rambaud, *L'âge classique 1140–1378: Sources et théorie du droit*, Histoire du Droit et des Institutions de l'Eglise en Occident 7 (Paris, 1965) pp. 487–88 and 506–507. It is not directly linked to a grant of exemption, and it appears in many grants to nonexempt houses, just as it is not found in numerous privileges for exempt houses: M. Pacaut, 'Roland

Bandinelli (Alexandre III)', in *Dictionnaire de droit canonique* 7 (1965) pp. 702–726. Buhot herself has recently associated herself with the view that the formula is merely a reservation of papal authority to alter a privilege: Lefebvre and Rambaud, *L'âge classique* 7:487–88 and 7:506–507.

[52] Francis R. Swietek and Terrence M. Deneen, 'The Episcopal Exemption of Savigny, 1112–1184', *Church History* 52 (1983) 285–98.

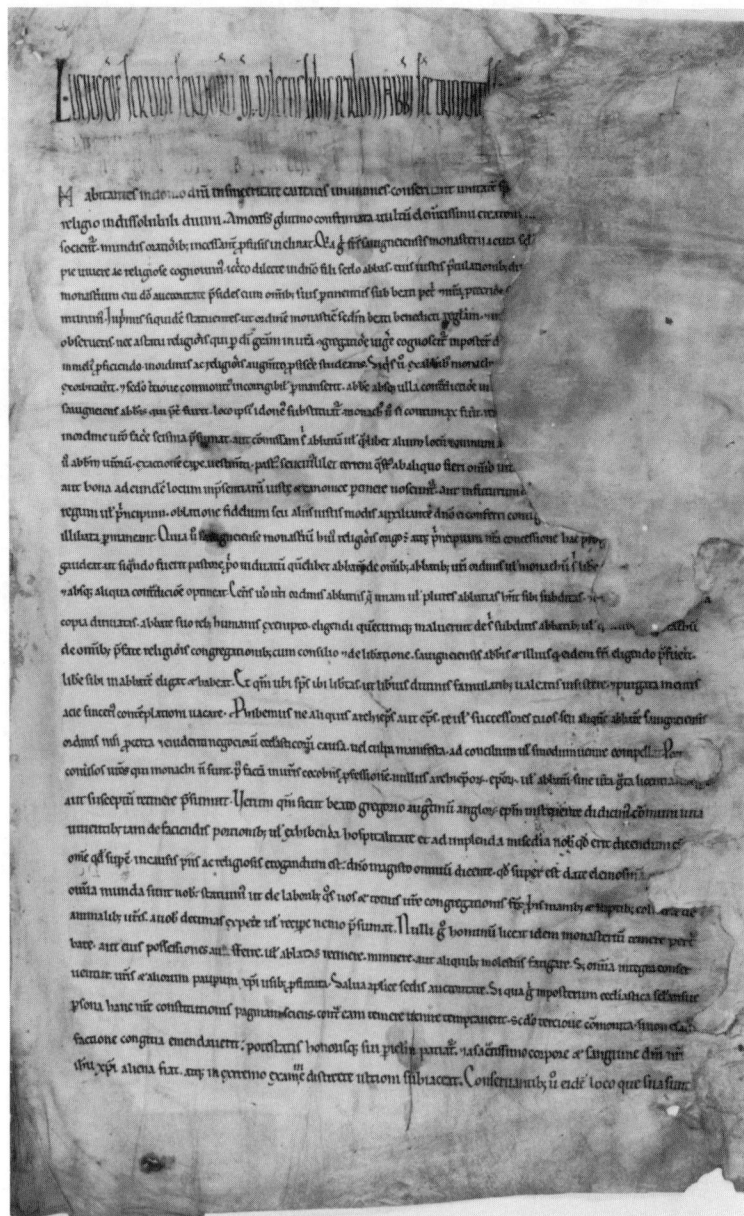

Paris, Bibliothèque nationale MS nouv. acq. lat. 2652, fol. 61r.

Paris, Bibliothèque nationale MS nouv. acq. lat. 2652, fol. 61v.

TOWARD A NEW PROVISIONAL EDITION OF THE STATUTES OF THE CISTERCIAN GENERAL CHAPTER c. 1119–1189

Chrysogonus Waddell, OCSO
Abbey of Gethsemani

IN HIS PANORAMIC synthesis of cistercian life and history, *The Cistercians: Ideals and Reality*,[1] Louis Lekai writes:

> The most important scholarly undertaking of the century was undoubtedly the publication between 1933 and 1941 of the statutes of the General Chapter from the beginning to the French Revolution (*Statuta Capitulorum Generalium Ordinis Cisterciensis*) in eight volumes, by Joseph Canivez. This work alone would have been enough to revitalize monastic studies both within and without the Order.[2]

Few students of cistercian history are likely to dispute Lekai's appraisal of this high achievement of Joseph Canivez, OCR, monk of Scourmont (d. 1952).[3]

This is not to say, however, that the Canivez edition of the *Statuta*[4] has been without its critics. Soon after the publication of the first three volumes in 1933, 1934, and 1935 respectively, Gebhard Rath, O. Cist., responded in the pages of *Cistercienser-Chronik*[5] with a rather severe, albeit objective critique of this major contribution to cistercian studies. With Rath, one may indeed wish that Canivez had provided us with a history of the cistercian order and its general chapters[6]—though one may also suspect that, given the enormity of the task before him, Canivez did well to address himself to the principal challenge of editing the cistercian texts, while leaving to other scholars such as Lekai the task of providing a synthesis of the history of the order and of its institutions. Rath was certainly justified, of course, in calling attention to the skimpiness of the codicological information supplied by Canivez,[7] and one can easily agree that the editorial principles of transcription adopted by Canivez admit of discussion.[8] As for occasional incorrect references,[9] these are certainly to be regretted—though in so mammoth an undertaking the relatively small number of these verges, for myself at least, on the quasi-miraculous. Exception must also be taken to a number of chronological references[10]—though here Rath himself almost certainly has no idea to what an extent this is true.

But even after we have accepted as justified these and other criticisms formulated by Rath, it remains true that the Canivez edition has brought together a wealth of material that would be otherwise inaccessible to most of us. And, while we may prefer a system of transcription more in keeping with modern scientific norms, it is also true that Canivez' transcriptions in no way affect the meaning of the texts (except in those rare instances where there is question of an error of transcription or of punctuation). It is only fair to note, too, that the full force of many of Rath's objections ought to be directed more to the earlier volumes of the edition than to the later ones.

Still, Canivez would himself be the first to express dismay that the first volume of *statuta*, published so many decades ago in 1933, is still the universally accepted point of reference for all discussion of the twelfth-century statutes of the general chapter. Perhaps it is the very excellence of the format and typography and the ease with which the statutes can be referred to—'Anno 1175, no. 23'—that has won this volume such universal acceptance even to the present day. Scholars of deservedly international repute continue to accept without much hesitation the chronology established by Canivez, even though this chronology errs at times by a margin of a quarter-century. Nor has anyone seemed to take seriously the problem of the critical apparatus, in which often only insignificant variants are indicated, while others of a more substantive nature are ignored. Again, Canivez would rejoice at the amount of new source material that has come to light since 1933 (thanks largely to the research of Jean Leclercq, OSB),[11] but which still remains to be exploited. Canivez was a pioneer who opened up to many of us a vast new territory; but it behooves us of a later generation to explore that territory in greater detail, to correct and fill in as often as possible the rough sketch-map drawn by Canivez, and to make creative use of newly discovered resources as they come to light almost year by year.

A NEW *STATUTA* PROJECT

Publication is projected, during the course of 1993–1994, of a new edition of general chapter statutes covering roughly the period 1119–1189. This material will appear in three volumes in the *Cistercian Liturgy Series* (CLS 23–25), edited by the undersigned and printed at Gethsemani Abbey, but distributed under the auspices of Cistercian Publications, Inc. The dedicatee of this edition is to be the dean of cistercianologists, Louis Lekai, O. Cist., for reasons so obvious as not to need spelling out. Of the three volumes, the first is devoted to an edition of each of the sources, transcribed as found in the corresponding manuscript (or, in some instances, in the printed source). The second volume is devoted to a synoptic edition of the material, so that the reader can see at a glance the various versions of essentially the same statutes. An attempt is made, too, to arrange this complex material in some kind of chronological order. But be it said straightaway that, in the present state of research, the problems touching on chronology often admit of no sure solution. Finally, the third volume provides notes on the individual texts. But there is no intention of offering a history of general chapters in western monasticism at large or in the cistercian order in particular. Neither is any attempt made to trace the evolution of the Cistercians as reflected in this legislation dating from the first seventy-five years of their corporate existence as an order.

A NEW PROVISIONAL *STATUTA* PROJECT

This three-volume edition is meant to be *provisional*, and this for three main reasons: 1, the limitations of myself and of the resources at my disposal; 2, the conviction that future systematic research will bring to light important new documents; 3, the further conviction that the present state of scholarship is so much in flux as to preclude the possibility, for the moment, of shaping up an edition that could serve as a sure and settled point of arrival for past research.

My own conviction is that a more definitive edition would require a collaborative effort—ideally on the part of both cistercian observances. Such a collective effort ought not to be by any means impractical, especially when we realize what even individual scholars such as Canivez or Lekai or Dimier have been able to accomplish. Care would be taken to define the parameters of the project, so that the period covered would not be excessive. Such a project would involve several individuals who would systematically examine likely source material in both libraries and archives. Obviously, not every possible *fonds* could be explored, and we can be sure that there will be manuscripts in abundance which Jean Leclercq will be identifying and calling to our attention from time to time. A few individuals skilled in textual criticism could be entrusted with the preparation of an edition which would conform to the highest standards of modern scholarship. Further, the exchange between scholars working as a team would help preclude the necessity of one lone individual having to make difficult editorial decisions that really require collective discussion by a group of peers.

Again, the collaboration of persons skilled in humdrum but essential tasks such as that of proof-reading would ensure the elimination of material errors of the kind that may perhaps mar CLS 23–25.

Accordingly, the present edition of *statuta* is in no way meant to mark a point of arrival, but rather a new point of departure.

A NEW PROVISIONAL *STATUTA* PROJECT

The title of the edition might have been somewhat more accurate had it been formulated so as to refer to 'statutes and *related material*'. By anyone's definition of 'statute', the vast bulk of material retained for this edition does indeed fall under the category of 'statute'. There are, however, certain texts offered by the sources which fall outside even a broad definition of 'statute'. When the scribe of a Tre Fontane manuscript adds to a series of *bona fide* statutes a text about abbatial elections taken from the *Summa Cartae caritatis*,[12] we may reasonably decide not to include such a text in the edition—though I have indeed included it. Similarly, one may question whether I should have included in the edition the several different forms of a text *De negligentiis*, that is to say, norms for correcting mishaps concerning the eucharistic species in the celebration of Mass.[13] Again, a few sources present texts which, to the best of my own understanding, are not general chapter statutes, but merely jottings made by this or that abbot on the occasion of his annual visit to Cîteaux. Thus, when we read in San Isidro, MS 1, f. 89v, the enigmatic words *Et in canpo thanéos*, we may infer not only that the scribe should have written *campo*, but that, given the heavy accent positioned over 'e', he meant to indicate that the word is to be pronounced 'ThaNEos' rather than 'THAneos'.[14] We are dealing, of course, with a snippet from Psalm 77:12b, and no doubt the abbot in question merely verified at Cîteaux where the accent should fall. So also, when we read in the same passage that the psalm-verse is *in penetralibus regum ipsorum* rather than *in penetralibus regum tout court*, or that the collect for the commendation of a deceased person reads *abluas indulgendo* rather than the simple imperative *ablue*,[15] we are not dealing with textual variants decreed by the current General Chapter, but simply with an individual abbot's verification of the correct reading of a text. Laon, Bibl. mun., MS 471 has any number of such texts, of which the most elliptical is surely: *In gradali plorabunt*[16]—which, being interpreted, means that in the Mass Book, the antiphon *Inter vestibulum* sung during the distribution of ashes before the Ash Wednesday Mass should read *plorabunt sacerdotes et levitae* rather than *plorabant sacerdotes et levitae*. Texts such as these, which are almost surely personal notes of individual abbots, might be better excluded from the edition—though in point of fact, I have included them.

A NEW PROVISIONAL EDITION OF STATUTA, C. 1119--1189

The *circa* is meant to qualify both the '1119' and the '1189'. Since the twelfth-century editor of the earliest recoverable collection of statutes claims, in the indices to these statutes, that the first ten are almost all taken from the 'institution of the first cistercian monks and from the Charter of Charity',[17] we cannot assign a reliable *annus a quo* for the series. 'Around 1119' represents a date *faute mieux*, since on 21 December 1119, Callistus II approved the Charter of Charity, by which time both the Charter of Charity and the 'institution' of the first Cistercians were already in existence.

As for the date '1189', this too is problematic. Originally the choice of 1189 as the cut-off point was determined chiefly by a practical consideration: a number of manuscript sources begin their statute-series precisely with the year 1190—as in collections from the abbey of Loos,[18] from Cîteaux itself,[19] from the Paris monastery of Feuillants (two manuscripts),[20] from the abbey of Wettingen.[21] The seventy-year span from c. 1119 to 1189 provides already more than a sufficient abundance of material, and by halting at 1189 it would be possible to avoid the expense of adding another five microfilms or sets or photocopies to my dossier. But it is precisely with the year 1189 that the principal sources, relatively concordant for the period 1180–1188, offer conflicting data. Part of the fault is, perhaps in two instances, attributable to errors on the part of the scribes or of the sources transcribed by the scribes.[22] But part of the fault probably lies in the fact that the general chapter of 1189 appointed an *ad hoc* commission consisting of the abbot of Cîteaux, the abbots of the first four daughter-houses, and still other abbots, to draw up a set of norms concerning land-acquisition, building projects, and other problematic areas of cistercian polity.[23] The text, dating originally from 1189, was confirmed by the chapter of 1190—but, it would seem, with modifications. The result? Manuscripts in which different versions of much the same material seem assignable now to 1189, now to 1190. Canivez, even with his many sources for the period beginning with 1190, was able to do no better than myself—as the alternative dates given in his critical apparatus for the 1190-series clearly indicate.[24] It should be noted, too, that the number of sources which supply dates for statute-series of the period 1180–1189 are relatively few.[25] If a second project is ever inaugurated for an edition of statutes from 1190 onward, the whole question of chronology for 1189 and 1190 will have to be addressed *ab ovo*. One of the merits of the present project, however, is that the reader is kept informed, thanks to the notes and commentaries in CLS 24–25, concerning all such problems and the tentative nature of the 'solutions' proposed.

THE EDITION OF THE TEXTS

The heterogenous nature of the source material can hardly be overstressed. Only a very few manuscripts offer chronological information. Some manuscripts offer texts that have been edited and systematically arranged for official incorporation into the order's customary. In other cases, local scribes have been responsible for their own unofficial editing and arrangement of material. Sometimes all we have is a series of dated or undated material containing, together with other general chapter decisions, texts which will later be incorporated into the *Ecclesiastica officia* or the laybrothers' *Usages*, but which will then disappear from the systematic collections. There are also several instances of occasional series written in successive hands and including jottings unrelated to the deliberations of the capitulants. To further complicate matters, three of the manuscripts have been misbound—not without raising problems concerning chronology.[26]

Given the complexity of the source-material, and given further the absolute impossibility of reducing all this mass of material to a single systematic collection arranged in a chronological order of the kind envisaged in the Canivez edition, I resolved to present to the reader each text exactly as found in the sources, and with a minimum of editorial intervention. It is this material that is contained in CLS 23.

Obviously, however, an attempt *should* be made to coordinate this material, to attempt, where possible, some kind of chronological arrangement, and to offer in some sort of synoptic form the various versions of basically the same texts. Such an edition would allow us to follow the work of the general chapters as the twelfth century progresses, to see the problems that arise, the solutions proposed. CLS 24 attempts to provide such an edition. Thanks to the prior edition of the individual sources in CLS 23, the reader can easily control at each step of the synoptic presentation the editor's use of the material.

But there is need for yet another volume to provide the more general reader with information needed to render a good number of the texts understandable. Let the following serve as an illustration for one of the numerous texts presented in synoptic form in CLS 24. This text is datable to 1157 on the basis of information provided by the only source with precise chronological indications for this period, that is, MON (= Montpellier, Bibl. universitaire, Ecole de médecine ms H 322; from Clairvaux). The indication MON 1157/9 tells us that this is the ninth statute in the series assigned by MON to 1157. The other four sources (identified by the abbreviations DIJ, ARS, LUZ, BEA/COL)[27] represent basically one and the same systematic collection, but without precise chronological indications. Here, in all four sources, the statute is fourth in a lengthy series that runs from sixty-two to seventy-two texts according to the individual manuscripts—the differences in numbering corresponding less to content than to the divisions indicated or not indicated by the scribes. The reader can see at a glance that, for the official systematic collection, the final incise of the text in MON has been amputated, and that, apart from this major variant, there are two others of apparently less import—*plus/amplius, quia/quam*:

MON 1157/9	Qvi lanam uel aliud uendunt . non ideo plus accipiant quia credunt . nec ultra quindecim dies ibi morentur.	
DIJ 4	Qui lanam uel aliud uendunt non ideo amplius	
ARS 4		plus
LUZ 4		plus
BEA/COL 4		amplius
DIJ 4	accipiant quia credunt.	
ARS 4	quia	
LUZ 4	quam	
BEA/COL 4	quam	

CLS 24 accordingly provides the reader with the means of comparing the various versions of the same text. And, for the reader interested in verifying the exact orthography and punctuation of the various scribes and editors, this is easily done by turning to the corresponding texts in CLS 23. But what is the significance of the variants? And what does the text mean? The commentary in CLS 25 attempts to respond to such questions. In the present text, the final incise of MON 1157/9 seems to authorize stays as long as two weeks at markets or fairs or other places of business—

a provision flatly contradicted by *Instituta* LI 'De nundinis' and other related texts. On the hypothesis that the MON text is authentic, we must conclude that the chapter of 1157 momentarily considerably extended the time-limit allowed for absences from the monastery or grange for business purposes, but that this broader provision was retracted at the latest when the statute entered into the systematic collection (some time a bit before 1180). But, as already indicated, this conclusion is contingent on the authenticity of the MON text, which is here supported by no other witness.

What, however, is the meaning of the text common to all five sources? 'Those who sell wool or anything else should not therefore accept more [*plus/amplius*] *because* [*quia*] they believe'? Or 'Those who sell...should not therefore accept more *than* [*quam*] they believe'? Neither is correct, since *credere* is here a technical term meaning 'to sell on credit'. The average latinist could not, of course, be expected to know this. And the scribe of LUZ as well as the editor of BEA/COL (Martène himself!) were similarly at a loss when they (or their sources) wrote *quam* instead of *quia*—a mistake easily made, since the orthographical signs for the two words are easily confused. So the note to this statute exegetes the text in these terms: 'Those who sell wool or anything else should not therefore accept more [money] *because* they sell on credit.' The text is a rather important one, since it shows that, in 1157, the General Chapter considered it usurious to increase the sales-price of goods sold on credit. Obviously, there would be no such statute unless goods sold on credit were indeed being marked up in price around 1157. In the present climate of the 'myth/reality' discussion, we can expect more than one scholar to seize on such a text to prove that early Cîteaux said one thing but did another. But this is the year of the Lord 1157, and we are not at 'early Cîteaux'. In 1157, cistercian abbeys are now counted by the hundreds all over western Europe. Huge numbers of communities founded under non-cistercian auspices have been affiliated with the order only recently. The charge of interest on credit-sales was as widespread a practice in the Middle Ages as it is now. And since, until 1157, there was nothing *specific* on the order's books, so far as we know, that addressed this particular question, there were doubtless many who in quite good faith did 'up the price' so often as credit was extended to the purchaser. Did they continue to do so after 1157? The 'myth/reality' or 'ideals/reality' scholar should therefore first demonstrate that, *after* 1157, Cistercians continued to sell on credit at higher prices. But before adducing this as an instance of the order's actual practice versus the order's theory, that scholar should also demonstrate that such a practice was sufficiently widespread as to involve more than just a few violators. We know, for example, of several instances of homicide within the order in the late twelfth century, but this does not mean that homicide was an accepted orderwide practice, or that the order proposed charity as the ideal while actually countenancing a policy of homicide. Still, it is indeed all too easy to show that, as the twelfth century progresses, actual practice sometimes goes counter to ideals formulated at an earlier period, and that there is an evolution that goes from prohibition to reluctant toleration and finally to unquestioning acceptance if not unconditional affirmation of practices contrary to the spirit and the letter of early Cîteaux. The present edition of the *statuta* helps us to trace the early progress of this evolution with a bit more clarity than was possible on the basis of earlier editions of *statuta*.

THE SOURCES AND THEIR ARRANGEMENT IN CLS 23

Here only the sketchiest of information can be provided concerning editorial choices discussed in detail in CLS 23–25.

PART I of CLS 23 is devoted to the earliest recoverable series of statutes known as the *Instituta Generalis Capituli apud Cistercium*. This is a complex body of systematically arranged material revised on several different occasions in the twelfth century. For this reason the present edition offers no less than three different transcriptions of basically the same material.

The first two transcriptions form a dual edition on facing pages. Six manuscripts form the basis of these two transcriptions. According to the working hypothesis adopted here, this systematic compilation would date to around 1147, the year which saw the affiliation to the order of the large Savigny congregation (some thirty houses) and the much smaller Obazine family. It was now necessary to provide a much enlarged order with copies of the customary and essential legislation, as well as of the order's liturgical books. A far-reaching revision of the order's liturgical books had but recently been completed,[28] and a sweeping up-date of the cistercian customary was a necessary concomitant of that revision. Since the customary-compilation included not only the customary proper (*Ecclesiastica officia*), but also an historical introduction (in this case, the *Exordium parvum* in an up-dated and somewhat expanded version) as well as the order's essential legislation (the *Carta caritatis* and general chapter statutes of permanent value), and also the *Usages* of the laybrothers, much of this material represents a c. 1147 revision of material dating back originally to an earlier period.

In particular, the *Instituta* represent, in the redaction under discussion, a systematic collection of general chapter decisions over a period ending before 1147, and beginning at an early but uncertain date. Of the five manuscripts chosen to form the basis of this edition, all offer basically the same version. But two of them, Ljubljana 31 and Donaueschingen 413, are more 'archaic' than the other three (Paris, Bibl. nat., mss n.a. lat. 430, lat. 4346, and lat. 4221) by reason of the arrangement of the material. Instead of an index of eighty-seven *capitula* followed by the corresponding statutes, all numbered consecutively, we find the material divided into three discrete sections: SECTION I consists of an index of twenty-seven *capitula*, but followed by twenty-eight statutes; SECTION II consists of eleven statutes without preliminary index; while SECTION III begins with an index of forty-eight *capitula* (forty-seven in the Donaueschingen manuscript) followed by forty-eight (or forty-seven) statutes. The numbering of the *capitula* and statute-texts is problematic, in that, at a later date (probably 1152, when further foundations were prohibited except with special authorization), four of the statutes dealing with foundations were eliminated, and later hands have attempted, with varying degrees of consistency, to re-number the statutes. The working hypothesis that I present in CLS 25 is that the three groups of statutes in the Ljubjlana and Donaueschingen manuscripts correspond to systematic collections dating respectively from the abbacies of Saint Stephen Harding and of the deplorable Guy, and from the first decade of Blessed Raynard's abbacy. (If I give no dates here, this is because, despite earlier studies of J. Marilier,[29] I believe that the date of Saint Stephen's resignation and the length of the abbacy of Guy require further discussion.[30])

Relegated to a section of *Addenda* is an edition of two documents which are, I suggest, somewhat peripheral to the matter at hand. The first is an edition of the *capitula* from Trent 1711, the manuscript which offers the only integral text of the earliest recoverable recension of our customary.[31] Where the later recension of c. 1147 offers complete texts of the *Exordium parvum*, the *Carta caritatis*, and of the *Instituta*, this earlier recension presents only much abridged versions of the corresponding material: the *Exordium Cistercii*, the *Summa Cartae caritatis*, and the *Instituta*. The interest of the *capitula* lies in the fact that the statutes which they abridge and re-arrange date from a period prior to the *Instituta* in their form of c. 1147. Still, it would be incorrect to edit these *capitula* as statutes *touts courts* rather than as what they really are, that is, an abridgement and systematic re-arrangement of select statutes.

The second *addendum* was edited by Martène and Canivez as a series of statutes dating from the chapter of 1134.[32]

They are no such thing, but simply a somewhat arbitrary selection of twelve texts excerpted by an unidentified scribe from the *Instituta* and the *Ecclesiastica officia* (only one of these twelve texts is not to be found in either of these sources). CLS 25 offers a careful analysis of this material, but it would be unhelpful to invest these *excerpta* with more importance than they deserve.

PART II of CLS 23, pp. 63–81, is devoted to statutes from the period 1152 to before 1159. There is an initial series recoverable from a manuscript from Cîteaux (Dijon 601) as well as a lost manuscript from Igny known only through the transcription in Martène-Durand, *Thesaurus Novus Anecdotorum*,[33] where the entire series is assigned (as in the Canivez edition)[34] to 1152. These two sources are edited in CLS 23 on facing pages. I am frankly somewhat dubious about the chronological classification of the final statutes in this series, a number of which seem to be variant forms of parallel statutes assignable in other sources to a period closer to 1180. But in the case of the Martène edition (followed by Canivez), the erudite Benedictine has concluded this series with a further eight statutes so obviously belonging to a much later period that I have excluded them from the CLS edition.

This same SECTION II contains, besides the systematic series described above, occasional statutes added by later scribes to four different manuscripts of our *Usages* (the recension datable to c. 1147). As already suggested earlier, it was also around 1152 that the version of the *Instituta* edited in SECTION I was modified: four statutes were eliminated, but another five were added; and a few of the older texts received minor revisions. During the next two decades, there were to be still further revisions.

SECTION III offers an important series of statutes arranged chronologically and dated by the scribe 1158–1161. The material is found in a manuscript of an abridged version of the *Usages* (recension from c. 1147), Montpellier, Bibl. Univérsitaire, Ecole de Médecine MS H 322. Thanks to a material lacuna, the series breaks off before the end of the 1161 statutes. On the hypothesis that the scribe's dates are correct, this manuscript is useful for helping clear up problems of chronology presented by other manuscripts without date-indications. The manuscript includes texts requiring revisions in the *Ecclesiastica officia*, the *Instituta*, and the *Usages* of the laybrothers. Such texts are absent from the systematic collections, since, once the revisions had been made elsewhere in the proper places, there was no reason to retain the corresponding statutes.

SECTION IV, CLS 23, pp. 93–126, is devoted to precisely such a systematic collection recoverable from five manuscripts but only four sources: one of the sources is the frequently mentioned Martène-Durand edition of *statuta*, based, for this particular series, on two lost manuscripts from Beaupré (diocese of Beauvais) and la Colombe (diocese of Bourges).[35] These statutes cover the period 1157 to a bit before 1180. Though the four sources are concordant in general, the variants are such as to justify the transcription *in extenso* of each source.[36] The mis-dating of this entire series, covering a period of more than two decades, is particularly unfortunate: Martène (followed by Canivez) assigns the whole series to 1157 because of his mis-reading of a scribe's introductory note:

> Anno ab Incarnatione Domini M.C.LVII. in capitulo generali haec coeperunt institui, ex quibus multa jam superioribus scriptis ubi potuimus inseruimus, cetera quae restant per capitula distinguantur, & praecedentibus, ut dictum est, capitulis adjungantur hoc modo.[37]

The sense of the text is this: the statutes which follow have 1157 as their *terminus a quo* (*Anno...1157...haec coeperunt institui*). From all this material, a great deal has been excerpted and inserted in texts positioned earlier in the manuscript (that is, the *Ecclesiastica officia*, the *Instituta*, the *Usages* of the laybrothers). The statutes which remain after the preceding revisions have been made are now written statute by statute with corresponding divisions in the format (that is, with paragraph- or *capitulum*-signs). And all this new material follows directly on the series of statutes contained earlier in the manuscript and dating from an earlier period.

This introductory note, reproduced with minor variants in a manuscript from the Paris monastery of the Feuillant congregation,[38] indicates clearly, then, that the manuscript in question contained texts whose *terminus ante quem* was 1157, and that the statutes, whose *terminus a quo* was 1157, were positioned immediately after those texts: A, before 1157; B, 1157 onwards.

But the scribe's note under discussion says nothing about a cut-off date 'before 1180'. This approximate date is arrived at by two considerations. The first is based on the fact that the same four manuscripts which present this systematic series also agree in following the same series with a systematic chronological series arranged year by year as of *1180*. It would seem, then, that, sometime before 1180, provisions were made for an official codification of pertinent statutes for the period 1157–1179 (or thereabouts), and, like the earlier expanded version of the *Instituta*, these statutes were arranged chronologically, but without indications of precise dates.

The second consideration is based on a heretofore enigmatic text offered by San Isidro, MS 1, f. 89v, in a series of texts datable to a period around 1175 or soon after:

> Pro usibus corrigendis conueniant loco et die quo decreuerint domnus cistercii [cisterti *ms.*] et IIII abbates priores cum VII aliis quos secum [sicut *ms.*] assciuerint et corrigant ea tantummodo que de transitu sancti bernardi constituta sunt.

Until I had seen the manuscript, I was sure that either the original transcription by Canivez was at fault,[39] or that the state of the manuscript was so problematic at this point that the transcription was partly conjectural. For it made but little sense to read that, in order to correct the *Usages*, the abbot of Cîteaux, the abbots of the first four daughter-houses, plus seven other appointees, would come together at the place and on the day agreed on to correct in the *Usages* 'only what been decided [or decreed] concerning the *transitus* of Saint Bernard' (who had just been canonized in 1174). Since the only reference to Bernard in the *Usages* would be to his twelve-lesson feast with two Masses, it seemed unlikely that a twelve-man commission, including the ranking abbots of the order, would be appointed and directed to convene in special session in order to correct a single prescription concerning Saint Bernard's *transitus*! What was at fault was not the text but my own mistranslation of the preposition *de*: the commission appointed to correct the *Usages* was directed to correct only what had been decreed *from the time of* or *after* Saint Bernard's *transitus* or death. This use of *de* may be relatively infrequent, but it is in keeping with both classical and medieval usage. In brief, a commission was appointed to correct in the *Usages* only what had been decreed from 1153 (the date of Bernard's death or *transitus*) up to the time of the appointment of the commission. The 'Usages' would include, of course, not only the *Ecclesiastica officia*, but all the other related material in the compilation, including the laybrothers' *Usages* and the *Instituta*. It is, then, almost certain that the systematic series of statutes under discussion, and printed in SECTION IV of the new edition, is the fruit of the Usages Revision Commission appointed soon after 1175.

It was probably at the same time that even the earlier *Instituta* were brought up to date, for the version presented by the order's official 'correctory' manuscript, Dijon 114,[40] differs from that of earlier manuscripts in a few particulars. Of particular interest is the *forma visitationis*, or 'Norms for Visitations'. The text, which is recoverable in two successive twelfth-century versions, was accorded a place among the other *Instituta*.[41] SECTION VI, then, offers the final version of the frequently up-dated *Instituta*.

SECTION VI, CLS 23, pp. 155–225, brings us to the annual series of statutes, dated and arranged chronologically, 1180–1189, by the same sources which offered the systematic but undated series printed in SECTION IV. The problem of the conflicting data for the year 1189 has already been touched on earlier.

SECTION VII, CLS 23, pp. 227–306, offers a considerable amount of previously unpublished material. The first series edited in this section, from a manuscript from Tre Fontane (Rome), that is, Paris, Bibl. nationale, MS n.a. lat. 1402, offers a series of statutes and related material edited by Canivez under the year 1154,[42] but actually dating, on the basis of comparison with other datable sources, from 1160 and 1161.

A customary manuscript from Signy, Charleville 108, unfortunately mutilated and lacunose in the final folios, yields some 108 statutes, including a fair amount of new material. Written in a single hand, this collection probably is due to the initiative of a local scribe, who picks and chooses material on the basis of no demonstrably objective norm. It is likely that he is shaping up his text on the basis of individual series of jottings and scraps of parchment, some of which have been arranged in the wrong sequence. The manuscript offers not only new texts, but also useful variant versions of texts known from other sources. Thus, while four of our sources provide an almost identical statute for 1157—*Nullus abbas guerrientibus aliquid det uel accomodet tempore guerre*[43]—the Charleville manuscript adds a specific reference to the gift or loan of horses and fodder: *Vt his qui inter se guerram exercuerint nichil neque frumentum neque equos tribuamus uel prestemus.* As for the periphrastic *his qui inter se guerram exercuerint* instead of the simple *guerrientibus* of the other sources, we would perhaps be reading too much into the Charleville long version to find it suggesting some sort of armed conflict between neighboring warlords. Still, it was precisely at this time that the lull in the hostilities involving Normandy, Brittany, Aquitaine, and England came to an end. No sooner had Henry II established his authority in England than he embarked on a vigorous campaign of territorial expansion across the Channel: the norman Vexin in the north, Brittany in the west, and the county of Toulouse in the south. Once again, as in the period of earlier hostilities, monasteries in disputed territories were especially vulnerable, and a policy of neutrality was without doubt the most prudent course to adopt. Given the historical context, then, a general chapter statute prohibiting aid to either side in what was, in effect, a civil war, was aimed less at toning up the level of monastic observance than at trying to ensure its survival.

In brief, since no effect is without a proportionate cause, we would do well to try to situate each statute within the historical context which brought it into existence. Take, for instance, the curious prohibition against the abbatial election of youngsters—youngsters whether in fact or in mere appearance: 'Prohibemus ne quis nimis iuuenis et puerili facie abbas constituatur', we read in an 1160 statute from the Montpellier (Clairvaux) manuscript.[44] The same occurs with insignificant variants in the manuscripts from the Paris Feuillants, Beaupré, and la Colombe, in a statute which Canivez assigns to 1157.[45] There is a yet more lapidary version of the same text—'Adolescentiores abbates non cito ordinentur'—in the series of statutes from Tre Fontane assigned by Canivez to 1154.[46] And the identical text is found in the Alcobaça manuscript inaccessible to Canivez. The text, which Canivez assigns variously to 1154, 1157, and 1160, belongs only to the general chapter of 1160, where the capitulant fathers, quite used to seeing new faces at the annual chapters, were nevertheless startled to see appearing for the first time in their midst the baby-faced, newly elected abbot of Hautecombe. Young Dom Henry de Marcy, former monk of Clairvaux, must have looked even younger than his very young years—something of an adolescent Truman Capote type. The cistercian chronicler Chrysostomus Henriquez was later to record that, within four years of his entry into Clairvaux, Henri was elected abbot of Hautecombe, much to the bemused wonderment of everyone: '... omnibus mirantibus Abbas Altecumbae est effectus'; for the lad was still taking mixt (the supplementary morning snack of bread provided for youngsters and those with special health needs) and had not yet started shaving: 'puer imbarbis et adhuc mixtum sumens.'[47] We in turn experience a bit of bemused wonderment at the extreme cruelty of the capitular fathers, who in the presence of the abbot-Wunderkind himself declared all such as him unsuitable candidates for abbatial election. Perhaps it was this initial rebuff that helped mold the character and polity of the beardless wonder-boy, who proved so effective an abbot at Hautecombe that he was elected abbot of Clairvaux in 1176, became a leader in the crusade against the Albigensians from 1178 onwards, was created cardinal-bishop of Albano in 1179, and died as papal legate while preaching the third crusade on 1 January 1189. Henri was aggressive, ruthlessly efficient, dedicated, and not particularly genial. Such was his strength of character, moreover, that he refused not just the abbacy of Cîteaux, but, in 1187, the papal tiara as well.[48]

In 1186, we meet with a further somewhat sarcastically formulated statute connected with our Cardinal Henri, though this connection is hardly in evidence in the Canivez edition (*Statuta* 1:103), where the text is edited as the first, or, rather, the first three of the statutes from 1186. That the editor provides no indication that several sources here give as a single statute what others give as three is a non-problem. Rather more problematical is Canivez' failure to note one of the really important textual variants essential for our understanding of the statute, which begins with the somewhat snide observation that 'There are some individuals who are upset because the brethren of our order—monks, laybrothers, and even abbots—eat two meals on Fridays from the Octave of Pentecost to the Exaltation of the Holy Cross [= 14 September] while they are with others who are fasting.' The text goes on (in statute 2 of the Canivez edition) to specify that Cistercians who have occasion to spend Fridays in a town should fast along with everyone else, and (in Canivez statute 3) that the Friday fast includes, in some regions, abstention from eggs and cheese and other milk products. For Cistercians inside the cloister, the dietary prescriptions of the *Rule* were somewhat less stringent: there was indeed a Wednesday and Friday fast beginning with Pentecost and continuing through the summer, but not if the brethren had to work in the fields, and not if the summer heat were oppressive.[49] But who are these 'some individuals' who are upset, and how is it that layfolk at large are bound to a Friday fast and abstinence from which the ascetic-minded Cistercians consider themselves exempt when outside their monasteries? All this is none too clear unless we take note of the important variants supplied by two manuscripts which reduce the lengthy text to the single proposition: 'Quicumque ordinis nostri ab octauis pentecosten usque ad festiuitatem sancte crucis . sexta feria moratur in uillis: ieiunet sicut nos ammonuit dominus albanensis.' The identical text is found in the manuscripts of San Isidro and of Lisbon, and the reference to the 'dominus albanensis' is, of course, to the cardinal-bishop of Albano, Henri de Marcy, who clearly has been brow-beating his cistercian brethren into conforming with the fasting practices of the laymen among whom they move. And now things fall into place. As part of the Church-wide program of moral re-armament aimed at combatting the evils of the day, the Church had enjoined on the faithful at large a series of dietary restrictions, including a weekly Friday fast. Henri alludes to this in a circular letter dated 1187: 'Et quidem mater vestra sacrosancta Romana Ecclesia statuit et decrevit omnibus sextis feriis, et in Adventu Domini in cibo quadragesimali clericis simul et laicis jejunandum... transgressores constitutionis hujus sacrorum reos canonum fore decernens.'[50] Cardinal Henri apparently took it ill that his own brethren were derogating the very norms he himself was enforcing on the clergy and laity of the Church at large.

The same mischief caused by misbinding is apparent in the much more important collection contained in the volume of *varia* from Vauclair (near Laon), Laon 246, ff. 93r–103v.[51] Not all the 233 texts edited in CLS 23 are statutes in the strict sense. But, even if we ignore the more dubious of these, this manuscript provides a large number of new texts. Scribe after scribe has contributed to this extremely complex collection of related material, which includes not only careful transcriptions of official texts but also highly idiosyncratic summaries and paraphrases of texts known from other sources.

Though unlike Laon 471, San Isidro de Dueñas, ms 1, from Santa Maria de Bujedo (near Burgos),[52] is a cistercian customary (recension of c. 1147). With respect to its additions it much resembles the Laon manuscript: many different scribes, texts of different kinds, folios out of proper sequence. There are some 137 texts from before c. 1190 transcribed in CLS 23—which leaves a large number of other texts utilizable for some future edition of statutes from 1190 onward. Some texts seem to be careful transcriptions of an official version of general chapter statutes; others seem to be personal summaries; still others are little more than personal memoranda concerning this or that particular point of liturgical usage.

Only the person who has read through this mass of heterogenous material will appreciate to the full the quasi-impossibility of reducing it all to some single continuous series of dated and systematically arranged statutes. Thus, the present edition offers the distinct disadvantage of being far less easy to consult than the Canivez edition. In that extremely practical edition, one could always refer to a statute under a specific year—'Anno 1157, no. 61', or 'Canivez 1157/61'. Again, the Canivez edition seems wonderfully clear and simple with its careful references to the sources used for each statute, and to the textual variants for each statute. But when we check the sources, we find ourselves wishing not only that Canivez had provided us with folio- and page-numbers, but also realizing that the arrangement of the material is often somewhat arbitrary, and that the variants noted in the apparatus hardly begin to do justice to the data furnished by the sources. True, Canivez' identification of persons and places in his second apparatus are extremely helpful. But we sometimes wonder why he has chosen one esoteric word to explain rather than a dozen others just as problematic for most readers, if not more so. Again, no annotator will be equally successful in his or her interpretation of all the difficult texts. Still, more than one scholar has perhaps been bemused by the editor's clarification of the term *ruptis* (= *colonus*, that is, a farmer) in the brief statute, 'Ruptis sicut interciditur incisio, ita combustio.'[53] It certainly throws light on cistercian attitudes towards peasants and tillers of the soil if the general chapter feels obliged to state that these socially disadvantaged persons really ought *not* to be maimed and branded by us Cistercians. But *ruptis* here means 'robbers', 'thieves', 'brigands'. And the text actually tells us that the Cistercians are here foreswearing the harsh physical punishment of mutilation and branding normally meted out to malefactors of that sort.

Obviously, it lay outside the scope of Canivez' mammoth undertaking to provide an exegesis of all problematic texts. But just as obviously, even the best possible edition of the texts of the *statuta* will remain a closed book to many readers unless a companion volume helps make those texts more readily accessible and calls attention to texts which, heretofore overlooked, might shed light on matters of current interest. Thus, in the context of present interest about the early order and cistercian nuns, attention might well be drawn to a statute dated (wrongly) by Canivez to 1157,[54] but which occurs towards the end of the official systematic series that stops a bit short of 1180.[55] The first part of the text prohibits the use of women for milking (and presumably for other related farming chores). But the second part of the text is about a quite different category of women: 'Qui vero iam velatas habent nullas ulterius recipiant'; 'Those who already have women religious [*velatas*] are not to receive any more in the future.' In the case of the women hired to do milking, all such hiring was forbidden for now and in the future, under pain of punishment for the responsible abbots, priors, and cellarers. In the case of women religious, however, nothing is said about a disavowal of those women religious for whom the order is already responsible. The prohibition concerns, rather, accepting responsibility for such women religious in the future. The text is of interest, since it shows that, in an official codification of the order's statutes dating from a bit before 1180, there was an implicit acknowledgement of continuing responsibility for groups of *velatae* who had been received prior to a date before, say, 1170/1179, or, at any rate, sometime before 1180. If this text has been overlooked, perhaps it is because there is no reference to it under the word *moniales* in Canivez' indices, but only under the word used for laywomen, *mulieres*. This is only one of many examples useful for deepening our knowledge of twelfth-century cistercian life and institutions.

In summary, then, CLS 23 offers an edition of the various *statuta* sources; CLS 24 attempts to correlate and arrange this material in some kind of coherent order that respects the chronological data, while CLS 25 provides notes useful for clarifying the meaning and the import of the texts edited individually in CLS 23 and synoptically (when possible) in CLS 24.

But to end where I began, the present edition of *statuta* is at best provisional, and the sooner it is superseded by a collective project of more definitive value, the happier I shall be. The Canivez edition was dedicated to a very great abbot of my own monastery, Dom Edmond Obrecht (d. 1935); and it is not without emotion that I frequently read, in the volume of the Canivez *statuta* that I always have at hand, the elegant dedication-formula couched in classical latinity, and followed by Canivez' own hand-written 'd.d. Auctor f. Joseph M^{ia} Canivez, O.Cist.ref'. It is now my own turn to dedicate another statute-project, modest though it is. And I know that Joseph Canivez, to whom this present edition owes so very much, would be more than happy to know that I am now dedicating it to a monk and scholar in the great tradition, a monk and scholar whose achievements have benefited countless persons within the cistercian family, but also outside it. And so—

R. P. LUDOVICO IULIO LEKAI, O.Cist.
inter omnes de rebus cisterciensibus scriptores
primatum tenenti
haec pauca e statutis capitulorum generalium
Ordinis Cisterciensis
recuperata et annotata
memor beneficiorum atque gratus
peramanter dedicavi.

NOTES

[1] The Kent State University Press, 1977.

[2] Lekai, p. 212.

[3] For a brief survey of Canivez' life and writings, see the obituary notice by Anselme Dimier, OCR, in *Revue d'histoire ecclésiastique* 48 (1953) 383–84.

[4] *Statuta Capitulorum Generalium Ordinis Cisterciensis ab anno 1116 ad annum 1786*, Bibliothèque de la Revue d'histoire ecclésiastique 9–14 B (Louvain: Bureau de la Revue, 8 vols., 1933–1941). Volume 1 will be referred to hereafter as Canivez, *Statuta* 1.

[5] 'Statuta Capitulorum Generalium Ordinis Cisterciensis ab anno 1116 ad annum 1786. Edidit D. Josephus-M^{ia} Canivez Ord. Cist. Ref.', *Cistercienser-Chronik* 48 (1936) 50–61.

[6] Rath, p. 51. Rath also stresses the importance of dealing with the pre-cistercian institution of general chapters, starting with Pachomius (d. 348).

[7] Rath, pp. 56–57.

[8] Rath, pp. 57–60. For Rath, the editorial policies adopted by the editors of the *Monumenta Germaniae historica* for their editing of diplomatic texts are proposed as normative; Rath, pp. 57 and 59.

[9] Rath, pp. 60–61.

[10] Rath, p. 59.

[11] Of the series of statutes noted in Leclercq's many inventories of cistercian manuscripts, published chiefly in *Analecta Sacri Ordinis Cisterciensis* from 1949 onward, most of those statutes date from the thirteenth century and later. For the purposes of the present edition, the two major twelfth-century series identified by Leclercq were presented by him in his article, 'Epîtres d'Alexandre III sur les cisterciens', *Revue bénédictine* 64 (1954) 68–82, with special reference to pp. 74–82 for the Vauclair MS, Laon, Bibl. mun. 471, and to p. 82 for the Alcobaça MS, Lisbon, Bibl. naçional, MS Alcobaça CXL–185.

[12] Paris, Bibl. nat. lat. n.a. 1402, f. 4v–5r; CLS 23, p. 231.

[13] The various texts recoverable from our manuscripts of statutes are based on canons *De missa* or *De eucharistia* in eleventh- and twelfth-century collections of canons, and were meant to be inserted in the order's missals. Laon 471, f. 102r, explicitly refers, for one of its variant versions, to the decrees of Pope Pius [II], cap. iii = CLS 23, p. 290, no. 157. Some manuscripts offer the integral text (as f. 78r of the Tre Fontane manuscript referred to above, note 12 = CLS 23, p. 232), while others provide only the incipit, as Paris, Bibl. d'Arsenal 785, f. 14r (= CLS 23, p. 189, no. 191), or Luzern, Staatsarchiv KU 544/1, p. 24 (= CLS 23, p. 265, no. 199).

[14] Contrary to the edition in Canivez, *Statuta* 1:85, anno 1175, no. 42, the transcription in CLS 23, p. 301, no. 42, retains the accent clearly

indicated by the scribe, and necessary for our understanding of the *raison d'être* of the prescription.

[15] San Isidro, MS 1, f. 89v (= CLS 23, p. 301, no. 40). On the basis of manuscripts recoverable from a much earlier period from the order's history, it can be confidently asserted that *in penetralibus regum ipsorum* and *abluas indulgendo* had always been the cistercian reading of these texts. Here there is no question of the general chapter touching up liturgical texts, but merely of a local abbot emending a few defective readings of the sort that can usually be found in even carefully copied liturgical manuscripts.

[16] Laon 471, f. 102v (= CLS 23, p. 291, no. 176).

[17] The text is retained in the indices of all the early versions of the *Instituta*: 'Hucusque capitula de institutione primorum monachorum cisterciensium et de carta caritatis fere omnia sunt sumpta' (= CLS 23, p. 2, lines 26–28; p. 3, lines 28–30; p. 129, lines 15–18).

[18] Lille, Archives 27 H, no. 70.

[19] Luzern, Staatsarchiv Luzern, MS KU 544/2, written for the swiss abbey of Sankt Urban in the eighteenth century, but based on *monumenta* from Cîteaux itself. For the background of the commissioning of this collection by the abbot of Sankt Urban, Dom Benedictus Schindler, see Gregorius Müller, O Cist., 'Aus Cîteaux in den Jahren 1719-1744: 47, Eine Abschrift der Statuten der Generalscapitel', *Cistercienser-Chronik* 13 (1901) 266–78.

[20] Paris, Bibl. d'Arsenal, MS 783 (40 J.L.); and Bibl. Mazarine, MS 1758 (2421).

[21] Mehrerau (near Bregenz), MS s.n., written between 1787 and 1788 by Viktor Frey, monk (and prior) of Wettingen (d. 1818). The manuscript is in three parts, according to the sources transcribed. Part I (1133–1189) merely transcribes the defective Martène edition; Part II (1190–1402) is based on an early, otherwise unidentified manuscript from the Salem archives; Part III (1403–1738) is based on original manuscripts and authentic copies.

[22] Dijon 601, where the series for 1189 is first written 'M°.C°.' and is then corrected in the margin by the addition: 'XC°.I.' The year-numbers become regularized only with 1192. The Martène edition, *Thesaurus Novus Anecdotorum* 4, cols. 1263–66, gives no hint of anything being out of order, but comparison with parallel sources suggests that series belonging to several different years have been edited here under the single date 1189.

[23] The protocol to the 1190 version begins, though in only two manuscripts: 'Anno ab Incarnatione Domini 1189 constituta sunt haec assensu et mandato Capituli generalis a D. Cisterciensi et quatuor primis abbatibus, et aliis quibusdam nominatis patribus Ordinis, confirmata autem a Capituli generalis apud Cystercium anno Domini 1190'; Canivez,

Statuta 1:117, anno 1190, no. 1. The text probably submitted by the *ad hoc* commission to the capitulants of 1190 is found in Troyes 1599 and San Isidro 1, and begins: 'Ego cisterciensis et coabbates nostri quibus iniunctum fuit. ex consensu et mandato capituli generalis ad locum diemque statutum conuenimus. ubi quanta potuimus diligentia. ad commodum et formam [famam, San Isidro] ordinis ista prouidimus obseruanda...' (CLS 23, pp. 261 and 310).

[24] Canivez, *Statuta* 1:117–22, nos. 1–16.

[25] Dijon 601, ff. 164v–78r; Paris, Bibl. d'Arsenal 785, ff. 5v–14v; Luzern, Staatsarchiv Luzern, MS KU 544/1, pp. 8–25; the Martène edition based on two lost manuscripts, *Thesaurus Novus Anecdotorum* 4, cols. 1251–66.

[26] All these and related questions are discussed in detail in the introductory section to CLS 23.

[27] DIJ = Dijon, Bibl. mun., MS 601 (304), from Cîteaux, late twelfth century; ARS = Paris, Bibl. de l'Arsenal, MS 785 (40 J.L.), a mid-seventeenth-century collection of *statuta* from the Paris monastery of Feuillants but copied from a lost manuscript of Cheminon; Luzern, Staatsarchiv Luzern, MS KU 544/1, the background of which is indicated above, note 19; BEA/COL = Martène-Durand, *Thesaurus Novus Anecdotorum* 4 (Paris, 1717), based on lost manuscripts from Beaupré (diocese of Beauvais) and la Colombe (diocese of Bourges).

[28] The *terminus ante quem*, 1147, is supplied by the account of the incorporation of Obazine and its dependencies into the cistercian order in 1147. According to the author of the *Vita S. Stephani Obazinensis*, Lib. II, cap. 13, one of the conditions for incorporation was the revision of Obazine's liturgical books, despite the fact that these books had already been copied from cistercian exemplars. Unfortunately, these cistercian exemplars dated from the period of *early* cistercian usage, and those earlier books had since been replaced by revised versions at an uncertain date—but obviously by 1147 at the latest. It was a case, then, of early Cîteaux as opposed to Cîteaux of a more recent date. For the text from the *Vita*, see Michel Aubrun, *Vie de saint Etienne d'Obazine*, Publications de l'Institut d'Etudes du Massif Central 6 (Clermont-Ferrand: Institut d'Etudes du Massif Central, 1970) pp. 114–15.

[29] Jean Marilier, 'Catalogue des abbés de Cîteaux pour le XIIe siècle', *Cistercienser-Chronik* 55 (1948) 1–11; the *summa capita* of his presentation appeared with a few modifications in his list of twelfth-century abbots, *Chartes et documents concernant l'abbaye de Cîteaux 1098–1182*, Bibliotheca Cisterciensis 1 (Rome: Editiones Cistercienses, 1961) pp. 26–27.

[30] For the beginning of Raynard's abbacy, Marilier refers to a single document witnessed by Raynard and dated (according to *Gallia Christiana* 4, *Instrumenta*, p. 240), before the 23rd or 25th of March 1134. For the resignation of Saint Stephen Harding, Marilier refers first to a text

from the *Exordium magnum* that is not date-specific, and then, without discussion, to p. 105 of Pérard, *Recueil de plusieurs pièces curieuses servant à l'histoire de Bourgone* (Paris, 1664), which refers to Stephen as still in office as of May 1133. Marilier understands the reference in the *Exordium magnum* to Guy's abdication to mean that his abbacy had lasted scarcely a month, though the text says only that Guy's unworthiness became apparent after hardly a month: 'Vix mensis praeterierat unus.' However, the text does add that his removal from office (deposition? abdication?) took place soon if not immediately afterward: 'eradicata est mox de paradisi Dei plantatio spuria.' But *mox* admits of so many shades of meaning—everything from 'immediately' to 'then' or 'in the next place' or simply 'afterwards', that it is dangerous to build a hypothesis on so shaky a foundation. (Though Marilier refers to the *Exordium magnum*, the text in question is actually just a minor revision of the much earlier account by Heribert in Liber II of his *De miraculis*, cap. 24, in the somewhat defective version printed in PL 185:1334AB.) Given the nature of available data, it might be perhaps a bit cavalier to dismiss the witness of the absolutely co-eval text by Ordericus Vitalis (followed here by Robert de Torigny), which refers to a two-year abbacy (*Historia ecclesiastica*, Pars III, liber viii, 444): 'Guido autem... officium aliquandiu uituperabiliter tenuit, et post duos annos insipienter reliquit.' 'Manifestement une erreur', comments Marilier. But is this necessarily so?

[31] The major portion of the manuscript, devoted to our customary proper, was edited by Bruno Griesser, O. Cist., 'Die *Ecclesiastica Officia Cisterciensis Ordinis* des Cod. 1171 von Trient', *Analecta Sacri Ordinis Cisterciensis* 12 (1956) 179–280. Of the various editions of the *capitula*, the most accessible (excluding that of CLS 23, pp. 55–59) are J. A. Lefèvre, 'La véritable consitution cistercienne de 1119', *Collectanea OCR* 16 (1954) 101–104; and Jean de la Croix Bouton, OCR, and Jean-Baptiste Van Damme, OCR, *Les plus anciens textes de Cîteaux* (Achel, 1974) pp. 121–35. The CLS 23 edition is the only one which draws attention to two lines of *capitulum XIIII*, 'Quibus diebus utimur quadragesimali cibo', where the original text has been erased and re-written by a later hand.

[32] For the Martène edition, see cols. 1143–44 of the Martène-Durand *Thesaurus Novus Anecdotorum* 4 (Paris, 1717); for the Canivez edition, *Statuta* 1:32–33.

[33] Cols. 1244–46.

[34] Canivez, *Statuta* 1:45–49.

[35] Martène-Durand, 4, cols. 1246–51.

[36] The other three manuscripts are: Dijon, Bibl. mun., MS 601, ff. 1595–164v; Paris, Bibl. de l'Arsenal, MS 785 (40 J.L.), ff. 1r–5v; Luzern, Staatsarchiv Luzern, MS KU 544/1, pp. 1–9.

[37] As transcribed in Martène-Durand, 4, cols. 1246E–47A.

[38] Paris, Bibl. de l'Arsenal, MS 785 (40 J. L.), p. lr: 'ANNO ab Incarnatione Domini centesimo quinquagesimo Septimo coeperunt ista constitui ex quibus aliqua superioribus scriptis inseruimus. Caetera quae restant per capitula distinguentur et praecedentibus ut dictum est capitulis adiungentur.' The Feuillant transcription is based on a lost manuscript from Cheminon. [39] *Statuta* 1:85, Anno 1175, no. 44.

[40] Sections of this important codex were edited by Philippe Guignard, *Les monuments primitifs de la Règle cistercienne*...(Dijon, 1878). The manuscript was written to provide a normative text of the order's liturgical books and essential legislation. This official *editio typica* served as the point of reference for the correction of variants found in other manuscripts.

[41] No. XXXIII of the *Instituta* in the revision canonized by the 'correctory', Dijon 114, f. 183v2–3; CLS 23, pp. 139–40; Canivez, *Statuta* 1:20–21. For an earlier redaction of the same, see CLS 23, pp. 243–44 (Lisbon, Bibl. naçional, MS Alcobaça CXL–185, ff. 171r–86v).

[42] Canivez, *Statuta* 1:56–59.

[43] Canivez, *Statuta* 1:60, anno 1157, no. 5.

[44] CLS 23, p. 88, no. 43; Canivez, *Statuta* 1:71, anno 1160, no. 2.

[45] Canivez, *Statuta* 1:62, anno 1157, no. 23; CLS 23, pp. 105, 121.

[46] Canivez, *Statuta* 1:58, anno 1154, no. 19; CLS 23, pp. 230, 248.

[47] From Lib. II, Distinctio xli of Henriquez' *Fasciculus Sanctorum Ordinis Cisterciensis* (Bruxelles, 1623), p. 409; re-printed in PL 185:1553A.

[48] For a detailed and masterly presentation of Henri's *curriculum vitae*, see pp. 1–55 of the richly documented study by Yves Congar, 'Henri de Marcy, abbé de Clairvaux, cardinal-éveque d'Albano et légat pontifical', *Studia Anselmiana* 43 (1958) 1–90; for Henri's election to the vacant abbey of Cîteaux, see pp. 25–26; for his refusal of the papal election of 1187, pp. 43–44.

[49] *Rule* of Benedict, 41, 2.

[50] Letter 31; PL 204:248BC. The date of the decree to which Henri alludes raises problems for the dating of our statute from 1186—the date given by all four manuscripts with indications of the year. Baronius, *Annales Ecclesiastici*, assigns to Gregory VIII the decree to which Cardinal Henri refers (vol. 19 of the 1869 Theiner edition, pp. 558–59, n. 17). Gregory's pontificate began on 21 October 1187 and ended a few months later with his death on 17 December. The decree, in which he enjoins a five-year universal fast on Fridays for the success of the third crusade, is unanimously attributed to Gregory VIII by numerous independent sources, which also agree on the date, 29 October 1187: see the many references in Jaffé-Wattenbach, *Regesta Pontificum Romanorum*...(Leipzig, 1888; Graz re-print, 1956) 2:529, n. 16018 (9984). The cistercian statute of 1186 antedates the decree by more than a year, and the incipit, *Solet movere nonnullos*, suggests that the criticism of the order on the

point of usage under discussion is a long-standing grievance. Either the date of the statute is wrong, or else Gregory VIII's decree *Numquam melius superni* of 21 October 1187 prescribes for a different intention (the third crusade) a practice already decreed by one of his predecessors. It is known that Gregory did indeed enact legislation drafted by his immediate predecessor, Urban III (1185–1187), but only the cistercian statute of 1186 presupposes the weekly Friday fast already in effect at that early date.

[51] For an analysis of the manuscript, see the article by Jean Leclercq, referred to above, note 11.

[52] The manuscript has been frequently and invariably identified as a manuscript from Matallana de Campos (diocese of Palencia), because of an *ex libris* signed by the important spanish bibliographer and historian, Roberto Muñiz (1739–1803): *Definiciones del ano 1134 en uso de Fr. Roberto Muñiz hijo del monasterio de Mantallana*. Quite overlooked is the much earlier original *ex libris* at the bottom of f. 102v: *Iste liber est sancte marie buxeti*, referring to Santa Maria de Bujedo de Juarros, founded (diocese of Burgos) at an uncertain date (1172?) from the Gascon monastery of l'Escale-Dieu (line of Morimond).

[53] Canivez, *Statuta* 1:64, anno 1157, no. 39.

[54] Canivez, *Statuta* 1:67, anno 1157, no. 58.

[55] CLS 23, p. 101, no. 58 (Dijon 601, ff. 163v–64r); p. 108, no. 56 (Paris, Bibl. d'Arsenal 785, f. 5r); p. 116, no. 65 (Luzern Staatsarchiv KU 544/1, p. 7); p. 125, no. 59 (Martène transcription of two lost manuscripts, *Thesaurus novus* 4, col. 1251).

CURRICULUM VITAE

LOUIS J. LEKAI, O. CIST.

Born February 4, 1916; Budapest, Hungary.
Secondary education: 1926–1934, Cistercian Gymnasium of Budapest
Entered the cistercian Abbey of Zirc: 1934
Philosophical and theological studies at the theological institute of the order, Zirc and Budapest, 1935–1941
Secondary teacher's certificate in history and geography, 1941, University of Budapest (MA equivalent)
PhD (*summa cum laude*), major in history, minor in philosophy; Peter Pazmany University of Budapest, 1942
Teacher in the Gymnasium of the Abbey in Eger, 1942–1947
Lecturer in history at the Law School of Eger, 1943–1944
Military service (chaplain), 1944–1945
Left Hungary for the U.S., October 1947 (U.S. citizen since 1953)
Assistant Professor of History, Canisius College (Buffalo), 1952–1956
Associate Professor of History, University of Dallas, 1956–1958
Professor of History, University of Dallas, 1958–1986

Prior of Our Lady of Dallas Abbey, 1969–1976
Recipient of research awards from the American Philosophical Association (Philadelphia)
Member of a dozen professional organizations.

BIBLIOGRAPHY OF PUBLISHED WORKS

by Louis J. Lekai

BOOKS

Hungarian Historiography, 1790–1830 [in Hungarian]. Budapest: University of Budapest Press, 1942.

The White Monks: A History of the Cistercian Order. Okauchee, Wis.: Our Lady of Spring Bank, 1953.

Les moines blancs: Histoire de l'ordre cistercien. Paris: Editions du Seuil, [1957].

Geschichte und Wirken der weissen Mönche. Köln: Wienand Verlag, 1958.

The Rise of the Cistercian Strict Observance in Seventeenth Century France. Washington, D.C.: The Catholic University of America Press, [1968].

The Cistercians: Ideals and Reality. [Kent, Ohio]: The Kent State University Press, [1977].

De orde van Cîteaux: Cisterciënsers en Trappisten: Idealen en werkelijkheden. Achel: Abdij, 1980.

Nicolas Cotheret's Annals of Cîteaux: Outlined from the French Original. Cistercian Studies 57. Kalamazoo, Michigan: Cistercian Publications, 1982.

Los Cistercienses: Ideales y realidad. Barcelona: Herder, 1987.
I cistercensi: Ideali e realtà. Florence:Certosa, Monaci cistercensi, 1989.
The Cistercians: Ideals and Reality, japanese trans. by Gabriel B. Asakura. Tokyo, 1989.

ARTICLES

'Historiography in Hungary, 1790–1848.' *Journal of Central European Affairs* 14 (1954) 3–18.
'The Beginnings of the Cistercian Strict Observance.' *The Catholic Historical Review* 41 (1955) 129–43.
'Cardinal La Rochefoucauld and the Cistercian Reform.' *The American Benedictine Review* 6 (1955–1956) 427–49.
'Cardinal Richelieu as Abbot of Cîteaux.' *The Catholic Historical Review* 42 (1956) 137–56.
'The Election of Claude Vaussin as Abbot of Cîteaux.' *Revue Bénédictine* 67 (1957) 201–219.
'The Cistercian General Chapter of 1651 and its Aftermath.' *Cîteaux in de Nederlanden* 9 (1958) 106–120.
'The Antecedents of the Apostolic Constitution of Pope Alexander VII: "In suprema."' *Analecta sacri ordinis Cisterciensis* 14 (1958) 117–26.
'Pope Alexander VII and the Cistercian Observances.' *The Catholic Historical Review* 45 (1959) 1–23.
'The Problem of the Authorship of Rancé's "Standard" Biography.' *Collectanea ordinis Cisterciensium reformatorum* 21 (1959) 157–63.
'The Cistercian Reform and the General Chapter of 1667.' *Revue Bénédictine* 70 (1960) 393–409.
'Abbot Jean Petit of Cîteaux and the Strict Observance.' *Analecta sacri ordinis Cisterciensis* 16 (1960) 120–42.
'The Unpublished Second Volume of Gervaise's "Histoire générale de la réforme de l'ordre de Cîteaux en France."' *Analecta sacri ordinis Cisterciensis* 17 (1961) 278–83.
'A Bibliography of Seventeenth Century Pamphlets and Other Printed Material Related to the Cistercian Strict Observance.' *Analecta sacri ordinis Cisterciensis* 19 (1963) 105–144.

'Moral and Material Status of French Cistercian Abbeys in the Seventeenth Century.' *Analecta sacri ordinis Cisterciensis* 19 (1963) 199–266.
'The Growth of the Cistercian Strict Observance in the Seventeenth Century.' *Revue Bénédictine* 73 (1963) 126–32.
'Cistercian Monasteries and the French Episcopate on the Eve of the Revolution.' *Analecta Cisterciensia* 23 (1967) 66–114.
'The Cistercian Order and the "Commission des Réguliers", 1766–1783.' *Analecta Cisterciensia* 23 (1967) 179–225.
'French Cistercians and the Revolution, 1789–1791.' *Analecta Cisterciensia* 24 (1968) 86–118.
'Hungarian Cistercians in America.' *The Records of the American Catholic Historical Society of Philadelphia* 79 (1968) 223–42.
'Motives and Ideals of the Eleventh-Century Monastic Renewal.' *Cistercian Studies* 4 (1969) 3–20. Also in *The Cistercian Spirit: A Symposium in Memory of Thomas Merton*, ed. M. Basil Pennington. Cistercian Studies 3. Spencer, Massachusetts: Cistercian Publications, 1970, pp. 27–47.
'Catalogue des pamphlets des dix-septième et dix-huitième siècles concernant la lutte entre les abbés de Cîteaux et les quatrepremiers pères de l'Ordre.' *Analecta Cisterciensia* 25 (1969) 107–128.
'The Abbatial Election at Cîteaux in 1625.' *Church History* 39 (1970) 30–35.
'The Rule and the Early Cistercians.' *Cistercian Studies* 5 (1970) 243–51.
'Introduction à l'étude des collèges cisterciens en France avant la Révolution.' *Analecta Cisterciensia* 25 (1969) 145–79.
'The Parisian College of Saint Bernard in 1634–1635.' *Analecta Cisterciensia* 25 (1969) 180–208.
'The Financial Status of the Parisian College of Saint Bernard, 1765–1790.' *Analecta Cisterciensia* 25 (1969) 209–244.
'The College of Saint Bernard in Paris on the Eve of the Revolution.' *Analecta Cisterciensia* 26 (1970) 253–79.

'The Cistercian College of Saint Bernard in Paris in the Fifteenth Century.' *Cistercian Studies* 6 (1971) 172–79.
'The Cistercian College of Sénanque in Avignon, 1496–1795.' *Cîteaux* 22 (1971) 40–47.
'The College of Saint Bernard in Toulouse, 1533–1791.' *Analecta Cisterciensia* 27 (1971) 157–211.
'The Question of the "College of Boulbonne" in Toulouse.' *Cîteaux* 22 (1971) 312–18.
'The College of Saint Bernard in Toulouse in the Middle Ages.' *Analecta Cisterciensia* 27 (1971) 143–55.
'The College of Saint Bernard in Paris in the Sixteenth and Seventeenth Centuries.' *Analecta Cisterciensia* 28 (1972) 167-218.
'The Cistercian College of Dole in the Seventeenth and Eighteenth Centuries.' *Revue Bénédictine* 83 (1973) 436–47.
'Le Collège Saint-Bernard de Toulouse au Moyen Age, 1280–1533.' *Annales du Midi* 85 (1973) 251–66.
'A Supplementary List of French Cistercian Pamphlets.' *Analecta Cisterciensia* 30 (1974) 188–92.
'Medieval Cistercians and Their Social Environment: The Case of Hungary.' *Analecta Cisterciensia* 32 (1976) 251–80.
'An Unknown French "Janauschek" of the Eighteenth Century.' *Analecta Cisterciensia* 33 (1977) 177–90.
'Germans and the Medieval Cistercian Abbeys in Poland.' *Cîteaux* 28 (1977) 121–30.
'Ideals and Reality in Early Cistercian Life and Legislation.' In *Cistercian Ideals and Reality*, ed. John R. Sommerfeldt. Cistercian Studies 60. Kalamazoo, Michigan: Cistercian Publications, 1978, pp. 4–29.
'The Acts of the Cistercian General Chapter of 1783.' *Analecta Cisterciensia* 34 (1978) 200–249.
'Banking at the Abbey.' *The Bankers Magazine* 161 (1978) 71–75.
'Le Collège St-Bernard de Toulouse (1533–1791).' *Annales du Midi* 91 (1979) 383–414.
'Nicolas Cotheret and the Conditional Nature of the *Privilegium romanum*.' *Cîteaux* 31 (1980) 1–7.

'The Events of the Cistercian General Chapter of 1765: According to the four proto-abbots.' *Analecta Cisterciensia* 36 (1980) 87–102.

'Studien, Studiensystem und Lehrtätigkeit der Zisterzienser', trans. M. and W. Marcour. In *Die Zisterzienser: Ordensleben zwischen Ideal und Wirklichkeit.* Schriften des Rheinischen Museumsamtes Nr. 10. Bonn: Rheinland-Verlag im Kommission bei Rudolf Habelt Verlag GmbH, 1980, pp. 165–70.

'Nicolas Cotheret and His History of the Abbots of Cîteaux.' In *Cistercians in the Late Middle Ages: Studies in Medieval Cistercian History 6*, ed. E. Rozanne Elder. Cistercian Studies 64. Kalamazoo, Michigan: Cistercian Publications, 1981, pp. 70–89.

'The Early Cistercians and the Rule of Saint Benedict.' *Mittellateinisches Jahrbuch* 17 (1982) 96–107.

'Zire 800 éve' [800 Years of Zirc]. In *Ciszterci Lelkiseg*, ed. Cistercian Abbey Our Lady of Dallas. Eisenstadt: Prugg Verlag, 1982, pp. 7–17.

'The Manuscript Tradition of Nicolas Cotheret's *Annales de Cîteaux.*' In *Melanges à la mémoire du Père Anselme Dimier*, ed. B. Chauvin, T. II: *Histoire cistercienne*, Vol. 3: *Ordre, moines*. Arbois: Puppilin, 1984, pp. 115–119.

'Nicolas Cotheret, *Annales de Cîteaux I.*' *Analecta Cisterciensia* 40 (1984) 150–303.

'Nicolas Cotheret, *Annales de Cîteaux II.*' *Analecta Cisterciensia* 41 (1985) 42–315.

'Nicolas Cotheret, *Annales de Cîteaux III.*' *Analecta Cisterciensia* 42 (1986) 265–330.

MISCELLANEOUS

Sixty articles in *The Salve Regina*, 1951–1963.

Seven articles in *The Catholic Encyclopedia for School and Home* (New York: McGraw-Hill, 1965).

Fifty articles in *The New Catholic Encyclopedia* (New York: McGraw-Hill, 1966).

Seventeen articles in *Dizionario degli istituti di perfezione* (Roma: Edizioni Paolini, 1974–1983).

Four articles in *Dictionnaire des auteurs cisterciens* (Rochefort: La Documentation Cistercienne, 1975).
Seventy-one articles in *Encyclopedic Dictionary of Religion* (Washington, D.C.: Corpus Publications, 1978).
One article in *Collier's Encyclopedia* (New York: Macmillan, 1990).
More than thirty-five reviews in *Analecta Cisterciensia* and *The American Catholic Historical Review*.

Book reviews and popular articles have not been included.

CONTRIBUTORS

Constance H. Berman, Professor of History at the University of Iowa, is a graduate of Carleton College and the University of Wisconsin-Madison. She has specialized in documents relating to medieval agriculture and the economic history of women's monasteries.

Constance B. Bouchard, Professor of History at the University of Akron, has published *Holy Entrepreneurs: Cistercians, Knights, and Economic Exchange in Twelfth-Century Burgundy*. She holds degrees from Middlebury College and from the University of Chicago.

Elizabeth Connor entered the cistercian monastery of Notre-Dame de Bon Conseil, Lévis, Québec, after studying classics. She is known for her translation of *The Mirror of Charity* of Aelred of Rievaulx, and for numerous studies on 'The Bernard of the North'.

Terrence M. Deneen, Associate General Counsel of the Pension Benefit Guarantee Corporation in Washington, D.C., holds degrees in history and law from the University of Illinois at Urbana-Champaign. He has published several collaborative articles on the history of Savigny.

E. Rozanne Elder is Director of the Institute of Cistercian Studies, Western Michigan University. Her doctoral dissertation at the Centre for Medieval Studies at the University of Toronto focused on the christology of William of Saint Thierry.

†John Tracy Ellis, late Professorial Lecturer in the Department of Church History at the Catholic University of America, received his S.T.D. from the Institut Catholique in Paris. Long recognized as the dean of

american catholic historians, he was the author of numerous books and articles.

Astrik L. Gabriel is Director of the Ambrosiana Microfilm and Photographic Collection at the University of Notre Dame, where he was for many years Director of the Medieval Institute. Well known for his studies on the history of universities, Canon Gabriel studied at the University of Budapest.

Thomas W. Jodziewicz, Chairman of the Department of History at the University of Dallas, has specialized in colonial american and american catholic history. He holds degrees from Providence College, Tufts University, and the College of William and Mary.

Zoltan Z. Kosztolnyik has focused his very productive research on his native Hungary. Currently Professor of History at Texas A&M University, he studied at New York University and Fordham University.

Bede K. Lackner is Professor of History at the University of Texas at Arlington and a confrère of Louis Lekai at Our Lady of Dallas Abbey. A student of the late Jeremiah F. O'Sullivan at Fordham University, he has explored the background of the cistercian reform and its origins.

Jean Leclercq, emeritus professor at the Gregorian University and Sant'Anselmo, Rome, renowned Bernard scholar, and indefatigable lecturer at monastic houses and universities around the world, is a monk of the Abbaye Saint Maurice in Clervaux, Luxembourg.

Meredith Parsons Lillich, Professor of Medieval Art at Syracuse University, specializes in medieval stained glass and monastic arts, and is editor of the series Studies in Cistercian Art and Architecture. She holds degrees from Columbia University, Cornell University, the Université libre de Bruxelles, and Oberlin College.

Contributors

John Lukacs, Professor of History at Chestnut Hill College, earned his doctorate at the University of Budapest. He has published widely in modern intellectual, diplomatic, and cultural history, historiography, and the philosophy of history.

John A. Nichols, Professor of History at Slippery Rock University, has published numerous articles on english cistercian nunneries and is the co-editor of the series Medieval Religious Women.

Thomas Renna is Professor of History at Saginaw Valley State University (Michigan) and a graduate of the University of Scranton, the University of Nebraska, and Brown University. His research interests reach from early monasticism through the Anabaptists.

Bernhard Schimmelpfennig is Ordinarius in Medieval History at the University of Augsburg. A graduate of the Free University of Berlin, he has specialized in the history of the papacy, of clerical sons and clerical criminals, as well as of Cistercians, and has also investigated the history of pre- and postcolumbian Mexico.

John R. Sommerfeldt, Professor of History and colleague of Father Lekai at the University of Dallas, is a graduate of the University of Michigan and was founding Director of the Medieval Institute at Western Michigan University. His research in the spirituality and intellectual history of the Middle Ages, Reformation, and Renaissance has focused on Bernard of Clairvaux.

Francis R. Swietek, Associate Professor of History and a colleague of Father Lekai at the University of Dallas, holds degrees in history and classics from Saint John's University and the University of Illinois at Urbana-Champaign. His research centers on medieval monasticism and medieval latin literature.

Chrysogonus Waddell, a monk of Gethsemani Abbey (Kentucky), studied liturgy in Rome and has concentrated his research on the history, documents, and music of the cistercian order from the precursors of Cîteaux to the present, with concentration on the eleventh, twelfth, and seventeenth centuries.

CISTERCIAN PUBLICATIONS, INC.
TITLES LISTINGS

CISTERCIAN TEXTS

THE WORKS OF BERNARD OF CLAIRVAUX

Apologia to Abbot William
Five Books on Consideration: Advice to a Pope
Grace and Free Choice
Homilies in Praise of the Blessed Virgin Mary
The Life and Death of Saint Malachy the Irishman
Love without Measure. Extracts from the Writings of St Bernard (Paul Dimier)
The Parables of Saint Bernard (Michael Casey)
Sermons for the Summer Season
Sermons on the Song of Songs I - IV
The Steps of Humility and Pride

THE WORKS OF WILLIAM OF SAINT THIERRY

The Enigma of Faith
Exposition on the Epistle to the Romans
Exposition on the Song of Songs
The Golden Epistle
The Mirror of Faith
The Nature and Dignity of Love

THE WORKS OF AELRED OF RIEVAULX

Dialogue on the Soul
The Mirror of Charity
Spiritual Friendship
Treatises I: On Jesus at the Age of Twelve, Rule for a Recluse, The Pastoral Prayer

THE WORKS OF JOHN OF FORD

Sermons on the Final Verses of the Song of Songs I - VII

THE WORKS OF GILBERT OF HOYLAND

Sermons on the Songs of Songs I-III
Treatises, Sermons and Epistles

OTHER EARLY CISTERCIAN WRITERS

The Letters of Adam of Perseigne I
Baldwin of Ford: Spiritual Tractates I - II
Gertrud the Great of Helfta: Spiritual Exercises
Gertrud the Great of Helfta: The Herald of God's Loving-Kindness
Guerric of Igny: Liturgical Sermons I - II
Idung of Prüfening: Cistercians and Cluniacs: The Case of Cîteaux
Isaac of Stella: Sermons on the Christian Year
The Life of Beatrice of Nazareth
Serlo of Wilton & Serlo of Savigny
Stephen of Lexington: Letters from Ireland
Stephen of Sawley: Treatises

MONASTIC TEXTS

EASTERN CHRISTIAN TRADITION

Besa: The Life of Shenoute
Cyril of Scythopolis: Lives of the Monks of Palestine
Dorotheos of Gaza: Discourses
Evagrius Ponticus: Praktikos and Chapters on Prayer
The Harlots of the Desert (Benedicta Ward)
John Moschos: The Spiritual Meadow
Iosif Volotsky: Monastic Rule
The Lives of the Desert Fathers
The Lives of Simeon Stylites (Robert Doran)
The Luminous Eye (Sebastian Brock)
Mena of Nikiou: Isaac of Alexandra & St Macrobius
Pachomian Koinonia I - III
Paphnutius: A Histories of the Monks of Egypt
The Sayings of the Desert Fathers
Spiritual Direction in the Early Christian East (Irénée Hausherr)
The Syriac Fathers on Prayer and the Spiritual Life (Sebastian Brock)

WESTERN CHRISTIAN TRADITION

Anselm of Canterbury: Letters I - [III]
Bede: Commentary on the Seven Catholic Epistles
Bede: Commentary on the Acts of the Apostles
Bede: Gospel Homilies I - II
Bede: Homilies on the Gospels I - II
Cassian: Conferences I - III
Gregory the Great: Forty Gospel Homilies
Guigo II the Carthusian: Ladder of Monks and Twelve Mediations
Peter of Celle: Selected Works
The Letters of Armand-Jean de Rance I - II
The Rule of the Master

CHRISTIAN SPIRITUALITY

Abba: Guides to Wholeness & Holiness East & West
A Cloud of Witnesses: The Development of Christian Doctrine (D.N. Bell)
Athirst for God: Spiritual Desire in Bernard of Clairvaux's Sermons on the Song of Songs (M. Casey)
Cistercian Way (André Louf)
Fathers Talking (Aelred Squire)
Friendship and Community (B. McGuire)
From Cloister to Classroom
Herald of Unity: The Life of Maria Gabrielle Sagheddu (M. Driscoll)
Life of St Mary Magdalene and of Her Sister St Martha (D. Mycoff)
The Name of Jesus (Irénée Hausherr)
Penthos: The Doctrine of Compunction in the Christian East (Irénée Hausherr)
Rancé and the Trappist Legacy (A.J. Krailsheimer)
The Roots of the Modern Christian Tradition
Russian Mystics (S. Bolshakoff)
The Spirituality of the Christian East (Tomas Spidlék)
Tuning In To Grace (André Louf)

MONASTIC STUDIES

Community & Abbot in the Rule of St Benedict I - II (Adalbert De Vogüé)
Beatrice of Nazareth in Her Context (Roger De Ganck)
Consider Your Call: A Theology of the Monastic Life (Daniel Rees et al.)
The Finances of the Cistercian Order in the Fourteenth Century (Peter King)
Fountains Abbey & Its Benefactors (Joan Wardrop)

TITLES LISTINGS

The Hermit Monks of Grandmont (Carole A. Hutchison)
In the Unity of the Holy Spirit (Sighard Kleiner)
Monastic Practices (Charles Cummings)
The Occupation of Celtic Sites in Ireland by the Canons Regular of St Augustine and the Cistercians (Geraldine Carville)
The Rule of St Benedict: A Doctrinal and Spiritual Commentary (Adalbert de Vogüé)
The Rule of St Benedict (Br. Pinocchio)
Towards Unification with God (Beatrice of Nazareth in Her Context, II)
St Hugh of Lincoln (D.H. Farmer)
Serving God First (Sighard Kleiner)

CISTERCIAN STUDIES

A Difficult Saint (B. McGuire)
A Second Look at Saint Bernard (J. Leclercq)
Bernard of Clairvaux and the Cistercian Spirit (J. Leclercq)
Bernard of Clairvaux: Man, Monk, Mystic (M. Casey) Tapes and readings
Bernard of Clairvaux: Studies Presented to Dom Jean Leclercq
Bernardus Magister
Christ the Way: The Christology of Guerric of Igny (John Morson)
Cistercian Sign Language
The Cistercian Spirit
The Cistercians in Denmark (Brian McGuire)
The Cistercians in Scandinavia (James France)
The Eleventh-century Background of Cîteaux (Bede K. Lackner)
The Golden Chain: Theological Anthropology of Isaac of Stella (Bernard McGinn)
Image and Likeness: The Augustinian Spirituality of William of St Thierry (D. N. Bell)
An Index of Cistercian Works and Authors in the Libraries of Great Britain I (D.N. Bell)
The Mystical Theology of St Bernard (Etiénne Gilson)
Nicholas Cotheret's Annals of Cîteaux (Louis J. Lekai)
The Spiritual Teachings of St Bernard of Clairvaux (J.R. Sommerfeldt)
Studiosorum Speculum
Wholly Animals: A Book of Beastly Tales (D.N.Bell)
William, Abbot of St Thierry
Women and St Bernard of Clairvaux (Jean Leclercq)

MEDIEVAL RELIGIOUS WOMEN
Lillian Thomas Shank and John A. Nichols, editors

Distant Echoes
Peace Weavers
Hidden Springs

STUDIES IN CISTERCIAN ART AND ARCHITECTURE
Meredith Parsons Lillich, editor

Volumes I, II, III, IV now available

THOMAS MERTON

The Climate of Monastic Prayer (T. Merton)
The Legacy of Thomas Merton (P. Hart)
The Message of Thomas Merton (P. Hart)
Thomas Merton: The Monastic Journey
Thomas Merton Monk (P. Hart)
Thomas Merton Monk & Artist (Victor Kramer)
Thomas Merton on St Bernard
Thomas Merton the Monastic Journey
Toward an Integrated Humanity (M. Basil Pennington et al.)

CISTERCIAN LITURGICAL DOCUMENTS SERIES
Chrysogonus Waddell, ocso, editor

The Cadouin Breviary (two volumes)
Hymn Collection of the Abbey of the Paraclete
Two Early *Libelli Missarum*
Molesme Summer-Season Breviary (4 volumes)
Institutiones nostrae: The Paraclete Statutes
Old French Ordinary and Breviary of the Abbey of the Paraclete: Text & Commentary (2 vol.)
The Twelfth-century Cistercian Psalter
The Twelfth-century Usages of the Cistercian Laybrothers

STUDIA PATRISITICA
Papers of the 1983 Oxford patristics conference edited by Elizabeth A. Livingstone

XVIII/1 Historica-Gnostica-Biblica
XVIII/2 Critica-Classica-Ascetica-Liturgica
XVIII/3 Second Century-Clement & Origen-Cappodician Fathers
XVIII/4 *available from Peeters, Leuven*

Cistercian Publications is a non-profit corporation. Its publishing program is restricted to monastic texts in translation and books on the monastic tradtion.

North American customers may order these books through booksellers or directly from the warehouse:
Cistercian Publications
St Joseph's Abbey
Spencer, Massachusetts 01562
(508) 885-7011
fax 508-885-4687

British and European customers may order these books through booksellers or from:
Brian Griffin
Storey House, White Cross
South Road, Lancaster LA1 4QX
England

Editorial queries and advance book information should be directed to the Editorial Offices:
Cistercian Publications
Institute of Cistercian Studies
Western Michigan University
Kalamazoo, Michigan 49008
(616) 387-8920

A complete catalogue of texts in translation and studies on early, medieval, and modern monasticism is available at no cost from Cistercian Publications.